Word Structure in **Ngalakgan**

I0881332

Word Structure in **Ngalakgan**

Brett J. Baker

CSLI PUBLICATIONS
Center for the Study of
Language and Information
Stanford, California

Copyright © 2008
CSLI Publications
Center for the Study of Language and Information
Leland Stanford Junior University
Printed in the United States
12 11 10 09 08   1 2 3 4 5

Library of Congress Cataloging-in-Publication Data

Baker, Brett J. (Brett Joseph), 1967–

Word structure in Ngalakgan / by Brett J. Baker.

p. cm.

Includes bibliographical references and index.
ISBN-13: 978-1-57586-562-1 (pbk. : alk. paper)
ISBN-10: 1-57586-562-9 (pbk. : alk. paper)
1. Ngalakan language—Morphology. 2. Ngalakan language—Phonology.
I. Title.

PL7101.N447B35 2008
499′.15–dc22   2008010503
CIP

Cover design by Damon Baker. Painting 'Love songs' by Willie Gudabi and Moima Willie, courtesy the artists, the artists' estate, and Alcaston Gallery, Melbourne. Photography by Michael Watson.

∞ The acid-free paper used in this book meets the minimum requirements of the American National Standard for Information Sciences—Permanence of Paper for Printed Library Materials, ANSI Z39.48-1984.

CSLI was founded in 1983 by researchers from Stanford University, SRI International, and Xerox PARC to further the research and development of integrated theories of language, information, and computation. CSLI headquarters and CSLI Publications are located on the campus of Stanford University.

CSLI Publications reports new developments in the study of language, information, and computation. Please visit our web site at
http://cslipublications.stanford.edu/
for comments on this and other titles, as well as for changes and corrections by the author and publisher.

Contents

Maps, tables and figures

Maps

Tables

Figures

Abbreviations

Agreement and noun class

1, 12, 2, 3:	1st, 1st incl., 2nd, 3rd person
m/MIN:	minimal number (roughly: non-plural)
a/AUG:	augmented number (roughly: plural)
F	feminine noun class
M	masculine noun class
NC	noun class
NEUT	neuter noun class
NFEM	non-feminine superclass (i.e. masculine, neuter, vegetable)
O	object
RESID	residual noun class (Ngandi and Wubuy)
S	subject (that is, Agent of a transitive or Subject of an intransitive verb)
VEG	vegetable noun class

Other grammatical abbreviations

ABL	ablative
ALL	allative
ART	article
AUX	auxiliary, finite verb stem
AVOID	marks an 'avoidance' form (used with certain classes of kin)
COM	comitative
DAT	dative
DIST	distributive
EPENTH	meaningless epenthetic element (Wubuy)
ERG	ergative
F/FUT	future
FNEG	future negative

GEN	genitive
IMMED	immediate
IN	incorporated noun
INST	instrumental
INT	interrogative clitic
INTENS	intensive
INTERR	interrogative particle
IRR	irrealis
ITV	intransitive verb
ITER	iterative
LAT	lative
LOC	locative
NP	nonpast
PC	past continuous
PNEG	past negative
POSS	possessive
POT	potential
PRNEG	present negative
PROX	proximal
PP	past punctual
PR	present
RED	reduplication
REL	relative/subordinator
RR	reflexive/reciprocal
SAP	speech act participant (1st and 2nd person referents)
sp	species
TOP	topic
TV	transitive verb
VBSR	verbaliser

Language groups

BGW	Bininj Gun-wok
(P)GN	(Proto-)Gunwinyguan (language family)
P-NgR	Proto-Ngalakgan-Rembarrnga
Dlbn	Dalabon
Jwyn	Jawoyn
Myli	Mayali
Ngkn	Ngalakgan
Ngdi	Ngandi
NPN	Non-Pama-Nyungan
PN	Pama-Nyungan
Rmba	Rembarrnga
Wby	Wubuy ~ Nunggubuyu

Kinship
Kinship terms are classificatory

Categories

Mo	mother
Fa	father
Zi	sister
Br	brother
So	son
Da	daughter
Ch	child
Si	sibling

Operators

+	elder
-	younger
m	male's
f	female's

Categories and operators can be combined to derive further categories, e.g. terms glossed 'FaFa' are those referring to persons in father's father's category; 'mCh' is 'male's children', including children of a man and his brother; 'mZiCh' is 'male's sister's children', and so on.

Conventions

Transcriptions
Orthographic forms are given in italic style. Underlying, phonemic representations are given in slashes. Surface, phonetic representations are given in square brackets. For example:

SR [yɛ́rkkega̰]
UR /yerkke-kaʔ/ = *yerrkge-gah*
ludaun
below-LOC

Occasionally, I quote Kriol translations of Ngalakgan data given by the speakers. These should not be regarded as full translations or glosses, they are mainly intended for those familiar with Kriol, and are only included where they shed light on a complex construction or interpretation. My transcriptions of Kriol have some inconsistencies with respect to segmental quality; this reflects the nature of the language, at least as spoken by my consultants.

In glosses, a period '.' separates two glosses corresponding to one item in the transcription, for example:

/ŋu-caŋ+an/
1mS-be.standing+PR

Boundary symbols

+	Root level boundary
-	Word level boundary
=	Clitic, or bound stem, boundary

Argument prefixes
Argument prefixes to intransitive verbs are often simply glossed with their person and number features, without the redundant 'S' specification. In transitive combinations of two prefixes, normally only the prefix with a specific argument role allomorph is glossed as such (which, where identifiable, always precedes a prefix which is not so-specified). Argument prefixes glossed 'x/y' indicate 'subject x' and 'object y'. The full set of argument prefix allomorphs are set out in Tables (2) and (3) in Chapter 4. The minimal/ augmented number system is discussed in Chapter 4, footnote 1.

Acknowledgements

This is a much revised version of my 1999 University of Sydney PhD thesis of the same title. It is my pleasure here to acknowledge the help—intellectual, financial, and emotional—I have received from the following people during work on this monograph and the thesis that preceded it.

Most importantly I would like to acknowledge the people of the Roper River. Even though 'Ngalakgan' is on the title page, I hope this work can be a testament to the richness of the cultural life of all the Roper mob. But in particular I must mention *Golokgurndu*, *Gerrepbere*, and *Nyulpbu*, who invested a great deal in me in the hope that something of their language would remain to pass on to their children and grandchildren. My debt to them cannot be repaid.

The financial support of the Australian Institute of Aboriginal and Torres Strait Islander Studies was crucial at various stages of the research that led to this work, particularly at the beginning. The Australian Research Council kept this research going between PhD and job, and several grants from the University of New England continued it thereafter. The support of these institutions is gratefully acknowledged. I would also like to thank the University of New England, and in particular my colleagues, for granting me the study leave (and several periods of 'down time') to work on this book. Thanks also to Vicki Knox for her painstaking editorial work.

There are some people who I must mention here because their intellectual influence on this work has been and continues to be so great. Much of the stimulus for examining the structure of Aboriginal languages came from Michael Walsh and Jane Simpson, who were inspirational teachers and researchers, and personal role models for me. The particular view of morphology presented here owes much to Mark Harvey and Toni Borowsky. Toni's immense knowledge of phonological and morphological theory, and her criticism at the PhD stage, were central in improvements to the structure, argument and expression of the thesis. Jane and Mark also played a big part in this. Mark has continued to be a great collaborator in the ideas presented herein; almost every page of this book bears the stamp of his impact on my thinking. To the extent that this book sheds some useful light on how the languages of this region operate, this is in large part due to the aforementioned scholars. Thanks also to my thesis examiners—Juliette Blevins, Nick Evans, and Armin Mester—and the editors and anonymous reviewers of CSLI, who provided, and have continued to provide, many insightful comments which led to numerous improvements in the final outcome.

Thanks to the staff of the Department of Linguistics and Applied Linguistics at Melbourne University, who were gracious enough to host me at the last minute on my study leave in 2005, during which time many of the analytical revisions were worked through. As I came to realise, this was the best place I could have chosen to rework the thesis. Thanks in particular to Nick Evans, Janet Fletcher, Rachel Nordlinger, Nick Piper, Lesley Stirling, and the Phonetics Lab crew—Hywel, Debbie and Mary—for making this time so intellectually stimulating and rewarding, and for making the three of us feel so welcome.

My year of study at the University of Massachusetts (1996-1997) was crucial to my development as a linguist and the work in this monograph. I'd like to thank my sponsors Ellen Woolford and John McCarthy, and other Faculty with whom I discussed the ideas contained herein, particularly Diamandis Gafos and John Kingston. I'd especially like to acknowledge the input of my fellow classmates, scholars, and friends John Alderete, Caroline Jones, and Rachel Walker. Many other scholars have provided useful discussion of the ideas in this book, including Eric Bakovic, Gavan Breen, Andy Butcher, Stuart Davis, David Nash, Ian Smith, Cheryl Zoll, and audiences at WCCFL16, BLS23, MIT, SUNY Buffalo, UBC, USC, ALS, and the Australian Linguistics Institute 2002.

Finally, and most importantly, my wife Karan has been my biggest supporter through all of this sustained effort. And it is to her that I dedicate this book, with love.

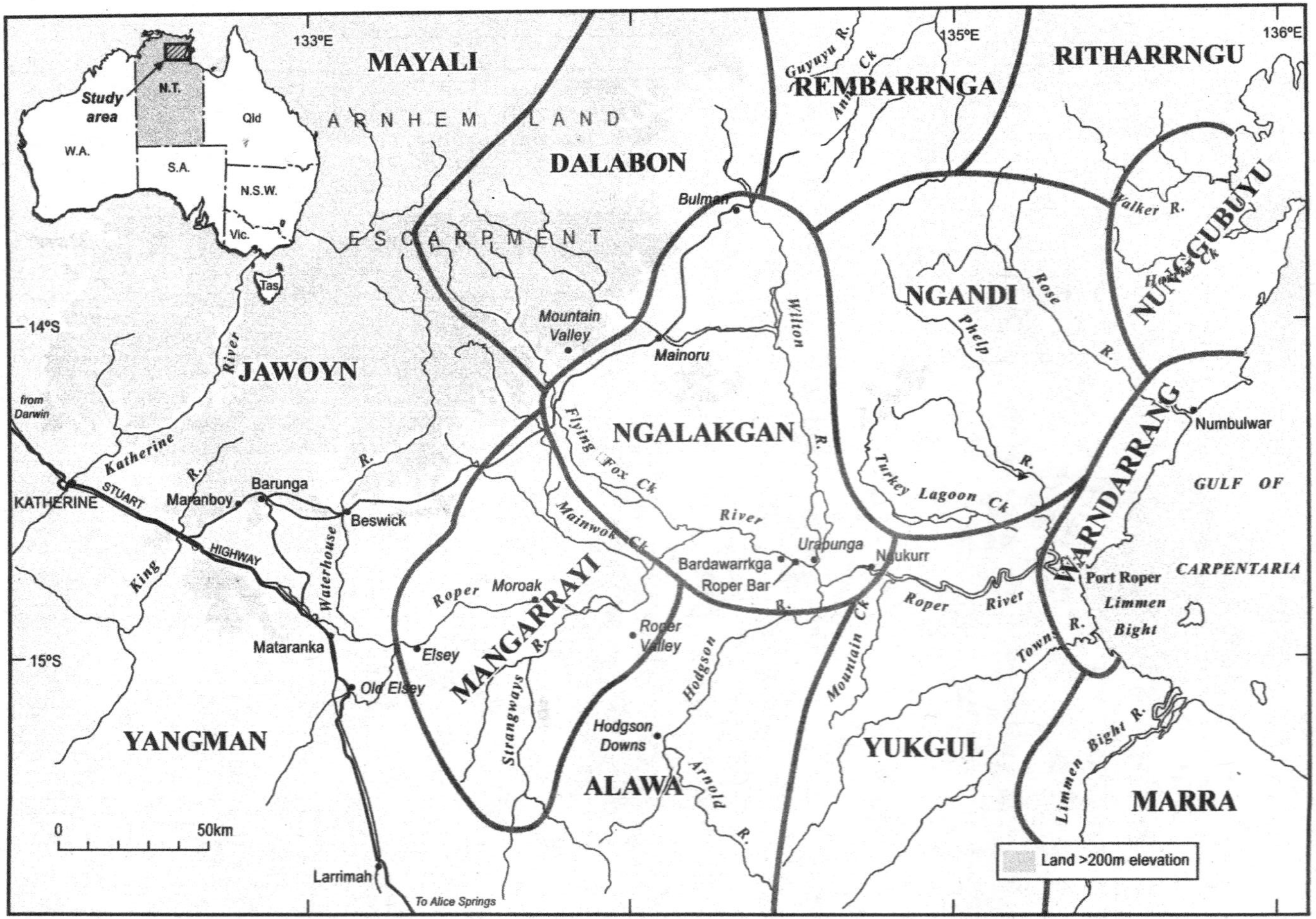

Map 1: The location of Ngalakgan in relation to neighbouring languages.

1

Introduction

Ngalakgan, like many languages of northern Australia, allows a high degree of complexity in word structure. The structure of phrases and sentences, by contrast, is quite 'loose'. There are no privileged positions for logical subject, object or verb in the sentence. All of this information is encoded in the morphology of argument and predicate expressions. Hence, the proper interpretation of complex words in Ngalakgan is crucial to an understanding of what speakers want to say.

Unlike many other polysynthetic languages such as Navajo and Slave (Rice 1989: 131), Ngalakgan is almost entirely agglutinating. There are very few morphophonemic alternations. Ngalakgan therefore provides an ideal testing ground for one of the most interesting questions in linguistics: to what extent are the words of polysynthetic languages like the phrases of configurational languages like English?

In this monograph I have two main aims. The first is to understand the nature of the morphological relations within words in Ngalakgan. In Chapters 3 and 4, I show that morphological relations in Ngalakgan are not all of a single type. But they are not unlimited in type either. Rather, just two kinds of morphological relations serve to enable us to account for the vast majority of semantic and phonological patterns in the language. I call these two types 'ROOT' level and 'WORD' level, following Selkirk (1982) and Borowsky (1990). ROOT-level relations are lexicalised, unproductive relations which are largely invisible to phonology and apparently inaccessible to speakers. WORD-level relations by contrast are productive, phonologically-active, and WORD-level morphemes may be isolated by speakers. The word structure of Ngalakgan is not unique, many Australian languages evince the same distinctions of morphological type that are crucial in Ngalakgan (see Baker and Harvey 2003).

My second aim is to understand some phonological processes that are restricted to Ngalakgan and its close neighbours and congeners. These processes depend on the nature of the stop contrast, and the behaviour of the glottal stop, described in Chapter 2. Understanding these processes provides an insight into the relationship between moraicity, syllabification, and gesture, which is not revealed by currently available data from any other languages.

Ngalakgan is quantity-sensitive for stress. But its quantity-sensitivity is of a type hitherto unknown to the literature on stress. Codas count for weight in Ngalakgan, but only if they are heterorganic to following consonants. Homorganic nasal-stop clusters, and geminates, fail to contribute weight to the preceding syllable. This runs directly counter to the predictions of Moraic Theory (Hyman 1985; Hayes 1989). I argue in Chapter 5 that the weightlessness of homorganic clusters derives from the fact that they are monogestural: this allows them to be exceptionally syllabified as onsets in Ngalakgan and in other Australian languages.

Both glottal stops and geminates are widely attested at morpheme boundaries both synchronic and historic in languages of the region where Ngalakgan was spoken. In Chapter 6 I argue that these articulations are well suited to function as 'boundary signals' in Trubetzkoy's (1969[1939]) sense, since they interrupt the largely continuous voicing which is characteristic of words in these languages. Ngalakgan and its congeners Ngandi and Rembarrnga restrict the distribution of these boundary signals according to prosodic domains, resulting in an unusual pattern of geminate alternation at suffix edges.

The data reported herein come from my fieldwork in the Northern Territory from 1994 until 2002. The last native speaker of Ngalakgan— *Nyulpbu* (Doreen Duncan)—passed away in 2004. In the following sections I describe some of the sociolinguistic, historical and theoretical background to the study. 1.1 describes some of the major typological features of Ngalakgan, its genetic relationships, the speakers and their social environment, and the data sources. 1.2 outlines previous work on Ngalakgan, and how the book fits into the current situation in Australian linguistics. The analysis is framed in terms of Optimality Theory (Prince and Smolensky 1993; McCarthy and Prince 1993a, b). 1.3 provides a brief introduction to this theory. An outline of the chapters is provided at 1.4.

1.1 The Ngalakgan people and their language

Ngalakgan is an Australian language, formerly spoken in the Roper River region of the Northern Territory (see the map preceding page 1).[1] Ngalakgan

[1] This map represents an estimate of the positions of languages in relation to each other and major land forms. Names of languages in the Gunwinyguan family are written using the standard

is classified by Alpher, Evans and Harvey (2003), as a member of the large 'Gunwinyguan' (GN) family of languages. GN is one of the better-established genetic groupings within the residual category of Non-Pama-Nyungan Australian languages (the distinction 'Pama-Nyungan' vs 'non-Pama-Nyungan' is originally due to unpublished claims by Hale: cited in e.g. Dixon 1980: 21; see Bowern and Koch 2004 for recent work on the subclassification of Australian languages). In Baker (2004), I show that Ngalakgan is most closely related to Rembarrnga within this family. I would describe their relationship as being closer than that between Standard French and Standard Italian. Indeed, there must have been a high degree of mutual intelligibility between these varieties in traditional times, even though the percentage of shared vocabulary is less than 50% (the percentage of shared verbs is much higher).

Both Rembarrnga and Ngalakgan are in turn quite closely related to the biggest, and most widely spoken language of the group, which is now known as Bininj Gun-wok (Evans 2003). Bininj Gun-wok (literally 'people's language') is the name given by Evans to a dialect chain consisting of named varieties such as Mayali, Kunwinjku, Kuninjku, Gundjeihmi, and Kune. BGW has received detailed attention from several researchers (e.g. Evans 1997, 1998, 1999; Bishop 2002; Stoakes in preparation), and will serve as a frequent point of reference for the discussion in this book.

1.1.1 Linguistic situation

During my time working with them, all three speakers of Ngalakgan were in regular contact with each other and with speakers of various other languages in the region. Apart from Ngalakgan, the most important languages in this area (the Roper River drainage basin and neighbouring areas) are presented in the list below, together with a primary reference for each.

Alawa	(Sharpe 1972)
Dalabon/Ngalkbon	(Capell 1962)
Jawoyn	(Merlan n.d.)
Kriol	(Harris 1986; Munro 2005)
Mangarrayi	(Merlan 1982)

---

orthography for Ngalakgan, presented in 2.7 (except 'Jawoyn', which uses the conventional spelling of [ɟawoʲɲ]). It should be noted that many of these languages have their own, distinct orthographic systems. The spelling of the Yolngu language Ritharrngu [ɻit̪t̪arŋu] is given in the standard Yolngu orthography, except that the digraph 'ng' is used rather than the Yolngu orthographic symbol 'ŋ' (which was not available when producing the map). The map should not be treated as a definitive description.

Marra	(Heath 1981)
Ngandi	(Heath 1978b)
Rembarrnga	(McKay 1975)

Kriol is an English lexifier creole which is the lingua franca of the majority of the Top End and the Kimberley regions. Rembarrnga is the language which appears to be most closely related to Ngalakgan (Baker 2004). Ngandi is a neighbouring GN language with many phonological and typological similarities to Ngalakgan, but these similarities are on the whole superficial: the verb paradigms of Ngandi are quite different to Ngalakgan and demonstrably related to neighbouring Nunggubuyu/Wubuy (Heath 1984; Baker 2004). However, it shares many important phonological features with Ngalakgan and Rembarrnga, such as the geminate/singleton contrast and geminate alternation. Marra and Alawa are two neighbouring Non-Pama-Nyungan languages which are not closely related to any other languages. There is no strong evidence for a relationship between these languages. Mangarrayi is possibly another GN language (Alpher et al. 2003), but quite divergent from them in many respects (Merlan 2003). It is probable that Ngalakgan speakers traditionally had some contact with Jawoyn and Dalabon also, both are GN languages. Dalabon appears to be somewhat closer to Bininj Gun-wok than other GN languages (Alpher et al. 2003), though it is not clear whether there is strong evidence for this (Baker 2004), and Jawoyn is probably related most closely to Warray (Harvey 2003).

Despite being closely related to Rembarrnga, and more broadly, BGW, there are several features which make Ngalakgan unique. With the exception of Dalabon, Ngalakgan has taken the separability of argument prefixes to the greatest extreme among Australian prefixing languages. Prefixes in Ngalakgan, unlike BGW, Ngandi, Wubuy and Rembarrnga, never regularly take stress accent, regardless of the length of the verb or noun stem to which they are attached. Ngalakgan is an interesting combination of 'western' and 'eastern' GN features. Like the western languages (Jawoyn, BGW, Dalabon, Rembarrnga) it has a highly transparent morphology-to-prosody iconicity, giving us the best environment for testing the 'phrasehood' of complex words. Unlike the western languages, but like the eastern languages Ngandi and Wubuy, it has a fully-functioning noun class system with four classes and agreement for both inanimate classes (among GN languages, only Ngandi and Wubuy show verb agreement for every noun class). Noun class prefixes, as in Wubuy, function as articles in Ngalakgan (Baker to appear), a feature which is very rare among Australian languages. In Ngalakgan and Wubuy, the different prefix forms mark distinctions which can be broadly described as 'focus/contrast' vs 'topic', but they also interact with polarity in interesting and unexpected ways. Among GN languages, Ngalakgan allows possibly the greatest degree of complexity in terms of number and type of constituents in words. It is polysynthetic on a similar order of complexity to Athabaskan languages (e.g. Slave: Rice 1989), but with a very simple lego-like agglutinative structure. Indeed, morphology in Ngalakgan can mostly be described as 'compounding'.

The following sections place Ngalakgan in its social and linguistic context. I will outline the descriptive contribution of the book: how it differs from the descriptive grammar of Merlan (1983), and from previously described patterns in other Australian languages.

1.1.2 Features of the language

The principal typological features of Ngalakgan are:

- Prefixation to predicates for up to two arguments, and to nominals for one of four Noun Classes.
- Suffixation for argument (Ergative, Genitive/Dative) and local-semantic roles (Locative/Allative, Ablative, Perlative), and number.
- A wide range of bound stems (previously analysed as 'prefixes' or 'clitics') performing modifying, quantificational (e.g. /man-/ 'group', /weleŋ-/ 'together', /koreʔ-/ 'alone'), derivational, and manner functions (e.g. /ɳamulu-/ 'really'), as well as applicatives such as /pak-/ which raise non-subcategorised arguments. Many of these bound stems can attach to both nouns and verbs, including the set of Dative pronouns which mark possession on nouns and benefactives on verbs.
- Productive compounding in both the nominal and verbal classes, including 'incorporation' of nominals and adverbials.
- Syntactically-free, pragmatically-determined word order.

Similar or identical patterns are found in Ngalakgan's closest relatives: Rembarrnga, Bininj Gun-wok, Dalabon, Wubuy, and Ngandi. See for example (Evans 2003) for recent descriptive work on this group of languages.

1.1.3 The speakers, their social environment, and the fieldwork

From available evidence, it seems that children have not acquired Ngalakgan fully since the 1930's. When I began work on Ngalakgaṇ, there were three fluent speakers left in the Roper communities in which I worked (those serviced by the Roper Highway). Since the submission of my thesis in 1999, all three of them have died. It is conceivable, though doubtful, that there still remain first language speakers in other communities with which I have had little or no contact such as Bulman. All three speakers I worked with were elderly at the time, in their seventies or early eighties. There are still several secondary speakers (some very fluent) among the Roper communities speaking various other languages, and a number of (at least) partial speakers at Bulman, on the Central Arnhem Highway; I am unsure of their level of command of the language.

1.1.4 Informants

There were three primary consultants for the fieldwork on which this book is based: †*Golokgurndu* (Roy James), †*Gerrepbere* (Splinter James), and †*Nyulpbu* (Doreen Duncan).[2]

My primary consultant throughout my period in the field was Roy, now deceased. He was perhaps in his late seventies or early eighties when I started working with him. Roy grew up and worked in the area of Roper Bar as a police tracker. In his early days he drove cattle to Queensland through the Barkly Tablelands. Roy lived at Bardawarrkga outstation, on land granted back to his clan under the Aboriginal Land Rights Act (NT 1976), together with some of his family, including his brother Splinter. Splinter was a few years younger than Roy, and deferred to him in all traditional matters including language.

Doreen lived in the community of Urapunga 30 kms to the east of Bardawarrkga. Doreen spent some of her childhood at Bulman, but as a young woman worked at Roper Bar. Doreen was particularly knowledgeable about both the names and uses of native plants. Much of the most interesting linguistic material I collected was based around this theme.

All three informants were fluent speakers of Rembarrnga and Ritharrngu. Doreen told me that Rembarrnga was her 'first' language, and was clearly her stronger language, though her primary familial affiliation is to Ngalakgan. Roy was also proficient in Mayali, Ngandi, Djinang and possibly other languages.

1.1.5 Fieldwork

The languages of elicitation were English, Kriol and (in later stages) Ngalakgan. Fieldwork was carried out at various locations—Katherine town, Bardawarrkga, Urapunga, Ngukurr—with Urapunga and Ngukurr being the most frequent bases. Total time spent in the field was around 18 months. Periods spent in the field, together with dated recordings, were as follows:

---

[2] The symbol '†' conventionally in Australian linguistics signals the name of a deceased person. These names should not be used in any context where there is a chance that the deceased's relatives or fellow community members could see or hear them.

1994	July-October	(Tapes 6/9/94-27/9/94)
1995	March-May	(Tapes 3/3/-16/5/95)
1996	January, March-August	(Tapes 4-10/1/96; 13/5-4/7/96)
1997	September	(Tapes 1/9/-12/9/97)
1998	October	(Tapes 13/10-15/10/98)
1999	October	(Tapes 13/10-22/10/99)
2001	July	(MD 27/6/01, 15-17/7/01)

Data taken from elicitation sessions are referred to by the date, tape number and side. For example: [1/6/96: 1A] refers to the session recorded on this date, tape number 1, side A. The majority of these sessions are transcribed and the transcriptions are lodged at the Australian Institute of Aboriginal and Torres Strait Islander Studies (AIATSIS) together with the recordings.[3]

Data taken from texts are cited with an abbreviation of the text title. These are as follows:

KD	'Kangaroo Dreaming': dreaming myth narrative relating to travels of the Plains Kangaroo ancestor (*jardugal/ garndalpburru*)
DP	A processual text: how to collect pandanus and 'sugar-bag' (wild honey)
DD	A processual text: how to make damper
Txt 1/6/96	A hunting narrative
QS	'Quiet Snake Dreaming': dreaming myth narrative relating to the travels of the Quiet Snake (Olive Python) ancestor (*gurrujardu/gurrijartbonggo*)

1.1.6 Data and methodology

Ngalakgan data I collected are primarily of two types: elicited words and phrases, and texts. Texts were often freely offered by speakers, particularly Roy. Roy provided many texts, some sacred ('Kangaroo Dreaming', 'Two Quiet Snakes') many secular—his favourite theme being hunting.

Doreen also provided some fine, succinct texts, which were all recorded as part of the ongoing language revival program at Urapunga school. They cover such themes as the traditional way to collect and prepare pandanus for weaving, preparing lilyseed bread, and making medicine from indigenous plants.

---

[3] The AIATSIS collection numbers for recordings up to and including 1997 are Baker_B02 and Baker_B03.

The tapes record a copious amount of elicitation. Elicitation of acceptability judgements however, as any fieldworker on Australian languages will attest, is a tricky business with Aboriginal consultants.[4] Luckily, both Splinter and Doreen were adept at objectifying linguistic data, and elicitation with Splinter in particular was very productive. Some interactive material was also recorded.

I have also had the privilege of working with many other people in these communities, who provided me with an insight into the range of linguistic variation in the area. I would particularly like to mention †*Dhitdenbuy* Thompson, †*Ginburr* Hall, †Alice Mirninggirri and especially Cherry Daniels, who acted as consultants for Ngandi. †*Garlbarr* (Dicky Darwin) also provided valuable data on Ngalakgan, though his primary linguistic affiliation was to Rembarrnga.

Much of the material for phonological elicitation was drawn from a lexical database of Ngalakgan, which is also archived at AIATSIS, along with all of the recordings made with speakers. The lexical database contains around 1300 words, and consists of the lexicon published in Merlan (1983) together with around 200 additions from my own fieldwork. Several lexical items recorded by Merlan were not recognised by my informants, but on the whole Merlan's lexicon (and her grammar) closely conform in most respects to the language that my informants spoke.

While this monograph discusses many aspects of the sound system of Ngalakgan, only certain aspects received instrumental phonetic analysis. In particular, the analysis of stress is based entirely on auditory, impressionistic evidence. While it is regrettable that no acoustic evidence is available to back up the claims made in this monograph, the lack of such data does not necessarily make the discussion dubious. Firstly, many of the claims made in the 1999 thesis on which this monograph is based were backed up by later acoustic analysis in other Australian languages, in particular (Bishop 2002). Bishop (2002: Ch 3.6) shows, for instance, that Bininj Gunwok distinguishes syllable weight and that this can affect the location of nuclear accent. Also, Bishop finds that the vowels of accented syllables in Bininj Gun-wok are 'centralised' with respect to the vowels of unaccented syllables, a claim made on the basis of impressionistic evidence in Baker (1999). Other claims in Baker (1999) have been backed up by the evidence of similar patterns in other Australian languages. For instance, a fluent second language speaker of Bininj Gun-wok, Murray Garde, has confirmed that this language has essentially the same system of quantity-sensitivity found in

[4] The reasons for this are sociolinguistic and pragmatic (Walsh 1997). Many Aboriginal informants tend to respond to the content of an utterance, rather than the form. This was true of Roy for instance.

Ngalakgan. I have found similar patterns of quantity-sensitivity in other languages of the southern Arnhem Land area also, such as Marra. This is highly significant: it means that the pattern of quantity-sensitivity found in Ngalakgan is not a quirk of a now-extinct language, but a systematic phonological pattern in need of explanation. Bininj Gun-wok is spoken by several thousand people, is being acquired by children, and is one of the few traditional Aboriginal languages whose number of speakers is expanding.

1.2 Previous work on Ngalakgan

The only published reference work on Ngalakgan is Merlan (1983): *Ngalakan Grammar, Texts and Vocabulary*. The lexical and grammatical analysis in this grammar form the basis for the discussion herein. Merlan based her initial fieldwork on unpublished fieldnotes on Ngalakgan by Jeffrey Heath, who worked on the neighbouring, related language Ngandi (Heath 1978b). Field tapes recorded by Merlan and Heath, and earlier researchers such as Graham McKay, are lodged at AIATSIS. (I did not make use of these tapes.) To my knowledge, Merlan has carried out no subsequent work on Ngalakgan since the publication of her grammar. Examples taken from Merlan (1983) are annotated as [M-*n*], where *n* is the number given to the example in that work.

The earliest substantial documentation of Ngalakgan is in Tindale (1928), a wordlist of 400 words in a number of languages of the Roper region, including Ngalakgan. Capell (1942: 387-389) included three pages on Ngalakgan grammar and vocabulary in his survey of North Australian languages. Frances and Howard Morphy worked with speakers of the language for a land claim under the auspices of the Northern Land Council, as anthropological consultants. Their unpublished land claim book *Yutpundji-Djindiwirritj* (1981) contains much valuable anthropological, historical, and social data and discussion, and some language material in the form of toponyms, kinship, subsection, personal and ancestor names.

1.2.1 Differences from previous work

This book extends the description and analysis of Ngalakgan in a number of areas. Here, I point out the differences between the current volume and the material covered in Baker (1999) and Merlan (1983).

Chapter 2, which is entirely new material, is a description and analysis of the phonotactics of Ngalakgan, extending the description of Merlan (1983) in a number of respects. Particular attention is paid to the nature of the glottal stop and the geminate/singleton realisation of oral stops. Consideration of neighbouring languages such as Burarra suggests that geminates in these languages are syllabified in the onset, rather than as coda-onset clusters. This proposal is confirmed by the behaviour of homorganic clusters for quantity, discussed in Chapter 5.

Chapters 3, 4, and 5 provide extensive description of stress in Ngalakgan. Merlan (1983) contains only a brief description of stress. What is included there does not diverge in most respects from the description given here. The analysis (though not the facts) of quantity-sensitivity presented in Chapter 5 is completely different from the analysis presented in Baker (1999: Ch 5) and previous work.

Chapters 3 and 4 are revised and expanded versions of Chapters 2 and 3 of Baker (1999). I have revised the description of morphological types in the lexicon, and described the lexicon itself in more formal detail. Both of these developments lead to more elegance in the analysis of stress in complex words in Chapter 4.

Geminate alternation is described in Merlan (1983: 25-6). In Chapter 6, I provide additional material leading to a different description of the process. This chapter is not significantly different from Chapter 4 of Baker (1999).

There are points on which Merlan (1983) and I differ. Merlan found a vowel length contrast in just one word /maːʔ/, the predicate form of attributive /maʔ/ 'good'. I did not find these two to be in contrast. I did find a contrast in length between open monosyllabic roots such as /po/ 'river' [boː], and corresponding vowels in all other environments: /pok/ 'creek' [bɔk]. But this contrast is entirely predictable, so I do not regard it as an underlying contrast.[5] This distinction is described and analysed in 3.1.2-3. Heath (1978b: 7) recognises a contrastive vowel length distinction in Ngandi in a handful of stems. McKay (1975: 26) notes that vowel lengthening is a predictable feature of monosyllabic roots in Rembarrnga, regardless of affixation. I follow McKay in this regard. Merlan and I also differ in the phonological analysis of what I call 'geminates' and she calls 'fortis' stops. This issue is discussed in detail in 2.3 and 6.1.

1.2.2 The book in the current Australian linguistic context

There has been comparatively little study of the prosody of Australian languages, though more has appeared since Baker (1999). To date, the only extended treatments of prosody in Australian languages are King (1998), Berry (1999), Bishop (2002) and Pentland (2004). King (1998) and Bishop (2002) are instrumental studies of intonation in Dyirbal and Bininj Gun-wok,

[5] This is not the only difference between Merlan (1983) and the present work, but it is one of the most important differences.

respectively. Pentland (2004) is an instrumental study of the phonetic correlates of stress in Warlpiri. In each case, the authors use the existing descriptions of stress in the published grammars—(Dixon 1972; Evans 2003; Nash 1986)—as the basis of their metrical analysis. Berry (1999) is a treatment of stress and other phonological phenomena mainly in Central Australian languages—Warlpiri and Arrernte—couched in Optimality Theory. Henderson (1998) is an extended treatment of phonology, morphology and prosody in Arrernte, addressing both phonetic and phonological evidence. Nash (1986) is a study of morphology in Warlpiri, and contains extensive sections on prosody and phonology. McDonald (1977) is a study of the phonetics and phonology of Yaralde, which includes a detailed treatment of stress and syllabification.

There are a few discussions devoted exclusively to the phonology of Australian languages. Dixon (1980: Ch 6) is a typological survey of phonological and phonotactic patterns. Hamilton (1996) is a survey and analysis of phonotactic patterns in Australian languages, building on and extending Dixon (1980). The account of Ngalakgan phonotactics presented in Chapter 2 of the current monograph takes these two studies as a basis for the analysis. Evans (1995) is a survey of Australian phonological patterns such as syllable structure, the range of segmental contrasts, dissimilation processes, and stress. Andy Butcher has produced papers and several unpublished manuscripts on the phonetics of Australian languages, mainly of the Northern Territory (Butcher 1993a, 1993b, 1995, 1999, 2004). Butcher's work informs the discussion of retroflexion in Ngalakgan in 2.2.2-3, and the analysis of geminates in 6.1. There are numerous shorter works on Australian phonology and prosody, for example (Hale 1976a; Wood 1978; Harvey 1991; Breen 1992; Blevins and Marmion 1994). Evans and Merlan (2004) is a study of stop contrasts in Arnhem Land languages, which makes extensive reference to the analysis presented in Baker (1999).

Two PhD theses have studied aspects of BGW from a phonetic point of view. Since BGW is so closely related to Ngalakgan, these theses are significant for the current monograph. Bishop (2002) is a detailed investigation of the intonation and metrical system of BGW. Bishop couches her analysis in Autosegmental-Metrical theory, with the use of the ToBI ('Tones and Break Indices') system of intonational transcription developed by Janet Pierrehumbert, Mary Beckman and associates (e.g. Silverman et al. 1992). Bishop bases her phonotactic and metrical analysis on Evans (2003). Evans proposes a somewhat different metrical analysis of BGW than I do of Ngalakgan, although the two systems are clearly related. Stoakes (in preparation) is a study of the articulation of consonants in BGW, particularly in Kunwinjku. Although the findings are preliminary, they potentially have a significant bearing on the nature of geminates and glottal stop in Ngalakgan.

1.3 Optimality Theory

The phonological analysis in this book is couched in terms of 'Optimality Theory' (OT) as set out in Prince and Smolensky (1993), McCarthy and Prince (1993a, 1993b, 1995), and subsequent works. This section offers a brief overview of the mechanics of the theory.[6]

1.3.1 The basic apparatus

OT differs from previous work in phonological theory in two respects:

(1) a. There are no phonological rules, rather, the grammar consists of well-formedness conditions ('constraints') which are of a very general sort, available to all languages.
  b. Output forms are evaluated simultaneously, rather than serially, for satisfaction of all of the constraints in the grammar.[7]
  c. Constraints are ranked and violable.

I take each of these points in turn in the discussion which follows.

Rule formalism in Chomsky and Halle (1968: *The Sound Pattern of English* , hereafter 'SPE') was of the following kind:

(2) A → B/ (X)___(Y)

The interpretation of (2) is that 'A becomes B in the environment of X (preceding) and/or Y (following)'.

In OT by contrast, it is hypothesised that all languages have access to a common store of phonologically natural conditions on well-formedness.[8] Instead of the rule in (2), there is a constraint stating that the configuration XAY is ill-formed (*XAY). Outputs are evaluated with respect to a large number of well-formedness conditions simultaneously: there is no rule ordering, and no 'constraint-and-repair' strategy.

One such putatively universal condition is that syllables should have onsets. This is formalised as a constraint—called 'Onset'—which has the

---

[6] For introductions to OT, see e.g. Kager (1999), McCarthy (2001).

[7] While simultaneous evaluation is a desideratum of OT, serial derivation is not ruled out, and is in fact a feature of the analysis in McCarthy and Prince (1993b). Cf. also Blevins (1997), McCarthy (1999).

[8] The use of well-formedness conditions is of course not restricted to OT; McCarthy and Prince (1993b) cite *inter alia* Kisseberth (1970), Haiman (1972), Stampe (1972), Sommerstein (1974), and Goldsmith (1990).

following definition (McCarthy and Prince 1993a: 30; Prince and Smolensky 1993: 16):

(3) ONSET *[$_\sigma$V 'Syllables must have an onset'

It may not be observably the case that every syllable in a given language has an onset, and the word-initial position in languages may often be onsetless. This occurs because any constraint may in principle be violated. The fact that Onset may be violated does not change the observable fact that in most languages, in most environments, syllables have onsets: the constraint 'Onset' is obeyed. Where Onset is *not* obeyed in a given environment, OT claims that there is some other constraint which overrides Onset (in that environment), and therefore, permits violation of Onset.

Much of the variation between languages resides in the ranking between constraints such as 'Onset' which ban illicit structures—'Markedness' constraints—and another set of constraints given the general term 'Faithfulness'. Markedness constraints drive alternations, Faithfulness constraints restrict them.

In OT, Faithfulness is the term given to constraints on the relation between two strings: input and output. *Underlying* and *surface* representations (UR, SR) constitute one pair of input and output strings, respectively. Other pairs proposed by McCarthy and Prince (1995) are *Base* (B) and *Reduplicant* (R), where 'Base' is the surface form of the stem which is copied by the reduplicant.

Faithfulness can be considered as a constraint on a Correspondence relation between the input and output, shown schematically as (4) (following McCarthy and Prince 1995: 252). In this example, the input and output are in perfect correspondence: at the surface, every segment finds some *correspondent* segment in the input.

(4)

Input	/fit/	'feet'
↑		
Correspondence		
↓		
Output	[fit]	

Now consider (5), in this form, perfect correspondence is not observed. The output form has a segment [ʔ] which is not part of the input form. In this case, Onset demands that the initial syllable of [itɪŋ] have an onset, and in the output, this onset is supplied by an 'epenthetic' segment: one which finds no input correspondent. In this example, Onset is satisfied, but perfect correspondence is violated; we say that Onset 'outranks' Faithfulness in this language.

(5)

Input	/itɪŋ/ 'eating'
↑	
Correspondence	
↓	
Output	[ʔitɪŋ]

Faithfulness, in McCarthy and Prince (1995), is now the term given to a 'family' of constraints which regulate any operations on a phonological string which cause it to differ from its correspondent. The three Faithfulness constraints which concern us here are given in (6):

(6)

DEP[endency]	'No epenthesis'
MAX[imality]	'No deletion'
IDENT[ity]([x])	'Segments in correspondence have identical features (optionally parametrised to some feature [x])'

The three Faithfulness constraints may be relativised to pairs of correspondents: Input-Output (IO) Faithfulness regulates the realisation of output representations based on some input, Base-Reduplicant (BR) Faithfulness, of reduplicants on some base, and Output-Output (OO) Faithfulness, of some output form on another (morphologically related) output form.

The second divergence of OT from SPE-based frameworks is simultaneity of evaluation. An Optimality Theoretic grammar evaluates candidate output forms with respect to their satisfaction of a large number of constraints simultaneously, relative to other candidates. The candidate which best satisfies the given constraint ranking is optimal for that grammar.

The set of candidate outputs is produced by a function called GEN (for 'Generator') in Prince and Smolensky (1993: 4), and candidates are *analyses* of the input 'admitted by very general considerations of structural well-formedness' (McCarthy and Prince 1993b: 1). These 'general considerations' in many cases amount to providing the underlying form with prosodic structure: stress and syllabification.

In (7), below, a *tableau* arrays an input, in slashes in the top left hand corner; a partial constraint ranking (left to right); and a selection of candidate outputs, below the double line. The input in (7) consists of the word presented previously in (5), which is onsetless in the underlying (input) form. In English, onsetless words are dispreferred: epenthetic glottal stop insertion is observed, as in candidate (a). This is the attested output corresponding to the input in (7).

Based on the input, we have two serious candidates for consideration apart from the attested form (a). Candidate (b) represents the 'Faithful' analysis, and candidate (c) satisfies Onset by deleting the initial vowel of /itɪŋ/. These candidates are 'evaluated' with respect to the three constraints given in (7): MAX, ONSET and DEP.

(7)

/itɪŋ/ 'eating'	MAX	ONSET	DEP
☞ a. [ʔ]itɪŋ			*
b. itɪŋ		*!	
c. tɪŋ	*!		

Candidate (b) faithfully realises the underlying form, so it satisfies both MAX and DEP. This candidate violates the constraint against onsetless syllables—ONSET—since the initial syllable of the surface form lacks an onset. Constraint violation is signalled by asterisks (*). Candidate (a), with an initial epenthetic segment, satisfies ONSET: the word has an onset at the surface. Epenthesis violates DEP. Since in this language epenthesis, rather than onsetlessness, is observed in this environment, we conclude that ONSET is ranked higher than DEP: it is more important that syllables have onsets than that they respect underlying forms.[9]

We can draw no conclusion about the ranking of MAX and ONSET based on this tableau. Both of the candidates which violate these forms are unattested, and the attested candidate violates neither: there is no 'ranking argument' for MAX and ONSET.[10] But since candidate (c) is unattested, MAX must be ranked above DEP, since onsetlessness is resolved in English by epenthesis, rather than deletion.

In the text, constraint domination is notationally represented with '>>'; as in 'ONSET >> DEP' 'ONSET outranks DEP'. Unranked constraints are separated by commas: 'MAX, ONSET'. In tableaux, ranking is signalled with solid boundaries between constraints (as between ONSET and DEP); a dotted boundary signals a lack of a ranking argument.

Note that constraint violation does not automatically exclude a candidate output from the running (exclusion is signalled by an exclamation mark (!) accompanying a violation mark). What is important is that a given candidate

---

[9] I have abstracted away from other issues, particularly the choice between potential onset segments.

[10] Additional information, such as the behaviour of /itɪŋ/ following a consonant-final word, will allow us to make further ranking arguments.

should violate constraints *minimally*. The attested candidate, which is signalled by the pointing hand (☞), is the candidate which is *optimal* with respect to the constraint ranking in this language. The other candidates, (b) and (c) are *less harmonic* than (a) because they violate constraints which are higher-ranked than the highest (given) violation incurred by (a).[11]

The foregoing has described the basic mechanics of the theory. Other aspects of OT will be introduced in the following chapters where they are appropriate to the discussion.

1.4 Outline of the chapters

The book can be divided into two parts. The first part—Chapters 2, 3 and 4—discusses issues that are relevant to a large number of Australian languages, not just Ngalakgan. The second part—Chapters 5 and 6—discusses some issues which are more peculiar to Ngalakgan and its near neighbours and genetic relations.

In Chapter 2 I introduce the segmental inventory (2.1) and phonotactics (2.2) of Ngalakgan. In 2.3, I discuss the phonotactics of geminates, concluding that they behave like clusters, but are syllabified in the onset, rather than across a syllable boundary. In 2.4, I examine the nature of laryngealisation in Ngalakgan, and conclude that the glottal stop is a phoneme which is consistently realised as post-laryngealisation of a preceding sonorant. This has implications for its phonotactic and phonological behaviour.

The metrical structure of roots and compounds is described in Chapter 3. I show that stress provides evidence for two types or 'levels' of morphology: the 'ROOT'-level and the 'WORD'-level (following Selkirk 1982; Borowsky 1990). When two words are compounded—are complex at the WORD-level—each word retains the metrical structure and the meaning that it has when independent. Words which are complex at the ROOT-level on the other hand have the same metrical structure as simple words. This reflects their semantic characteristics: the constituents of ROOT-complex words do not necessarily make a compositional contribution to the semantics of the whole word. Chapter 3 also justifies the distinction between stress and pitch accent in Ngalakgan: not every strong beat in a word is associated with distinctive pitch.

Chapter 4 describes the prosody of bound morphemes in the language. I show that WORD-level affixes and bound stems constitute independent domains for prosodic structure, a characteristic which Ngalakgan shares with

---

11 Following Prince and Smolensky (1993) I avoid use of the phrases 'less optimal', 'more optimal', and use 'less harmonic', 'more harmonic' instead, reserving 'optimal' for the best output.

many other Australian languages such as Warlpiri (Nash 1986) and Diyari (Austin 1981). As a result, every WORD-level suffix and bound stem which is two syllables long or more receives its own stress. Monosyllabic suffixes and bound stems (from minor syntactic categories) can only be stressed if they precede another monosyllabic suffix or clitic.

Pitch accents in Ngalakgan are associated with two positions in words: their primary affiliation is to roots of major syntactic categories (N, V, Adj). They have a secondary affiliation with the last strong beat in a word. They cannot ordinarily be associated with any other positions. As a result, suffixes and left-binding stems can be associated with distinctive pitch, but prefixes and many right-binding stems cannot be. This characteristic distinguishes Ngalakgan from other languages of its genetic group (Gunwinyguan), in which prefixes can be stressed only if the root is monosyllabic (see e.g. Evans 2003: 99). Ngalakgan provides further evidence that meaningful parts of words (morphemes) which are not themselves words, can nevertheless have the prosodic characteristics associated with words (cf. Aronoff and Sridhar 1983; Rubach and Booij 1990).

Chapter 5 discusses the basis of syllable quantity effects on stress in roots. The quantity sensitivity found in Ngalakgan and, as I show, other neighbouring languages, is of a kind hitherto unknown to the metrical literature. Stress is attracted to syllables with codas, but only codas which are heterorganic to any following consonants count for weight. Geminates, and homorganic nasal-stop clusters, do not attract stress to the preceding syllable. I argue that syllabification in Ngalakgan and neighbouring languages is gesturally—rather than timing—based: homorganic clusters are syllabified in the onset. The only consonants which might contribute weight to a syllable are thus those which cannot be place-linked to a following consonant and therefore must be syllabified as codas.

Chapter 6 discusses further aspects of the nature and distribution of geminates in the language, and in particular the unusual process of geminate alternation. I argue that Ngalakgan has a single series of stops, like the majority of Australian languages. These stops also occur as geminates, which in most respects behave like geminates in other languages. This analysis is contrary to that of Merlan (1983), who proposes two series of stops in Ngalakgan: fortis and lenis. The phonetic correlates of geminates and singletons are examined in 6.1.

Geminates, and glottal stops, are commonly found at morpheme boundaries (6.2). I regard both as 'boundary signals' in Trubetzkoy's (1969[1939]) sense: elements that help a hearer to segment a word or phrase into its constituents.[12] In this way, geminates and glottal stops perform a similar

[12] This Prague school notion was taken up by Firth (1949), and more recently Cléirigh (1998)

function to the stress patterns described in Chapters 3 and 4. Each morpheme is distinguished not only by prosodic patterns, but also by characteristic syllabic structures and segments. Geminate alternation (6.3) is a process which reinforces this relationship, by preventing incorrect parses.

Chapter 7 is a summary of the main claims of the book, together with a flagging of some issues for future research.

---

has extended the idea to a systemic-functional analysis of Irish.

2

Issues in the segmental inventory of Ngalakgan

This chapter has two aims. The first is to provide a survey of the phoneme inventory and the segmental phonotactics of Ngalakgan, as a general introduction to the sound system of the language which will be important in later chapters. The second is to critically evaluate in particular the status of two processes—gemination and laryngealisation—whose representation and status in the grammar has proven problematic. My intention here is to propose a new analysis for both of them, one which makes sense of their interactions with phonotactics and quantity-sensitivity. The former is examined in detail here, while metrical quantity is the subject of Chapter 5.

2.1 Segment inventory

Table (1) on the following page presents the underlying consonant inventory assumed in this work.

Minimal and near minimal pairs for the phonemes given here are presented in Merlan (1983). I will not repeat her evidence for the most part. Ngalakgan has previously been described as having a fortis/lenis contrast in its inventory of oral obstruents (Merlan 1983). In Baker (1999), I described the language as having a single series of obstruents, which could be realised as singletons in any position in the word, or as geminates just in word-medial positions. The major cue to the contrast is stricture duration. The nature of the stop contrast is discussed more fully in section 2.3 below and in Chapter 6.

	Labial	Apico-alveolar	Apico-post-alveolar (retroflex)	Lamino-alveo-palatal	Dorso-velar	Glottal
Stop	p	t	ʈ	c	k	ʔ
Nasal	m	n	ɳ	ɲ	ŋ	
Lateral		l	ɭ			
Tap/trill		r				
Approx.	w		ɻ	j		

Table 1: Consonant phonemes

Stops are represented phonemically with a voiceless symbol though the voicing of simple stops varies according to segmental context and place of articulation (and varies accordingly in the phonetic representations of examples). Geminate stops are represented phonemically with double voiceless stop symbols.

I will now briefly discuss the articulation of these consonantal segments. Note however that I have not carried out extensive instrumental studies of Ngalakgan, and my comments are necessarily impressionistic. I will discuss place of articulation first, followed by manner. I rely here on Hamilton (1996) and especially Butcher (1993a), the latter being an instrumental study of a range of Australian languages including some (such as Bininj Gun-wok—BGW) closely related to Ngalakgan.

2.1.1 Place of articulation

Like many Australian languages, Ngalakgan has a large inventory of coronals. There are two contrastive apical articulations: alveolar and retroflex. Articulatory research on speakers of nearby, related languages such as Bininj Gun-wok is presented in Butcher (1993a, 1995). Butcher's research indicates that in Australian languages with an apical contrast, the most consistent correlate of the contrast is the tongue gesture involved, rather than passive place of articulation. In apico-alveolars, the tongue is raised to touch the closest point on the alveolar ridge. In apico-retroflexes, by contrast, the tongue tip is drawn back and touches the palate usually in the postalveolar region, then moves forward, releasing at a point and in a tongue configuration very similar to that of apico-alveolars (see also Henderson 1998).

This 'ballistic' quality of retroflexes can help to explain much of their characteristic phonological behaviour. Because their release characteristics are nearly identical to apico-alveolars, without a preceding vowel, retroflex consonants are nearly impossible to distinguish from alveolars. Even with a preceding vowel they can be difficult to distinguish depending on speaker, speech rate, and phonological, prosodic and morphological context. I have found however, that the apical contrast in Ngalakgan is certainly clearer than that of neighbouring Alawa.

The apicals contrast with a single laminal series which to my ears sounded consistently lamino-postalveolar. Languages with this kind of single laminal are also described in Butcher (1995). He shows that the stricture is formed by raising the blade of the tongue towards the rear of the alveolar ridge, typically extending at midline for a distance of around 10mm.

The articulation of the other contrastive places is not particularly noteworthy. Stops differ in their release quality when intonation phrase-final to some extent: the dorsal and laminal tend to have an audible release, while the labial and apicals tend not to. However, I would say that the articulation of laminals is more variable than the other stops, with the exception of retroflexes, and both certainly deserve fuller investigation.

The nasals, as far as can be determined, are articulated in essentially the same way as the corresponding stops except that the velum is lowered (this is the conclusion of Butcher 1993a, on the basis of his investigation of several Australian languages). In other work (1999), Butcher suggests that speakers of Australian languages do not nasalise vowels in anticipation of following nasals, suggesting the velum is lowered late. Further work by Marija Tabain, Gavan Breen and Andy Butcher (2004), suggests that a lack of VC coarticulation in general is characteristic of many Australian languages.

2.1.2 Manner

It is useful to distinguish several manner classes among consonants, for the purposes of phonotactics (2.2), as well as phonological processes:

(1)	a. Stops	[–son, –cont]	/p t ʈ c k ʔ/
	b. Sonorants	[+son]	/m n ɳ ɲ ŋ l ɭ r ɻ w j/
	c. Nasals	[+son, –cont]	/m n ɳ ɲ ŋ/
	d. Continuants	[+son, +cont]	/l ɭ r ɻ w j/[1]

[1] Throughout the book 'continuant' refers to the set {vowels, liquids and glides}. I will refer to nasals, glottal stop and supralaryngeal obstruents collectively as 'non-continuants'. This follows Australianist practice (e.g. Morphy 1983), although it is not the standard application of the term 'continuant'. Stevens (1998: 249) for example defines continuancy in the following terms: 'the articulator that forms the constriction creates a complete closure (the feature [–continuant]) or a partial closure [+continuant]). In the latter case, continuous turbulence [sic]

Stops and nasals have already been described. Geminates are described in 2.2.The glottal stop is described below in 2.4.

Among continuants, Ngalakgan has a relatively large inventory of liquids, and no fricatives, as is typical of Australian languages (Hamilton 1996). There are two apical laterals, contrasting for retroflexion, and two ‘r’ sounds: the tap/flap/trill /r/ and the glide /ɻ/. The tap varies somewhat according to position in the word, and especially with respect to neighbouring consonants, though perhaps not as much as other Australian languages. Between vowels it is an apical tap, much like that of American English. Speakers of Australian English and even Kriol speakers commonly confuse it with an intervocalic stop ‘d’ (and hence loans such as ‘medicine’ become [mɪɾiccɪn] in Ngalakgan and Kriol). Preceding stops, it can have a brief trill quality (though no more than a few oscillations are heard), and appears to be articulated more with the blade than the tip. The trill quality is more pronounced when word final; however in this position it can also approach the articulation of a fricative, with the sides of the blade sustaining contact with the palate while the midline is grooved.

2.1.3 Vowels

The vowel inventory is presented in Table (2).

	Front/unrounded		Back/rounded
High	ɪ ~ i		ʊ ~ u
Mid	ɛ ~ e		ɒ ~ ɔ ~ o
Low		a ~ æ ~ ɐ	

Table 2: Vowel phonemes

The most usual allophones of each vowel are given. Each vowel has at least two allophones—‘centralised’ and ‘peripheral’—though these are most distinct for the non-low vowels.[2] The auditory distinction between the two

noise is formed near the constriction.’ Stevens includes the fricatives of English in this class, as well as /r/, but not /l/, which he classes as [–continuant] for reasons I do not understand, given that the articulation of /l/ does not form a complete closure.

2 The auditory distinction between the two major allophones of the low vowel [a] and [ɐ] is not very clear in Ngalakgan. The third allophone [æ] I have heard before alveolars in a few instances, e.g. before /l/ in /palmo/ [bǽlmo] ‘whack (small game animal, to stun or kill it)’ and both /r/ and /ʈ/ in /caraʈatpuwa/ [ɟæ̀raɖǽtpuwa] ‘chestnut rail’, as well as after the laminal stop occasionally in e.g. /cacabaɻŋʔ/ [ɟǽɟæbaɻŋ̃] ‘yesterday’. But this allophone [æ] does not appear consistently in these environments for all lexical items, e.g. /carppic/ [ɟárppic] ‘thigh’,

is roughly like that between 'lax' or 'open', and 'tense' or 'close' vowels, respectively, in English. In open monosyllables, as in (2)a, vowels are both peripheral (though not as tense as English [o] in /oʊ/) and phonologically long (see 3.1.3).[3] In open final syllables of polysyllabic morphemes, (2)b, vowels are somewhat peripheral but short. Elsewhere, (2)c-d, vowels are mostly lax. Vowels can be especially centralised (at least to my ears) in stressed syllables; see also Bishop (2002: 233-234).

(2)				
	a.	/po/	'river'	[boː]
	b.	/ɻapo/	go+PP	[ɻábo]
	c.	/pok/	'creek'	[bɒk]
	d.	/pot/	'fly'	[bɔt] ~ [bɔᵊt]

Only the mid back vowel appears to have the two lax allophones shown in (2), other vowels just have one lax allophone. The usual allophone of /o/ is a mid-back lax vowel written [ɔ], though this vowel is not long, unlike in English. Before velars, particularly in closed monosyllables as in (2)c, the mid-back vowel is relatively low and less rounded, similar to Australian and British English [ɒ] in *rock*. Before apicals, the most typical allophone of /o/ is higher, more rounded and can be longer; it will be represented with the elsewhere allophone [ɔ]. Before the apico-alveolar stop, one can often hear movement of the formants indicating a brief central offglide around [ə].

Diphthongs found in Ngalakgan are presented in Table (3). Phonemically, these represent the combination of every vowel followed by either of the two semivowels /j w/, except that phonemic combinations of homorganic vowel+semivowel are not found. These would be phonetically indistinguishable from long versions of these high vowels—however, there are no environments where these two vowels occur long in Ngalakgan, all long vowels are [–high].[4]

The same inventory is found also in BGW (Evans 2003: 75). Evans provides several arguments that the phonetic offglide should be regarded as a

---

/pala-cakku/ [bàlaɟákku] 'lefthand side', /palak/ [bálak] 'MoMoBrCh', and many others. I have never heard these items pronounced with the higher front allophone.

[3] That is, as opposed to vowels which are lengthened for stylistic reasons. For example, a common discourse device in this area is to lengthen the last vowel of a verb, to indicate temporal or spatial extension or duration: [ɟɪrbʊ̀ɪppʊɪjnɛ́:::ɲ] /jir-pujppujɳe+ɲ/ (1aS-singe+[burn+]PP) 'we singed it (for a long time)' (see e.g. Heath 1984 for discussion of this phenomenon in Nunggubuyu). Here the vowel is not phonologically long, and is accordingly realised not in the peripheral, but in the central allophone [ɛ].

[4] The exception is the heteromorphemic long /i/ vowel which occurs when a stem ending in this vowel takes the Ergative suffix /-jiʔ/, e.g. /mu-wacci-jiʔ/ 'VEG-sun-ERG' heard as [muwaˈcciḭ].

phonological semi-vowel/approximant, rather than a vowel. These arguments are reviewed in 2.5.

/j/-final		/w/-final	
	uj [uɪ]	iw [ɪʊ]	
ej [eɪ]	oj [oɪ]	ew [ɛʊ]	ow [oʊ]
	aj [aɪ]		aw [aʊ]

Table 3: Diphthongs in Ngalakgan

2.1.4 The stop contrast and the glottal stop

Throughout this monograph I assume that the stop contrast should be interpreted as one of geminate vs. singleton, although (as shown in 2.3.2) geminates do not have the syllabification that we would expect: rather, they are syllabified entirely in the onset. I suggest that this 'dual nature' of the stop opposition in Ngalakgan and related languages such as Rembarrnga and Bininj Gun-wok, is what has led to the differing analyses, depending on the level at which authors focussed their attention—segmental, or syllabic (cf. Evans and Merlan 2004). Moreover, as later sections and Chapter 6 will show, the difference between geminate and singleton stops cannot be characterised in terms of a single controlling feature such as duration or voicing. Rather, different correlates of the distinction play distinct roles in the phonology of Ngalakgan and other Northern languages such as Rembarrnga, Ngandi, and Bininj Gun-wok. The phonetics of the stop contrast is discussed in 2.3.1, and their phonological representation in 2.3.3. The phonological status of the glottal stop is discussed further below in 2.4. Like the oral stop contrast, its distribution, phonetics and phonological behaviour are all problematic for a simple segmental account.

Before dealing with these matters, I first discuss the phonotactics of consonantal segments in general in Ngalakgan.

2.2 Syllabification and phonotactics

This section provides an overview of phonotactics in Ngalakgan; for more detailed exemplification of attested patterns, see Merlan (1983). As we will see in Chapter 5, understanding the nature of syllable structure is crucial to providing a meaningful account of quantity-sensitivity in Ngalakgan and related languages. In what follows, I draw on Hamilton (1996), Dixon (1980), and Steriade (1999b).

2.2.1 Phonotactic positions

The general schema for syllable and word structure in Ngalakgan and nearby languages is in most crucial respects the same as that first proposed for Australian languages by Dixon (1980: 159-78). The following characterisation is due to Hamilton (1996: 75), who develops Dixon's proposals in more detail, with reference to a bigger sample of Australian languages than was available to Dixon (1980). Hamilton in addition uses theories of perceptual and articulatory markedness in order to account for the observed regularities in Australian phonotactics.

The consonantal phonotactics of Australian languages can in most cases be described in terms of five phonotactic positions, shown in (3):

(3) a. $C_{init}V(C_{inter}V)^*(C_{fin})$
b. $C_{init}V(C_1C_2V)^*(C_{fin})$

where,

C_{init} is a word-initial consonant
C_{inter} is an intervocalic consonant or monogestural cluster (see below)
C_{fin} is a word-final consonant
C_1 is a pre-consonantal consonant
C_2 is a post-consonantal consonant
and C_1C_2 are heterorganic

Hamilton, following Dixon (1980), shows that each consonantal position is associated with a distinctive and characteristic range of segmental possibilities. The core range of segmental possibilities at each position is very similar across the continent, varying mainly in the extent of additional contrasts permitted.

In Ngalakgan, the following segmental contrasts are associated with these positions. The first three types are relatively straightforward:

C_{init} Any consonant except the tap/trill /r/ and the glottal stop /ʔ/. Geminates are not found initially (2.3.2), and the apical contrast is neutralised in this position (2.2.2), with conditioned alternation between alveolar and retroflex realisations.
Initial consonants are optional in Ngalakgan: there are several vowel-initial words, all of them conjunctions, and all of them polysyllabic.[5]

[5] Blevins and Marmion (1994) suggest that this is one word class which is a prime candidate for initial consonant erosion, due to a combination of position-in-utterance and perceptual factors.

C_{inter} Any consonant or monogestural cluster except the glottal stop /ʔ/.
C_{fin} Any consonant; geminates are not found word-finally.

In addition to single consonants, C_{inter} can host all the monogestural clusters in the language. By ‘monogestural cluster’ I mean a geminate, or a homorganic nasal-stop cluster; those sequences which correspond to two timing slots but involve a single oral gesture. Furthermore, as discussed in 2.2.2, apical clusters must be monogestural, that is, made with a single tongue gesture. The only apical clusters then are nasal-stop clusters sharing place of articulation, that is /nt, ɳʈ/. There are no apical clusters permitted apart from these. So potential clusters /lt, ɭʈ, ltt, ɭʈʈ, ɭt, lʈ .../ are all banned in Ngalakgan, though /lt, ɭʈ/ are possible in neighbouring Marra and Alawa. These lateral+stop clusters, though homorganic (involving the same phonological place of articulation feature) are not, strictly speaking, monogestural (Hamilton 1996: 95), because the liquids in these clusters are not produced with the same gesture as the following stop (where ‘gesture’ is defined in terms of Browman and Goldstein 1989). Chapter 5 demonstrates that this difference is recognised in the weight system of Ngalakgan and related languages such as Kuninjku.

	p	t	ʈ	c	k	m	ŋ	w	j
p	pp								
t	tp	tt							
ʈ	ʈp		ʈʈ	ʈc	ʈk				
c	cp			cc					
k	kp				kk				
m	mp								
n	np	nt		nc	nk	nm			
ɳ	ɳp		ɳʈ	ɳc	ɳk	ɳm	ɳŋ	ɳw	
ɲ	ɲp			ɲc	ɲk	ɲm			
ŋ					ŋk				
l	lp				lk	lm	lŋ		lj
ɭ						ɭm	ɭŋ		ɭj
r	rp				rk	rm	rŋ	rw	
ɻ				ɻc		ɻm	ɻŋ		ɻj
w									
j						jm	jŋ	jw	

Table 4: Intramorphemic, word-medial clusters with two segmental timing positions

Table (4) (on the previous page) illustrates both heterorganic and homorganic clusters with two timing units, that is, it does not include clusters of geminates with other segments (these are examined separately below). The data here is derived from Merlan (1983: 13). The leftmost column corresponds to the first segmental timing position, the topmost row corresponds to the second segmental timing position.

As in other Australian languages, heterorganic clusters are common in the Ngalakgan lexicon. Furthermore, with few exceptions, heterorganic clusters, even those which are unattested intramorphemically, are not subject to assimilation processes across morpheme boundaries (Hamilton 1996: 19). The following data illustrate the first point. Of 1268 monomorphemic roots attested so far in Ngalakgan, 508 (40%) have a cluster of some kind —heterorganic or homorganic. 238 (19%; close to half of all clusters found) have a heterorganic cluster, whether medially or finally. 161 roots have a medial heterorganic cluster—13% of the lexicon.

Heterorganic clusters fall into several types, depending on the manner of articulation of C_1 and C_2.[6] I limit my remarks here to monomorphemic roots, ignoring reduplicated forms (whether frozen or productive). There is a general tendency for C_1 to be sonorant, and C_2 to be non-sonorant; this is a cross-linguistic generalisation (the 'syllable contact law' of Murray and Vennemann 1983). In terms of place, the overwhelming pattern in all Australian languages is for C_1 to be coronal, and for C_2 to be non-coronal (Hamilton 1996: 118). This is true of Ngalakgan. Where C_1 is coronal, C_2 may be a consonant with any non-coronal place of articulation. Some examples illustrating common clusters are: /peɳpereɲ/ 'ghost gum sp.' (*Eucalyptus papuana*), /warcaʔ/ 'forage', /muɳcum/ 'shoulder', /munpic/ 'woman's pubic covering', /munku/ 'follow'. Notably absent from the C_2 position in Table (4) are coronal sonorants: apart from /j/, these are never found intramorphemically in the second position of clusters. In 2.6, I discuss some phonological alternations involving these segments in C_2 of heteromorphemic clusters.

Apart from these common types, C_1 may also be a non-coronal nasal or oral stop in just a handful of clusters: /ŋm/ in two words—/kurŋmuŋ/ 'greedy' and /waɻŋmele/ 'hip', /kp/ in /ʈakparara/ 'green pandanus frog' (an onomatopoeic word), and /kc/ in /kajakciŋiweɳ/ 'cranky, bad-tempered'.[7] The latter (recorded by Merlan), at least, appears to be historically complex but there is no clear etymology. In addition, speakers did not recognise the term

---

6 The behaviour of glottal stop, when viewed as a segment, falls outside the characterisation presented here. It is discussed separately below, in 2.4.

7 Although in the first two words, there is a triconsonantal cluster involved, the second consonant is still a 'C_1' under Hamilton's definition. Of course, it is also a 'C_2' under the same set of definitions. I consider triconsonantal clusters further below.

when I attempted to record it. Merlan (1983: 15) in addition lists /ŋp/ as a possible cluster, providing /ʈaŋpon/ (the name of an ethnolinguistic group to the immediate north-west of the Ngalakgan) as an example. This name is clearly complex, even for Ngalakgan speakers: /ʈaŋ/ is recognised as Bininj Gun-wok for 'mouth', and /bon/ as the ethnonym.[8] Apart from these, there are a number of words with a cluster of labio-dorsal glide and following consonant, typically /k/ or /ŋ/. These include [goʊkko] 'Mother's Mother' [kinship category], and [ɻoʊno] or [ɻo:no], a placename, which contrast with forms such as /ɻok-kaʔ/ [ɻɒkka̤] 'pandanus-LOC' and /poɳo/ [bɔɳo] 'another'. The correct phonemic analysis of these forms is still unclear. Tentatively, I would analyse them as /kowkko/ and /ɻowno/, respectively. I have omitted doubtful or marginal examples of clusters such as these from Table (4).

Table (5) gives the attested medial clusters of continuant followed by what I call monogestural clusters: geminates or homorganic nasal-stop clusters.

	pp	tt	ʈʈ	cc	kk	mp	nt	ɳʈ	ɲc	ŋk
l	lpp			lcc	lkk					
ɭ	ɭpp				ɭkk					
r	rpp			rcc	rkk	rmp				rŋk
ɻ	ɻpp			ɻcc	ɻkk					
w					wkk					
j	jpp				jkk					

Table 5: Continuant+monogestural clusters

Clusters involving continuants plus geminates are common in the lexicon, e.g. /palkkiɲ/ 'salty; dangerous', /puɻppa/ 'water lily' (*Nymphaea violacea*), /kulcci/ 'mortar'; see Merlan (1983) for further examples. Examples of continuants plus homorganic nasal-stop clusters are rarer, (4) provides all the attested examples, along with the only other two forms involving a trisegmental cluster of any kind (again, ignoring forms with laryngealisation as the 'third segment'), which have already been mentioned.

[8] This ethnonym has a variety of forms, reflecting regular correspondences among the language groups neighbouring the Dalabon. /taŋbon/ is the BGW term (BGW /taŋ/ 'mouth'); the Ngalakgan term is /ʈalapon/, equivalent to the actual Dalabon term for the language (whose autochthonous term for 'mouth' is /tala/); the Ngalakgan term for mouth is cognate /ɟala/. The Jawoyn term is /ŋalkbon/, with Jawoyn /ŋalk/ 'mouth'. The Rembarrnga typically use the term /buan/, a cognate (with Rembarrnga vowel-breaking: see Baker 2004) of what is probably the original ethnonym (though Evans 2003 suggests that the /bon/ portion is just the Dalabon 'go' (NonPast) stem).

(4) /warmpaja/ 'anywhere, everywhere'
/warŋku/ 'for that reason, thus'
/waɻʈŋmele/ 'hip'
/marŋki/ 'unknowledgeable, inexpert'
/ŋurŋki-/ 'jealous' (verb stem)
/kurŋmuŋ/ 'greedy'

Notably, all trisegmental clusters fall into one of two types: a liquid followed by a homorganic nasal-stop cluster, or a liquid followed by the sequence /ŋm/. I return to these forms after discussing final clusters.

Ngalakgan, and many other Northern languages, differ from the general Australian template in two respects: (i) many roots and words are monosyllabic, and (ii) clusters are attested word finally as well as medially; some examples are presented in (5), and the full complement in Table (6).[9]

(5) a. /poʈewk/ 'bad'
b. /peɻʈemelk/ 'shoulder blade'
c. /piccurk/ 'tuber sp.'

	p	t	ʈ	c	k	m	n	ɳ	ɲ	ŋ
l	lp				lk					lŋ
ɭ					ɭk					ɭŋ
r	rp				rk					rŋ
ɻ	ɻp				ɻk					ɻŋ
w					wk					
j					jk					

Table 6: Attested word-final clusters

Since the attested range of clusters in word-final position is more restricted than that found medially, and since the presence of a consonant preceding a word-final consonant also restricts the possibilities at the latter position, it seems best to propose a third, distinct word pattern for these languages:

---

[9] I use the term 'Northern' languages to refer to those—mainly Non-Pama-Nyungan—languages of the northern half of the Northern Territory (i.e. north of a line drawn from the Victoria River across to the Barkly tablelands), and the Kimberley region of Western Australia, which have similar typological and phonological profiles.

(6) $$C_{init}V(\begin{Bmatrix} C_1C_2V \\ C_{inter}V \end{Bmatrix})C_3C_4$$

The possible segments at C_3 and C_4 are a subset of those found in C_1 and C_2. In general, C_3 must be a liquid or glide and C_4 must be a stop (nasal or oral), and furthermore can only be the dorsal nasal [ŋ] or oral stop [k], with [p] also found in a handful of forms.[10] That is, a sequence of continuant+ non-continuant where C_1 and C_2 differ in major articulator. The continuants in Ngalakgan are /r, l, ɭ, ɻ, w, j/. The apical liquids and glide rule out apicals in C_2 as a consequence. In addition, the labio-dorsal and palatal glides cannot be followed by a labial or lamino-palatal consonant, respectively; that is, the sequences /wp/, /wm/ and /jc/, /jɲ/ do not occur. In the case of the laminals, these sequences would be difficult to distinguish from /Vc/ and /Vɲ/ in any case, since the major perceptual cue for laminals in codas is a preceding palatal offglide from the vowel.

With one exception, the first two positions of all of the medial trisegmental clusters presented above can be described as a subset of the attested possible word-final clusters. All of these clusters, except for one, start with liquid plus dorsal nasal. The sequence liquid plus labial nasal does not occur word-finally in Ngalakgan, hence /warmpaja/ does not fall under the general pattern. However, it makes sense in terms of the analysis (presented in 2.3.3) that monogestural clusters are onsets; indeed, its occurrence medially is otherwise inexplicable in terms of syllabic licensing.

We will now examine the only major pattern of phonological place alternation which is dependent on phonotactics—the neutralisation of apical contrasts—following which I present an analysis of place phonotactics in general.

2.2.2 Neutralisation of the apical contrast

Apical consonants in Ngalakgan contrast for alveolar and postalveolar place of articulation, but only following vowels, as in many languages (Hamilton

---

[10] With the onomatopoeic exception of /korpkorp/ 'kookaburra', words with final clusters involving /p/ are only found in the verbal lexicon: /warp/ 'to tell a lie', /walp/ 'to get lost', /waɻp/ 'be full up with food', /ʈeɻp/ 'to be sleepy'. All of these forms are from the open conjugation of verbs (see Chapter 3), and can therefore be pronounced as words in the Present tense, which takes -Ø inflection in this conjugation. The Present tense form is also the citation form for speakers. There is but one example of a morpheme-final cluster involving /c/, it too is from the verbal lexicon: /wiɻc+jo/ 'be on either side of'. In this case, the form is a bound stem (see Chapter 3), and hence cannot be pronounced as a word.

1996: 48).[11] Root-internally, the contrast distinguishes minimal and near-minimal pairs:

(7)	a. /paɳarʔ/	[baɳaɽ]	'marble tree'
	b. /wa**n**ar/	[wanar]	'rock ring-tailed possum'

Without a preceding vowel, apicals either neutralise to postalveolar, or assimilate completely in place of articulation to a preceding apical (8). There are no words like those in (9). Indeed, I know of no languages where such a contrast is possible.

(8)	a. /kaɳ̟ʈ̟a/	[gaɳ̟ɖ̟a]	'lower leg'
	b. /cakanta/	[ɟaganda]	'female plains kangaroo'

(9)	a. */kaɳ̟ta/	[gaɳ̟da]
	b. */cakanʈ̟a/	[ɟaganɖ̟a]

In roots, nasal+stop clusters of apicals must be fully homorganic. This is despite the fact that heterorganic nasal+stop clusters (of coronal+peripheral place of articulation) are relatively common. There are no morpheme-internal homorganic liquid+stop clusters in the language, as noted above in 2.2.1.

The contrast is neutralised word-initially. After a pause, apicals are alveolar, as in (10)a-c. Following a vowel, apical-initial stems and words are postalveolar-initial, as in the prefixed examples in (10)d-f. Square brackets enclose the phonetic realisation in each case.[12]

(10)	a. [**n**]aŋkuru 'saltwater crocodile'	d. ɳu-ku-[**ɳ̟**]aŋkuru M-TOP-crocodile 'the crocodile'
	b. [**n**]occo 'grass' (generic term)	e. ku-[**ɳ̟**]occo NEUT-grass '(some) grass'

---

[11] Apicals can also be postalveolar after a vowel+glottal stop sequence both root-internally and hetero-morphemically. The reason for this is discussed in 2.4.

[12] Butcher (1995), based on palatographic evidence from Warlpiri, Ngaanyatjarra, Murrinh-Patha, Guugu Yimidhirr, and Nyangumarta, has proposed that neutralised apicals are gesturally distinct from both contrastive apico-alveolars and apico-postalveolars. Rather, he claims, neutralised apicals are in fact articulated at a distinct place midway between the alveolar and post-alveolar regions, with an apical, rather than sublaminal, gesture. I have no data on this issue in Ngalakgan. But I note that Butcher only discusses the articulation of word-initial apicals in isolation (Butcher p.c. has confirmed this); he does not discuss the effect of preceding vowels on the articulation of neutralised apicals.

c. [**n**]e+ɲ	f. ŋu-ku-[**ɳ**]e+ɲ
burn+PP	1mS-NEUT-burn+PP
'[someone] burnt it'	'I burnt it'

I represent the initial-apical in words as underlyingly postalveolar (following Merlan 1983: 9). A neutralisation of postalveolar to alveolar is straightforward to motivate on perceptual grounds. Since the primary cue for retroflexion is 'r-colouring' on the preceding vowel (Hamilton 1996: 48; Anderson 2000), in the absence of a preceding vowel, postalveolars are difficult to distinguish from alveolars. Neutralisation of the apical contrast in word-initial position is phonetically-grounded therefore (Steriade 2001). There is no such motivation for the opposite position: that underlying apico-alveolars are regularly realised as postalveolar following vowels.

2.2.3 Analysis of place phonotactics

In what follows, I provide a constraint-based analysis of the major phonotactic patterns affecting place of articulation, following Hamilton (1996). Hamilton proposes that the following two hierarchies together determine the major phonotactic patterns observed in Australian languages:

(11) a. [place] tied to release cues:
*[place]^{VC} >> *[place]^{CV} >> *[place]^{VCV}

b. [place] tied to attack cues:
*[place]^{CV} >> *[place]^{VC} >> *[place]^{VCV}

The hierarchy distinguishes the perceptibility of place features depending on whether they are cued primarily (or only) by release, or by attack. The majority of obstruent place features are cued primarily by release, since the properties of the burst alone are usually sufficient to identify the place of articulation of stops (Hamilton 1996: 50; citing Repp 1976; Fujimura, Macchi and Streeter 1978; among others).[13] However, in the case of retroflex stops, the most reliable cue is in the vowel formant transitions of the attack, where the falling F3 contour is highly distinctive of these stops (what is described as 'r-colouring' on the preceding vowel) (e.g. Dave 1977; Dart 1991; Ladefoged and Maddieson 1996). By contrast, the release of retroflex apicals is often indistinguishable from that of apico-alveolars (Dave 1977; Butcher

[13] When the consonants in spliced V-C and C-V transitions have different places of articulation, with a gap equal to that typical of a single stop, listeners generally "hear" only the consonant cued by the C-V transition.'(Hamilton 1996: 50)

1993a; Henderson 1998). The lamino-postalveolar stops are distinctively cued both in attack (with raised F2) and in release (Hamilton 1996).

The hierarchy in (11)a states that place features which are cued mainly by release (the major articulator nodes labial, dorsal, apical, laminal) are most perceptible in an intervocalic context, and least perceptible in a context lacking release, such as preceding a consonant of a distinct place of articulation (and possibly also word-final position, depending on whether stops are released in this position). In this context, only the vowel formant transitions of the attack can be used as cues for the obstruent's place of articulation. Obstruents in a pre-consonantal position are those which are most vulnerable to assimilation, as shown in numerous studies. Wilson (2001) is a recent, perceptually-based account of this pattern.

The hierarchy in (11)b states that place features which are cued mainly by attack (the minor articulator nodes apico-retroflex, and lamino-post-alveolar), are most perceptible in an intervocalic context, and least perceptible in a context lacking attack cues: that is, following pause or a consonant of a distinct place of articulation. Apical consonants consistently fail to show contrast in initial position in languages with such a contrast medially; see Steriade (2001) and Hamilton (1996) for Australian examples. They also fail to contrast following non-apical consonants. Following apicals, they undergo total assimilation, as shown in 2.2.2.

Note that whether place of articulation is cued mainly by release, or mainly by attack, all places of articulation are most easily perceived in an intervocalic context, since both the vowel formant transition cues and the burst cues are available for the perception of place features. This is why, Hamilton argues, the intervocalic position in Australian languages consistently licenses the full range of segmental contrasts, while other positions in the word fail to do so. In many Australian languages, this effect is quite extreme. For instance, in Kalkatungu (Blake 1979), which has a typical Australian phonotactic system, there are six places of articulation in stops (the same as Ngalakgan with the addition of lamino-dental), but these six contrast only in intervocalic position (which includes homorganic clusters, recall). The apical contrast is neutralised in initial position (as is typical of Australian languages, as discussed in 2.2.2), while only labials and dorsals can occur in the second position of a heterorganic cluster, and furthermore the possibilities in word-final position are heavily restricted.

On the basis of this kind of evidence, Hamilton argues that licensing by prosodic position ('onset', 'coda', etc) cannot describe the typical Australian phonotactic system. The intervocalic position is an 'onset', but it is not the only onset position. There is no way, in prosodic licensing terms, to uniquely identify the intervocalic onset as a privileged position of contrast in distinction to the other onset positions in the word (C_{INIT} and C_1). Rather, such distinctions in phonotactic licensing as exist must be described in terms of segmental strings.

This generalisation is true of Ngalakgan, just as it is of most Australian languages: retroflex consonants are only found post-vocalically in Ngalakgan, and geminates are only licensed between continuants. Hence, the intervocalic position is the only phonotactic position that licenses the full range of segmental contrasts.[14] Other phonotactic positions license a subset of these contrasts.

Rather than describe phonotactic possibilities in terms of syllable positions such as onset and coda then, we are forced to use statements ranging over strings of types of segments. Steriade (2001) argues that many of the common phonotactic patterns found crosslinguistically arise from speakers' knowledge about the potential confusability of segmental contrasts in particular phonotactic positions. For instance, one common phonotactic pattern is for stops to fail to contrast for voice finally in words. Steriade argues that this results from the knowledge that speakers obtain that voiced stops are difficult to distinguish from voiceless stops in this environment. She proposes that such knowledge, what she calls the 'P-map' ('P' for 'perceptibility'), consists of a ranking of the perceptibility of segmental contrast pairs in different phonotactic environments according to relative similarity:

> The P-map is the repository of speakers' knowledge, rooted in observation and inference, that certain contrasts are more discriminable than others, and that the same contrast is more salient in some positions than in others ... One can conceive of the P-map as a set of statements, each of which assigns a similarity value to a contrast realized in a specific context. (Steriade 2001: 236)

The P-map generates phonological constraints of fixed rank, (on a partly language-specific basis, according to the segmental contrasts and the phonotactic contexts found) in the form of Correspondence constraints between underlying and surface realisations:

> ... Rankings among correspondence constraints (McCarthy and Prince 1995) must be indexed to the perceived similarity of the input-output differences they refer to. A correspondence constraint prohibits a certain type of difference between a lexical form and its surface realization: but, as we have seen, some differences are more salient than others. The proposal is that if two contrasts a-b and x-y differ in perceived salience in a given language, the correspondence constraints "a must not surface as b" and "x must not surface as y" are predictably ranked relative to each other: the more salient contrast projects the higher ranked constraint. (Steriade 2001: 239)

---

[14] The exception to this characterisation is the glottal stop. The glottal stop, exceptionally, is not licensed intervocalically. It can only occur word-finally or preceding another consonant, and must follow a sonorant. Its distribution is examined further in 2.4.1 below.

In the case of the apical contrast in Ngalakgan, we find that the contrast is 'best' maintained intervocalically. That is, if a language contrasts apicals anywhere it will be in the intervocalic position. Other positions of potential contrast are more marked. Only a handful of Australian languages maintain a contrast initially in words, and even less allow it following a non-apical consonant. None allow it following an apical consonant, as already noted.

These facts suggest that the following universal ranking obtains for apical stops (Steriade 2001: 237, 240):[15]

(12) Ident(retro) / V ʈ V >> Ident(retro) / V ʈ # >> Ident(retro) / # ʈ V

We can read this ranking in the following terms: 'It is more preferable to maintain the feature [retroflex] for apical stops in the environment of preceding vowel and following consonant than it is to maintain the feature [retroflex] for apical stops in the environment of preceding consonant and following vowel'.

These Correspondence constraints, as is typical in OT analyses, interact with Markedness constraints. In this case, they interact with the array of Markedness constraints banning implementation of *any* segmental constrasts, among which are those referring specifically to apicals. In cross-linguistic terms, it would seem that apico-alveolars are the unmarked term in this contrast. Apico-alveolars are found in a majority of the world's languages, but contrastive retroflexes have a more limited distribution (Ladefoged and Maddieson 1996). In addition, an alveolar realisation of an apical is more articulatorily neutral, in that it involves less displacement of the tongue, than is a retroflex.[16] Hence the ranking in (13) should be universal, where the monovalently specified marked configuration [apical, retroflex] dominates the unmarked [apical] (not contrastively specified).

(13) *[apical, retroflex] >> *[apical]

To see how these constraints interact, consider the example in (10), repeated here.

---

[15] Steriade's actual constraints are of the form 'Ident(anterior) / V[__, apical, stop] C' etc. I have modified these for ease of readability using the format of perceptual constraints introduced by (Hamilton 1996). Following the latter, I have also eliminated reference to the feature [anterior] in favour of monovalent features referring to major articulators: [apical] and [retroflex]. The implications of this move are explored elsewhere (Harvey and Baker 2005).

[16] 'Retroflexion, as well as involving adjustment away from the longitudinal convexity of the neutral tongue configuration, also involves displacement of the active articulator relative to the neutral passive articulator.' (Laver 1994: 141).

(14) a. [**n**]occo
'grass' (generic term)

b. ku-[**ɳ**]occo
NEUT-grass
'(some) grass'

We find the underlying retroflex only in environments where it follows a vowel. Elsewhere, it is either realised as apico-alveolar or assimilates completely to a preceding apical. We can capture this behaviour by inter-ranking the Correspondence and Markedness constraints referring to apicals in typical fashion. In (15), we find that the underlying retroflex is prevented from appearing in utterance-initial position because it violates *[apical, retro] but doesn't trigger the higher-ranking Correspondence constraint referring to retroflexes in postvocalic contexts.

(15)

/ɳocco/ 'grass'	ID/VʈV	*[apical, retro]	ID/ Vʈ#	ID/ #ʈV	*[apical]
☞ a. [nocco]				*	*
b. [ɳocco]		*!			

In (16), where this root follows a vowel in the word the retroflex can surface because it is now subject to the higher-ranking Correspondence constraint, even though it violates the same Markedness constraint against retroflexes as before.

(16)

/ku-ɳocco/ 'grass'	ID/VʈV	*[apical, retro]	ID/ Vʈ#	ID/ #ʈV	*[apical]
a. [kunocco]	*!				*
☞ b. [kuɳocco]		*			

We would expect similar, but opposite behaviour from contrasts that are cued mainly in release, and not in attack. Hamilton (1996) demonstrates this is the case with the lamino-dental vs. apico-alveolar contrast found in many Australian languages (but not Ngalakgan). These stops have near-identical formant cues in the V-to-C transition. In languages which distinguish them, overwhelmingly these stops fail to contrast in word-final and pre-consonantal position, unless they are part of a monogestural cluster. This pattern can be accounted for in a similar manner to the apical pattern discussed here, except that the Identity contexts would be the opposite for the dental/alveolar contrast.

In the following sections I describe the distribution of geminates and other stop clusters.

2.3 The phonology of the stop contrast

Ngalakgan contrasts two kinds of stop articulations; I will argue in what follows that this is a singleton vs. geminate contrast. I will also propose that there is no single phonological feature that serves to distinguish geminates from other articulations. Rather, they are crucially distinguished along two dimensions: being monogestural, and having two timing positions. In the first respect they are like simple stops, in the second, like clusters. This dual nature is characteristic of geminates (e.g. Kenstowicz and Pyle 1973; Hayes 1986), and can account for their phonotactics and their phonetic characteristics in Ngalakgan as well as neighbouring languages, as I will show.

Roots contrasting for these realisations of obstruents are presented in (17), (18), and (19); (a) and (b) in each case are near-minimal contrastive pairs.

(17)	a.	/kacca/	[gáˈcca]	‘nothing’
	b.	/kacaʔ/	[gáɟa̠]	‘dog’
(18)	a.	/ŋappa/	[ŋáppa]	‘better’
	b.	/ŋapak/	[ŋábak]	*Eucalyptus grandifolia*
(19)	a.	/marcci/	[márcci]	‘ghost; paleskinned person’
	b.	/maɻci/	[máɻɟi]	‘hand’

The contrast between singleton and geminate stops is only possible between continuants. In non-contrastive positions—before and after non-continuants, and word-peripherally—the geminate/singleton contrast is not possible, as discussed in 2.3.2.

2.3.1 Phonetics of the stop contrast

Chapter 6 shows that the only consistent acoustic parameter of the stop contrast in Ngalakgan is stricture duration. Table (7) below presents average durations for post-tonic singletons and geminates ordered by place of articulation (taken from Baker 1999). The number of tokens is given in parentheses, followed by the average duration in milliseconds (ms). It can be seen that geminate stops at all places are at least twice the length of the corresponding singleton stop, with the exception of apico-alveolar singletons, for which there are no data. In the case of the retroflexes, the duration difference between geminates and singletons is 4:1. Similar ratios are presented by Butcher (1993a: 11) for stop contrasts in six languages of central Arnhem Land.

	Labial	Apico-alveolar	Apico-retroflex	Lamino-alveo-palatal	Dorsal
Geminate	(9) = 194	(5) = 139	(2) = 226	(2) = 228	(35) = 211
Singleton	(7) = 71		(23) = 48	(4) = 64	(6) = 63

Table 7: Average durations of geminates and singletons

A contrast between two series of stops is found in many languages of the 'Top End' of the Northern Territory.[17] The contrast has been interpreted in at least four ways:

(20)
a. A voicing contrast (Glasgow 1981)
b. A fortis/lenis contrast (Heath 1978b; Merlan 1983; Jaeger 1983; Butcher 2004; Evans and Merlan 2004)
c. A geminate/singleton contrast (McKay 1975, 1980, 1984; Baker 1999)
d. A long/short contrast (Evans 2003; Green 1995)

In all cases, researchers have noted that duration is the primary acoustic correlate of the distinction, though there are also said to be additional factors involved in the articulation of the fortis stop, such as increased tension (Jaeger 1983) or increased intraoral pressure (Butcher 2004).

Section 2.3.2 shows that the distribution of geminates in words follows if we regard them as obstruent clusters, suggesting the geminate analysis is the right one. However, there are other factors to consider. Firstly, the quantity-sensitivity system of Ngalakgan (as well as neighbouring languages like Bininj Gun-wok), as well as some of the phonotactic facts, suggests that they are syllabified in the onset, along with homorganic nasal-stop clusters; see 2.3.3. Secondly, as discussed in Chapter 6, geminates are commonly found in the initial position of some roots and suffixes in Ngalakgan and other languages of Arnhem Land, suggesting that they have arisen as boundary marking phenomena in these cases. Thirdly, if it is the case (as Butcher 2004 suggests) that the intraoral pressure which is characteristic of fortis stops in Arnhem Land languages cannot be derived from a simple mathematical

[17] This name refers to the region of the Northern Territory roughly bounded by the coast along the north, east and west, and the Roper and Victoria rivers to the south. The languages of this region, while highly diverse in genetic terms, show many phonological and morphological similarities.

effect of duration of obstruents, then this too would argue in favour of an underlying contrast.[18]

2.3.2 Distribution of geminates in syllable structure

In this section I demonstrate that the distribution of geminates follows if we regard them as clusters. As discussed in 2.2.1, the contrast between singleton and geminate stops is only possible between continuants. In non-contrastive positions—before and after non-continuants, and word-peripherally—geminates are not possible.

Segments contrast with each other for place of articulation in word-medial, -final and -initial position. Example (21) shows a three-way contrast between stops and the glottal stop in word-final position.[19]

Segments contrast word-finally

(21)	a. /ʈer**p**/	b. /ʈer**k**/	c. /ʈer**ʔ**/
	[dɛrp]	[dɛrk]	[dɛr̰]
	'tie'	'cut'	'hard'

Stops contrast for place in initial position also, as shown in (22), although in this position the contrast in apicals is neutralised, as described in 2.2.2.

(22)	a. /**ʈ**ac-ca/	b. /**k**acca/	c. /**p**acca/
	[dáˈcca]	[gáˈcca]	[báˈcca]
	'cut-FUT'	'nothing'	'hit.PRES'

Geminates do not have the same distribution in words as singletons. Geminates only contrast with singletons word-medially, as in (23).

Inter-continuant geminate vs singleton contrast

(23)	a. /ma**rcc**i/	b. /ma**ɻc**i/
	[marcci]	[maɹɟi]
	'white person'	'hand'

Like geminates, clusters of [–cont] segments only contrast with single stops in word-medial position, as shown in (24) and (25).

---

[18] (Stoakes In preparation) has found further evidence for this proposal, in Gunwinjgu (a dialect of BGW). See Chapter 6 for discussion.

[19] All stops contrast for place word-medially and finally, the examples in (21) demonstrate the contrast for three stops with a minimal triplet.

Inter-continuant nasal-stop cluster vs single stop

(24) a. /ca**ŋk**u/ b. /ca**k**u/
[ɟaŋgu] [ɟagu]
'fresh meat' 'lefthand'

Intervocalic stop-stop cluster vs single stop

(25) a. /ca**ʈp**a/ b. /ca**ʈ**a/
[ɟaʈpa] [ɟaɖa]
'firstborn' 'twirl firedrill.PRES'

Geminates and non-continuant clusters both contrast with singletons in the same position in words: medially, between continuants.

However, the distribution is 'defective'. Not all clusters of continuant plus geminate stop contrast with the same cluster involving a singleton stop. Table (8) shows the attested clusters of continuants with singleton and geminate stops

Geminates allow a greater variety of continuants in preceding C_1 position than do singletons. Clusters of continuants and singletons are limited to just five types: clusters of /l, r/ with /p, k/, and in addition /ɻc/. There are no clusters of singletons with the retroflex lateral /ɭ/ or with the glides /w, j/. In addition, in attested clusters of continuant and stop, geminates are overwhelmingly preferred over singletons.[20] Merlan (1983: 5) suggests that this points to a historical allophonic conditioning factor determining the distribution of singletons and geminates.

	p	t	ʈ	c	k
l	lp				lk
ɭ					
r	rp				rk
ɻ				ɻc	
w					
j					

	pp	tt	ʈʈ	cc	kk
l	lpp			lcc	lkk
ɭ	ɭpp				ɭkk
r	rpp			rcc	rkk
ɻ	ɻpp			ɻcc	ɻkk
w					wkk
j	jpp				jkk

Table 8: Clusters of continuant with singleton and geminate stops

20 There are 19 attested examples of morpheme-medial continuant+singleton stop clusters in the lexicon, as in /pulkut/ 'kurrajong (*Brachychiton sp.*)', /karpe+/ 'crawl', but 68 attested examples of continuant+geminate clusters, as in /palkkiɲ/ '"cheeky", dangerous, bitter'.

Singleton stops do not contrast with geminates in word-final or -initial position. There are no words like that in (26)a below, ending in a contrastive geminate, nor are there any words ending in clusters of [–continuant] segments (26)b-c.

(26) a. */ʈerpp/ b. */ʈetk/ c. */ʈent/

The fact that no words end in nasal+stop clusters (homorganic or otherwise) is somewhat surprising, given that word-final heterorganic clusters such as /lk/ are relatively common. I return to this issue below in 2.3.3.

Similarly, there are no words like those in (27) in Ngalakgan, beginning in geminates, stop+stop or nasal+stop clusters.

(27) a. */tterp/ b. */tkerp/ c. */nterp/

There are however, several bound morphemes which begin in geminates, nasal-stop clusters, or glottal stop-consonant clusters:

(28) a. /-kkaʔ/ LOC
b. /=ŋki/ 2mDAT
c. /-ʔwala/ ABL

There are no morphemes beginning in any other kind of cluster, such as a heterorganic cluster, though other Australian languages such as Warlpiri and Western Desert have such forms.

Suffixes beginning with these clusters can never be words. The two bound stems beginning in nasal-stop clusters, one of which is shown in (28)b, can on occasion be pronounced as words. On these occasions, the nasal is not pronounced, as in the second pronunciation of /ŋkore/ 'we (inclusive, non-minimal)' in (29). Square brackets surround Intonational Phrases in this case, that is, a pause precedes the second pronunciation of /ŋkore/, which is under contrastive intonation here.

(29) [ŋumijak̯ɔ̀rickɔ́re][21] [gɔ́re ŋumugɔ́ric]
/ŋu-mu-caʔ-koric=ŋkore, ***ŋkore*** ŋu-mu-koric/
1mS-VEG-now-grind-12aDAT 12aDAT 1mS-III-grind
'I'm grinding it now for us, I'm grinding it *for us*.' [2/7/96: 1B]

[21] The realisation of the VEG prefix, underlying /mu-/, as [mi] here is due to the following laminal. Fronting of the high back vowel before laminals is regular, particularly in prefixes, but only in unmonitored speech.

For similar examples, with bound stems from the same set in related languages, see (McKay, 1975: 108) for Rembarrnga and (Evans 2003: 268) for Bininj Gun-wok.

With respect to their distribution in words, then, geminates are like clusters, and unlike single segments, almost all of which contrast in both initial and final position, as well as intervocalically, as we have seen.

Geminates, nasal+stop, glottal stop+consonant and stop+stop clusters arising at morpheme boundaries are realised faithfully if they follow a continuant, as in the (a) examples below. But if the underlying cluster follows a [–cont] segment, the underlying medial nasal, oral or glottal stop is deleted from the output, as shown in the (b) forms.

		Post-continuant geminate		Post-obstruent geminate → C
(30)	a.	/copa**l-kk**aʔ/ [ɟobálkka̰] MMBS-LOC	b.	/waɲca**t-kk**aʔ/ [waˈɲɟátka̰] arm-LOC
		Post-continuant NC cluster		Post-obstruent NC cluster → C
(31)	a.	/copa**l**=**ŋki**/ [ɟobálŋgi] MMBS=2mDAT	b.	/waɲca**t**=**ŋki**/ [waˈɲɟátki] arm=2mDAT
		Post-continuant ʔC cluster		Post-obstruent ʔC cluster → C
(32)	a.	/copa**l-ʔkV**n/ [ɟobál̰gan] MMBS=DAT	b.	/waɲca**t-ʔkV**n/ [waˈɲɟátkan] arm=DAT
		Post-continuant heterorganic CC cluster[22]		
(33)	a.	/ma**lk**=**p**ore/ [màlkpɔ́re] subsection=3aDAT		

Underlying, heteromorphemic clusters of three [–cont] segments are simplified at the surface by deleting the middle segment. Geminates behave like an obstruent sequence or cluster for this syllabification process, and not like a segment. If geminates were segments, we might expect the outcome of (31)b (repeated here as (34)a, with geminate represented as long stop) to be (34)b:

---

[22] There is no (b) form corresponding to (33)a because there are no morphemes beginning or ending in heterorganic obstruent clusters.

(34) a. /waɲcat-**kː**aʔ/
b. *[waˈɲɟátkːa̰]
arm-LOC

The pattern whereby the middle of three obstruents deletes is a cross-linguistically common repair for such strings. Steriade (1999a) suggests that in a string $VC_iC_jC_kV$ of three obstruents:

> C_i is sufficiently distinguishable from the immediately preceding vowel. Moreover, since this vowel carries C_i's cues to place and voicing, it provides information distinguishing C_i from other consonants, including C_j, which might have occurred in the same position. Therefore C_i is not confusable with either the V or the following C_j, hence it is not confusable with Ø. The medial C_j, on the other hand, is confusable with Ø: as no vowel is adjacent to C_j, the string $VC_iC_jC_kV$ contains less information allowing the listener to differentiate C_j from any other stop that might have occurred in the VC_i __ C_kV position, *including from* C_i *or* C_k. If C_j is confusable with either one of the adjacent stops, then the string $VC_iC_jC_kV$ is confusable with $VC_i{:}C_kV$ or $VC_iC_k{:}V$ and hence with VC_iC_kV. And therefore C_j is more confusable with Ø, than C_i [is? BB]. We reach in this way the unsurprising conclusion that, if cluster simplification targets the C that is most confusable with Ø, then it will operate in this case at the expense of the medial C_j. (Steriade 1999a: 30-31)

To derive the patterns of medial consonant deletion, Steriade (ibid.) proposes the following constraints:[23]

(35) C//V: 'Every C is adjacent to a V'

(36) Max[–cont]/_K: 'Obstruency must be realised in the output in environment K'

The universal markedness relation she proposes is the following:

(37) Max[–cont]/V_C >> Max[–cont]/C_C

[23] Steriade (2002: 22) characterises her Correspondence constraints thus:
MAX and DEP constraints refer to P-map differences of the form Δ(x-Ø)/_K, where x is a phonological property (e.g. a segment) and K is a context where x occurs in one representation and its absence occurs in a related representation. Thus MAX segment/_K, could be paraphrased as: "There is no Δ(Ø-C) between I and O, such that I contains C in K and O contains Ø in K' and K corresponds to K'."

This states that it is more desirable (or more perceptible) to realise pre-consonantal obstruents after vowels than after consonants.

With C//V ranked between the two Max constraints, in a similar pattern to the retroflex constraints, we derive the effect that medial obstruents, but no other consonants, are deleted in multiconsonant strings. This is what we observe in the Ngalakgan case (and many other languages, such as Macedonian: Groen 1977).[24]

(38)

/waɲca**t-k$_i$k$_j$**aʔ/ arm-LOC	MAX[–CONT] /V_C	C//V	MAX[–CONT] /C_C
☞ a. [waɲcatk$_j$a̰]			*
b. [waɲcatkka̰]		*!	
c. [waɲcakka̰]	*!		

In languages that have underlying word-initial geminates, we can observe the same ranking in action. In Swiss German, for example, Kraehenman (2001: 138) says that word-initial geminates are realised as such just if there is a preceding voicing context, otherwise (in phrase initial position), they are degeminated.

(39) a. I han [ə kk]utsche gsee
[i han ə kkutʃə ksee]
'I have seen a coach' (Kraehenmann 2001: 135)

b. #[k]utsche
'coach'

The same constraint ranking will account for the deletion of nasals (31) and glottals (32) between obstruents. In the case of nasals, there are in addition articulatory reasons for this behaviour. Nasals, being sonorants, require 'spontaneous voicing' (Chomsky and Halle 1968). Spontaneous voicing is not possible between obstruents, because the obstruction of airflow entailed by obstruents makes voicing difficult to maintain. However, I will not pursue this line of analysis further here, since the constraints given in (35)-(37) will account for the same output with all four kinds of clusters.

---

24 In 2.4.3 below I examine further tri-consonantal contexts, involving glottal stop.

2.3.3 Geminates as onsets

Despite the fact that the distribution of geminates can be described in similar terms to clusters, in other respects geminates (and homorganic nasal+stop clusters) do behave like single segments. In particular, both these monogestural sequences appear to be syllabified as onsets not just in Ngalakgan but in many Australian languages. One piece of evidence for this is that, even though Ngalakgan and other languages of Arnhem Land are quantity-sensitive for stress, neither geminates nor homorganic nasal-stop clusters contribute weight to the preceding syllable. The simplest explanation for this pattern is that monogestural clusters, exceptionally, syllabify as onsets; see Chapter 5 for further discussion of this proposal.

There are phonotactic facts in neighbouring languages which independently provide evidence for this analysis. I make the simplifying assumption here that the phonemic inventories and phonotactics of central and southern Arnhem Land languages are essentially of the same kind, the differences being ones of degree.[25] This is the approach of Dixon (1980) and Hamilton (1996). Here I will discuss one language group in particular: Burarran, spoken immediately to the east of Kuninjku (a BGW dialect), and to the north of Rembarrnga, and constituting a separate group of Northern languages.[26] In most respects, the phonology of Burarran languages is very similar to that of Gunwinyguan languages. Both language groups contrast two sets of stop articulations at the same places of articulation, both languages have very similar morphological structures, similar phonotactic constraints, and have essentially the same consonant and vowel inventories, except that laryngealisation has only marginal phonemic status in Burarran. Butcher (1993b) has carried out instrumental work on languages in both groups, including Burarra and Gurr-goni, and concluded that the phonological and phonetic basis of their stop contrast was essentially identical.

Where the Burarran languages differ from Gunwinyguan languages is in allowing geminates to occur after nasals (Green 1995: 46); Gurr-goni examples from (Green 2005), Burarra examples from (Glasgow n.d.):

---

25 The major exception to this statement however is the Daly languages in the western Top End. The stop contrast here appears to be based primarily on voicing (Reid 1990; Butcher 2004), and has a different phonotactic distribution to the stop contrast in other Top End languages. In Ngan'gityemerri for instance (Reid 1990), fortis and lenis stops contrast initially as well as medially. Many Daly languages also have contrastive fricatives at one or more places of articulation, unlike most other Top End languages.

26 Green (2003) argues that the closely related Burarran languages, of which Gurr-goni is a member, belong to a language family she calls 'Maningridan', which together with Gunwinyguan and perhaps some other languages descend from an ancestor she calls 'Proto-Arnhem'.

(40) a. /mit-ce**nkk**iʈi/ 'brains; cycad' [Gurr-goni]
b. /ɲa**ŋkk**ura/ 'archerfish'

(41) a. /ko**mkk**akka/ 'old man' [Burarra]

This possibility is not attested in Gunwinyguan languages. If the basis of the stop contrast in Burarran is the same, in other respects, as that in Gunwinyguan, then we must consider this phonotactic pattern more carefully. In the first place, it raises problems for a straightforward analysis of geminates as coda+onset clusters, since syllable-final nasal-stop clusters—whether homorganic or heterorganic—are not possible in Burarran or Gunwinyguan languages (nor in the vast majority of Australian languages).[27]

(42) a. */cenk/
b. */ɲaŋk/

Geminates are also found after homorganic liquids (Green 1995: 30):

(43) a. /-ʈə**ɭʈʈ**əɭ/ 'bald' [Gurr-goni]
b. /puɳʈu**ltt**ul/ '*Varanus* sp., a kind of goanna'
c. /manto**ɭʈʈ**oɭ/ 'bush passionfruit' (*Passiflora foetida*)

Again, if we regard geminates as coda+onset clusters, then the syllable preceding the geminate would bė an illicit syllable in Gurr-goni, since liquid +apical stop is not a licit coda cluster elsewhere in the language.

(44) a. */ʈəɭʈ/
b. */ʈult/

What this means is that a structure like that shown in (45), where a geminate is divided between syllables, is not a licit structure for Gurr-goni, since the first syllable is not a possible syllable type.

(45)

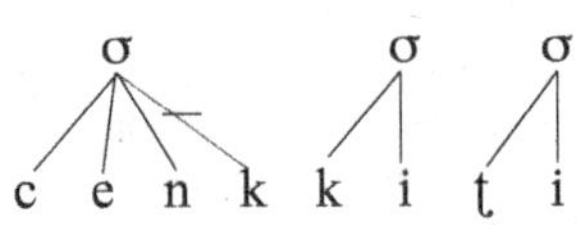

[27] Butcher (p.c.) confirms that the duration contrast in post-nasal stops in Burarra and Gurr-goni is comparable to that in post-liquid and post-vocalic contexts, i.e roughly twice as long as the singleton stops. So these are not simply voiceless stops.

On the other hand, if we regard geminates in Gurr-goni and the Burarran languages generally as onsets, then the resulting structure makes both syllables licit.

(46)

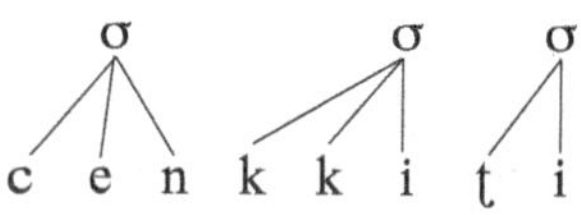

In sum, the phonotactic distribution of geminates provides conflicting evidence for their phonological status. On the one hand, in string-theoretic terms they are clearly clusters: they cannot occur word-initially or -finally, and following other obstruents they lose a timing position. On the other hand, at least in neighbouring languages (as well as in other Australian languages such as Warumungu (Simpson 1998) and Kukatj (Breen 1992), they occur following sonorants in clusters which would not be licit coda+onset clusters otherwise in the language.[28] I suggest here that these contradictory behaviours can be captured by analysing the 'long stop' as a *geminate onset*: a monogestural cluster of two segmental timing units, but syllabified in the onset rather than as a coda+onset cluster. This analysis is developed further in Chapter 5.

2.4 The glottal stop

The distribution of the glottal stop is more restricted than any other segment in Ngalakgan and other Northern languages which have this phoneme; it can only follow sonorants—vowels, nasals, and the set of consonantal continuants {r, ɻ, l, ɭ, w, j}—and can only occur as the final element in a syllable coda. The glottal stop is realised as creaky voice on the preceding vowel or sonorant consonant. Glottal closure is optional, depending on position of a morpheme in the word and utterance.[29]

(47)
a.	[bɔ́ll̰] ~ [bɔ́ll̰ʔ]	/pol̰/	'track'
b.	[wɛ́ɛ̰] ~ [wɛ́ɛ̰ʔ]	/wḛ/	'water'
c.	[jɛ́rɛ̰] ~ [jɛ́rɛ̰ʔ]	/jerḛ/	'below; downriver'

---

[28] For instance, in Warumungu (Simpson 1998), a language which is similar to Warlpiri, we find roots such as /wiɳkkalki/ 'dingo' and /nanttu/ 'humpy', despite the fact that coda clusters such as /ɳk/ and /nt/ are not possible in this language.

[29] This was first noted by Merlan (1983: 6): 'in spectrographic analysis of ordinarily-paced speech, the Ngalakan glottal shows up mainly as stretches of 'creaky voice', not characterised by any abrupt glottal closure'.

The transcription [ll̰] in (47) represents an articulation of [l] with an initial fully voiced period followed by a period of creaky voice. That is, sonorants are post-laryngealised in Ngalakgan, rather than pre-laryngealised.[30] Throughout the book I have represented these simply as [l̰].[31] The transcription [ɛɛ̰] ~ [ɛɛ̰ʔ] represents a long vowel articulation, the second half of which is articulated with creaky voice optionally followed by glottal closure. These articulations contrast with examples like (47)c. Here, the final syllable is not long, and the transcription [ɛ̰] represents a short vowel followed a period of creaky voice. Final glottal constriction in utterances can be extremely long: 200 ms of creaky voice or constriction before audible release is not unusual in this position.

I have never heard these forms pronounced, as in (48), *without* coarticulation.

(48) a. *[wɛʔ] b. *[bɔlʔ]

Words such as those in (47), then, do not contain sequences of vowel or sonorant followed by glottal stop, but rather vowel or sonorant with (partly) coarticulated glottal constriction.

The glottal stop in Ngalakgan is clearly phonemic (Merlan 1983: 7): the presence of laryngealisation serves to distinguish minimal pairs, both simple (49)-(50) and complex (51)-(52).[32]

(49) a. [lɛr]
/ɭer/
'fall'

b. [lɛr̰]
/ɭerʔ/
'set alight'

(50) a. [máɳiɲ]
/maɳiɲ/
'help'

b. [máɳiɲ̃]
/maɳiɲʔ/
'make'

---

[30] Preliminary results from (Stoakes In preparation) suggest that this is true of BGW, with the proviso that the timing of glottal constriction within closure is somewhat variable, though it never precedes the oral closure (where the phonemic input is /Xʔ/).

[31] Following (Pullum and Ladusaw 1986), I have placed the creaky voice diacritic above segments with a descender {ɲ̃ŋ̃ɳ̃ɻ̃ɭ̃}.

[32] There are no minimal pairs for laryngealisation to be found among nominal roots. All minimal pairs come from the class of verbs. Verb roots must be obligatorily affixed, either for person, or for TAM. However, speakers do use roots such /ɭer/, /ɭerʔ/, /maɳiɲ/, /maɳiɲʔ/ (all from the open verb class) as citation forms. Verbs from the closed classes, such as /ma/ 'get', even when inflected for tense, are much less amenable to citation as roots in this way.

(51) a. [gumá:] / /ku-ma/ / NP-get.NP / 'he/she/it gets it'

b. [gumáa̰] / /ku-maʔ/ / NEUT-good / 'it [NEUT] is good'

(52) a. [nugumɔ́kkɔl] / /ɳu-ku-mokkol/ / M-TOP-father / 'my father'

b. [nugumɔ́kkɔl̰] / /ɳuku-mokkol-ʔ/ / 1mS/2aO-father-VBSR / 'I call you (pl.) "father"'

The presence of laryngealisation is the only perceptible difference between these pairs of words. While the phonemic status of the glottal stop is not at issue, its phonological representation remains problematic.

In particular it is not clear whether the glottal stop should be represented as a segmental phoneme (as in Merlan 1983; Baker 1999), or as some kind of feature of the syllable (as in Wood 1978 discussing Yolngu languages, cf. Evans 2003: 87 discussing BGW), or even whether we should propose a set of laryngealised sonorants and vowels in Ngalakgan, as in many Native American languages (e.g. Kwakw'ala: Boas 1947). In order to assess these questions, we need to consider the distribution of the glottal stop in syllables, and its interaction with morphological structure.

2.4.1 The distribution of the glottal stop

The distribution of laryngeal segments in Northern languages is unique in several respects (see Harvey 1991 for general discussion). As described above, laryngeal segments in Ngalakgan have a restricted distribution: they must follow a sonorant (vowel, liquid, approximant, or nasal), and within morphemes cannot immediately precede a vowel. In terms of syllable structure, then, they must be the final coda in a syllable. That is, while words such as (53) are possible, words such as (54) are not.

(53) /poɭo̰/ 'hollow log', /poɭ̃/ 'carry', /peɭŋ̃/ 'foliage', /ka̰war/ 'chase'

(54) */peɭ̃ŋ/, */kaw̰ar/, */po̰l/

Laryngeal segments are unique in Ngalakgan (and in most other Northern Australian languages which have them) in not being able to appear intervocalically, unlike all other consonantal segments.[33]

[33] Glottal stops can be intervocalic in Wagiman (Wilson 1999: 174), in a handful of words which are almost certainly historically complex, including 'half a dozen' nouns of the shape

Furthermore, laryngeal segments make no contribution to the description of possible segment sequences in Ngalakgan, beyond what has been presented above. That is, there appear to be no co-occurrence restrictions between the glottal stop and any other segments, apart from the general distributional restriction that they must follow a sonorant and cannot precede a vowel: all possible syllable final sequences which are attested without final laryngealisation are also attested with final laryngealisation, with few exceptions. For example, final consonant clusters can be described in terms of continuant+ non-continuant sequences where the non-continuant must differ in major place of articulation (and furthermore cannot be /m/). All these clusters are attested in laryngealised and non-laryngealised versions.

(55) a. /paɻŋ/ 'dangerous' b. /cacapaɻŋ̃/ 'yesterday'

(56) a. /calŋ/ 'spinifex' b. /calŋ̃/ 'right up to'

(57) a. [no examples][34] b. /waccaɭŋ̃/ 'mud'

As Wood notes (1978: 96, with reference to Yolngu), if we analyse laryngealisation as a stop phoneme, then forms such as those in (55)-(57) would be the only syllable-final nasal+stop clusters in the language.

In Baker (1999), I argued that the best analysis of the glottal stop was as a segment, rather than a syllabic feature, because of the behaviour of stem-final laryngeals under affixation. Ngalakgan contrasts with Rembarrnga in this respect. In Rembarrnga, a laryngeal segment originating in the stem in (b) can surface in a syllabic position following a dorsal nasal originating in the suffix. Hence, laryngeals can be disassociated from the stem with which they were introduced into a word.

CVʔVn e.g. /waʔan/ 'water' (cf. Ngalakgan /weʔ/), and forms of the 'say/do' verb. Some phonetic realisations of common Ngalakgan words also have intervocalic or pre-vocalic glottal stop: /wurʔwuruŋu/ 'old people' is most commonly [ʊr̠ʔʊrʊŋu] and /kaʔwar/ 'chase' is [gaʔar]. In the case of /wurʔwuruŋu/, the prevocalic form arises because of the common deletion of homorganic glides preceding high vowels in Australian languages (Dixon 1980: 146). Deletion of /w/ before /a/ is found in Wubuy/Nunggubuyu (Heath 1984), though is not attested regularly in Ngalakgan apart from this word.

[34] The exceptions to this statement are the sequence /rŋ/, which only occurs in non-laryngealised versions in the data, and the sequence /ɭŋʔ/, which only occurs in *laryngealised* versions. The sequence /rŋʔ/ is found in BGW (Evans 2003): /kurŋʔ/ ~ /kurŋ/ 'mother-in-law', /ŋaɳarŋʔ/ 'black cockatoo', and the reduplicated root /narŋʔnarŋ/ in /mim-narŋʔnarŋ/ 'droopy eyed' (/mim/ 'eye'). On the other hand, the sequence /ɭŋ/ which is absent in the Ngalakgan corpus is found in BGW: /koɭŋ/ 'Carpentaria palm', though not the laryngealised version /ɭŋʔ/. It is quite likely in both cases that these are accidental gaps due to the limited lexical corpus available in each language.

(58) a. [ɟabuɻŋgə] 'your "cousin"' [Rembarrnga]
/capuɻ=ŋkə/ WIMOBR=2mDAT
b. [mobalŋ̰gə] 'your knee'
/mopalʔ=ŋkə/ knee=2mDAT

McKay (1975: 37-39) argues that laryngeals in Rembarrnga are a feature of the syllable in so-specified words, partly on the basis of this behaviour.

While laryngeals in Ngalakgan can be 'invisible' to processes of spreading (see 2.4.2 which follows), they do not display the freedom of syllabification shown in Rembarrnga. As we saw in 2.3.2 above, where suffixation or compounding of nasal-stop clusters would result in a sequence of three obstruents, the medial obstruent deletes rather than metathesising with the laryngeal:

(59) a. [dɔdɔ́ɪ̰gi] 'your "uncle"'
/ʈotojʔ=ŋki/ MOBRSOCH=2mDAT
b. *[dɔdɔ́ɪŋ̰gi]

In (59), the glottal of the stem causes deletion of the initial nasal in the cluster which begins the bound pronoun. In Rembarrnga we would expect resyllabification for such an input, giving (59)b. The deletion of the nasal in (59)a can be analysed in the same way as the deletion of the first timing unit of a geminate in a suffix following a stop-final stem described in 2.3.2.

However, laryngeals do superficially behave as a syllabic feature in other morphologically complex environments. In particular, where stems with final laryngealised vowels are followed by apical-initial stems, the first stem is realised with a final laryngealised retroflexed vowel followed by a retroflexed apical segment:[35]

(60) a. [gugɔ̰́˞ ɳan]
/ku-koʔ+ɳa+n/
IRR-have+SEE+PR
'she/he/it has it'
b. [gujaa̰˞ ɳàmuluɻúŋa]
/ku-caʔ-ɳamulu-ru+ŋa/
IRR-now-really-cook+FUT
'it'll really get cooking now'

[35] The articulation is one where the tongue tip is retracted while the tongue body forms the vowel articulation. So, a retroflexed vowel, rather than vowel+glide sequence.

This could indicate that laryngeals indeed remain unaffiliated to syllable structure until a late stage in the derivation, as suggested by McKay (ibid.). Alternatively, the forms in (60) could just be the result of oral/glottal timing overlap. If glottal constriction is timed to occur during the articulation of a preceding sonorant, but can also overlap with the constriction of a following sonorant, then we would observe the pattern in (60) in the case of retroflexes. Auditorily, this pattern also appears to be true of some reduplicated forms where laryngeals in a short syllable precede sonorants. The typical pronunciation of /meʔme/ 'got' is as shown in (61). Here, the glottal constriction audibly overlaps with the labial closure of the following nasal, but ceases before release of the labial constriction, giving a pre-laryngealised quality to the nasal.

(61) [mɛ̰m̰ɛ]
/meʔ+me/
RED+get.PP

Rather than examples such as (60) and (61) providing evidence for the freedom of laryngeals then, they may simply be examples of anticipatory coarticulation effects from the following consonant.

There is one other morphological process involving the glottal stop which is relevant to the question of their phonological status, the derivation of Future and Irrealis forms of open class verbs (also discussed in Merlan 1983), discussed in the following section.

2.4.2 The morpho-phonology of the open class Future and Irrealis inflection

The behaviour of laryngealisation is central to one highly productive process of verb inflection.[36] The open conjugation class of verbs forms the Future and Irrealis with affixes whose elsewhere forms are /-ɻa/ and /-ɻe/ respectively. The suffixes have these forms following vowels, see (63) below. In consonant-final stems, these verb inflections are formed by geminating the final supralaryngeal consonant of the stem (Merlan 1983: 120; a cognate inflectional paradigm is found in Rembarrnga: McKay 1975); hence glottal stops are invisible to this process. Example (62) demonstrates the pattern found with consonant-final stems, including stems derived from Kriol, as in the (d) example.[37]

[36] It is also central to various reduplication processes, and is implicated in processes of degemination and delaryngealisation, both discussed in Chapter 6.

[37] The Irrealis inflection is identical to the Future, except that the vowel of the inflection is /e/ rather than /a/.

		Present	Future		
(62)	a.	[buɭ]	[buɭɭa]	/puɭ/	drown-FUT
	b.	[wulup]	[wuluppa]	/wulup/	bathe-FUT
	c.	[maɳi̤ɲ]	[maɳi̤ɲɲa]	/maɳi̤ɲ/	help-FUT
	d.	[laɪdɪmap]	[laɪdɪmappa]	/ɭajtimap/	set alight-FUT (Kriol < English *light 'im up*)

The elsewhere (and historically original) form of the FUT suffix—/-ɻa/ ~ /-ja/—is shown in (63). This is the form selected by vowel-final (polysyllabic) stems.[38]

(63) [mungu]   [munguɻa] ~ [munguja]
/munku/   follow-FUT

I discuss below why this form cannot be regarded as the form underlying the suffixes to consonant-final stems, however.

In the case of stems which have a final laryngealised sonorant, the inflection is realised as gemination of the final sonorant position. In these forms, the glottal constriction is relaxed before release of the sonorant, unlike laryngealised sonorants in codas (where glottal constriction is released after the oral constriction), and the sonorant closure duration is longer than in ordinary intervocalic sonorants.

(64) a. [maɳi̤ɲ̃]   [maɳi̤ɲ̃ɲa]
/maɳi̤ɲʔ/   make-FUT
b. [bawʊn̰]   [bawʊn̰na]
/pawunʔ/   leave-FUT
c. [dul̰]   [dul̰la]
/ʈulʔ/   set.alight-FUT

The constriction of the sonorant is maintained throughout the glottal constriction, and is released as the onset of the following syllable.

Similarly, stems in which a final glottal stop follows a vowel behave just like vowel-final forms:

		Present	Future
(65)	a.	[jukka̰]	[jukka̰ɻa] ~ [jukka̰ja]
		/jukkaʔ/	go ahead-FUT

[38] Vowel-final polysyllabic thematic stems are rather rare: besides those here, Merlan cites /marcca/ 'to be starving', /mi̤ɲci/ 'to remember, think', and /jalala/ 'to slide down'; none of which have turned up in my data (/mi̤ɲci/ only in the PP form /mi̤ɲci-mi̤ɲ/ and a compound form /mi̤ɲci-pu+/ 'know, be knowledgeable'). /munku/ is a commonly-occurring verb.

b. [warɟa̰] [warɟa̰ɹa]
/warcaʔ/ search-FUT
c. [jana̰] [jana̰ɹa] ~ [jana̰ja]
/janaʔ/ do what?-FUT

What we do *not* get, following glottal-final stems, is gemination of the glottal:

(66) a. [jukka̰] *[jukka̰ʔa]
/jukkaʔ/ go ahead-FUT
b. [warɟa̰] *[warɟa̰ʔa]
/warcaʔ/ search-FUT

The realisation of the suffix following vowel-final stems (ignoring glottal stops) varies according to the place of articulation of the vowel. Stems which end in a mid-vowel are only attested with suffixes in a homorganic glide (67)a-c, while those ending in /a/ vary between /j/ and /ɹ/ initial suffixes.

(67) a. [dɛɭḛ] [dɛɭḛja]
/teɭeʔ/ move-FUT
b. [leḛ] [leḛja]
/ɭeʔ/ search for-FUT
c. [bælmo] [bælmowa]
/palmo/ whack-FUT

Stems ending in /i/ can similarly vary between /j/ and /ɹ/ initial suffixes (68); however I have not heard the high back vowel followed by homorganic glide in the suffix. The only frequent example of a high back vowel-final stem is /munku/, which only takes suffixes in /ɹ/ or /j/ (63), as with the high front vowel. But I did not explicitly test this possibility with speakers.

(68) [jinḭ] [jinḭɹa] ~ [jinḭja]
/jiniʔ/ do/say thus-FUT

Merlan (1983: 120) claims that in monosyllabic open roots, there is no consonant between stem and suffix, presenting the following form as an example (=my (67)b):

(69) a. /ɭeʔ/ /ɭeʔ-a/
look.for look.for-FUT

According to Merlan, monosyllabic roots differ from other roots, which take /-ɻa/.

Phonologically, vowel sequences within words, without intervening glides, are entirely absent in Ngalakgan and the majority of Australian languages. On phonological grounds then, structures such as those in (69) are unlikely. In addition to the impossibility of vowel sequences, glottal stops are not attested intervocalically in Ngalakgan and most other Northern languages.

Phonetically, there is a difference however between a sequence /eʔa/ and /eʔja/. In the latter, glottal constriction is released before the release of the glide constriction. This is what I hear in the attested Ngalakgan forms. Further instrumental research is required to answer this question definitively.

The mid-vowels are the only vowels that can occur in monosyllabic open roots such as that in (69), and thus it appears accidental under Merlan's analysis that it is they that condition homorganic glides. But the fact that mid-vowels in polysyllabic stems such as /palmo/ also take a homorganic glide-initial suffix (and not the /j/ or /ɻ/ form) suggests that it is mid-vowels which are the conditioning factor for homorganic glides in the suffix. I can think of no good reason why mid-vowels should only allow homorganic glides but high vowels vary between /ɻ/ or /j/ regardless of place.

Stems ending in the glides {ɻ, j} take /a/ as the suffix, but do not geminate:

(70)	a.	[ɲaɻ̰]	[ɲaɻ̰a]
		/ɲaɻʔ/	die-FUT
	b.	[wai]	[waija]
		/waj/	have a rest-FUT

I have one example of a /w/-final thematic verb in future inflection (no examples are provided by Merlan (1983: 120) in the relevant section discussing the process), this example was repeated a number of times with a geminate /w/:

(71)	[guɖiw̰wagan]	/ku-ʈiwʔ-Ca-kan/	
	'so he'll fly'	NP-fly-FUT-PURP	[3/7/96]

I have a number of examples of /r/-final stems which were realised without perceptible lengthening:

(72)	[lɛr̰]	[lɛr̰a]
	/ɭerʔ/	set alight-FUT

In addition, the same informant, when repeating an /r/-final form slowly, supplied the onset with [r] as well (I represent the pause here):

(73) [lɛr̰ ... ragan] /ŋu-ku-ɭer?-Ca-kan/
'[so] I can light it' 1mS-IV-light.up-FUT-PURP [2/7/96: 1B]

It is possible to analyse the underlying form of the Future suffix as /-ɻa/, with surface forms undergoing obligatory assimilation to preceding supralaryngeal place of articulation. This is almost certainly the historical origin of the inflection in Ngalakgan and Rembarrnga (Baker 2004). It is noteworthy that the speaker in (73) filled the onset with /r/, rather than /ɻ/, however. The tap/trill /r/ is entirely absent word-initially in Ngalakgan (as in most Australian languages: Hamilton 1996), while the retroflex glide /ɻ/ is not uncommon as an onset in Ngalakgan. This suggests that speakers regard the underlying form of the Future inflection as a copy of the preceding stem-final consonant, rather than a retroflex glide undergoing obligatory total assimilation under contiguity.

Synchronically then, it may be preferable to regard the FUT inflection as a process of suffixation of a vowel /-a/ or /-e/ accompanied by gemination of the final supralaryngeal segment of the stem, presumably because of the dominance of Onset over Faithfulness, with constraints banning geminate versions of some segments: the coronal glides /ɻ/, /j/, and the tap /r/. There are good reasons why /r/ should be restricted from gemination. The typical realisation of this segment intervocalically, as noted, is a tap: an articulation with a necessarily very brief closure phase. A geminated [ɾ], that is a tap with a sustained closure, would be indistinguishable from the apical stop /t/, typically realised as [d] intervocalically. Constraints banning coalescence of morphemes and/or phonemes should rule out such a possibility. The reason for the restriction on geminate glides is most probably to be found in universals of gemination according to consonant manner. If it is the case that gemination is easiest to perceive in obstruents, and hardest in approximants, then the differences in behaviour of these segments in this process in Ngalakgan follow. I omit a formal analysis here. In the following section, I propose a phonological representation of the glottal stop in Ngalakgan which accounts for its distribution and behaviour in words.

2.4.3 The phonological representation of glottal stop

I show here that the behaviour of glottal stop can be accounted for if we adopt the representation in (74), as a non-continuant root segment lacking place features, and having only the laryngeal specification [creaky voice]:

		Glottal stop
(74)	Root node	[–cont]
		|
	Place node	[ ]
		|
	Laryngeal node	[creak]

The usual specification for glottal stops is [constricted glottis] (e.g. Stevens 1998). However, there appears to be an articulatory difference between the syllable-initial glottal stops found in English and German, and the syllable-final creaky voice found in Ngalakgan and other languages of the Top End. As we have seen, glottal closure is a potential but not a necessary realisation of this segment. Hence, it would seem that glottal adduction, rather than constriction, is the articulatory specification we need. Barring articulatory investigations of speakers of Top End languages with this kind of glottal stop, however, I will refer to 'creaky voice' as the feature in question since it has the advantage of being descriptively accurate.

The behaviour of glottal stops in obstruent clusters follows if we regard them as [–cont]. Like other [–cont] segments, they condition degemination in a following morpheme. However, unlike other [–cont] segments, they can be coarticulated with preceding sonorants. Their ability to do this derives from their zero place specification: unlike all other segments, coarticulation of sonorants together with creaky voice does not obscure place cues sufficiently to prevent recovery of the phoneme in perception. Finally, if we regard laryngealisation as spreading or coarticulation of [creaky voice] rather than glottal stop, then their phonotactic distribution makes sense. Since creaky voice can be described in terms of 'vocal folds that are tightly adducted but open enough along a portion of their length to allow for voicing' (Gordon and Ladefoged 2001: 386), creaky voice presumably requires a voicing environment in order to be perceived itself. This can be encoded as a series of perceptual/articulatory constraints:

(75) *[creak]/[–son] >> *[creak]/[+son, –cont] >> *[creak]/[+cont, –syll] >> *[creak]/[+syll]

As is usual with such an approach (Steriade 2001; Blevins 2003), these constraints interact with Faithfulness constraints demanding realisation of underlying [creak]:

(76) IDENT[creaky voice]: 'A segment with [creaky voice] specification in the input must have creaky voice in the output'

In Ngalakgan, the ranking which obtains is (77), where creaky voice is maintained on every carrier segment except non-sonorants:

(77) *[creak]/[–son] >> **IDENT[creaky voice]** >> *[creak]/[+son, –cont] >> *[creak]/[+cont, –syll] >> *[creak]/[+syll]

What this set of constraints does *not* explain is the syllabic position of creak, why we do not find creaky voice pre-finally in clusters, for example:

(78) a. */peʔŋba/ [bḛŋba]
b. */peʔlŋa/ [bḛlŋa]

The constraints in (77) only specify the allowable carrier segments for creak, not their relative position in strings of segments. We have seen that the stringwise constraints on the occurrence of creak are quite strict.

It could be simply that such clusters are banned because of the [–cont] characteristic of glottal stop: non-continuant segments cannot be followed by continuants within the syllable, nor can any segments at all occur between two non-continuants, as in (78)a. Gordon and Ladefoged (2001: 395) suggest that such sequences are perceptually ill-formed: non-modal articulations reduce the recoverability of cues to place of articulation, and as such are dispreferred preceding consonant articulations that are themselves not immediately followed by vowels. In (78), for example, the cues for /ŋ/ and /l/ are in both cases obscured by preceding glottal stop and following heterorganic consonant. By delaying glottal adduction until immediately prior to a following onset, as is typically the case in Ngalakgan, speakers ensure maximal recoverability of cues for all consonants, as well as the glottal adduction itself.

One way to encode the string-based constraints on laryngealisation is in terms of a constraint series demanding Correspondence to an input [creak] feature in varying contexts, à la Steriade, shown in (79):

(79) Max[creak]/V_C >> Max[creak]/[+son]_C >> Max[creak]/[–cont]_C

The constraint ranking states that it is more desirable to realise creaky voice after vowels or sonorants than non-continuants, in contexts where a consonant follows. Interspersed with the constraints we have already proposed on realisation of [creak], as shown in (80), we derive the effect that laryngealisation is limited to post-sonorant contexts.

(80) Max[creak]/V_C >> Max[creak]/[+son]_C >> *[creak]/[–son] >> **IDENT[creaky voice]** >> *[creak]/[+son, –cont] >> *[creak]/[+cont, –syll] >> *[creak]/[+syll] >> C//V >> Max[creak]/[–cont]_C

2.4.4 The timing of laryngealisation

Section 2.4.3 above suggested that, although the glottal stop is necessarily coarticulated with a preceding sonorant, it nevertheless occupies a distinct root note on the skeletal (timing) tier (see Chapter 5 for further discussion). The question is an important one to answer, since the alternative is that Ngalakgan (and other Northern languages) have an independent series of laryngealised vowel and sonorant phonemes. Unit phonemes like this, according to Sagey (1990), should occupy a single timing position. Complex segments, however, should occupy two timing positions. If the glottal stop is an independent phoneme of Ngalakgan, we would expect it to contribute an extra timing position to the syllable.

In order to answer this question, we would need acoustic data from Ngalakgan (or related languages) with speech timing held relatively constant, in order to decide whether sonorant+laryngeal sequences were longer than instances of the sonorant segment in question alone. At this stage, there is not enough data of the required kind to address the question properly. However, the data available, though preliminary, suggests that laryngeal segments do contribute an additional timing slot. My data here comes from 31 words of Ngalakgan, some with repetitions, recorded as citation forms.[39] Each syllable was analysed for duration of all segments, f0, RMS amplitude, and VOT of stops. The total number of syllables in the corpus was 159. 19 of these syllables contain a measurable laryngealised vowel. The average duration of the laryngeal portion alone was 81 ms., and the average duration of the preceding vowel was 76 ms. The complete morphological and phonetic representations are presented in (81) and the actual tokens involved are presented below in Table (9).

(81) a. [jirgʊ̀rʊŋgʊ̰́miɲ]
/jir-kuruŋkuʔ-miɲ/
1ex.pl-walk-AUX.PP
'we walked'

b. [jírkka̰pɪ̀ra̰]
/jirkkaʔ-piraʔ/
1ex.pl-DU
'us two (exclusive)'

f. [jukkḛ́ɟḭ]
/jukkaciʔ/
'quickly'

g. [mɛ̀lɛ̰ɻú:]
/Ø-meleʔ-ɻu/
3sg-LEST-burn.PR
'it might burn'

---

39 The recordings were made on a Sony cassette Walkman, and then digitised and analysed on a Sun Sparc station running XWaves at the UMass phonetics lab.

c. [bàʈʈaɻáʊwḭ]
/paʈʈa-ɻaw?-ji?/
COMIT-hair-COMIT
'[it has] hair, is hairy'

d. [numɛ̀lɡ̰ɳé:ppɪra̰]
/ɳu-mele?-ɳe-ppira?/
2pl-lest-cook.PR-DU
'you two should cook it'

e. [numɛ̀lɡ̰ɳé:]
/ɳu-mele?-ɳe/
2pl-lest-cook.PR
'you should cook it'

h. [nuwìɾɟ̰é:ppìɾa̰]
/ɳu-wiri?+je-ppira?/
2pl-take.out-PUT.PR-DU
'you two take it out'

i. [ɟinibɐkjé:ppìɾa̰]
/jini-pak-je-ppira?/
2pl/1sg-APPL-put.PR-DU
'you two put it [there] for me'

j. [ɟándḁka̰]
/canta?-ka?/
tree-LOC

	Utterance	Syll #	Onset	V	V dur.	Creak dur.	Total
1	jirgʊ̀rʊ**ŋg**ʊ́mḭɲ	4	ŋg	ú	52.50	81.44	133.94
2	jirgʊ̀rʊ**ŋg**ʊ́mḭɲ	4	ŋg	ú	106.13	63.25	169.38
3	jírk**ka̰**pìra̰	2	kk	a	65.94	66.00	131.94
4	bàʈʈa**ɻáʊ̰**wḭ	3	ɻ	áʊ	52.25	86.55	138.80
5	bàʈʈaɻáʊ̰**wḭ**	4	w	i	102.94	75.12	178.06
6	numɛ̀**lɡ̰**ɳé:ppɪra̰	3	l	e	57.12	22.13	79.25
7	mɛ̀**lɡ̰**ɻú:	2	l	e	59.50	117.13	176.63
8	numɛ̀**lɡ̰**ɳé:	3	l	e	50.63	93.87	144.50
9	nuwìɾɟ̰é:ppì**ɾa̰**	3	ɾ	i	100.06	61.56	161.62
10	nuwìɾɟ̰é:ppì**ɾa̰**	6	ɾ	a	69.31	13.34	82.65
11	jukké**ɟḭ**	3	ɟ	i	44.00	40.63	84.63
12	mɛ̀lɡ̰ɻú:	2	l	e	67.69	76.19	143.88
13	nuwì**ɾḭ**jé:ppìɾa̰	3	ɾ	i	78.44	38.00	116.44
14	nuwìɾɟ̰é:ppì**ɾa̰**	6	ɾ	a	61.81	230.50	292.31
15	jinibakjé:ppɪ̀**ɾa̰**	6	ɾ	a	122.25	130.25	252.50
16	ɟá**ndḁ**ka̰	2	nd	a	64.81	96.62	161.43
17	ɟándḁ**ka̰**	3	k	a	68.94	315.75	384.69

Table 9: Durations of vowels and glottal constriction in a sample of acoustically analysed Ngalakgan words

Note that, with the exception of numbers 1, 2, and 4, all occurrences of glottal stop fall in unstressed syllables. The average duration of unstressed vowels in open syllables in Ngalakgan is between 50-60 ms. Hence, if we were to regard these vowels as laryngealised, the combined durations of vowel plus creak (given in the final column) would in most cases greatly exceed the normal range for modal unstressed vowels. Many tokens would instead fall within the range of phonologically long vowels. In this sample, there were 9 tokens of phonologically long vowels, and the average duration of these tokens was 120 ms. I conclude on the basis of this preliminary data that glottal stops occupy a distinct timing slot from the preceding sonorant (where this is a vowel), though their articulation in every case is that of an additional laryngealisation feature on a preceding sonorant, rather than a distinct glottal stop. These two characteristics, I suggest, can account for their prosodic and phonological behaviour in Ngalakgan and other Northern languages.

2.5 The syllabification of glides

Following vowels, [j] diphthongises the peak:

(82)	a.	/ŋej/	[ŋeɪ]	'name'
	b.	/leʔ-ja/	[lḛ́ɪja]	'look for-FUT'

This is true of [j] even when it is intervocalic:

(83)	a.	/kajapam/	[gáˈjabam]	'bush orange' (*Capparis* sp.)
	b.	/kojo/	[góˈjo]	'freshwater crocodile'

The syllabification of the labio-dorsal glide [w] varies. Syllabifed exclusively as a coda (that is, when not followed by a vowel), it also causes (or is realised as) diphthongisation:

(84)	a.	/kowk/	[goʊk]	'humpy' (shelter)
	b.	/poʈewk/	[bɔɖɛ́ʊk]	'bad'
	c.	/ʈiʈipaw[a]pa/	[díɖibàʊba]	'lotus bird'

(Example (c) here shows syllabification of underlying onset as a coda.)
Intervocalically however, no diphthongisation is perceived:

(85)	a.	/calawarcca/	[ɟalawarcca]	*[ɟalauwarcca]	'full, brimming'
	b.	/cawaɳʈa/	[ɟawaɳɖa]	*[ɟauwaɳɖa]	'whiskers'

The retroflex glide [ɻ] is exceptional: alone among consonants, it can be syllabic (and cf. Evans 2003: 86):

(86) a. /kiɳalk/ [gɻ̩ɳalk] 'white/straw-necked ibis'
b. /ʈuɻ̃/ [dɻ̩ɻ̃] 'sit down'

Further, an underlying [postalveolar] feature on a postvocalic segment can be realised as a *pre*-vocalic onset, creating a surface obstruent-glide cluster:

(87) a. /ʈaɻʔ/ [dɻa̰] 'tree (generic)'
b. /kiɳalk/ [gɻɨɳalk] 'white/straw-necked ibis'
c. /kiɳʈar/ [gɻɨɳɖar] 'cross cousin'

Perhaps more surprising is the shifting of retroflexion through an onset into the following vowel, as in (88):

(88) /malaʈiʔ/ [málaɖɻ̃] 'wedge-tailed eagle'

On the basis of such behaviour, as well as distributional restrictions, Evans (2003: 86) proposes that retroflexion be analysed as an autosegment of the syllable node, along with laryngealisation.

The alveolar tap/trill /r/ has some ambisyllabic characteristics, although the evidence from Ngalakgan is mainly distributional. As in many Australian languages, and other languages (e.g. Basque: Hualde 1991), it is restricted to postvocalic, and morpheme-medial or -final position. In this respect, it is the only such contrastive segment, apart from the glottal stop, which is never found in root-initial position.

The evidence for /r/ ambisyllabicity is stronger in other Australian languages. In closely-related languages to the north of Ngalakgan, such as Bininj Gun-wok (Evans 2003: 107), /r/ alternates with stem-initial underlying /t/ (or /d/):

(89) a. /ŋani-taŋiɲ/ [ŋanidáŋiɲ]
1duS-stand.PP 'we two (exclusive) stood'
b. /ŋa-taŋiɲ/ [ŋaɾáŋiɲ]
1sS-stand.PP 'I stood'

/r/ therefore has a similar distribution in BGW to the tap allophone [ɾ] of /d/, /t/ in English (Kahn 1976), except that [ɾ] and [d] are contrastive in BGW and Ngalakgan, though the tap [ɾ] and stop [d] are not contrastive in English:

(90) a. sough[ɾ]Ed 'sought Ed'
b. ci[ɾ]y 'city'

Evans (2003: 76-77) discusses several pieces of evidence for the interpretation of phonetic diphthongs as vowel+glide sequences rather than vowel+vowel sequences in BGW. One argument relies on the behaviour of glides in reduplication. This argument applies also to Ngalakgan, though in a different reduplication pattern to the one that Evans examines. In Ngalakgan, there are several reduplication patterns. One of the more productive patterns targets an initial CVCV portion of the stem:

(91) a. [ŋʊruɖʊ̀muɖʊ́mur̠a]
/ŋuru-**ʈumu**-ʈumurʔ-a/ /ʈumurʔ-a/
12aS-ITER-break.up-FUT break.up-FUT
'we will go around breaking up (sticks for the fire)' [2/7/96:1A]

b. [bʊruwɔ̀rowɔ́roʊkmiɲ]
/puru-**woro**-worowk-mi+ɲ/ /worowk-mi+ɲ/
3aS-ITER-jump.along-AUX+PP jump.along-AUX+PP
'they jumped along' [KD: passim]

c. [bʊruwʊ̀luwʊ́lʊppa]
/puru-**wulu**-wulup-pa/ /wulup-pa/
3aS-ITER-bathe-FUT bathe-FUT
'they are going to splash around'

When the stem contains a vowel+glide sequence in the second syllable, the reduplicant copies just the nucleus, rather than the whole diphthong.

(92) a. [bʊrubɔ̀ɖebɔ́ɖɛʊk]
/puru-**poʈe**-poʈewk/ /poʈewk/
3aS-ITER-bad bad
'they are very bad'; or: 'they are habitually bad' [3/7/96]

One other source of argument for glides as consonants is the behaviour of glides for phonotactics (Evans 2003: 77): the distribution of semivowels follows if we include them in the class of continuants, as shown in 2.2.1. In particular, the existence of a vowel+glide sequence precludes the possibility of a following continuant in the same syllable. That is, we find examples such as (93) as possible words, where a glide is followed by [–cont] segment within the coda, but not (94), as Evans notes.

(93) a. /poʈewk/ 'bad'
b. /wojk/ 'to fish'[40]

---

[40] As in BGW, /j/-final sequences are more constrained that /w/-final ones. (93)b is the only example where /j/ is followed by another segment in the syllable (except /ʔ/), while there are several examples like (93)a, where /w/ is followed by a further coda segment.

(94) *a. /pewl/
*b. /wojr/

Finally, there is evidence from vowel harmony that similarly excludes offglides from the nucleus. The Dative/Genitive/Relative suffix /-ʔkVn/ in Ngalakgan copies the final vowel in the stem:

(95) a. [ŋʊɾuɻábɔn̰kɔn]
/ŋuru-ɻapon-ʔkon/
12aS-go.PR-REL
'when we go'
b. [bʊrmuɭɛ́r̰lɛr̰kɛn gʊnguŋóɪ]
/pur-mu-ɭerʔ-ɭerʔ-ʔkVn kun-ku-ŋoj/
3aS-VEG-ITER-set.alight-REL NEUT-TOP-fire
'when they light the fire' [9/9/97: 1A]

However, when the final syllable of the stem contains a phonetic diphthong, only the nuclear vowel is copied:

(96) a. [ŋʊɾuwárɟa̰ɻa mumáɪ̰kan]
/ŋuru-warcaʔ-ɻa mu-maj-ʔkan/
12aS-forage-FUT VEG-veg.food-DAT
'we're going to look around for food' [2/7/96: 1/2A]
b. [jɪɾiŋéɪ̰kɛn]
/jiri-ŋejʔ-kVn/
1a-get.up.PR-REL
'when we get up' [13/10/99:1A]
c. [jɪɾiwóɪkkoɪkkɔn]
/jiri-wojk-wojk-kVn/
1a-ITER-fish.PR-REL
'when we fish here and there' [13/10/99:1A]

Further discussion of the syllabification of semivowels (including the retroflex glide /ɻ/) can be found in 2.6, which follows.

2.6 Inter-morphemic clusters and assimilation

In 2.2.1, I noted that heterorganic clusters are common in the lexicon of Ngalakgan, as in other Northern languages. In heterorganic clusters within morphemes, there is no assimilation. Unlike more well-known languages such as English, clusters of underlying heterorganic nasal+stop do not undergo place assimilation. Thus /cuɳku/ 'back' contrasts with /cuɳʈupolʔ/ 'small rock wallaby (*Petrogale*) sp.' contrasts with /cuŋ-pun/ 'build a bough shade' (PRES; /cuŋ/ 'bough shade') contrasts with /cuŋ-gun/ 'bough shade-DAT' and so on.

Clusters across morpheme boundaries in Ngalakgan, with a couple of well-defined classes of exceptions, likewise surface without loss of distinctive place or manner features. The exceptions fall into two types: coronal +coronal clusters, and non-continuant+continuant clusters, both of them dispreferred sequences in Australian languages (Hamilton 1996).

Apico-alveolar+laminal clusters tend to merge with homorganic laminal clusters at the surface in Ngalakgan, as in other Australian languages. Clusters of underlying morpheme final /n/ and morpheme-initial /c/ tend to assimilate to the homorganic laminal cluster [ɲɟ] at the surface, though perhaps only in unmonitored speech. This cluster is rather difficult to distinguish from the heterorganic /nc/, the only consistent cue is a raised second formant in the VC transition, heard as a raising of preceding vowel often with a brief [ɪ] offglide. The two are in contrast in the lexicon; there are two monomorphemic examples of /nc/: /kancu/ 'straightaway' and /kancari/ 'bony bream', contrasting with near-identical strings such as /aɲci/ 'and now' and /ŋaɲca/ 'all the way'. However, it is not uncommon for Australian languages to lack a contrast between these two clusters (Hamilton 1996: 118); Warlpiri is an example.

Similarly, as noted by Merlan (1983: 29), clusters of the apical plus laminal stop are indistinguishable in many cases from a laminal geminate. She provides the following examples:[41]

(97) a. [guɟɛ́cci̠]
/ku-cet-ciʔ/
NP-pluck.out-FNEG
'he can't/won't pluck it out'
b. [guŋʊ́ɻcci̠]
/ku-ŋuʈ-ciʔ/
NP-stop-FNEG
'he can't/won't stop'

In apical+laminal clusters then, assimilation is leftwards (anticipatory).

Intermorphemic clusters of two apicals must be entirely homorganic at the surface, with the place features (apico-alveolar/postalveolar) determined by the first segment in the cluster. In other words, assimilation is rightwards (perseverative):

---

41 The representations here are my own, rather than Merlan's.

(98) a. /ŋun-ɳe/ [ŋunːeː]
1mO-burn.PR ‘it burns me’

Note that, as described in 2.2.2, morpheme-initial apicals (in word-level morphemes) are neutralised for place features in any case. And so (98) is the only possible example of assimilation to apical place.

The second class of assimilations concerns inter-morphemic clusters where the second consonant is a glide. Synchronically, there are few good examples of clusters of this type. There are two glide-initial affixes, /-jiʔ/ Ergative/ Instrumental, and /-wi/ Lative. However, as in many Australian languages, homorganic glide+vowel sequences like /ji/ are ill-defined, and can often be realised simply as the corresponding vowel where there is a preceding consonant. As with the historical process which derived the Future and Irrealis inflection of open class verbs (2.4.2), elision of the initial glide typically results in gemination of a preceding stop:

(99) a. [bàʈʈabɔ́ɳɖɒkkḭ]
/paʈʈa-poɳʈo**k-jiʔ**/
COMIT-woomera-INST
‘with a woomera [spear thrower]’
b. [jɪɾɪɳŋàɾiɲgùl̰gúl̰mɻiɲ muɻɒ́kkḭ]
/jiriɳ-ŋariɲ-kulʔ-kulʔ-miɻiɲ mu-ɻo**k-jiʔ**/
1aO-hand-ITER-jab-AUX.PC
‘it kept jabbing our hands, the pandanus’ [DP]

When the final segment of the stem is a lateral, we find variation between deletion and faithful realisation of the following glide as in (100).

(100) a. [bàʈʈaɖákkuɭḭ] ~ [bàʈʈaɖákkuɭjḭ]
/paʈʈa-ʈakkuɭ-jiʔ/
COMIT-axe-INST
‘with an axe’ [DP]
b. [numókkolḭ] ~ [numókkoljḭ]
/ɳu-mokkol-jiʔ/
M-father-ERG
‘my father’ (Ergative case) [2/9/97:1A]

Where the final segment is the tap /r/, then only deletion is observed, as in (101):

(101) a. [bàʈʈaŋálpporḭ]
/paʈʈa-ŋalppor-jiʔ/
COMIT-egg-INST
‘with [its] eggs’ [DP]

b. [wíɭmuri̠]
/wiɭmur-jiʔ/
three.pronged.spear-ERG [2/9/97:1A]

When the final segment is a nasal, the glide appears to be realised faithfully for the most part (102)a-b, although following the apico-alveolar nasal deletion is more typical, presumably to avoid confusion with the laminal nasal (c).

(102) a. [bàʈʈabíɳɟi̠]
/paʈʈa-piɳ-jiʔ/
COMIT-rock-INST [9/9/97:1B]

b. [ɟumánaŋɟi̠]
/cu-manaŋ-jiʔ/
F-mother-ERG [2/9/97:1A]

c. [jáɾamani̠]
/jaraman-jiʔ/
horse-ERG [12/9/97:1A]

The affix /-wi/ has not been observed to participate in any alternations; however, it is quite rare in my data and I did not explicitly test it for alternations.

The inflecting verb /ɻapo+/ 'go' alternates with a palatal glide-initial form /japo/ just where it follows the person prefix /ɲiɲ-/ '2sg': [ɲiɲjabo] 'you went'. No other /ɻ/-inital verbs were observed to undergo this alternation (cf. Merlan 1983: 28); it appears to be a lexicalised formation.

2.7 Orthography

The following tables present the orthography currently in use in schools for teaching Ngalakgan. Orthographic representations are not used in this monograph, except for the spelling of names. The orthography follows that developed by Batchelor College for the Katherine region languages (e.g. Jawoyn) in most respects, and is similar to orthographies used by Diwurruwurru-jaru (the Katherine Language Centre) for teaching traditional languages in schools.

	Front	Central	Back
High	i		u
Mid	e		o
Low		a	

Table 10: Orthographic vowels

	Labial	Apico-alveolar	Apico-retroflex	Lamino-alveo-palatal	Dorsal	Glottal
Simple stops	b...p	d...t	rd...rt	j...tj	g...k	h
Geminates	...pb...	...td...	...rtd...	...tjj...	...kg...	
Nasal	m	n	rn	ny	ng	
Lateral		l	rl			
Tap		rr				
Approximant			r	y	w	

Table 11: Orthographic consonants

The main features to note are the following.

- Lenis, singleton stops are written *b d rd j g* syllable-initially, and *p t rt tj k* syllable-finally. This accords with the usual phonetic realisations in these environments.
- Fortis, geminate stops are represented by digraphs combining the syllable-final and syllable-initial symbols: *pb td rtd tjj kg.*
- Apicals in non-contrastive positions are written as alveolars. Non-contrastive positions are morpheme-initially (following a word-level '-' or '#' boundary), and in the second position of clusters. Accordingly, clusters of postalveolar segments are written with a single preceding *r*; hence *rnd*, *rtd* represent [ɳɖ], [ʈʈ] respectively. Non-homorganic clusters of apical segments do not occur; such clusters arising at morpheme boundaries are obligatorily assimilated at the surface (see 2.2.2).
- *h* is a glottal stop [ʔ], realised as laryngealisation (creaky voice) on a preceding sonorant as described in section 2.4.
- *nk, rnk* represent heterorganic alveolar nasal+dorsal stop and postalveolar nasal+dorsal stop, i.e. [ng], [ɳg] respectively, whereas the homorganic cluster [ŋg] is written *ngg*. Similarly *nj* and *ntj* are homorganic [ɲɟ] and heterorganic [nɟ] respectively (the latter cluster is quite rare).

3

Root and Word

Ngalakgan morphology is classically agglutinative: words can consist of many morphemes, each morpheme having a relatively consistent function or meaning, and a relatively consistent form. Morphophonological rules are rare. It is an open question in linguistics whether and to what extent words in such languages correspond to phrases in languages such as English, which have comparatively little morphology.

This chapter establishes a fundamental difference between two kinds of morphological relations in Ngalakgan, which I will call 'root-level' and 'word-level', following Selkirk (1982), and Borowsky (1986). This distinction has correlates in both prosody and productivity. I show that the metrical structure of free words is retained under productive compounding, but not in lexicalised, unproductive, compounds.

This chapter, then, provides the first basis for an argument that the lexicon of speakers of Ngalakgan (and, by extension, that of speakers of similar Australian languages) distinguishes between these two kinds of relations. In particular, I propose that productive morphemes are listed in the lexicon individually, where they are available to be combined with other lexical elements in some kind of combinatorial system (a version of such a system is described in 3.4). Forms which are (historically) derived with unproductive, irregular or lexicalised morphology are listed in their entirety. The elements of such forms, while bearing some historical relationship to other words in the lexicon, are not subject to synchronic combinatorial rules (following Jackendoff 2002, among others). The implications of this view of morphology for Optimality Theory are explored in 3.8.1.

I begin by outlining the basic prosodic patterns in simple words, in 3.1. I then show that for elements which are surface words, the metrical structure they have when independent is retained in compounds, in 3.2. Compounds of this kind are called WORD-compounds. WORD-compounds contrast with 'ROOT -compounds' which have the same metrical organisation as simple words, as shown in 3.3.2. ROOT-compounds are lexicalised compounds, with largely idiosyncratic interpretations, whereas WORD-compounds are semantically compositional: the meaning of the compound is derived straightforwardly from the meanings of its constituent morphemes.

3.1 Simplex words

On the whole, Ngalakgan has a trochaic stress system. In simple, monomorphemic words, stress is initial. Most monomorphemic words are disyllabic or trisyllabic.

		Disyllables		
(1)	a.	/pere/	[bɛ́ɾe]	'brisket'
	b.	/polo/	[bɔ́lo]	'old person'
	c.	/poɲi/	[bɔ́ɲi]	'now'
	d.	/kara/	[gáɾa]	'high up'
	e.	/kaja/	[gája]	'same-sex sibling's child'
	f.	/kiʈi/	[gíɖi]	'young girl'
	g.	/kojo/	[gójo]	'freshwater crocodile'
	h.	/cala/	[ɟála]	'mouth'
	i.	/cele/	[ɟɛ́le]	'urine'
	j.	/ceŋe/	[ɟɛ́ŋe]	'teat, breast, milk'
	k.	/ciwi/	[ɟî́wi]	'liver'
	l.	/colo/	[ɟɔ́lo]	'inside meaty part'
	m.	/coɳe/	[ɟɔ́ɳe]	*Terminalia canescens*
	n.	/maŋa/	[máŋa]	'throat, neck'
	o.	/maʈu/	[máɖu]	'paperbark coolamon' (a vessel)
	p.	/maɭa/	[máɭa]	'centipede'
	q.	/mira/	[míɾa]	'head'
	r.	/ŋaʈa/	[ŋáɖa]	'uncircumcised boy'
	s.	/ŋoro/	[ŋɔ́ɾo]	'flower'
	t.	/ŋuru/	[ŋʊ́ɾu]	'catfish sp.'
	u.	/ɻere/	[ɻɛ́ɾe]	'camp' (N)
	v.	/ɳamu/	[námu]	'woman's child'
	w.	/ɳaʈi/	[náɖi]	'frog sp.'
	x.	/ɳimi/	[ními]	'arse'
	y.	/ɻoro/	[ɻɔ́ɾo]	'east'
	z.	/were/	[wɛ́ɾe]	'who?'; 'somebody'
	aa.	/wiɳi/	[wíɳi]	'shortnecked freshwater tortoise (*Emydura*) sp.

bb. /wolo/	[wɔ́lo]	'cooked, ripe'
cc. /jele/	[jɛ́le]	'animal hole'
dd. /kaɻe/	[gáɻe]	'Eucalyptus sp.'
ee. /ɲili/	[ɲíli]	'fog'

The examples in (1) represent all the disyllabic, open-syllabled roots which can occur as words.[1] All the trisyllabic open-syllabled examples are presented in (2). Again, stress is on the initial syllable. There is no stress on the final syllable.

	Trisyllables		
(2)	a. /picuʈu/	[bíɟuɖu]	'whirlwind'
	b. /puluki/	[búlugi]	'bullock, cow'
	c. /kamala/	[gámala]	'sky'
	d. /caworo/	[ɟáwoɾo]	'patrilineal clan'
	e. /ceraʈa/	[ɟɛ́raɖa]	'women's ceremonial singing'
	f. /cilara/	[ɟílaɾa]	[unidentified tree sp.]
	g. /malaʈi/	[máladi]	'wedge-tailed eagle'
	h. /munaŋa/	[múnaŋa]	'European'
	i. /muwaʈa/	[múwaɖa]	'canoe'
	j. /ŋuɭiri/	[ŋúɭiɾi]	'black duck sp.'
	k. /walama/	[wálama]	'face'
	l. /waʈija/	[wáɖija]	'multiparous woman'
	m. /weleɲe/	[wɛ́lɛɲe]	'young girl'; 'female'
	n. /jiŋoro/	[jíŋoɾo]	'all around'
	o. /makara/	[mágaɾa]	'white clay'
	p. /wamara/	[wámaɾa]	'freshwater tortoise sp.'
	q. /ciwuru/	[ɟíwuɾu]	'wild cassava'
	r. /palara/	[bálaɾa]	'string'
	s. /komoɭo/	[gɔ́moɭo]	'white crane'

In the next section, I account for these patterns of prosodic structure.

3.1.1 Analysis of simplex forms

The prosodic form of simple words in Ngalakgan derives from constraint satisfaction and general principles of prosody. The general principles I assume are 'Prosodic Licensing' (Itô 1986), the 'Prosodic Hierarchy' and 'Strict Layering' (Selkirk 1980, 1995), and 'Foot Binarity' (Prince and

[1] I discount frozen reduplicated forms such as /ʈaʈa/ 'sugarbag (native honey)'. There are a handful of roots about which I have insufficient knowledge to include here: e.g. /moŋo/ 'animal lair'.

Smolensky 1993: 47; cf. Prince 1980). I outline these briefly here, before moving on to an analysis of the metrical structure.

All morphological forms are subject to Prosodic Licensing. This is the proposal that all lexical words require some kind of prosodic structure in order to be pronounced (e.g. Selkirk 1980; Itô 1986). Prosodic structure is organised into a hierarchy of prosodic constituents: the Prosodic Hierarchy, as in (3). The form of the Prosodic Hierarchy in (3) follows that in (Selkirk 1995); in particular, it assumes three superordinate prosodic constituents above the Foot (the Utterance is not a prosodic constituent of the same kind, in that it does not have specific tonal characteristics). Arguments for this structure are provided in 3.2.3.

The Strict Layering hypothesis (e.g. Selkirk 1984) says that a prosodic constituent at level *n* must immediately dominate a prosodic constituent at level *n*-1. So any PRWD constituent must dominate some Foot constituent. I assume, following (McCarthy and Prince 1993b) and (Selkirk 1995), a version of Strict Layering which is factored into violable constraints, such that the Prosodic Hierarchy 'expresses the domination relations among the prosodic constituents, but it does not express relations of immediate domination' (McCarthy and Prince 1993b: 5).

(3)	Utterance	
	Intonational Phrase	(IP)
	Phonological Phrase	(PPH)
	Prosodic Word	(PRWD)
	Foot	(Ft)
	Syllable	(σ)
	Mora	(μ)

Selkirk's (1995: 443) proposal for decomposing the Strict Layering Hypothesis into constraints is repeated here as (4):

(4) *Constraints on Prosodic Domination*
(where C^n = some prosodic category)

(i)	*Layeredness*	No C^i dominates a C^j, $j > i$, e.g. "No σ dominates a Ft."
(ii)	*Headedness*	Any C^i must dominate a C^{i-1} (except if $C^i = \sigma$), e.g. "A P[r]Wd must dominate a Ft."
(iii)	*Exhaustivity*	No C^i immediately dominates a constituent C^j, $j < i-1$, e.g. "No P[r]Wd immediately dominates a σ."
(iv)	*Nonrecursivity*	No C^i dominates C^j, $j = i$, e.g. "No Ft dominates a Ft."

Selkirk proposes further that while Layeredness and Headedness hold universally (i.e. are unviolated), Exhaustiveness and Nonrecursivity may be both violable and relativised to particular constituents of the Prosodic Hierarchy. In particular, she allows for violations of Exhaustiveness with respect to the domination of syllables by PRWD directly (bypassing the foot), to allow for syllable 'extrametricality', and for violations of Nonrecursivity with respect to PRWD (cf. also Nespor and Vogel 1986; Rubach and Booij 1990). The syllable node must always dominate some mora, but not everything it dominates must in turn be dominated by a mora. The syllable node dominates onset directly in the representation assumed by e.g. Hayes (1989), McCarthy and Prince (1993a, b) and adopted here.

Prosodic licensing in OT takes the form of a general constraint 'MCAT ≈ PRWD' (McCarthy and Prince 1993a: 139; cf. Prince and Smolensky 1993: 43). This constraint makes sure that words *qua* lexical entries (strings of segments) are realised as words *qua* prosodic constituents.

(5) MCAT ≈ PRWD 'A member of the morphological category "MCat" is a Prosodic Word', where MCat = Root, Stem, Lexical Word

For the moment, it is sufficient to regard the 'MCat' referred to in the constraint as a 'lexeme', that is a 'lexical word' in McCarthy and Prince's terminology. The question of the identity of MCat in this constraint as it pertains to Ngalakgan is addressed more carefully in following sections.

Metrical feet are binary, as encoded in the constraint FTBIN presented in (6). FTBIN rules out monomoraic, trisyllabic, and 'unbounded' feet (Halle and Vergnaud 1987).

(6) Foot Binarity(FTBIN) 'Feet are binary at some level of analysis (mora μ, syllable σ)'

From the Prosodic Hierarchy, Strict Layering, and FTBIN, it then follows that PRWDs are minimally bimoraic. And since lexemes are required to be PRWDs, by MCAT ≈ PRWD, then every lexeme must also be bimoraic at the surface (McCarthy and Prince 1993a; Prince and Smolensky 1993).

MCAT ≈ PRWD does not say anything about the form of feet, or their association with particular edges of words or morphemes (foot 'directionality'). The form of feet is decided by constraints given the general term 'Foot Form' (Prince and Smolensky 1993: 53, 63).[2] In Ngalakgan, feet are necessarily trochaic, and hence the constraint applicable is the one given in (7).

---

[2] In Prince and Smolensky (1993), FTFORM is a cover term for distinct constraints determining headedness (left/right) called 'RhType=T' (trochaic rhythm) and 'RhType=I' (Iambic Rhythm).

(7) Foot Form:Trochaic (FTFORM) 'Feet are left headed'

Given the FTBIN constraint in (6), the only allowable foot in Ngalakgan is that shown in (8) (where 's' 'w' label 'strong' or 'head' and 'weak' or 'tail' branches, respectively, of the foot).

(8)

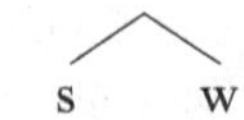

Trochees are *bimoraic* in Ngalakgan. The moras can be associated to each of two syllable peaks, giving disyllabic feet as in (9).

(9)

Disyllabic foot

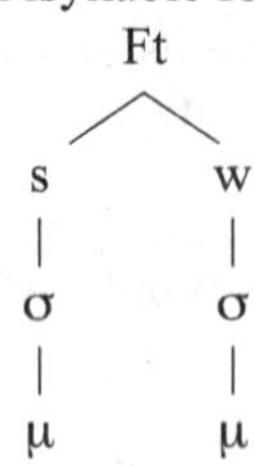

Otherwise both moras can be associated to the same syllable: where one mora is associated to a peak and the other to a coda, or both moras are associated to the peak, giving monosyllabic, 'heavy' feet as in (10).

(10)

Monosyllabic heavy foot

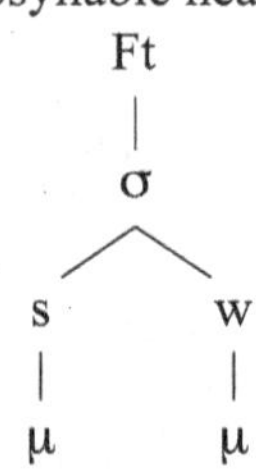

The definition of syllable weight in Ngalakgan is a complex issue, and is discussed in Chapter 5. For the purposes of this chapter and the next, the only heavy syllables considered will be those where the vowel is long.

The fact that stress is initial in all of the disyllabic and trisyllabic words above is determined by the following constraint:

(11) ALIGNL(PRWD, FT): 'Align the left edge of every Prosodic Word with the left edge of some foot'

ALIGNL encodes the observation that PRWDS are always left-headed in Ngalakgan, modulo the effect of heavy syllables (Chapter 5).

All of these constraints are active in deriving a trisyllabic form like /cérața/, as shown in (12). Foot boundaries are shown with parentheses, PRWD boundaries with square brackets.

(12)

/cerața/ 'women's ceremony'	FTBIN	FTFORM	MCAT ≈ PRWD	ALIGNL (PRWD, FT)
☞ a. [(céra)ța]				
b. [ce(ráța)]				*!
c. [ce(rațá)]		*!		*
d. [(cérața)]	*!			
e. [(céra)(tà)]	*!			
f. cerața			*!	

I have only shown a few of the possible parses here. None of these constraints conflict. The constraints are therefore unranked—represented by the dotted boundary.

FTBIN and FTFORM rule out any parse which includes feet which are iambic (right-headed), as in (12)c, or which are less or more than binary (12)d, e. MCAT ≈ PRWD rules out the 'Null Parse' in (12)f, where a morphological form is not supplied with any prosodic realisation at all. ALIGNL(PRWD, FT) prefers left-headed words, and so picks (12)a over the misaligned (12)b. I have assumed that this constraint is evaluated gradiently: the grammar assigns a violation mark for every syllable separating the left edge of the PRWD from the left edge of a foot.

All simple polysyllabic words are derived straightforwardly with the constraints presented in this section, modulo the effect of syllable weight (examined in Chapter 5). In the following section, I examine monosyllabic words, which present their own challenges.

3.1.2 Monosyllabic words

All monosyllabic roots in Ngalakgan are required to correspond to a bimoraic minimum, as proposed above. A monosyllabic word consisting of an underlyingly short vowel, such as /ce/, the Ngalakgan word for 'nose', cannot satisfy the word minimality requirement: this word is not bimoraic. These words present a problem then: they cannot be parsed Faithfully without violating MCat ≈ PrWd.[3]

A short vowel, according to Moraic Theory, is a vowel which is associated to one mora. The word in (13) violates FtBin because a minimum of two moras is required to form a foot.

(13)

```
        Ft
        |
        σ
        |
        μ
        |
      /ce/     *[ɟe]   'nose'
```

Since the word in (13) must be parsed by PrWd, and every PrWd must dominate a foot, and every foot must be minimally bimoraic, the outcome for Ngalakgan (and many other languages) is that the smallest possible word (the *minimal word*) is bimoraic. This is shown in (14).

(14)

```
       PPh
        |
       PrWd
        |
        Ft
        |
        σ
        |\
        μμ
        |/
      /ce/     [ɟeː]   'nose'
```

In (14), the word satisfies the FtBin requirement because it is realised with a bimoraic, that is long, vowel. (15) presents examples of underlying monosyllabic, open-syllabled roots, pronounced with long vowels in surface forms.

(15)	a. /ce/	[ɟeː]	*[ɟe]	'nose'
	b. /po/	[boː]	*[bo]	'river'
	c. /ke/	[geː]	*[ge]	'man's child'

---

[3] The reasons for adopting an underlying short vowel are discussed more fully in §3.1.3. I postpone considerations of 'Richness of the Base' (Prince and Smolensky 1993, Ch 6) until then.

CV words cannot be realised with a short vowel at the surface. These examples are the only CV roots which can occur unaffixed. Aside from the three nouns, there are nine inflected verb forms which are CV words. These do not occur without a prefix, however, as discussed in Chapter 4, inflectional prefixes are never stressed and never count towards the bimoraic minimum. So CV verb roots must also surface with long vowels.[4]

In monosyllabic closed roots the vowel is short. This is true regardless of whether the coda is a sonorant (16), or a stop (17).[5]

(16)	a.	/lel/	[lɛl]	*[leːl]	‘aquatic plant sp.’
	b.	/wom/	[wɒm]	*[wɔːm]	‘black plum’ (*Vitex glabrata*)
	c.	/pim/	[bɪm]	*[bɪːm]	‘white ochre’
	d.	/piɳ/	[bɪɳ]	*[bɪːɳ]	‘rock; money’
	e.	/puɳ/	[bʊɳ]	*[bʊːɳ]	‘knee’
	f.	/ker/	[gɛr]	*[gɛːr]	‘kurrajong’ (*Brachychiton paradoxum*)
	g.	/koɲ/	[goɲ]	*[goːɲ]	‘kangaroo (generic)’

(17)	a.	/pot/	[bɔt]	*[bɔːt]	‘fly’
	b.	/kot/	[gɔt]	*[gɔːt]	‘paperbark’
	c.	/ɻok/	[ɻɒk]	*[ɻɔːk]	‘pandanus’
	d.	/pok/	[bɒk]	*[bɔːk]	‘small creek’
	e.	/pak/	[bak]	*[baːk]	‘pond algae’
	f.	/mic/	[mic]	*[miːc]	‘louse’
	g.	/muc/	[muc]	*[muːc]	‘Rainbow Serpent’ (a mythological figure)

[4] McKay (1975: 26) makes a similar observation for Rembarrnga. He notes that no contrasting pairs of short vowel/long vowel are available, and that ‘all words consistently pronounced with noticeably lengthened vowels are monosyllables’. He provides the following examples, of which he notes just one is a closed syllable: [ɭɛːn] ‘ground honeycomb’; the others are [piː] ‘man’, [mɔː] ‘knee’, [mɛː] ‘vegetable food’, [ɻɛː] ‘[class of animals]’, [bɛː] ‘north’. He notes further ‘these words regularly have long vowels, even when inflected with suffixes’. Changes in the vowel systems of Ngalakgan and Rembarrnga have led to the situation where cognates which are monosyllabic or monophthongal in one language may be disyllabic or diphthongal in the other, and vice versa. For the monophthongal Rembarrnga items cited above, cf. Ngkn cognates /maj/ ‘vegetable food’, /ɻaj/ ‘meat; class of meat animal’, /paj/ ‘north’, all of which are realised with a diphthong nucleus [aɪ] ~ [aj]. Some monosyllabic Ngalakgan roots with a monophthongal nucleus correspond to disyllables in Rembarrnga: Ngkn /po/ Rmba /puwa/ ‘river’; Ngkn /po/ Rmba /puwa/ ‘hit’ (PP); Ngkn /koɲ/ Rmba /kuweɲ/ ‘kangaroo (generic)’; Ngkn /ɳe/ Rmba /ɳiya/ ‘burn’ (PR).

[5] The variation in mid-back vowel allophony here is not phonemically significant: it depends on the place of articulation of the final consonant. Vowel allophony is discussed in Chapter 2.

Glottal stop codas in CVC words are a separate case. These are examined in Chapter 5.

The list of monosyllabic roots with sonorant codas in (16) is not exhaustive, but the examples in (17) represent all the monosyllabic nominal roots with obstruent codas in my data.[6]

The next section presents an OT analysis of the monosyllabic words.

3.1.3 Analysis of monosyllabic words

In this section I argue that the long vowels in CV words are not present in underlying forms, but are realised in satisfaction of MCAT ≈ PRWD and FTBIN: a condition called 'word minimality' in McCarthy and Prince (1986).

Is there any evidence for the opposing view—that is, that the long-vowel form in (15) [ɟeː] *is* the underlying form? If long vowels were contrastive in some environment in Ngalakgan, then we would be forced to postulate an underlying vowel contrast in the language. But the distribution of long and short vowels is entirely predictable, and therefore I assume that there is no underlying contrast, but rather, the surface realisation of vowels is an outcome of constraint satisfaction.

Long vowels in Ngalakgan only occur in monosyllabic open roots, and in no other environment. Vowels in every other position are short. Long vowels and short vowels are in complementary distribution; therefore, they are allophones of the same underlying phoneme (Trubetzkoy 1969[1939]: 49). Vowel length is non-distinctive in Ngalakgan.

The long allophone of vowels is the marked allophone. It occurs in an environment which must be specified: in monosyllabic, open roots. The short allophone occurs in the elsewhere case, every root which is not monosyllabic, or is monosyllabic but closed. The environment which conditions the distribution of the long allophone is more restricted than that which describes the distribution of the short allophone, so I assume the latter is unmarked with respect to the former. Therefore, we can postulate the constraint ranking shown in (18) (cf. Harvey and Borowsky 1991: 91).

(18) *[V:] >> *[V]
'Long vowels are marked with respect to neutral (non-long) vowels'[7]

---

[6] There are one or two additional words of this form in Merlan (1983) whose realisation I am unsure of: e.g. /cet/ 'stone oven'.

[7] I avoid using 'short' here to characterise the non-long member of this opposition, since vowels can be distinctively short in opposition to a neutral vowel also (e.g. Ossetic: Abaev 1964).

This constraint ranking, like markedness constraints in general (Prince and Smolensky 1993: 3, 187-188; McCarthy and Prince 1995), is held to be universal on the grounds that:

(19) a. There are more languages lacking in (contrastive) long vowels, than there are possessing them.
b. Long vowels are often more restricted in their distribution than short vowels.[8]

Thus, the restricted and predictable distribution of long vowels, and their complementarity with short vowels, leads to the conclusion that the UR of the root for 'nose' is /ce/, and for 'man's child' is /ke/, with short vowels.

A surface realisation with a long vowel in Ngalakgan violates constraints on the relation between the *input* and the *output* in OT. The relevant constraint here is IO-IDENT[mora], regulating the length of segments in the output with respect to the input (Urbanczyk 1995; McCarthy and Prince 1995: 265; McCarthy 1995):

(20) IO-IDENT[mora]: 'Vowels in the output must have the same moraic affiliation as their correspondents in the input'

IO-IDENT[mora] checks that segments which are underlyingly monomoraic are monomoraic in surface form, and likewise that underlyingly bimoraic segments are bimoraic at the surface, on the assumption that length is encoded in underlying moraic affiliation (e.g. Hayes 1989).[9]

The distribution of long vowels in monosyllabic words can be derived in the form of an OT tableau, as in (21). I have given both the phonemic and phonetic representations for the candidate forms. The phonemic form is surrounded by parentheses, representing a foot. The fact that the surface form—the attested output—is [bo:] and not [bo] constitutes a ranking argument for the domination of FTBIN over both IDENT[mora] and *[V:]. Even though candidate (a) violates both *[V:] and IDENT, it is considered better than candidate (b), which surfaces with a short vowel, because candidate (b) violates FTBIN. Candidate (c) does not parse the word as a foot, satisfying FTBIN (spuriously) but fatally violating MCAT ≈ PRWD.

---

[8] We might also add the following observation: 'Every language which has long vowels also has short vowels, but not vice versa'. However, there is an element of circularity in this claim which I am not willing to delve into.

[9] For this chapter and the following one I will assume the only moraic elements allowed—outside of monosyllabic words—are vowels; the issue of moraic consonants is addressed in Chapter 5.

(21)

/po/ 'river'	MCAT ≈ PRWD	FTBIN	IDENT[μ]	*[V:]	*[V]
☞ a. $(po_{\mu\mu})$ ~ [bo:]			*	*	
b. (po_{μ}) ~ [bo]		*!			*
c. po_{μ} ~ [bo]	*!				*

Since FTBIN is decisive in the evaluation of candidates in (21), IDENT[mora] can do no work. The same hierarchy will derive the correct output even if we assume the input has a long vowel, as shown in (22). Regardless of whether the UR has a long vowel or a short vowel, the outcome must have a long vowel, because of the dominance of MCAT ≈ PRWD and FTBIN in the language.

(22)

/po:/ 'river'	MCAT ≈ PRWD	FTBIN	IDENT[μ]	*[V:]	*[V]
☞ a. $(po_{\mu\mu})$ ~ [bo:]				*	
b. (po_{μ}) ~ [bo]		*!	*		*

Are there any principles which can decide which is more likely to be the underlying form? Considerations of 'Lexicon Optimisation' will lead learners to postulate an underlying form with a *long* vowel. Lexicon Optimisation is defined by Prince and Smolensky (1993: 192) as follows.

(23) Lexicon Optimisation:

Suppose that several different inputs I_1, I_2, ..., I_n when parsed by a grammar G lead to corresponding outputs O_1, O_2, ..., O_n, all of which are realised as the same phonetic form Φ—these inputs are all *phonetically equivalent* with respect to G. Now one of these outputs must be the most harmonic, by virtue of incurring the least significant violation marks: suppose this optimal one is labelled O_k. Then the learner should choose, as the underlying form for Φ, the input I_k.

The idea behind the principle is that, of two or more possible sources of a surface form, learners should postulate the one which incurs the minimal violation with respect to the other potential inputs, an idea Prince and Smolensky attribute to Stampe (1972; cf. also Hale 1973). Unbridled Lexicon Optimisation predicts that underlying forms are the same as surface forms in any language, as far as possible.

Comparing the two tableaux (21) and (22), it can be shown that postulating an underlying form with a long vowel, as in (22), results in an evaluation which is minimally disharmonic. In (22), the attested form violates only the markedness constraint *[V:]. In (21), the attested form violates both *[V:] and IDENT[mora]. Therefore, of the two potential inputs, that with the long vowel, in (22) induces the least significant violations, compared to (21). According to Lexicon Optimisation, the learner should postulate an underlying form with a long vowel.

Balancing Lexicon Optimisation is something Prince and Smolensky dub 'Minimal Redundancy': 'to the maximal extent possible, information should be excluded from the lexicon which is predictable from grammatical constraints' (Prince and Smolensky 1993; cf. Kiparsky 1982). This principle will lead learners to postulate a *short* vowel underlyingly, since the long vowel realisation is entirely predictable, based on the constraints constituting the grammar. I suggest that Minimal Redundancy outweighs Lexicon Optimisation in this case. Long vowels are only found in environments where their form is entirely determined by constraints which are needed anyway: FTBIN and MCAT ≈ PRWD. Therefore, I conclude that the underlying form has a short vowel. This results in a grammar which is more parsimonious.

In CVC words there are no long vowels at the surface. I interpret this to mean the coda is moraic. CVC words satisfy FTBIN on that assumption. Candidate (c) in (24) is optimal because it constitutes a bimoraic foot, unlike (b), and it does not violate *[V:], unlike (a). Since long vowels are unattested in CVC roots, I assume the input has a short vowel. In that case, candidate (a) also violates IDENT[μ].

(24)

/le$_\mu$l$_\mu$/ 'aquatic plant sp.'	MCAT ≈ PRWD	FTBIN	IDENT[μ]	*[V:]	*[V]
a. (le$_{\mu\mu}$l) ~ [lɛ:l]			*!	*	
b. (le$_\mu$l) ~ [lɛl]		*!	*		*
☞ c. (le$_\mu$l$_\mu$) ~ [lɛl]					*

I have assumed an *input* in (24) in which the coda is moraic. Importantly, candidate (c) is optimal regardless of whether the coda is underlyingly moraic or not—so this assumption does not affect the outcome. The reasoning here follows again from Lexicon Optimisation (Prince and Smolensky 1993, Ch 9). Given that codas *can* be moraic, there is no reason to restrict their presence in the input: OT is unable to achieve this because of the 'Richness of the Base' hypothesis (Prince and Smolensky 1993, Ch 6).[10]

3.1.4 Words with four or more syllables

This section describes the stress patterns in simple words of more than three syllables. I will refer to such words as 'polypedal', because they must be parsed by more than one foot. Each quadrisyllabic word with open syllables divides neatly into two disyllabic feet, each of which is left-headed: trochaic. These forms therefore provide the best evidence for trochaic rhythm in words.

There are fifteen quadrisyllabic roots with all-open syllables for which I have stress data. Initial primary stress is observed in 8 of the 15 forms; these are shown in (25).[11]

(25)	a.	/paɻamunu/	[báɻamʊ̀nu]	'sand goanna'
	b.	/paɻaŋari/	[báɻaŋàɾi]	'Mitchell's water goanna'
	c.	/paʈikuluʔ/	[báɖigʊ̀lṵ]	*Eucalyptus ferruginea*
	d.	/purukulu/	[bʊ́ɾugʊ̀lu]	'snake sp.'
	e.	/kaɳamuru/	[gáɳamʊ̀ɾu]	'"long-nose" native bee'
	f.	/kaɳawaraʔ/	[gáɳawàɾa̰]	'tree-dwelling goanna sp.'
	g.	/karatata/	[gáɾadàda]	'chest brace'
	h.	/ŋoɭomoro/	[ŋɔ́ɭomɔ̀ɾo]	'nail-tailed wallaby'

I have not heard these forms pronounced with alternative stress patterns.

Seven of the fifteen roots vary in pronunciation between initial and penultimate stress; these are shown in (26).

(26)	a.	/kurucaʈu/	[gʊ̀ɾuɟáɖu] ~ [gʊ́ɾuɟàɖu]	'olive python'
	b.	/camaɭara/	[ɟàmaɭáɾa] ~ [ɟámaɭàɾa]	'the Pleiades'
	c.	/ciriʈiti/	[ɟɪ̀ɾɨɖídi] ~ [ɟíɾɨɖɪ̀di]	'fly catcher'
	d.	/ŋalaʈara/	[ŋàlaɖáɾa] ~ [ŋálaɖàɾa]	'archer fish'
	e.	/ʈarapija/	[dàɾabíja] ~ [dáɾabɪ̀ja]	'black cockatoo'
	f.	/wariʈila/	[wàɾɨɖíla] ~ [wáɾɨɖɪ̀la]	'hooked boomerang'
	g.	/kuɳɲara/	[gʊ̀ɳɲáɾa] ~ [gʊ́ɳɲàɾa]	*Ficus racemosa*

10 What Prince and Smolensky call Richness of the Base is the assumption that there are no principled limits on the amount of structure that can be posited in the input. All possible inputs for any given output are subject to evaluation according to the Lexicon Optimisation proposal. Given the obvious complexities in this notion I will not go into it here.

11 Syllables which are open except for a glottal stop count as open syllables; see Chapter 5 for discussion.

I have given all the forms for which I have reasonably clear intuitions or recordings of stress variants here. The generalisation then is, any form which takes penultimate primary stress also has a variant with initial primary stress.

The tonal characteristics of each type differ. Forms with an initial primary stress have a single salient pitch movement:

H

báɻamùnu

(27) /paɻamunu/ 'sand goanna'

Forms with a penultimate primary stress always have a salient pitch movement on the initial syllable as well as the penultimate syllable:

H H

gùruɟáɖu

(28) /kurucaʈu/ 'olive python'

There are just a few simple words longer than four syllables, none of them entirely composed of open syllables. Example (a) in (29) presents the only pentasyllabic form with mostly open syllables, and (b) the only sextisyllabic form. Both forms have initial primary stress.

(29)	a. /woroŋomoloʔ/	[wɔ́rɔŋɔmɔ̀lo̰]	'grass sp.'
	b. /kaɻaŋkaŋaɳini/	[gáɻaŋgàŋaɳìni]	'large wallaby sp.'

Monomorphemic roots in Ngalakgan almost always have some stress on the first syllable, unless the second syllable is heavy. In disyllabic and trisyllabic forms, initial stress is also primary. In quadrisyllabic words, the initial stress may be primary or secondary, but in either case it is associated with a pitch movement.[12] In longer words, stress is initial also. A formal account of these patterns is given in 3.2.3. First, I turn to a description of word compounds. I will show that polypedal roots and compounds have a similar prosodic structure.

---

[12] The lack of a pitch accent on a secondary stress following any main stress appears to be a general characteristic of intonational phrasing; see Truckenbrodt (1999). It is probable that further investigation of the nature of intonational phrasing in Ngalakgan will reveal the alternant placement of primary stress within polypedal roots to be determined at the Intonational or Phonological Phrase level.

3.2 WORD-compounds

Section 3.1 has shown that monomorphemic words always have stress on their initial syllable. When monomorphemic words are compounded—in a 'WORD-level compound'—each WORD retains the stress accent on its initial syllable. Prosodic structure therefore reflects the morphological structure of WORD-compounds. A similar relationship between stress and the structure of compounds is found in many other languages, for example English (e.g. Selkirk 1984), and Malayalam (Mohanan 1986).

There is also a class of 'ROOT-compounds' which we will see in 3.3.3 have just one stress on their initial syllable, like simple words. There are no prosodic indicators of internal morphological structure in ROOT-compounds. This accords with their semantic characteristics: they are non-compositional for the most part.

WORD-compounds also have a distinctive superordinate prosodic structure, where metrically strong positions are associated to salient pitch movements, like the polypedal roots in the previous section. Based on the prosodic characteristics of WORD-compounds, in 3.2.3 I propose three distinct levels of metrical and prosodic constituency: Foot, Prosodic Word, and Phonological Phrase, each of which has its own structural and intonational characteristics.

3.2.1 Examples of WORD-compounds

Compounding is a productive process in Ngalakgan, applying to all major lexical categories: noun+adjective, noun+verb, adverb+verb. There are numerous examples in the data, of which the following is a sample. The examples in (30)-(35) are composed of two elements, each of which can also occur alone as an independent word.[13]

Disyllable+disyllable

(30)	a.	/kuɳʈu-kakkeŋ/	[gùɳɖugáḳkɛŋ]
		country-far	'long way'
	b.	/ɭaŋka-kaɲaʔ/	[làŋgagáɲa̰ʔ]
		billabong-small	'little billabong'
	c.	/kuɳʈu-jocconŋ/	[gùɳɖujɔ́ccɔŋ]
		country-not.sacred	'"clear" country'
	d.	/mala-poɳo/	[màlabɔ́ɳo]
		group-another	'different group'
	e.	/piɲi-ŋolkko/	[bìɲiŋɔ́lkko]
		water-big	'big water'

[13] There are some exceptions to this statement, which I return to below.

Disyllable+trisyllable

(31) a. /kuɳʈu-cappuru/ [gʊ̀ɳɖuɟáppuɾu]
country-sacred ‘sacred country’
b. /colkko-porama/ [ɟɔ̀lkkobɔ́ɾama]
ground-good ‘good ground’

Disyllable+monosyllable

(32) a. /kuɳʈu-maʔ/ [gʊ̀ɳɖumáa̼]
country-good ‘good country/place’
b. /colkko-ʈeɻʔ/ [ɟɔ̀lkkoɖɛ́ɻ̃]
ground-hard ‘hard ground’
c. /(ku-ku-)piɲi-wurk/[14] [bɪ̀ɲiwʊ́rk]
NP-NEUT-water-swallow ‘he swallows water’
d. /(ku-ku-)piɲi-ŋalʔ/ [bɪ̀ɲiŋál̼]
NP-NEUT-water-rise ‘the water is rising’
e. /(ku-ku-)mili-ŋalʔ/ [mɪ̀liŋál̼]
NP-NEUT-water-rise ‘the water is rising’
f. /(ku-)piɲi-cow/ [bɪ̀ɲiɟóʊ]
NP-water-flood ‘the water is flooding’
g. /weja-maʔ/ [wèˈjamáa̼]
shade-good ‘good shade’

Monosyllable+disyllable

(33) a. /polʔ-keŋkeŋ/ [bɔ̀l̼gɛ́ŋgɛŋ]
track-long ‘long footprint’
b. /polʔ-caɻuk/ [bɔ̀l̼ɟáɻʊk]
track-short ‘short footprint’
c. /ɻum-poɳo/ [ɻʊ̀mbɔ́ɳo]
law-different ‘(in a) different way/manner’
d. /weʔ-palkkiɲ/ [wɛ̀ɛ̼bálkkiɲ]
water-salty/dangerous ‘saltwater; beer’
e. /(ku-)po-wana/ [bòːwána]
NP-river-follow.FUT ‘will follow the river’

Monosyllable+monosyllable

(34) a. /weʔ-maʔ/ [wɛ̀ɛ̼máa̼]
water-good ‘freshwater’
b. /ceɲ-jarʔ/ [ɟèˈɲjár̼]
fish-lots ‘lots of fish’

---

[14] Prefixation with the NonPast prefix /ku-/ is obligatory for verbal predicates in the present tense with 3rd person non-plural subjects. As shown in Chapter 4, inflectional prefixes such as these are consistently without stress in Ngalakgan; they do not affect the prosodic structure of the rest of the word.

		Trisyllable+monosyllable	
(35)	a.	/caʈukal-jarʔ/	[ɟàɖugaljár̠]
		kangaroo-lots	'lots of kangaroos'
		Trisyllable+disyllable	
	b.	/miɻppara-kaɳaʔ/	[mɨ̀ɻpparagáɲa̠]
		child-small	'a small child'
	c.	/ŋaɲcuɭa-poʈewk/	[ŋàɲɟuɭaboɖɛ́ʊk]
		eye-bad	'bad eyes'
	d.	/Ø-miɻppara-ɳaniɲ/	[mɨ̀ɻpparaɳániɲ]
		3/3m-child-see.PC	's/he saw a child'

3.2.2 Compounding morphology

The constituents of WORD-compounds retain the morphological and semantic characteristics that they have in other environments. Each element in a WORD-compound is typically a freely-occurring word.

(36)

WORD

WORD WORD

WORD-compounding is a morphological operation on WORDs, a 'WORD-level' operation. The structure in (36) is equivalent to a rule of the following form (cf. Selkirk 1984: 76):

(37) WORD → WORD + WORD

That is, WORDs in Ngalakgan are recursive: they can in turn consist of WORDs.

Note that 'WORD' in this formulation refers to a morphological, not a phonological category. In particular, it is not meant to be equivalent to Prosodic Word. I provide reasons in 3.2.3, which follows, to think that in fact compounds are Phonological Phrases, not Prosodic Words. As in Selkirk (1984), the morphological categories WORD and ROOT define sets (or 'levels') over which phonological processes may be applied. The phonological processes applicable to each category may be partly language-specific.

I assume here in most respects the general grammatical architecture of Jackendoff (1997), where the elements of the lexicon as well as the permissable operations performed in the lexicon determine the shape of words and their compositional meanings. In this model, along with words, and idioms, productive morphemes are also listed in the lexicon. There is no 'morphological component' as such, but neither, in a sense, is morphology clearly separated from syntax, except in the sense that the rules producing these respective structures are for the most part disjunct (see Ackema and Neeleman 2004 for a similar view). It is the interface between the lexicon and the phonology which together produce the surface characteristics of words in Ngalakgan, as I show in the remainder of this chapter.

WORD-level operations are fully productive in the grammar of Ngalakgan. However, since the word 'productive' has been used in different ways by different authors (see Carstairs-McCarthy 1992), I define more carefully what I mean here. The morphological relationship between each element in a WORD-compound can be characterised as in (38):

WORD-level characteristics

(38) a. Freedom of appearance
b. Lack of morphophonemic selectional requirements
c. Compositional contribution to meaning

'Freedom of appearance' (a) encodes the fact that each element of a WORD-compound is a word which can appear in many other compounds. Secondly (b), there are no idiosyncratic morphophonemic requirements which obtain between the elements of WORD-compounds; the combination of words to form WORD-compounds is in principle unrestricted. Lastly (c), each element in a WORD-compound retains the meaning that it has as a word, and words in compounds are interpreted in a standard fashion, with the right-most stem of a major lexical category (N, V, or ADJ) constituting the head (the basis for inflection).

Productive operations such as compounding in Ngalakgan can be captured by general rules which mention only information of categorial type ('N', 'V') and broad classes of morphology ('WORD', 'AFFIX') and nothing more. In particular, they should not need to mention the identity of specific morphemes, nor to specify the phonological form or interpretation of outputs. The rule in (37) is a rule of this type. However, it is not sufficient for deriving the semantic and syntactic behaviour of its output. I address this issue more fully in 3.5.

The characteristics listed in (38) are also true of other WORD-level processes in Ngalakgan—reduplication and affixation. Reduplication is examined in 3.4, while affixation is the topic of Chapter 4.

3.2.3 Prosodic characteristics of WORD-compounds

The prosodic structure of WORD-compounds provides evidence about the nature of prosodic constituents in Ngalakgan. I show that there are distinct

Prosodic Word (PRWD) and Phonological Phrase (PPH) constituents; PRWDS are left-headed and PPHs right-headed.

WORD-compounds have a distinctive prosodic structure. Each of the words of the compound is stressed as a word. In the compound as a whole, the first element takes secondary stress, while the second takes primary stress, as shown in (39).

(39) /kuɳʈu-cappuru/ [gʊ̀ɳɖuɟáppuɾu]
country-sacred 'sacred country'

Unlike the polypedal roots discussed in 3.1.4, in WORD-compounds the second stress accent is always the primary one; these words do not show variation in the relationship between secondary and primary stress.

We can see from the examples in (40) the stress that each of these words has in isolation. Comparing (39) and (40), we can see that whatever metrical pattern a word has in isolation is retained in the metrical structure of a compound in which it appears.

(40) a. /kuɳʈu/ [gʊ́ɳɖu] 'country'
b. /cappuru/ [ɟáppuɾu] 'sacred'

Each stem in a compound is therefore a distinct metrical domain. This is because each stem is subject to MCAT ≈ PRWD and ALIGNL(PRWD, Foot). Therefore, each stem must minimally constitute a bimoraic foot, and each stem is associated with an initial stress.

Here we must consider the status of lexical stems which are not free. In McCarthy and Prince (1993b: 139), 'MCAT' includes 'root, stem, lexical word'. The morphological categories which are required to be realised as Prosodic Words in Ngalakgan are productive stems, but are not all free forms (which is what I understand 'lexical words' to refer to). For instance, in examples (c-f) from (32), the two morphemes meaning 'water', /piɲi-/ and /mili-/, are both bound, WORD-level stems. They are not 'words' because they cannot occur alone, but must be compounded with some other (WORD-level) element. In all other respects, they have the characteristics of WORD-level morphology: freedom of appearance, lack of morphophonemic restrictions, and compositional contribution to meaning. While the vast majority of WORD-level stems are free forms, there is a large set of forms which are (mostly) bound, with a diverse set of functions which I label 'bound stems'. The characteristics of bound stems are explored in Chapter 4.

In Ngalakgan, the morphological class which is subject to MCAT ≈ PRWD I will call 'Morphological Words' (MWDS). A 'Morphological Word' is a WORD-level stem from the major lexical categories (Noun, Verb,

Adjective). WORD-level stems, whether bound or free, are listed in the lexicon with their own subcategorisation frames and consistent interpretations. Stems of these categories can head complex words, as shown in 3.5.

The difference between bound and free stems reduces to a specification in their phonological subcategorisation frames: bound stems require a WORD to follow (or precede) them, as do affixes, while free stems do not. Hence, the entry for the bound stem /mili-/ 'water', will look like this (following Jackendoff 1997, Ch 5):

(41) a. b.

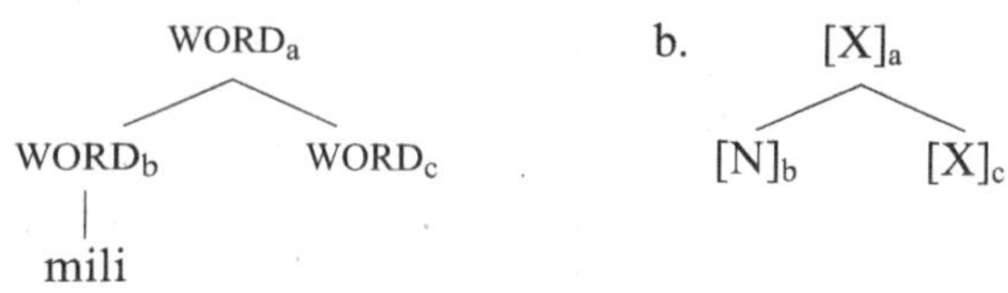

c. [[$_{\text{Entity}}$ *water*]$_b$]$_a$

In Jackendoff's model, lexical entries are triplets of phonological, syntactic and semantic representations, linked to each other by coindexation (the subscripts in (41)). The first representation in (41), (a), what Jackendoff calls the 'morphophonological' representation (Jackendoff 1997: 110), states that there exists a lexical entry for Ngalakgan speakers for an element with a pronunciation represented by /mili/, that this element is a phonological WORD, and that it must occur preceding another element which must also be a phonological WORD. The (morpho)syntactic representation in (b) says that /mili/ is of syntactic category 'N', and that the complex word containing /mili/ can be of any syntactic category. Other principles of the grammar, such as the Head-Right Principle (see (87), 3.5), will ensure that this is a lexical category: N, V or ADJ. Finally, the morphosemantic representation in (c) says that in the complex word containing it, /mili/ contributes an argument of the ontological type 'Entity', with whatever lexical semantic meaning can be attributed to 'water' in the lexicon, to the compositional interpretation of the word.[15] This representation is true of other bound WORD-level stems of 'N' category in Ngalakgan: these are all stems which must be followed by another WORD-level stem.[16]

Given lexical entries of this form, we can define an MWD in the following way:

---

[15] I have not addressed the semantics of lexemes themselves here; see e.g. Goddard and Wierzbicka (2002) for concrete proposals.

[16] Bound verb stems behave differently, taking obligatory constituents to the left. Given this, we expect to find forms which consist of two bound forms, a right-binding stem attached to a left-binding stem. Such compounds exist in Ngalakgan, e.g. /ŋun-paṯṯa-me/ 1mO-APPL-get.PP 'it got away from me'; see 4.5.4 for discussion.

(42) MWD: A lexical entry whose morphophonological form is dominated by the category 'WORD', and whose morphosyntactic form is assigned to a lexical category (V, N, ADJ).

This definition rules out all affixes and a-categorial bound stems, as well as bound stems from minor categories such as PRO and ADV. I return to this issue in 3.5, and show that this definition of MWD can derive the prosodic differences between the various morphological categories of Ngalakgan.

The MCAT ≈ PCAT constraint relevant then to Ngalakgan is given in (43):

(43) MWD ≈ PRWD: 'Every Morphological Word corresponds to a Prosodic Word'

This constraint will ensure that in compounds, WORDS consisting in turn of more than one WORD, each WORD will have the prosodic characteristics associated with WORDS independently.

In a compound, each stress is associated with a distinctive, salient pitch movement, as shown in (44).[17]

bìɲiɟóʊ
(44) /piɲi-cow/
water-flood 'water is flooding'

I call these salient pitch movements 'pitch accents' (following Pierrehumbert 1980). The distribution of metrical heads and pitch accents is not necessarily the same. In the word in (45) below, there are three metrical feet but only two MWDs, and there are correspondingly only two pitch accents. Only those metrical prominences which are associated with pitch accents are marked with accent diacritics (secondary ` and primary ´) in examples.

	(.	x)	3	PPH
	(x .)	(x .)	2	PRWD
	(x .) (x .)	(x .)	1	Foot
(45)	kàrakkara	cáŋan		
	together	stand.PR		

[17] The NP prefix /ku-/ is obligatory in Present tense, the representation in (41) abstracts away from such extraneous elements.

The distinction between metrical structure, pitch accents, and secondary vs primary accent in a word suggests three levels of prosodic structure. The first level ('Foot') corresponds to 'rhythmic prominence': the prominence given to syllables because of their organisation into rhythmic (metrical) feet, following Liberman and Prince (1977). At the second level ('Prosodic Word'), prominent syllables have tonal characteristics. At the third level ('Phonological Phrase'), the only prominent syllable is the one which is associated with primary stress, corresponding to the tonic accent.[18]

The three prosodic constituents—Foot, PRWD, and PPH—are subject to distinct constraints. The Foot is subject to constraints FTBIN and FTFORM as discussed previously. The PRWD and PPH constituents are subject to distinct *Alignment* constraints.

While the Phonological Phrase is characterised by right-headedness, Prosodic Words are left-headed: they are both regulated by Alignment constraints referring to prosodic 'peaks'—which are local metrical maxima (McCarthy and Prince 1986: 9):

(46) ALIGNL(PK, PRWD): 'Align the peak left in a PRWD'

(47) ALIGNR(PK, PPH): 'Align the peak right in a PPH'

These two constraints define two prosodic domains within which peaks are computed. The PPH is defined over the whole word, is right-headed, and determines the position of primary stress. Being the superordinate constituent, the PPH may be recursively embedded (I follow Ladd 1996 here).

The other domain, the PRWD, is smaller than or equal to the PPH. It is left-headed, and determines secondary *as well as* primary stresses. PRWDs may not be recursively embedded—as we would expect, being the domain of contrastive tonal effects—though there may be more than one PRWD per PPH. PRWDs must form adjacent, non-embedded domains.

I assume that only the heads of feet can be associated with pitch accents. I encode this as a constraint 'Peak-to-Head' (cf. the 'Continuous Column Constraint' of Prince 1983).

(48) PK-TO-HEAD: 'Peaks (at level $n+1$) are associated to metrical heads (at level n)'

[18] Acoustic study of Ngalakgan is at a preliminary stage, and I present this as my impressionistic view, based on 10 years familiarity with the language. Similar structures for complex words are proposed by Bishop (2002) and Pentland (2004), acoustic studies of the closely related Bininj Gun-wok and the distantly related Warlpiri, respectively.

We have seen that the location of feet, and thereby heads, is determined by morphological structure. Hence, given MWD ≈ PRWD, and ALIGNL (PRWD, FT), we derive MWDs with the form shown in (49). The leftmost metrical head of each MWD is projected as the peak at the PRWD level, by ALIGNL(PK, PRWD).

```
          (x      .    )          (x      .   )      PRWD
          (x   .) (x   .)         (x    .) (x   .)   Foot
(49)  [MWD(μ   μ)(μ   μ)...]-[MWD(μ   μ) (μ  μ)...]
```

By ALIGNR(PK, PPH), the rightmost of these strong positions will realise primary stress, and the other position will realise secondary stress:

```
          (.                        x            )   PPH
          (x      .    )          (x      .   )      PRWD
          (x   .) (x   .)         (x    .) (x   .)   Foot
(50)  [MWD(μ   μ)(μ   μ)...]-[MWD(μ   μ) (μ  μ)...]
```

With PK-TO-HEAD undominated, I assume that ALIGNL(PK, PRWD) and ALIGNR(PK, PPH) are only violated when a peak is projected from any foot which is non-initial in MWD. For instance, if the second head at the foot level of (50) were to realise the local PRWD peak this would violate ALIGNL. Any other realisation of the peak would violate PK-TO-HEAD.

The effects of the various constraints can be seen in consideration of a simple example such as that in (51).

None of the constraints shown here are in conflict. The word has two metrically strong positions, each associated with the initial syllable of an MWD, by MWD ≈ PRWD and ALIGNL(PRWD, FT). The rightmost of these must be projected to primary stress, by ALIGNR(PK, PPH). Candidate (a) violates this constraint thereby. I assume candidate (d) violates MWD ≈ PRWD because it is not true that every MWD—there are two—corresponds to its own PRWD domain (there is just one of these). While this is a representational difference, it allows the distribution of PRWDs and PPHs to be described uniformly.

I assume certain possibilities are ruled out by universals of metrical organisation, governed by an undominated constraint I have simply called 'WORDFORM'. A form such as (51)c, where each prosodic word receives a primary stress is ruled out by what Liberman and Prince (1977: 262) call 'Culminativity', the fact that 'each word or phrase normally has a single strongest syllable bearing the main stress' (Hayes 1995: 24).

(51)

/kuɳʈu-cappuru/ country-sacred	WD FORM	MWD ≈ PRWD	ALIGNL (PRWD, FT)	ALIGNR (PK, PPH)
a. [(kúɳʈu)]-[(càppu)ru]				*!
☞ b. [(kùɳʈu)]-[(cáppu)ru]				
c. [(kúɳʈu)]-[(cáppu)ru]	*!			
d. [(kùɳʈu)-(cáppu)ru]		*!		
e. [(kúɳʈu)]-[ca(ppúru)]			*!	

The characteristics of compounds then are the characteristics of words, and in particular polypedal words with penultimate stress. Stress is hierarchically organised and culminative: resulting in a single peak. In a morphologically-complex form, each stressed syllable corresponds to the initial syllable of a WORD. In this way, the location of pitch accents provides the learner with a good indication of the structure of complex words. Stress therefore has what Trubetzkoy (1969[1939]) called a 'demarcative' function in Ngalakgan.

The more complex example of (45) above is analysed in (52). A form, as in (52)c, where each foot in a PRWD realises a distinctive pitch accent violates ALIGNL(PK, PRWD), since at least one peak is not leftmost. But it is probably to be ruled out by Culminativity as before in any case, since within each domain, stresses should be hierarchically organised.

(52)

/karakkara-caŋa+n/ together-stand+PR	ALIGNL (PRWD, FT)	ALIGNL (PK, PRWD)	ALIGNR (PK, PPH)
a.[(kára)(kkara)]-[(càŋan)]			*!
☞ b. [(kàra)(kkara)]-[(cáŋan)]			
c. [(kàra)(kkàra)]-[(cáŋan)]		*!	

Rarely, complex words may consist of more than two MWDs. In these cases, a preference for no more than two pitch accents overrides MWD ≈ PRWD, at least in some cases. Compounds with more than two stems are rare, and so the maximum number of pitch accents in a word is normally two. The only attested examples from my data with more than two pitch accents are given in (53):[19]

[19] I do not fully understand the derivation of this word. The translation given for (53) here is the one my informant offered. Similar constructions are found in other Roper languages.

(53) a. [gugàmalagàɾakkaɾaɟáŋan]
/ku-kamala-karakkara-caŋ+an/
NP-cloud/sky-together-stand+PR
'daylight breaks out' [28/6/96: 2B]

b. [ɟuɳàmulugɛ̀rŋeɳána]
/cu-ɳamulu-kerŋe-ɳa+na/
2mS-really-body-see+FUT
yu labta faindim prabli
'You'll have to find that animal properly.' [2/9/97: 1B]

c. [ŋubugɛ̀rŋebʊ̀ɽnanɪkkɔ́ɾo]
/ŋu-pu-kerŋe-purʔ+ɳa+ni+kkoro/
1mS-3a-body-know+SEE+IRR+PRNEG
'I don't know them' [3/9/97]

Ideally in complex words, there is just one leftmost MWD and one rightmost MWD. Such forms maximally satisfy MWD ≈ PRWD and the Alignment constraints on peaks in PRWDs and PPHs. A series of three PRWDs, as in /kàmala-kàrakkara-cáŋ+an/, disrupts this symmetry. Such forms are avoided: most complex words in Ngalakgan contain no more than two pitch accents.

Forms such as (53) are reminiscent of phrases with repeated prenuclear accents discussed by Ladd (1986: 321). As Ladd notes, repetition of what appears to be the same pitch accent within a single domain (here, Phonological Phrase) is not something we expect from the Pierrehumbert (1980) model of intonational phonology. But it is what we expect if a complex word (a PPH) in Ngalakgan can consist of more than one PRWD, and if each of these PRWDs can potentially project their own pitch accent.

The behaviour of MWDs—as independent metrical domains—is a symptom of an endemic characteristic of Ngalakgan and many other Australian languages: that productive morphemes are subject to metrical independence. This notion is explored further in Chapter 4, where I discuss the idea that all elements of the lexicon, not just 'words', are required to correspond to PRWDs in Ngalakgan and other Australian languages.

3.2.4 Summary

This section has shown that WORD-level stems—MWDs—retain their prosodic characteristics when compounded. These complex words in turn have distinctive, and consistent, prosodic characteristics. While PRWDs form left-headed and concatenative tone domains, PPHs are right-headed and culminative metrical domains. In Pierrehumbert's (1980) model, we can say that

PPHs contain a single nuclear accent but may have zero or more prenuclear accents of the same type.

In the next sections I examine the phonological, semantic and prosodic characteristics of ROOT-level morphology, which are quite different from that of the WORD-level.

3.3 ROOT-morphology and prosody

In the following sections I show that the prosodic and semantic characteristics of words in Ngalakgan can be captured by the generalisation in (54).

(54) Stems which are ROOT-complex are prosodically equivalent to simple WORDs.

ROOT-level morphology is invisible to prosodic constraints.

In what follows I firstly discuss the distributional and semantic characteristics of ROOT-morphology in the lexicon. I then show that for all ROOT-morphological processes—affixation, compounding, and reduplication—the statement in (54) is true. I do this by describing the prosodic characteristics of ROOT-complex words, and comparing these to the prosody of words which are complex at the WORD-level.

3.3.1 ROOT-level morphology

Consider the set of forms in (55). Corresponding to the surface word in (a), there is no freestanding word such as [buː] 'hit'.

(55) a. [bʊniɲ] '(he/she/it) was hitting (s.t/s.o)'
/pu+niɲ/
hit+PC
b. *[buː]
/pu/

The morphemes in (a), which can be identified on the basis of recurrent patterns in verb morphology, are in a ROOT-level relationship, represented by a '+' boundary symbol. Those in a WORD-level relationship are separated by a '-' boundary symbol.

ROOT-affixation, ROOT-compounding, and ROOT-reduplication all create ROOT-level stems out of elements that cannot be words by themselves. Some of these stems are subject to further derivation, in order to create WORDs. Others can surface as WORDs without further derivation. The process of ROOT-affixation is represented schematically in (56) (and compare the preceding diagram in (36)):

(56)

Root compounding is represented in (57):

(57)

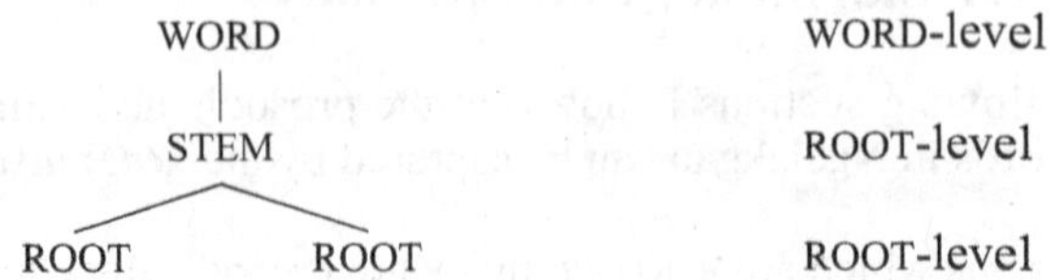

The most important set of forms in the class of bound roots are the 32 inflecting verb roots—such as /pu+/ 'hit' and /ma+/ 'get'. This class is called the *finite* verb class. All other verbal predicates in the language inflect by means of a construction which is morphologically a compound, using one of these roots as an inflected 'auxiliary'.

The affixes to finite verb roots are paradigmatically highly irregular, idiosyncratic and unproductive. It is not the case that all of a verb's inflectional forms can be predicted given any of the others. Consider the following representative sample for instance:

	'hit'	'get'	'stand (itv)'	'crawl'	'chop'
	√pu+	√ma+	√ca(ŋ)+	√karpe+	√co+
PP	poʔpo	meʔme	ca+ɲ	karrpe+ɲ	ce
PR	pu+n	(maʔ)ma	caŋa+n	karrpe	co
PC	pun+iɲ	maŋ+iɲ	caŋan+iɲ	karrpen+iɲ	coŋ+iɲ
FUT	pun+a	maŋ+a	caŋan+a	karrpen+a	coŋ+a
IRR	pun+i	maŋ+i	caŋan+i	karrpen+i	coŋ+i
RR	pu+jci- ~ pu+jcci+	maŋi+cci+			coŋi+cci+

Table 1: Some finite verb inflectional paradigms

Some inflections have a predictable realisation in *most* verbs. For almost all finite verbs, the Future and Irrealis inflections are equal to the Past Continuous, with /+a/ and /+i/ substituted for /+iɲ/.[20] We can therefore identify

20 There are four exceptional verbs which do not display this regular relationship. The verb /caʈe/ 'twirl firedrill', for example, has PC /caʈi+ɲ/ but FUT, IRR in /caʈiŋ+a/, /caʈiŋ+i/

a Non-Past (NP) stem, equivalent to the inflected form minus these three inflections. For the verb /ma+/ 'to get', for instance, the NP stem is /maŋ+/. In some cases, the NP stem can surface as a word, typically with a Present/Evitative interpretation (in the case of /pun/, the NP of the 'hit' verb, for instance). In other cases, it cannot (as with /maŋ/) (see Baker 2004; and Baker and Harvey 2003, for a discussion of the historical importance of the NP stem in various Australian languages).

The relationship between these three inflections (PC, FUT, IRR) and the older ones—Present and Past Punctual—is much less regular. A number of verbs show an ablaut relation between the PR and PP, as in /co/ 'chop' PR, vs. /ce/ PP. Other verbs have an overt PP suffix, e.g. /ca+ɲ/ 'stood' (PP), cf. /caŋ+an/ 'be standing' (PR). Some verbs have both an overt suffix and ablaut changes in the stem: /ŋow+iɲ/ 'ate' (PP), cf. /ŋu+n/ 'eat' (PR).

It *is* possible to group the conjugations into inflection classes of paradigms showing some broad correspondences (as does Merlan 1983). But the inflectional forms of finite verb roots, with the possible exception of the Future, Irrealis, and Reflexive-Reciprocal forms, are irregular enough to warrant that each verb paradigm be separately listed in the lexicon in full. Since there are just 32 finite verbs, and 6 distinct inflectional forms for most verbs (around 192 forms), this is not such a great hardship for the learner. Hence, lexical entries for finite verbs will have the following form (again following Jackendoff 1990, 1997: Ch 5):[21]

(58) WORD$_a$ [V]$_a$ [$_{Situation}$ PASTCONT [$_{Event}$]]$_a$

/maŋiɲ/ [V] T

PC

The difference between ROOT-complex forms such as (58) and WORD-complex forms such as (41) in the lexicon is that in forms such as (41) there are *n* elements of the lexicon which are combined by reference to a rule

respectively. Similar irregularities are found in the cognate conjugation in Rembarrnga. The form of the Future and Irrealis inflections in Ngalakgan and Rembarrnga are of comparatively recent origin. They serve to distinguish these two languages from their nearest genetic relatives —Bininj Gun-wok (Kunwinjku, Mayali), Dalabon and Jawoyn—which do not have a regular correspondence like this between PC, FUT and IRR (or their equivalents); see (Baker 2004).

[21] In Jackendoff's entries for morphologically complex forms, and for affixes, feature percolation is expressed in the top-most node of the entry, so the morphosyntactic form of the word in (58) would have a top-most node containing both 'V' and also the information [+PC]. However, he notes (1997: 131, fn. 1) that it may not be necessary to encode feature percolation in lexical representations, if this is accomplished by some general property of the grammar (as in Lieber 1992 or HPSG models). I have taken the latter option here.

external to (41), which also applies to many other elements of the lexicon. By contrast, in (58), there is no rule referred to here and no independent lexical elements to which it refers.

The inflected forms of finite verb roots are thus amenable to the 'full-listing' approach (Jackendoff 1975, 1997; cf. Aronoff 1976), since the rules and subcategorisations required to generate inflected forms from separately listed roots and affixes would not appreciably increase the parsimony of the grammar. More importantly however, by making ROOT-level roots and affixes separate entries, we would be claiming that they have the same kind of psychological status as WORD-level roots and affixes. On many grounds, clearly they do not, as the following sections will demonstrate.

The selectional requirements operating between ROOT-level forms are much more specific than those between WORD-level forms, and this is what allows us to derive the difference between them formally. Bound roots such as /pu+/ 'hit' are not free to take any affix that attaches to a verb. And conversely, the inflectional affixes attached to finite roots are subject to their own paradigmatic restrictions. If we were to list the inflectional affixes of finite verbs separately in the lexicon, they would require diacritics to match them to specific morphological classes of finite verbs, as in (59).

(59)

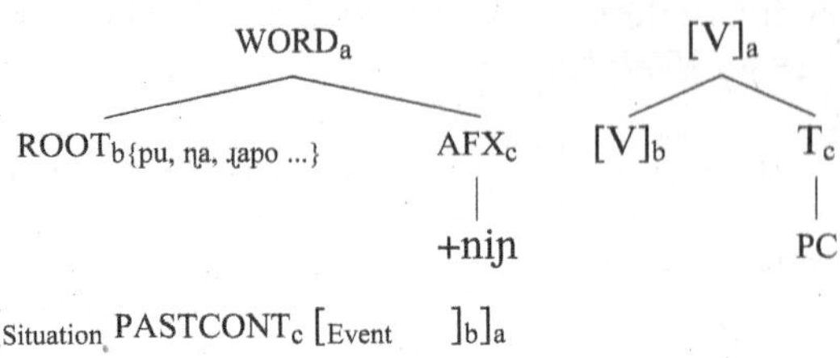

In (59), I have expressed this restriction as a diacritic feature in the morphophonology, listing the set of roots which take this affix. Other approaches (e.g. Aronoff 1994) would propose a diacritic listing a morphological class, with the membership of the class to be listed somewhere else in the lexicon.

Note that the paradigmatic restriction expressed in (59) is not the same as a subcategorisation frame, such as might be expressed for the WORD-level affix /-kkaʔ/ 'Locative', shown in (60). Unlike the inflectional affixes to finite verbs, WORD-level affixes such as case suffixes do not require a restriction to a particular set of morphological forms. The subcategorisation frame in their lexical entries merely expresses the requirement that they attach to a word which is syntactically a nominal expression:[22]

---

[22] Actually, this formalism both under- and over-generates, since nominals have a 'templatic' structure wherein case suffixes attach outside both optional Dative pronouns and number suffixes e.g. /ɳu-kakka=ŋki-ppulu-**kkaʔ**/ MASC-brother=2mDAT-PL-LOC 'to your brothers'.

(60) 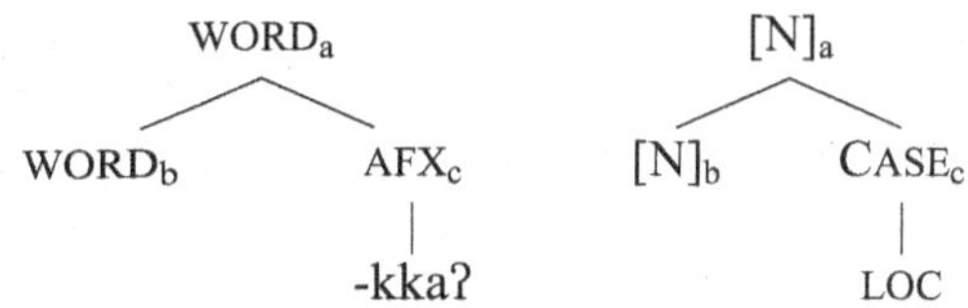

$[_{Entity}$ LOC$_c$ $[_{Entity}$ $]_b]_a$

This difference in the selectional requirements between WORD-level and ROOT-level affixation is one reason to think that they belong to two distinct components of the grammar, as argued by Jackendoff (1997), Aronoff (1976), and others (e.g. Pinker and Prince 1991; Clahsen 1999). Before discussing what such a grammar might look like (in 3.5), I first discuss the other major kind of ROOT-level relation: compounding. ROOT-level compounds show characteristically non-compositional interpretations, as discussed in the following section.

3.3.2 ROOT-compounds

There are around 150 verbs attested in Ngalakgan which are formally ROOT-level compounds. ROOT-compounds have idiosyncratic meanings, and often consist of at least one root which is not found elsewhere in the morphology. Some examples are given in (61)-(62).

(61)	a. /koʔ+**ɳa+niɲ**/	[gɔ́ɳaniɲ]	'had' (PC)
	b. /**ɳa+niɲ**/	[náɲiɲ]	'saw' (PC)
	c. */koʔ/		
(62)	a. /wi+**ɳa+n**/	[wíɳan]	'forgets' (PR)
	b. /**ɳa+n**/	[nan]	'sees' (PR)
	c. */wi/		

I will refer to the initial element in a verb compound (whether ROOT- or WORD-level) as the *coverb*, in contrast to the *finite* verb, which is the final element. It is the finite verb which hosts the inflection of the verb compound. Coverbs constitute a distinct word class in many Australian languages (Wilson 1999; Schultze-Berndt 2000), as well as some languages of East Africa (e.g. Amharic: Amberber 2002); (see Amberber, Baker, and Harvey 2007 for general discussion).

The entry in (60) would rule out such structures, unless we allow for recursive WORDs formed by affixation. However, such structures conflict with the pattern of affix stress described in Chapter 4. There are some suggestions about how to resolve this problem in 3.5.

In the ROOT-compound /koʔ+ɳa+/ 'to have', we recognise the root /ɳa+/ 'to see'. The ROOT-compound /koʔ+ɳa+/ inflects exactly like the finite verb /ɳa+/. This is the case with all ROOT-compounds—the inflection of the whole is that of the final finite verb root. However, the meaning of the ROOT-compound does not include, or is not derived from, the meaning of the second member /ɳa+/ 'to see' in any obvious way. For this reason, in glossing root compounds, the meaning of the finite verb is in small caps style: /wi+ɳa+n/ 'forget+SEE+PR'.

The same remarks apply to (62) and other root compounds, although occasionally the compound does bear some (unpredictable) relationship with the meaning of the verb root (Merlan 1983: 111); some examples are presented in (63). These compounds with the root /ɳa+/ 'to see' all have denotations in the domain of sensory perception and (by extension) epistemology.

(63) a. /pop+ɳa+/ 'to smell'
b. /ʈic+ɳa+/ 'to look hard at'
c. /purʔ+ɳa/ 'to know'

The first element of such compounds typically has no status whatsoever outside the compound. There is no element /koʔ/ (or /wi/ or /purʔ/ or /ʈic/) which occurs otherwise in the lexicon of Ngalakgan with any component of the meaning of the ROOT-compounds in (63). There are occasional exceptions however. The element /pop/ for instance can also be a verb stem in its own right: /pop-mi+/ 'to be smelly'.[23]

ROOT-compounds therefore contrast with WORD-compounds, as in (64), in which each element occurs in many other complex environments with the same interpretation:

(64) a. /**ŋej**/ 'name (N)'
b. /ŋur-pu-**ŋej-wu+na**/ 'we will give them names'
12aS-3a-name-give+FUT
c. /ŋun-**ŋej-wi+ɳa+n**/ 'he's forgotten my name'
1mO-name-forget+SEE+PR
d. /pur-kunʈu-**ŋej+pu+n**/ 'they name the country'
3aS-country-name+HIT+PR

The free root /ŋej/ 'name' can occur alone as a noun, as in (a). It can be incorporated, to form a compound verb as in (b) and (c), where its contribution to the meaning of the word remains constant. Example (d) shows that it also occurs in ROOT-compounds, itself compounded at the WORD level with

23 The finite root /-mi+/ (no meaning) is the verbaliser for the open ('thematic') verb conjugation discussed in Chapter 2.

a noun /kuɳʈu/ 'country'. In this case, the meaning of the ROOT compound is not recoverable from the meaning of the parts. The meaning of /ŋej+pu+/ does not derive in any obvious way from the meaning of 'hit'; rather, it has a fixed, idiosyncratic interpretation like other ROOT-compounds.[24]

The morphophonological structure of ROOT-compounds is schematised in (65), for the compound verb /wi+ɳa+n/ 'forget (PR)':

(65)

WORD — WORD-level

ROOT wi+ — STEM — ROOT-level

ROOT ɳa+ — AFFIX n — ROOT-level

ROOT-compounding creates WORDs. The WORD constituent in (65) is predicted to behave like other, morphologically-simple WORD-level stems. That this is the case is shown in the following section.

3.3.3 Prosodic characteristics of ROOT-morphology

Words consisting of bound root+affix have the prosodic characteristics of simple words: disyllabic, trisyllabic and quadrisyllabic forms have initial stress (in quadrisyllabics initial stress is secondary, primary stress is penultimate). This is shown in the examples in (66)-(68), and compare the simplex words in 3.1.

Disyllables

(66) a. /pu+ni/ — [bʊ́ni]
hit+IRR — 'he/she wants to hit it'

b. /ka+ŋiɲ/ — [gáŋiɲ]
take+PP — 'he/she took it'

c. /co+ŋiɲ/ — [ɟɔ́ŋiɲ]
chop+PC — 'he/she was chopping it'

---

24 Around half of the compounds with /pu+/ 'hit' have a first element which occurs elsewhere as a word. Typically the /pu+/ element 'verbalises' the meaning of the noun, as here. In the related GN languages Warray and Jawoyn, /pu+/ is a productive 'Factitive' auxiliary, with a meaning 'cause X to come into being', where X is a noun. It can for instance take loanwords from English in Warray (Harvey 1986 and p.c.): /ʈejp-pu+/ 'make a [cassette] tape [recording]'. Many /pu+/ compounds in Ngalakgan also have this kind of interpretation: /cuŋ+pu+/ 'build a bough shade' (/cuŋ/ 'bough shade'), /cele+pu+/ 'urinate' (/cele/ 'urine'). But this process seems no longer to be productive in Ngalakgan. The analogous loanword example to Warray occurs in Ngalakgan as /ʈejp-maɳiɲʔ-mi+/ 'make a tape', where /maɳiɲʔ/ 'make, build' is a WORD-level verb stem of the open conjugation.

	d.	/karpe+ɲ/ crawl+PP	[gárbeɲ] 'he/she crawled'
		Trisyllables	
(67)	a.	/ɻapo+niɲ/ go+PC	[ɻáboniɲ] 'he/she was going'
	b.	/curuwe+ɲ/ rush+PP	[ɟʊ́ruweɲ] 'he/she was rushing'
	c.	/jini+ŋi/ 'say/do (thus)+IRR'	[jíniŋi] 'he/she should say/do it like that'
	d.	/maɲi+cci+ɲ/ get+RR+PP	[máɲicciɲ] 'he/she got him/herself'
		Quadrisyllables	
(68)	a.	/curuwen+iɲ/ rush+PC	[ɟʊ̀ruwɛ́niɲ] 'he/she was rushing'
	b.	/maɲi+cci+ni/ get+RR+PC	[màɲiccíni] 'he/she got him/herself'

Affixed forms which are ROOT-complex contrast prosodically with words affixed at the WORD-level, as the contrast between (69) and (70) shows. Nouns take only WORD-level affixes. ROOT-level affixes are restricted to the class of inflecting verb roots.[25]

		Verb		*Noun*
(69)	a.	[ɟáŋana] /ca+ŋana/ stand+FUT 'will stand'	b.	[gè:ŋíni] /ke=ŋini/ son=1mDAT 'my son'
(70)	a.	[bʊ́ni] /pu+ni/ hit+IRR 'might hit'	b.	[bɔ́:wi] /po-wi/ river-LAT 'along the river'

[25] This might lead one to suppose that the distinction I draw here between WORD-level and ROOT-level relations is in fact more properly a distinction between nominal and verbal inflection. This would be an erroneous assumption to make. While it is clear that, in historical terms, ROOT-level inflection is more widely attested in the verbal lexicon, it is not restricted to it. For one thing, inflected verbs can also take WORD-level affixes (such as number and complementiser suffixes, pronominal argument prefixes and bound stems). For another, in other Australian languages, ROOT-level affixation is found also in the nominal word class. An example from the Gunwinyguan language Warray is discussed in Baker and Harvey (2003).

Examples (69)a and (70)a are complex at the ROOT-level but not the WORD-level, so they are realised with a single, initial stress, and the initial syllable is short. Words like this contrast with forms such as (69)b and (70)b which are complex at the WORD-level. Both contain a MWD which is monosyllabic and open, followed in (69)b by a WORD-level bound stem, and in (70)b by a WORD-level suffix. The MWD must constitute a PRWD, and so it must be realised with a long vowel. (The prosody of affixes and bound stems is discussed in detail in Chapter 4.) The difference between the two kinds of words is shown in (71).

(71)

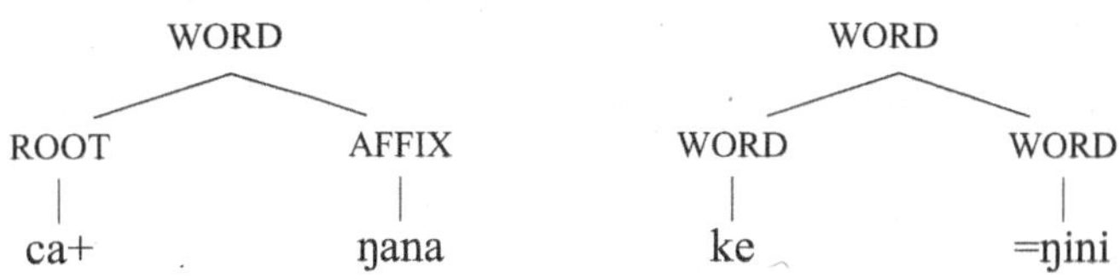

The vowels of the monosyllabic open roots /ca+/ and /pu+/ of the (a) examples are not long at the surface, and the following affix is not stressed. The word as a whole takes a single stress. The roots of ROOT-affixed words, then, are not MWDS, and are not themselves required to constitute PRWDS.

The same pattern is observed in ROOT-compounds. Disyllabic and trisyllabic compounds have a single stress on the initial syllable of the compound. Examples (72) and (73) illustrate the ROOT-compound stress pattern.

		Disyllables	
(72)	a.	/koʔ+ɳa+n/	[gɔ̰́ɳan]
		have+SEE+PR	'has'
	b.	/woc+ma/	[wɔ́cma]
		steal+GET.PR	'steals'
	c.	/ɭak+po/	[lákbo]
		split+HIT.PP	'split'

		Trisyllables	
(73)	a.	/koʔ+ɳan+iɲ/	[gɔ̰́ɳaniɲ]
		have+SEE+PC	'had'
	b.	/ɭak+pu+na/	[lákbuna]
		split+HIT+FUT	'will split'
	c.	/piɲce+ppo/	[bíɲɟɛppo]
		quarter+HIT.PP	'quartered [a carcass]'
	d.	/jiniʔ+ka+n/	[jínḭkan]
		say+TAKE+PR	'tells someone to'
	e.	/kaŋaʔ+wo/	[gáŋa̰wo]
		ask+GIVE.PP	'asked'

In the examples in (74) which follow, the contrast between the prosody of WORD and ROOT-level compounds is made clear. Disyllabic compounds which are complex at the ROOT-level, such as (72)a (repeated here as (74)a), contrast with the double-headed prosody of forms which are complex at the WORD-level, as in (74)b. ROOT-compounds therefore contrast with WORD-compounds, which take a stress on each WORD-level constituent.

(74)	a.	[gɔ̰́ɳan] /koʔ+ɳa+n/ have+SEE+PR	b.	[wɛ̰̀gmá̰a̰] /weʔ-maʔ/ water-good

Similarly, trisyllabic ROOT-compounds (75)a, (76)a contrast with trisyllabic WORD-compounds (75)b, (76)b. Trisyllabic ROOT-compounds have a single initial stress, while trisyllabic WORD-compounds have two stresses: one on each WORD-level constituent.

(75)	a.	[gɔ̰́ɳaniɲ] /koʔ+ɳan+iɲ/ have+SEE+PC	b.	[ŋɔ̀o̰mánʲiɲ] /ŋoʔ-maŋ+iɲ/ guts-get+PC
(76)	a.	[míɲɟɪppʊn] /miɲci+ppu+n/ remember+HIT+PR	b.	[mɛ̀lḛɳán] /meleʔ-ɳa+n/ lest-see+PR

Note that trisyllabic ROOT-compounds behave in the same way regardless of their constituency at the ROOT-level. In WORD-compounds, by contrast, the location of stress depends on the internal constituency. A form, as in (75)b, with a final disyllabic MWD has penultimate stress, whereas a form with a final monosyllabic MWD has final stress, as in (76)b.

3.3.4 WORD-reduplication and ROOT-reduplication

Reduplication is considered in detail in Chapter 6. Here, I review the main differences between reduplication at the WORD-level and the ROOT-level, which are similar to those between compounds of each type.

CVʔ is one of the most common reduplicant shapes in Ngalakgan. Reduplication is prefixal in all except a couple of rare cases.[26] At the WORD-

[26] There are two cases known to me of infixal CVʔ reduplication: /jiɲkon/ 'today, right now' was reduplicated as /jiɲkoʔkon/ [(j)íɲgɔ̰gon] by my informants; Merlan (1983: 217) records a more usual form /jiɲkojiɲkon/ with the meaning 'just now, recently'. Merlan (1983: 195) also records a reduplicated form of /kamiɲcikko/ 'all the time' as /kamiɲciʔcikko/. It is unclear

level, this reduplicant shape is attested with polysyllabic inflected verb forms, adverbs, and quantifiers; but no nouns. Nouns are only attested with other reduplication patterns (exemplified briefly in Chapter 6).

WORD-level reduplicants do not carry their own consistent, lexically-specified meanings. Rather, interpretation is partially dependent on the meaning of the base, and to some extent on the rest of the context. In predicates of motion or activity, in adverbs of manner, and in nouns, reduplication is interpreted as Distributive: distribution of the event in time, space, or participants. In stative or attributive predicates or modifiers, and in adverbs of time, reduplication is interpreted as Intensive.

(77) presents some examples of CVʔ WORD-reduplication. The reduplicant is in bold in the phonemic representations:

(77)			
	a.	[màa̰máŋiɲ] /**maʔ**-maŋ+iɲ/ DIST-get+PC 'got here and there'	[máŋiɲ] /maŋ+iɲ/ get+PC 'got'
	b.	[ɟùṵɟʊ́ɾuwɛn] /**cuʔ**-curuwe+n/ DIST-rush+PR 'rushing here and there'	[ɟʊ́ɾuwɛn] /curuwe+n/ rush+PR 'rushes'
	c.	[wàa̰wáŋgiɲ] /**waʔ**-waŋkiɲ/ DIST-one 'one at a time'	[wáŋgiɲ] /waŋkiɲ/ one 'one'
	d.	[jàa̰jappánʔɟa] /**jaʔ**-jappanca/ DIST-two 'two at a time'	[jappánʔɟa] /jappanca/ two 'two'
	e.	[ĵɪɪ̰jɪppʊ́ɲɟa] /**jiʔ**-jippuɲca/ INTENS-long.ago 'a very long time ago'	[jɪppʊ́ɲɟa] /jippuɲca/ long.ago 'a long time ago'

The reduplicant constitutes a bound WORD-level stem: an MWD. Like other WORD-level operations—compounding and affixation—reduplication is (a) freely available, (b) does not take or select for idiosyncratic forms, and (c) has a regular, compositional interpretation.

---

what motivates these unusual forms. It does not appear to be stress, stress is initial in /jiɲkon/, and initial and penultimate in /kamiɲcikko/.

ROOT-level reduplication is restricted to the paradigms of certain CV verb roots. It fulfils particular Tense-Aspect-Mood categories in the verb, in particular, the simple Present, and the Past Punctual. Tables (2) and (3) provide paradigms of these verbs.

	'hit' *pu	'give' *wu	'see' *ɳa
PP	**poʔpo**	**woʔwo**	**ɳaʔɳa**
PC	puniɲ	wuniɲ	ɳaniɲ
EVIT/HABIT	pun	wun	ɳan
PRES	pun ~ punupun	wun ~ wunuwun	ɳan ~ *ɳanaɳan

Table 2: Reduplicated CV verb roots (N-conjugation)

	'burn' (tv) *ɳe	'chop' *ce	'get' *ma	'put' *je	'bite' *pe	'burn' (itv) *ɻu
PP	ɳeɲ	**ce ~ *ceʔce**	**meʔme ~ *me**	jeɲ	peɲ	ɻuɲ
PC	ɳeŋiɲ	coŋiɲ	maŋiɲ	jeŋiɲ	peŋiɲ	ɻuŋiɲ
EVIT/HABIT	ɳe	co	ma	je	pe	ɻu
PRES	**ɳeʔɳe**	**co ~ *coʔco**	**maʔma**	**jeʔje**	**peʔpe**	**ɻuʔɻu**

Table 3: Reduplicated CV verb roots (NG-conjugation)

What we find from examining these tables is that the occurrence of reduplication in CV roots is not predictable. While the PP form of the verb /ma/ 'get' is reduplicated, the PP form of /co/ 'chop' cannot be, even though they are a minimal pair and from the same conjugation. Likewise, the simple PRES forms of most of the monosyllabic verbs of this conjugation have reduplicated forms, but again, not /co/.

In addition, reduplication in monosyllabic verbs does not have the kind of meaning associated with reduplication elsewhere in the language—Distribution, or Intensification. Rather, the reduplicated forms fill particular slots in the TAM paradigm of these verbs. Furthermore, reduplication elsewhere in the language is always optional. But in these TAM functions in monosyllabic verb roots, the reduplicated forms are obligatory in most cases.[27]

[27] The PP forms are obligatorily reduplicated, unless there is a preceding compounding stem; see 4.5.4. The PRES forms are in some variation between reduplicated and non-reduplicated forms. In the EVIT 'lest' and HABIT meaning, reduplication is not observed (contra Merlan

Prosodically, there are differences between WORD and ROOT-level reduplication as well. WORD-level reduplication produces words with the prosodic structure of compounds, as in (78):

(78)

a.	[mà̰amáŋiɲ]	[máŋiɲ]
	/**maʔ**-maŋ+iɲ/	/maŋ+iɲ/
	DIST-get+PC	get+PC
	'got here and there'	'got, was getting'
b.	[ɟùṵɟʊ́ruwɛn]	[ɟʊ́ruwɛn]
	/**cuʔ**-curuwe+n/	/curuwe+n/
	DIST-rush+PR	rush+PR
	'rushing here and there'	'rushes'
c.	[jɛ̀ɛ̰jɛ́ŋiɲ]	[jɛ́ŋiɲ]
	/**jeʔ**-jeŋ+iɲ/	/jeŋ+iɲ/
	DIST-put+PC	put+PC
	'put here and there'	'put, was putting'
d.	[nɛ̀ɛ̰ɳɛ́ŋiɲ]	[nɛ́ŋiɲ]
	/**ɳeʔ**-ɳeŋ+iɲ/	/ɳeŋ+iɲ/
	DIST-burn+PC	burn+PC
	'was burning here and there'	'burnt, was burning'

In (78)a, the reduplicant /maʔ/ is a PRWD: it has a long vowel, and takes its own pitch accent. The base is another PRWD: it too is minimally bimoraic, and takes a pitch accent. In ROOT-level reduplication, by contrast, neither the reduplicant nor the base constitute a PRWD. The surface forms of some of the ROOT-reduplicated forms in Tables (2) and (3) are shown in (79):

(79)

a.	[bɔ̰́bɔ]	d.	[wɔ̰́wɔ]
	/poʔ+po/		/woʔ+wo/
	RED+hit.PP		RED+give.PP
	'hit'		'gave'
b.	[ná̰ɳa]	e.	[mɛ̰́me]
	/ɳaʔ+ɳa/		/meʔ+me/
	RED+see.PP		RED+get.PP
	'saw'		'got'

1983: 98, possibly this represents a dialect difference between our informants). In the simple PRES, most of these verbs can apparently be reduplicated or not, it is not clear what (if any) the difference in meaning is. There are also apparently differences between verbs. The verb /ɻu/ 'burn, (intransitive)' is typically unreduplicated, though I have heard it reduplicated once. The verb /ma/ 'get', however, is typically reduplicated in the simple PRES unless there is a preceding stem.

c. [ŋɛ́ŋɛ]
/ŋeʔ+ŋe/
RED+burn.PR
'burns'

f. [mámа]
/maʔ+ma/
RED+get.PR
'gets'

ROOT-reduplicated verbs do not consist of two PRWDs, unlike WORD-reduplicated forms. Rather, they have just a single stress, on the reduplicant, and no vowel lengthening. The base then, does not constitute a PRWD. I assume that this is because the ROOT-reduplicated forms are all listed in the lexicon. There is no facultative process of CV reduplication in the synchronic grammar of Ngalakgan, though presumably there was in the past. As already noted, the CV verb roots which have reduplicated forms are not predictable.

In some cases, the CV base of the reduplicated form is not an MWD. This is true of the PP forms /+po/, /+wo/ and /+me/. These forms never appear as words, unlike the PRES/EVIT forms. The PP CV roots can only occur in ROOT-reduplications, or in compounds. Curiously, they can occur in both ROOT and WORD-compounds. Some instances of the latter are examined in Chapter 4.

The differences between reduplication at the WORD and ROOT-levels are what we would expect, given the differences between WORD and ROOT-compounding examined in the preceding section. I now discuss how these distinctions are to be modelled in the lexicon.

3.4 The Ngalakgan lexicon

The prosodic differences between WORD-level and ROOT-level forms follow straightforwardly given a difference between them in the lexicon. I follow Jackendoff (1997), among others, in assuming a simple two-way difference between complex words in the lexicon. What I have called WORD-level relations correspond to Jackendoff's 'productive morphology', Clahsen's (1999) 'combinatorial operations' and Pinker's (1999) morphological 'rules'. Forms which are complex at the WORD-level are produced by simple symbol concatenating rules of the type familiar since Chomsky and Halle (1968). For instance, given the existence of a lexical entry such as (60), repeated here as (80), in the lexicon of Ngalakgan speakers, we can predict that any noun which is also a WORD should be able to take the affix /-kkaʔ/ to derive a form interpreted with a Locative relation.[28] This is indeed the case. Every noun for which a Locative interpretation makes sense can in fact take this affix. There are no special idiosyncrasies attached to the form or the interpre-

[28] And hence, bound nominal stems such as /mili-/ 'water' cannot take this affix.

tation of this affix and its derived forms. The interpretation of N-/kkaʔ/ words is entirely compositional.[29]

(80)

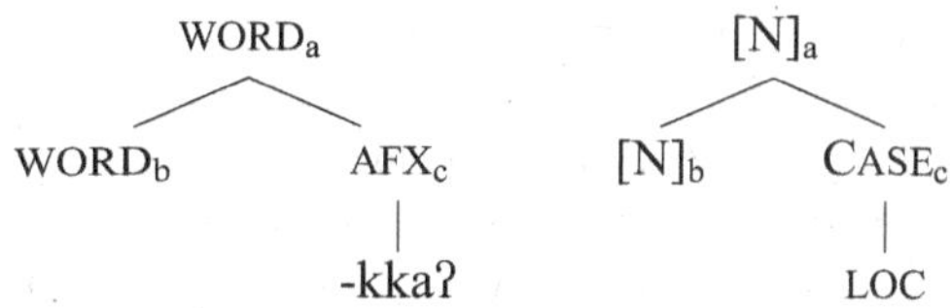

$[_{\text{Entity}}\ \text{LOC}_c\ [_{\text{Entity}}\ ]_b]_a$

The same analysis applies to WORD-compounds, prefixed forms, and all other WORD-complex forms. In all cases, the constituents of such forms can be freely combined with other WORD-level forms (subject to semantic and pragmatic naturalness), and the interpretations of such forms are straightforward given the meanings of the WORD-level constituents. Morphology at the WORD-level in Ngalakgan is fully productive, so far as can be determined.

The alternative view—known as the 'Strong Lexicalist' hypothesis (Chomsky 1970)—is to assume that the outputs of all morphological operations are 'lexically listed'. But there are good reasons to suppose that this is not the case. In (81), I give a rough indication of the number of morphemes which can fill each position in a complex verb form. The positions correspond to pronominal argument prefix 1, pronominal argument prefix 2, bound stems (of which there may be two or more), incorporated noun, finite verb (including verb compounds).

7- 7- 30 (-30) -50 -1000
(81) /ɳu-ku-caʔ-ɳamulu-caŋku-ru+ŋa/
2aS-NEUT-IMMED-really-meat-cook+FUT
'you've got to cook the meat properly now'

[29] In fact, case suffixes can also attach to V and ADJ as well as N, though it is not entirely clear what the limits on this affixation are (if any). While the REL suffix /-kVn/ (derived from the DAT/GEN suffix) is the general subordinating/relativising suffix, other local case suffixes have been observed in complementising or subordinating functions also; for a general discussion of this possibility in Australian languages, see Hale (1976b), Nordlinger (1998, 2006). An example of the use of this case suffix in a verb is shown here:

/pikur puru-poʈo-poʈop-miɲ-kaʔ/
person 3a-DIST-cross-AUX.PP-LOC
thei bin olweis krosim, olpipul yuno? enibodi, thei bin olweis krosim thet krik
'[that's] where people used to cross' [KD: 171]

Based on these figures, we can derive a conservative estimate of 2.2 billion possible combinations, just for verbs. It seems unlikely that speakers would have this many words stored in their brains. Moreover, it would make languages such as Ngalakgan (and Turkish, and Inuit, and Navajo and any number of other highly agglutinative languages) look very different to languages such as English, whose speakers would need a much smaller store of memorised words (Hankamer 1989 makes a similar argument).

More troubling than this though, a theory that demanded that only words be stored in the lexicon (and not bound morphemes), would make a theory of productivity more cumbersome. As Jackendoff (2002: 156) points out, such a theory would require that, 'when one hears a new noun stem like *wug*, one immediately adds not just *wug* but also *wugs* to one's long-term store'. Based on the estimates given above for Ngalakgan verb forms, this would mean adding over 70,000 forms to one's memory upon hearing a new verb stem. Worse, because two of these positions are open (the position for incorporated nouns, and the position for verbs), the number of potential verbs in Ngalakgan is also infinite; *ipso facto*, verb forms cannot be stored.

Finally, there is evidence from speech production in Ngalakgan that speakers can and do segment words into their individual (WORD-level) constituents. Example (82) illustrates two instances where (different) speakers slowed down their speech artificially, for my benefit.

(82) a. /jiriɳ-pi-pak-woc+ma/ [jíɾɨɳ]^[bi:]^[bak]^[wɔ́cma]
1aO-3a-APPL-steal+GET.PR 'they always steal from us'
normal speech: [jɪɾɨɳbibakwɔ́cma]

b. /ŋur-ku-kamala-ɳa+n-cci/ [ŋʊr]^[gu:]^[gámala]^[nánɟi]
12aS-NEUT-sky-see+NP-FNEG 'we can't see the view'
normal speech: [ŋʊrgugàmalaɳánɟi]

Note, firstly, that speakers do not break words up into syllables or feet and, secondly, that the ROOT-compound /woc+ma/ 'steal' is treated as a single item. There are numerous similar examples from the elicitation sessions. Such behaviour is entirely unexpected under Strong Lexicalist assumptions, though it seems natural under the view that productive morphemes are stored as lexical entries. In short, it seems more profitable and intuitively credible to think that WORD-complex forms in Ngalakgan are produced and interpreted by symbol-concatenating devices 'on line', in speakers' working memories.[30]

---

[30] This does not rule out short-to-long term storage of complex words, such as those which are frequently used. Clahsen (1999) provides psycholinguistic evidence for this proposal.

The equivalent of my ROOT-complex forms are what Jackendoff labels 'semi-productive or unproductive' (2002: 158-159). Jackendoff notes that the outputs of this kind of morphology are unpredictable. Based on the present tense form of a verb in English, for example, one cannot predict with any degree of certainty what the simple past tense or perfective participle form will be. In addition, the existence and meanings of forms derived by derivational morphology in English (which is largely unproductive) cannot always be predicted. Jackendoff (2002: 158-159) discusses the semi-productive rule of denominal verbalisation in English, producing alternations such as *butter, to butter, shelf, to shelve*. While it is true that there is a generalisation in the meanings of such verbs, it is not possible to predict *which* components of the potential meaning are in fact the ones that speakers allow. While one can shelve books, for example, one cannot shelve a clock.

> The upshot is that the outputs of semiproductive rules must be listed (at least in part) in long-term memory; they cannot be a product of free combination. Hence in this case the notion of a "lexical rule" a rule applying "in the lexicon" makes sense. Such a rule expresses a generalization in the relationship among pairs of lexical entries. But it does not apply to all entries that satisfy its conditions, nor does it fully predict the information in one member of a pair, given the other. Thus, unlike fully productive morphology, this sort of rule captures the original intention behind "lexical redundancy rules". (Jackendoff 2002: 159)

ROOT-complex words in Ngalakgan are clearly outputs of the same kind of semiproductive rules that Jackendoff discusses. Their products are unpredictable: we cannot predict with any certainty the PP form of any finite verb based on its NP form. We *can* predict with reasonable certainty the forms of the FUT and IRR based on the NP, but we would be wrong in some cases. In addition, the meanings of ROOT-complex forms are in many cases unpredictable and idiosyncratic. While /koʔ+ma+/ means 'show', /koʔ+ɳa+/ means 'have', even though the finite verb /ma+/ means 'get' independently, and /ɳa+/ means 'see', while the distinct open conjugation verb /koʔ-mi+/ means 'go away'.

Therefore I assume that the only elements having separate entries in the lexicon of Ngalakgan speakers are those which are WORD-level forms. ROOT-level morphemes, by contrast, have no independent existence in the lexicon.

3.4.1 The elements of the lexicon

In Chapter 4, I discuss the nature of bound morphemes in Ngalakgan more carefully. Preempting the discussion somewhat, we will find that the elements of the lexicon can be classified in a fashion illustrated in Table (4) below. I refer to the lexical entries as *lemmas*.

	Categorial elements		A-categorial elements
Morphosyntactic categories:	Major categories: N, V, ADJ	Minor categories: ADV, PRO, PART	
Label:	'Stems'	'Stems'	'Affixes'
Is a MWD:	yes	no	no
V-lengthening to attain minimum word:	yes	no	no
Necessarily assigned a pitch accent:	yes	yes	no

Table 4: Classes of *lemmas* in the lexicon

Stems, whether associated to major or minor categories, can be either bound or free. The distinction is not especially relevant to prosody in Ngalakgan. Affixes are necessarily bound.

Example (83) below illustrates the kinds of lexical entries which correspond to the elements illustrated in Table (4). A discussion follows.[31]

(83) a.

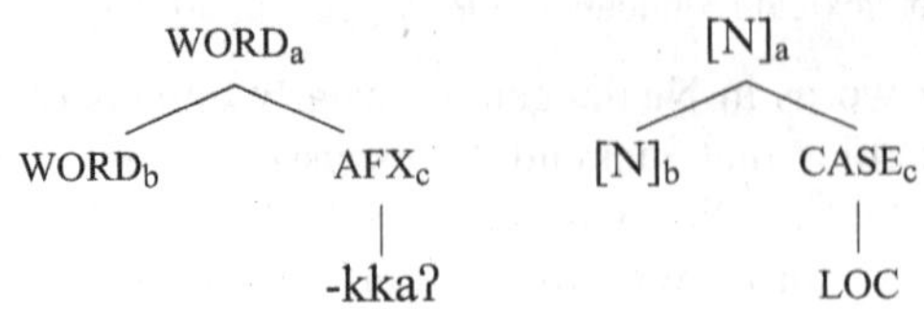

$[_{Entity}\ LOC_c\ [_{Entity}\ ]_b]_a$

b.

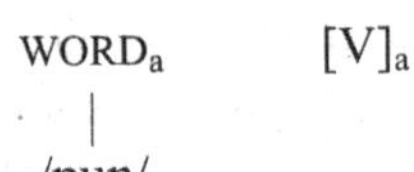

$[_{Situation}\ PRES\ [_{Event}\ CAUS_A\ [_{Event}\ INCH\ [_{State}\ BE\ ([\ ]_A,\ AT\ [\ ]_A])]]]]_a$ ('hit')

c.

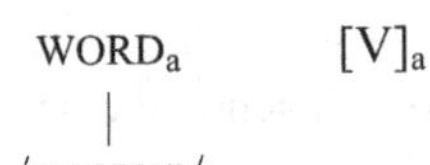

$[_{Situation}\ PRES\ [_{Event}\ CAUS_A\ [_{Event}\ INCH\ [_{State}\ BE_{Comp\text{-}}([SHELTER]_A\ (AT\ [BOUGHS]_A]))]]]]_a$ ('build bough shade')

[31] Here I again follow Jackendoff (1990, 1997). The Lexical Conceptual Structures (LCSs) of these entries are extrapolated from the LCSs of corresponding English lexical items discussed in the former.

d. WORD$_a$ [V]$_a$

/koʔɳaniɲ/

[$_{\text{Situation}}$ PC [$_{\text{State}}$ BE ([THING]$_A$ AT [THING]$_A$])]]$_a$ ('had', PC)

e. WORD$_a$ [N]$_a$

/ŋej/ $\begin{bmatrix} \text{N} \\ \text{class : I/IV} \end{bmatrix}$

[$_{\text{Entity}}$ PART OF [$_{\text{Entity}}$]]$_a$ ('name')

We have already met the lexical entry of the affix in (a). Example (b) is a ROOT-complex verb form in present tense, with the English gloss 'hit'. Example (c) is a ROOT-complex verbal compound, which happens to include the same inflected root as (b), but there is nothing in this entry which captures this. It is true that all verbal ROOT-compounds inflect for tense in the same way as the verb root which they contain, as noted in 3.3.2. This feature can be captured by lexical redundancy rules of the sort examined in Jackendoff (1997: 129) or Pinker and Prince (1988). I have not developed this mechanism here, partly because it is not essential to the analysis of the phonology presented herein.

Notably, ROOT-complex forms such as /koʔɳaniɲ/ 'have (PC)' have no internal structure, as far as this model of the lexicon is concerned. Judging by the behaviour of Ngalakgan speakers, this model is psycholinguistically valid, since such forms are never broken down into their constituent parts by speakers, unlike WORD-complex forms.

Now that we have an idea of the difference between WORD-level and ROOT-level morphology in lexical terms, we can define the notion of 'MWD' more succinctly:

(84) An MWD is a stem dominated by WORD in the morphophonology, and a major lexical category in the morphosyntax.

In (83) for instance, all of the entries apart from /-kkaʔ/ LOC carry morphosyntactic features indicating whether they belong to the category 'N', 'V', 'ADJ' and so on. Although the exact number and nature of word classes in Australian languages (and languages generally) is in some dispute, there is no question that there are such classes and that they have distinct formal and semantic characteristics (see for example Dixon 1980; Heath 1984; M. Baker 2003 for discussion). Affixes, I assume, do not carry categorial signatures of the same type (contra Lieber 1992). Rather, they carry subcategorisation requirements that specify the category of stems to which they can be attached.

Stems can also be dominated by minor categories, the most significant of these are 'PRO', 'DET' and 'ADV'. The prosodic behaviour of these elements is discussed in the following chapter, but in short, all bound stems behave much like WORDs, without being free forms, and without the requirement that they constitute Prosodic Words.

We can derive this behaviour if in their lexical entries, minor class bound stems are associated to 'WORD' in the morphophonological representation, but are not (immediately) dominated by a major lexical category in the morphosyntax, hence they fail to be treated by the phonology as Morphological Words, according to the definition of Morphological Word in (42).[32]

(85)

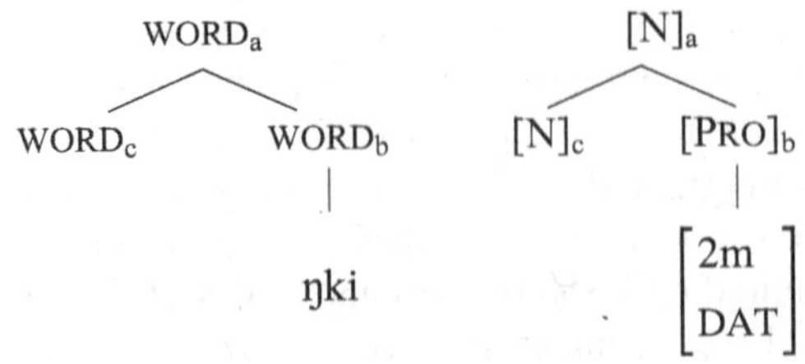

$[_{\text{Entity c}}$ OF/FOR $[_{\text{Entity}}$ 2min$]_b]_a$

In (85), the Dative pronoun /=ŋki/ '2sgDAT' is dominated by WORD in the morphophonology. This implies that these forms should have some of the prosodic and phonological characteristics of words. That this is so is demonstrated in Chapter 4. The morphosyntactic representation however tells us that this bound stem is not one of the major lexical categories (V, N, ADJ), but rather a 'PRO'. Hence, it cannot constitute a 'Morphological Word' for the phonology. As a consequence, Dative pronouns (and other minor class bound stems) do not undergo vowel lengthening in order to meet minimum Prosodic Word requirements. Chapter 4 demonstrates that this is the case.

In addition to this model of the lexicon, which gives us exactly one kind of output—WORD-level morphemes—we also require a mechanism which will handle the number, order and nature of morphemes in complex words.

3.5 Structure in complex words

Like the majority of Australian languages, Ngalakgan is non-configurational according to the usual criteria (Hale 1983; Austin and Bresnan 1996); that

32 Note that this is only true of bound stems. Minor class items which are words, such as independent pronouns, are (minimally) parsed as Prosodic Words in Ngalakgan.

is, there are no requirements that words constituting notional phrases appear together, or at all, nor are there dedicated configurations for the major grammatical functions of the clause (subject, object, verb phrase). Instead, as in many Australian languages, discourse considerations appear to be the major determinant of word order and referent realisation (zero anaphora vs overt realisation of various kinds) (Mushin and Baker To appear).

In such languages, it has been observed, words commonly take on the kinds of functions that phrases carry in configurational languages such as English (e.g. Bresnan 2001: 6). And hence, we can talk of morphology and syntax being 'in competition' to realise the grammatical and lexical categories of the clause (Foley 1991; Jackendoff 1997; Bresnan 2001; Ackema and Neeleman 2004). Two implications follow from this notion. One is that words might be very complex in languages where lexical and grammatical categories are preferentially realised morphologically, rather than phrasally. The other is that phrasal syntax itself might be quite impoverished, even to the extent that a language could display no phrasal syntax at all. Both characteristics are true of Ngalakgan. Indeed, Ngalakgan displays a level of word complexity at the upper end of the scale found among Australian languages. For instance, it allows complexity in nominal word structures which exceeds that found in BGW and Wubuy. Conversely, it has very little evidence for phrases (and cf. Heath 1986 on Wubuy)

Both nominal and predicational words in Ngalakgan may be highly complex, involving multiple stems and affixes on both sides of the head. Since words can be complex, we need some mechanism to ensure that morphemes are pronounced in the correct order. As is true universally, morphemes cannot be reordered within words in Ngalakgan. Templates are the most common way of expressing morphological selectional restrictions in grammars of Australian languages (see e.g. Merlan 1983: 93). The template in (86) presents the maximal structure and order of morphemes in words of nominal category in Ngalakgan (cf. Evans 2003: 133 on BGW).

(86) N → (NC-) (Bound stem-) N (-Dative pronoun) (-Number) (-Case)

Templates, unlike tree structures, make no predictions about headedness or selectional relationships within words. In some cases, this aspect of templates has been used to advantage—e.g. the description of Warlpiri auxiliary complexes in Simpson and Withgott (1986), who argue that these forms lack a morphological head. However, such an analysis is inappropriate for Ngalakgan, since all complex words have a designated head, which determines the morphosyntactic behaviour of the word.

In general, words are right-headed in Ngalakgan, as we have seen with the verb compounds presented in Chapter 3. More particularly, it is the right-most stem with a major categorial signature which determines the category of the word. Other morphemes realise arguments, modifiers or grammatical categories of this head, and may occur either to the left or the right of this stem. These characterisations can be encoded in the following principle of interpretation for Ngalakgan words (the Head-Right Principle):

(87) The rightmost MWD in a complex word is the morphosyntactic head.

In these terms, there are three formal categories of complex words in Ngalakgan—nouns, adjectives and verbs. Complex noun words are necessarily headed by a noun, with or without additional morphemes. The morphological template for nouns can be justified partly in morphoprosodic terms, and partly in terms of scope (cf. Rice 2000). Stems, including bound stems, must occur inside affixes. This determines the relative order of Dative pronouns (which are left-binding stems), as opposed to number and case suffixes. While all nouns take overt case suffixes, only certain lexical classes of nouns take overt number morphology. In general, only nouns referring to humans can take such morphology. Hence, the factor that determines the relative order of number and case suffixes appears to be either selectional restrictions or scope. These considerations suggest a structure such as (88) for complex nouns, where 'K' represents a case-marking head (following Bittner and Hale 1996), Num represents the number-marking head, and the Dative pronoun projects to a modifier of the lexical head /jappa/.

(88)

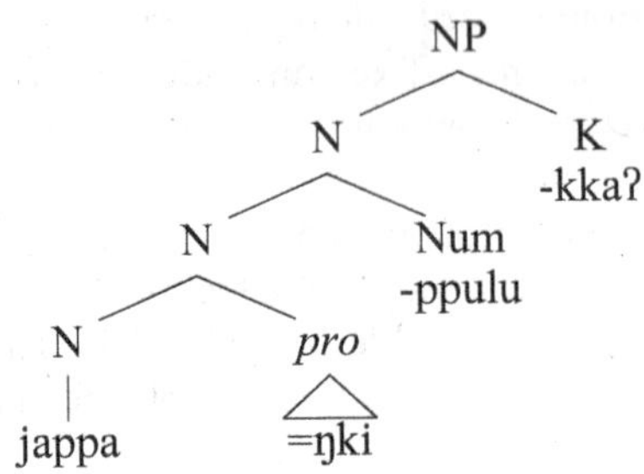

/jappa=ŋki-ppulu-kkaʔ/
sister=2mDAT-PL-LOC
'with your (sg.) sisters'

I have labelled the bound Dative pronoun as '*pro*', which is designed to be reminiscent of the 'little *pro*' arguments of verbs in Romance languages. Like pronominal argument prefixes, Dative pronouns can be referential regardless of whether an independent nominal with which they are coindexed is realised overtly. Indeed, for Speech Act Participants (SAPs)—1st and 2nd person referents—independent realisation in an overt pronoun is marked. Independent pronouns are largely used for contrastive purposes in discourse in Ngalakgan (Baker 2002).

Moreover, the features contributed by the Dative pronoun do not merge with those of the head. In this word, for example, the Dative pronoun has a grammatical number of singular (or minimal), while the NP as a whole has plural number. In a feature percolation analysis, such as that of Lieber (1992) or Bresnan (2001), such a construction would generate a feature 'clash' in the matrix representing the values of the grammatical categories of the highest projection dominating the word. It is for this reason, among others, that the Dative pronouns must be recognised as morphemes in the classical sense, and not merely as 'spell-out' rules like those suggested by Spencer (2003) and other authors (see Chapter 7 for further discussion of this claim).[33]

It remains to determine where in this structure the Noun Class prefixes might attach. I suggest that Noun Class prefixes are of category 'D' and that they take NPs as complements, forming a DP, as in the following structure:

(89)

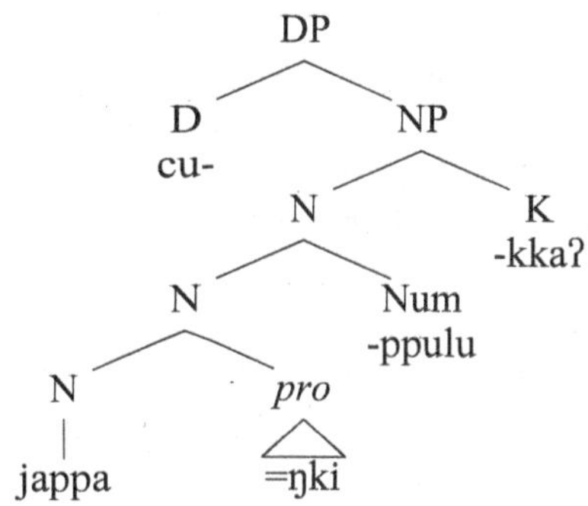

/cu-jappa=ŋki-ppulu-kkaʔ/
F-sister=2mDAT-PL-LOC
'with your (sg.) sisters'

The justification for this is as follows. Firstly, I have argued elsewhere (Baker To appear) that Noun Class prefixes in Ngalakgan, Wubuy and Marra are determiners, whose form conditions interpretations of NPs in terms of Topic and Focus relations with the predicate, operators such as negation and interrogation, and surrounding discourse. This suggests that it is the Noun Class prefixes which have the widest scope, within the nominal word. Secondly, in Wubuy and Marra the form of Noun Class prefixes is determined by the case function of the NP, as well as its gender. This suggests that Noun

[33] This might appear to conflict with the characterisation of Dative pronouns given in 3.4, where I used the representational fact that Dative pronouns are not dominated by a lexical category to derive their behaviour in prosody (discussed in more detail in Chapter 4). However, the same is true of pronominal argument prefixes. While these are undoubtedly phonological affixes, they nevertheless can be independently referential (Baker 2002), and so must be dominated by something like '*pro*' (or NP) at some level of representation.

Class prefixes must be attached higher in the word than case. Presumably this was historically true of Ngalakgan as well (as suggested by Merlan 1983); but I find no reasons to think this is a synchronically valid description of their function in Ngalakgan.

The nominal compounds exemplified in 3.2.1 are all compounds of the form 'N-ADJ', where the second member, and head of the compound, is of the adjectival class. That these compounds are headed by the adjective, rather than the noun, can be demonstrated with respect to inflectional possibilities: nominal compounds, but not common nouns, can be predicates. In (90), the compound takes a suffix /-ʔmolk/, for Present/Past Negative, which otherwise occurs in this meaning only on what Merlan (1983) calls 'nominal predicates' (which are adjectives, in the main). So it can occur on /cappuru/, but not /kuɳʈu/, (91). It also occurs on verbs but just with the Past Negative meaning.

(90) /ku-kuɳʈu-cappuru kuɳmaɳʔ ŋu-ɻapon-ci/,
NEUT-country-sacred maybe 1m-go.PR-FNEG
'it might be sacred country, I can't go [there],'
/ku-kuɳʈu-cappuru-ʔmolk kuɳmaɳʔ/,
NEUT-country-sacred-PRNEG maybe
'it might not be sacred ("dear") country,'
/ku-kuɳʈu-mocce, ŋu-ɻapon, warmpaja/
NEUT-country-clear 1m-go.PR anywhere
ai kin gu eniwe, nomo diawan
'it's clear country, I can go anywhere [there].'

(91) */ku-kuɳʈu-ʔmolk/
NEUT-country-PRNEG
(intended) 'it is not country'

Of nouns, only those referring to human status/age grades (/poloʔ/ 'old person', etc) and kin terms can readily take *predicate forms* of this kind, as shown in (92), with overt Inchoative auxiliary. Other kinds of nouns (species terms, 'generic' terms, implement terms) cannot take predicate forms (here I follow Heath 1984: 152; cf. Merlan 1983: 58; Evans 2003: 120):

(92) /ŋajkkaʔ koʔje **ŋu-miɻppara-meniɲ**/
I here 1m-child-INCH.PP
'I was a child' [M: 3-125]

Existence or identity can be predicated of (apparently) any noun. (93) is a Ngalakgan example, and (94) a Wubuy one, both from naturally occurring discourse (Wubuy example from my own fieldnotes).

(93) /ku-laŋga   koʔje/
NEUT-billabong   there
'there's a billabong there'

(94) /matamu   mana-jirpaɻa,   a-ciici-jiɲuŋ/   [Wubuy]
VEG.PROX   VEG.TOP-ironwood   NEUT-sore-DAT
dijan iya ayinwud tri, im blanga so
'this is ironwood, it's [used] for sores'   [31/5/04: tk1]

In the latter case, the species name is patently not a predicate grammatically, since it takes a Noun Class prefix, in this case /mana-/. The 'topic' (Heath's 'continuous') NC prefixes in Wubuy function as determiners, as they do in Ngalakgan. They are therefore only found on words referring to entities; never on verbs. So we need to distinguish the semantic distribution of predicates from the grammatical one. Hence, compounds have the morphosyntactic properties (the distribution) of adjectives, rather than nouns.

If we allow that compounds are adjectives, then the other properties follow, since adjectives as a class can be referential (cf. Hale 1983 on Warlpiri):[34]

(95) **/ŋolkko**   ŋu-pawunʔ-miɲ/
big   1m-leave-AUX.PP
bigmob ai bin libim
'I left a big [amount].'

(96) /jekke   ɳu-ku-ceɲ   mokkol   ku-ɻaponʔ/
INTERR   M-TOP-fish   father   NP-go.PR
'Dad, any fish [here]?'
/ŋolkko   ceceparŋʔ   ŋu-ɳaniɲ,   **ŋolkko**   ku-ɻapon/
big   yesterday   1m-see.PC,   big   NP-go.PR
O bigmob fish im wokabaut
'I saw a lot yesterday, a big [amount] moving around'   [2/9/97: 1B]

Thus, the same complex word can have either nominal or predicate functions in the clause, and this choice determines whether a word takes Noun Class prefixes or pronominal argument prefixes, as shown here.

(97) a. /ɳu-ku-pikur-maʔ/   'the good man'
M-TOP-person-good
b. /ŋu-pikur-maʔ/   'I'm a good man'
1m-person-good

[34] These examples are not ideal unfortunately, because the interpretation is quantificational rather than attributive. I am not sure why. See Bittner and Hale (1995) for relevant discussion.

(98)

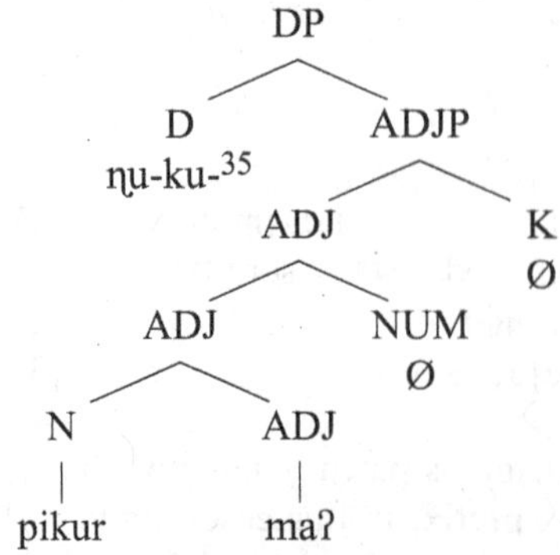

(99)

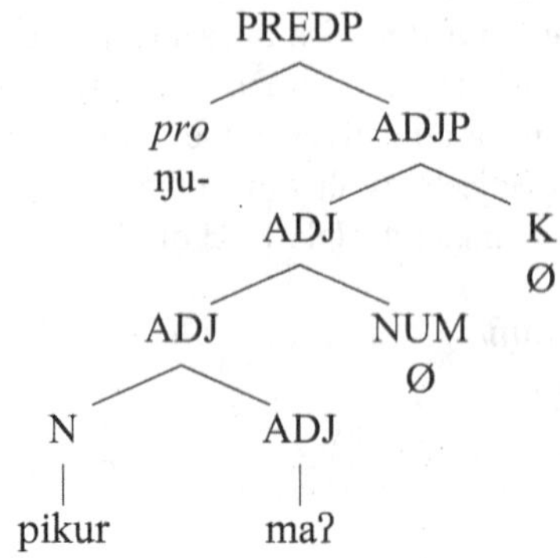

All nominals must belong to some Noun Class, even if this class is covert in particular tokens, and likewise all predicates must take a pronominal argument prefix. I have represented this argument prefix as a *pro* head, which, like the 'little *pro*' inflections on verbs in Spanish and Italian, can be referential independently of any co-occurring coreferential NP (Baker 2002). This *pro* specifies a phrase I have labelled 'Predicate Phrase', which is designed to encompass both verbal and adjectival predicates (since these have largely identical structures). As with Dative pronouns, independent pronouns coreferential to pronominal argument prefixes of Speech Act Participants are ill-formed, except under conditions of contrastive emphasis. This suggests that these pronominal argument prefixes, at least in the case of SAPs, saturate the argument positions of predicates. The situation for 3rd person prefixes is somewhat different, as I have argued elsewhere (Baker

[35] I have not analysed the complex determiner /ɳu-ku-/ M-TOP here. But it has a different interpretation and distribution to the simple determiner /ɳu-/ M, e.g. the topic form is obligatory on nouns under the scope of interrogative or negative operators; see Baker (To appear).

2002). These prefixes are genuine 'agreement' markers, since coreferential NPs are not interpreted contrastively. Nevertheless, in the absence of any coreferential NP, 3rd person agreement markers may also saturate the argument positions of a predicate; as in Spanish and Italian, overt NPs in argument positions are not obligatory.

I will not provide extensive argumentation for the hierarchical structures proposed here, since the particular structure we choose is not relevant to the matter, which is how to make sure that the order of morpheme classes is determined somehow. The structures in (98) and (99) will do this job, but other structures will do just as well, provided they capture the same scope, selectional and functional characteristics.

These general structures for complex words will constrain the free merger of morphemes listed in the lexicon which, as discussed in 3.4, carry their own phonological, syntactic, and semantic specifications and selectional properties. In (100), we see the entry for the head /jappa/ 'sister'. This is an inherently relational noun, as suggested in the LCS. Inherently relational nouns are the most common hosts of Dative pronouns (besides kinterms, we find body parts, and other partonyms, in this class).

(100)

WORD$_a$	$[N]_a$
|	|
/jappa/	[N, class: FEM]

$[_{Entity}$ KIN OF $[_{Entity}\ ]]_a$

Example (101) shows the lexical entry of a Dative pronoun, repeated from 3.4. In phonological terms, a Dative pronoun is a kind of WORD, while in syntactic terms, it is an affix of category 'PRO'. In 3.4, I justified this 'mixed' classification in terms of the behaviour of bound stems: they are phonologically word-like, but fail to behave as morphological heads of words (unlike bound nominal and verbal stems); that is, Dative pronouns do not determine the morphosyntactic behaviour of the word—they can attach to both nouns and verbs.[36]

---

[36] I have therefore modified the entry for /=ŋki/ from (85) to capture the idea that Dative pronouns, like case suffixes, can attach to WORDs of category X, to form WORDs of category X. In actuality, X ranges only over the major lexical categories N, V and ADJ.

(101)

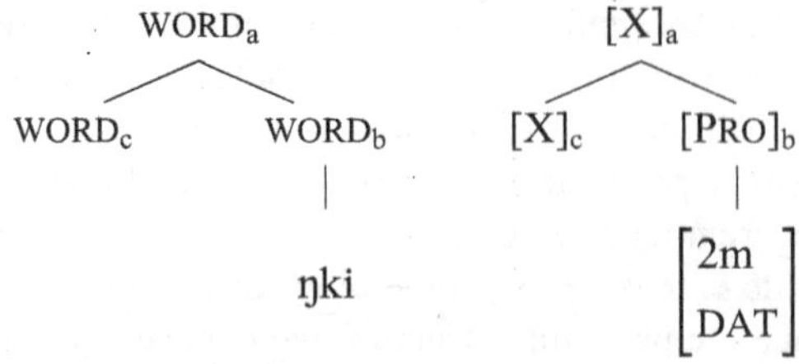

[$_{Entity\ c}$ OF [$_{Entity}$ 2min]$_b$]$_a$

The lexical entries for Dative pronouns specify that they can merge with WORDs of category 'X' to form relational structures where the referent of the Dative pronoun is the possessor of the referent of X (or the beneficiary of the event, where X = V). This information is only realised in the semantics /conceptual structure however: as far as the syntax is concerned, nouns with bound Dative pronouns are still nouns. Hence, merging (100) with (101) produces (102). Here, the N of (100) has merged at the empty X place in the syntactic representation of (101), with concomitant fill-in of the associated phonological and semantic features.

(102)

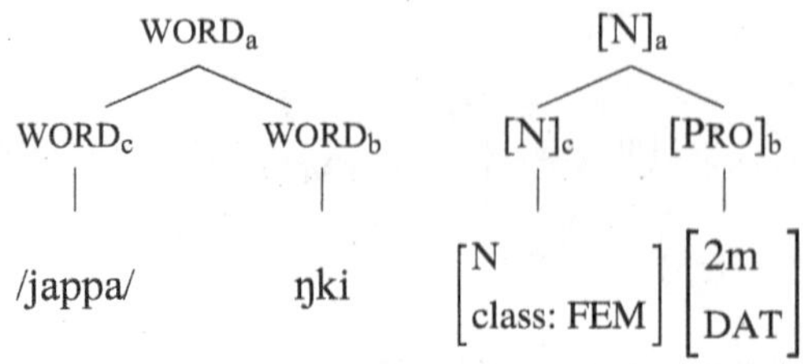

[$_{Entity}$ KIN$_c$ OF [$_{Entity}$ 2min]$_b$]$_a$

(103) presents the lexical entry for a case suffix /-kkaʔ/, also repeated from 3.4. Case suffixes are phonological affixes (unlike Dative pronouns), which attach to WORDs of category 'X' to form WORDs of category 'X' which are specified for a case relation in conceptual structure. Hence, the empty position in (103) can merge with (102) to form (104).

(103)

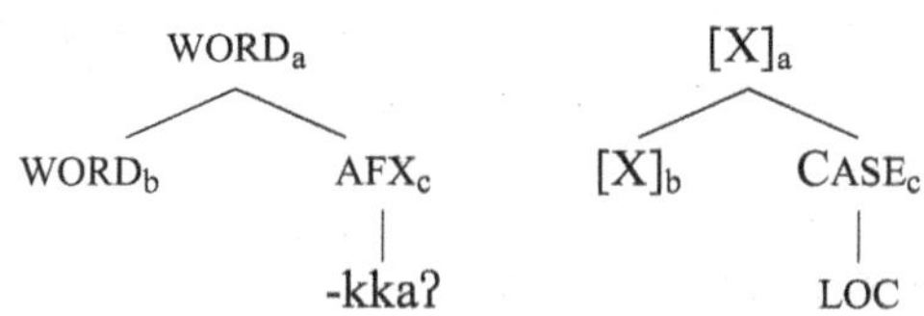

[$_{Entity}$ AT$_c$ [$_{Entity}$]$_b$]$_a$

(104)

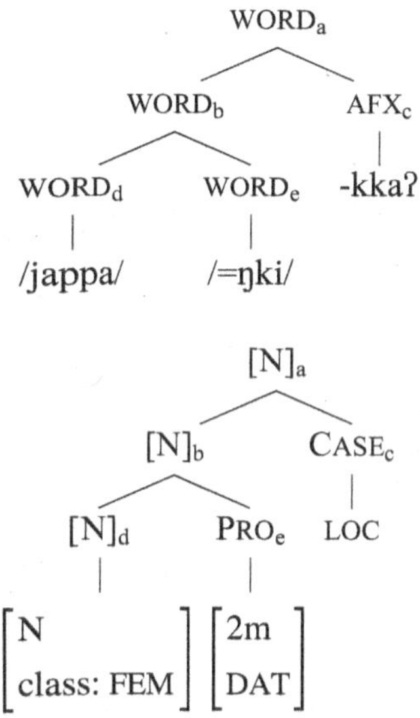

[$_{\text{Entity}}$ AT$_c$ KIN$_d$ OF [$_{\text{Entity}}$ 2min]$_e$]$_a$

Thus, the combination of independent lexical entries for productive morphemes, together with a morphosyntactic (or 'word syntax') structure such as (89) constraining the maximal structures for words, will together produce the kind of language that we observe Ngalakgan to be.

3.6 The analysis of ROOT-complex forms

Given the model of the lexicon proposed in 3.4, the prosodic facts of ROOT-complex forms follow straightforwardly from the constraints already discussed. An affixed, reduplicated or compounded ROOT consists of a single MWD, that is, a single lexical entry. Although it has not been explicitly discussed to my knowledge, the constituent morphemes which are assessed in the input to OT grammars are outputs from the lexicon (see Baker 2005 for further discussion of what kinds of constituents might be inputs to an OT grammar). ROOT-level boundaries are therefore invisible to OT constraints.

By MWD ≈ PRWD then, a ROOT-compound is only required to correspond to a single PRWD and a single foot. This is shown in tableaux (105) and (106) below. Tableau (105) presents an analysis of a WORD-compound. In (a), each MWD is separately footed; separate footing is a prerequisite to separate PRWD-hood, by the Prosodic Hierarchy hypothesis. To not do so, as in candidate (b), violates MWD ≈ PRWD. This is the case even though candidate (a) here violates the constraint against a short vowel:long vowel correspondence—IDENT[mora].[37]

(105)

/ŋoʔ-maŋ+iɲ/ guts-get+PC	FTBIN	ALIGNL (PRWD, FT)	MWD ≈ PRWD	IDENT[μ]
☞ a. [(ŋoːʔ)]-[(maŋiɲ)]				*
b. [(ŋoʔ-ma)ŋiɲ]			*!	
c. (ŋoːʔ)-[(maŋiɲ)]			*!	*

Tableau (106) presents the analogous ROOT-compound form. Candidate (b) is the best option in (106) because the PRWD, and hence the foot, is left-aligned to the only morpheme which is 'visible' to prosody: the ROOT-compound /koʔ+ɳan+iɲ/ meaning 'have (PC)'. This constituent is footed only once, because to build a heavy foot on the initial syllable /koʔ/ violates the constraint against long vowels. Violation of this constraint is licensed in (105), because of higher-ranked MWD ≈ PRWD. In (106)a, it is an unnecessary violation of Correspondence and hence (b) is the optimal candidate.

(106)

/koʔɳaniɲ/ 'have (PC)'	FTBIN	ALIGNL (PRWD, FT)	MWD ≈ PRWD	IDENT[μ]
a.[(koːʔ)(ɳaniɲ)]				*!
☞ b. [(koʔɳa)niɲ]				
c. [koʔ(ɳaniɲ)]		*!		

In sum, it appears that there are two types of morphological relations in Ngalakgan: WORD-level and ROOT-level. WORD-level morphemes are listed in the lexicon, with simple lexical entries, whose subcategorisation frames refer only to syntactic categories, not lists of morphemes. This last characteristic is a formalisation of the morphological productivity of WORD-level forms: they can attach to anything with the right syntactic category, where the resulting form would be morphologically and semantically coherent. By contrast, ROOT-level forms would have to have highly specific lexical entries if they

[37] The possible candidate where glottal stop bears the mora is ruled out by other constraints examined separately in Chapter 5.

were to be separately listed, and moreover, the lexicon would need to list the meanings of the resulting forms in many cases anyway.

The preceding sections have shown that there is a clear prosodic contrast between ROOT-compounds and WORD-compounds. ROOT-compounds have the prosodic characteristics of simple words, whereas WORD-compounds retain the prosodic characteristics of each of their constituent words. The prosodic contrast reflects the morphosemantic contrast: ROOT-compounds are lexicalised, WORD-compounds are productive. ROOT-compounds have idiosyncratic meanings, and their constituents are often not found in other morphological contexts. WORD-compounds have compositional meanings, and are formed from constituents which are commonly attested in a range of morphological environments. The same distinctions are true of the reduplication patterns discussed in 3.3.4.

I now turn to the characteristics of the apical contrast in words. The distribution of this contrast correlates with internal as well as external root and stem boundaries, and with the ROOT-level/WORD-level distinction in affixes. It is therefore an independent test of the morphological constituency proposed in preceding sections, though ROOT- and WORD-level stems (as opposed to affixes) are not distinguished by the distribution of apical distinctions. It will also be important for establishing the constituency of affixes in Chapter 4, and the effect of glottal stops on neighbouring consonants, in Chapter 5.

3.7 Phonological correlates of compounding: the distribution of apical distinctions in words

Chapter 2 discussed the neutralisation of apical distinctions at certain phonotactic positions in Ngalakgan. The same distribution is observed in complex words, both at the ROOT- and WORD-levels. An apical-initial stem is postalveolar when it follows a vowel or vowel+glottal stop, (107)a-c, (108)a but alveolar when it follows a (non-postalveolar) consonant (107)d, (108)b. In these examples, I have shown the phonetic realisation of the apical in question within the phonemic form.

(107) a. /cu-ɳamulu-kerŋe-[**ɳ**]a+na/
[ɟuɳàmulugɛ̀rŋeɳána]
2mS-really-body-see+FUT
'you'll have to really look for an animal'

b. /ŋu-ku-wi+[**ɳ**]a+n/
[ŋuguwíɳan]
1mS-NEUT-forget+SEE+PR
'I forget it [name: NEUT]'

c. /pur-koʔ+[**ɳ**]a+n/
[burgɔ̰́ɳan]
3aS-have+SEE+PR
'they have some'

d. /ŋu-pu-ʈic+[**n**]a+na-ppiraʔ/
[ŋubuɖɪcnanappíra̰]
1mS-3a-stare.at+SEE+FUT-DU
'I'll stare at those two'

(108) a. /ku-mili-[**ɳ**]e+ɲ/
[gumı̀liɳéɲ]
NEUT-water-burn+PP
'(he) boiled the water'

b. /jir-pujppuj+[**n**]e+ɲ/[38]
[jɪrbʊ̀ɪppʊɪnéɲ]
1aS-burn.hair+BURN+PP
'we singed the hair'

Note that the alveolar/postalveolar distinction does not correlate with WORD-level/ROOT-level distinctions in the case of stems, since both WORD-level (107)a and ROOT-level compounds (107)b-c behave in the same way.

Morpheme-initial apicals assimilate to the POA of preceding apicals; (109)a-b show assimilation to preceding alveolars, and (109)c-d to preceding post-alveolars.[39]

Prefixed word

(109) a. /ŋun-[**n**]e+ŋa/
1mO-burn+FUT
'it'll burn me'

c. /ŋuruɳ-[**ɳ**]e/
12aO-burn.PR
'it burns us'

WORD-compound

b. /jir-ɻalʔ-[**n**]e+ŋa/
1aS-hair-burn+FUT
'we have to burn the hair now'

d. /ŋun-puɳ-[**ɳ**]e+ŋa/
1mO-knee-burn+FUT
'It's going to burn my knee'

---

[38] I have confirmed this form acoustically. The spectrogram shows a brief period of voicelessness between the diphthong [ʊɪ] and the following apical [n]. This indicates either that the palatal off-glide is a fricative in this position or that the nasal is prestopped (see Butcher 1999 for further discussion of this feature of Australian languages). The diphthong shows no trace of depression in the third formant, which is the usual indicator of retroflexion, and I can hear none.

[39] There are no examples in my data of apical-initial stems following an apico-postalveolar-final *stem* (as against postalveolar-final prefixes, which are common). I regard this as a lacuna in the data, rather than an important fact. The example in (109)d is an invented one which is consistent with the facts otherwise.

In stems, then, apical distinctions are neutralised in initial position, with the unmarked realisation being postalveolar. The WORD-level and ROOT-level distinction is irrelevant in this case, stems at both levels behave in the same fashion.

While stems behave alike in terms of apical neutralisation, apical distinctions are distributed differently in suffixes, depending on whether they attach at the ROOT or WORD-levels. In addition, WORD-level suffixes may be distinguished from bound stems in terms of this feature.

ROOT-suffixes have the only morpheme-initial apicals which do not show alternation between alveolar and postalveolar: they are always apico-alveolar (Merlan 1983: 9).

(110) a. /pu+**n**iɲ/ [buniɲ] *[buɳiɲ]
hit+PC 'was hitting'
b. /caŋa+**n**a/ [ɟaŋana] *[ɟaŋaɳa][40]
stand+FUT 'will stand'

Apico-postalveolar realisations of verb ROOT-level suffixes are unattested. There are 32 attested finite verb roots, with 5 distinctive tense suffix categories (for most verbs) giving a total of 192 inflected forms. Of the 32 roots, 17 have a paradigm in which the Present, Future, Irrealis, and Past Continuous inflections are built on a suffix beginning, arguably, in an apico-alveolar nasal /+n/. Therefore, of 192 forms, 85—or just under half—involve an affix which is apico-alveolar. The apical initial inflections found in examples like /puniɳ/ have been reconstructed to the GN level by Alpher, Evans and Harvey (2003). They reconstruct no inflectional suffixes with initial retroflex segments. This alone is good evidence that such morphemes have no independent psycholinguistic existence for speakers: all productive apical-initial morphemes undergo this alternation otherwise.

Several bound stems are apical-initial. They behave in the same way as roots and words: initial apicals are neutralised in favour of apico-postalveolar. In (111)a, bound stem /ɳamulu-/ 'really' is apico-postalveolar initial following vowels, but apico-alveolar following a consonant (111)b.

(111) a. /cu-[**ɳ**]amulu-kerɲe-ɳa+na/
2mS-really-body-see+FUT
yu labta faindim prabli
'You'll have to really find an animal.' [2/9/97: 1B]

---

40 The morpheme division in inflected roots is open to some dispute. An alternative analysis would have the NonPast stem /caŋan/ taking a Future suffix /+a/; see Baker (2004) for discussion.

b. /macci poʈewk-me+ɳ [**n**]amulu ku-ɻapo+n-ciʔ/
indeed bad-be+PR really NP-go+PR-NEG
'He's bad [i.e. sick], he really can't get around.' [31/5/96: 1B]

The examples in (112) show the same range of behaviour for the bound Dative pronoun /-ɳowi/ (3NFEMDAT) 'his, its'. The initial apical is post-alveolar following a vowel, as in (112)a, and alveolar following a non-post-alveolar consonant, as in (112)b. Bound stems behave like roots and words with respect to apical neutralisation.

(112) a. /ku-ce=[**ɳ**]owi/
NEUT-nose=3NFEMDAT
'his nose'

b. /cu-palak=[**n**]owi/
F-WIMO=3NFEMDAT
'his mother-in-law'

While many ROOT-suffixes are apical-initial, there are no apical-initial WORD-suffixes at all (Merlan 1983: 9). Therefore we find a three-way contrast in the distribution of apical distinctions in bound morphemes. Initial apicals in ROOT-affixes are always apico-alveolar, those in bound stems are apical-neutral (like free WORD-level stems), while apical-initial forms are unattested in WORD-suffixes. The distribution of apicals in the various categories of bound morphemes is presented in Table (5). The number on the left in each cell represents the number of tokens in each morphological category ('ROOT-suffix' etc) which have an initial segment of the type given in each column, over the number of entire tokens in the category.

	Apico-alveolar	Apico-retroflex (neutralised)	Non-apical
ROOT-suffix	85/192	0/192	107/192
WORD-suffix	0/9	0/9	9/9
WORD-prefix	0/30	5/30	25/30
Left-binding WORD stems	0/16	2/16	14/16
Right-binding WORD stems	0/17	1/17	16/17

Table 5: Distribution of apical distinctions among bound morphemes

The neutralisation and distribution of apical distinctions at morpheme boundaries provides additional phonological evidence of internal morphological constituency in complex words, and of the WORD-level/ROOT-level distinction in affixes.[41]

---

[41] Heath (1978b, 1984) uses differences in the distribution of apical contrasts in initial positions of morphemes as a heuristic for morphological constituency in Ngandi and Nunggubuyu, though he does not recognise a general two-way difference in morphological relations in these languages. My experience with Ngandi and Nunggubuyu suggests that these

3.8 Implications[42]

I have shown that there are a number of characteristics which distinguish WORD-level and ROOT-level relations in Ngalakgan. WORD-level affixes, reduplicants, and stems attach to stems which are 'words', for all prosodic and semantic purposes. WORD-level stems must be minimally bimoraic if they are from the major lexical categories. WORD-level stems constitute a stress domain independent of other WORD-level stems. All productive morphological relations in Ngalakgan are at the WORD-level.

By contrast, ROOT-level affixes, reduplicants, and stems attach to stems which are not necessarily words. ROOT-level stems do not necessarily constitute independent stress domains, nor need they be minimally bimoraic. The combination of ROOT-level morphemes is always subject to arbitrary selectional restrictions.

In Ngalakgan, the distribution of apicals is also sensitive to the distinction between WORD-level and ROOT-level relations. Inflected verb roots behave like monomorphemic forms in terms of apical neutralization and stress. This is true generally of words which are complex at the root-level: they pattern as if they had no internal morphological structure.

I follow Selkirk (1982), Borowsky (1990) and others in allowing for just two 'levels' or types of morphological relations: Root and Word. Furthermore, I predict that for those phonological patterns where two types of complex words are distinguished, that ROOT-complex forms will show the same patterns as simplex forms; whereas in WORD-complex forms, at least one constituent of the word will itself have the characteristics of a simplex word. In this respect, I differ from versions of Lexical Phonology which allow for, in principle, *n*-ary levels of morphological structure within complex words. For example, Kiparsky (1982) proposes three levels for English, while Mohanan (1986: 28, 68) allows for four in both English and Malayalam.

I have proposed above that there is a direct relationship between productivity and morphological relations. Specifically, I propose that productive morphology is necessarily a WORD-level relation in Ngalakgan, while ROOT-level relations are necessarily unproductive. To some degree, this separation between unproductively and productively-derived forms is implicit in the Lexical Phonology literature. For example, Kiparsky summarises the model thus:

---

languages, and indeed many Australian languages, can nevertheless be described in these terms; a preliminary attempt in this direction is Baker and Harvey (2003), where we compare morphological relations in Ngalakgan and Warlpiri.

42 This section is based on Baker and Harvey (2003: 30-2).

> The first level comprises the affixes which have usually been associated with the + boundary. ... This level includes derivational suffixes such as *-al, -ous, -ity, -th,* and inflectional suffixes such as those in *kept, met, hidden, children, addenda, indices, foci* as well as "ablaut", "umlaut", and other stem changing morphology as in *teethe, bleed, bathe, teeth, lice*. To the second level we assign # boundary ("secondary") derivation and compounding. Such derivational suffixes as *-hood, -ness, -er, -ism, -ist* belong here. The third level takes care of the remaining "regular" inflection (*leaped, pleated, books, conundrums, indexes, crocuses,* etc.). (Kiparsky 1982: 5)

Evidently, the morphemes listed as level 1 are unproductive whereas those listed as levels 2 and 3 are productive. However, this is not a theoretical claim of the model. A similar connection is also implicit in Borowsky's model of English phonology (Borowsky 1990). She states that 'All rules which are marked for a particular [morphological] domain of application apply at level 1 only' (Borowsky 1990: 13). Given that unproductive patterns are necessarily restricted in their domain of application, they will be confined to level 1. However, again no theoretical claim is made concerning relations between productivity and phonological patterns.

Mohanan notes that the association between productivity and phonological patterns is worthy of further investigation:

> The reader will have noticed that affixation at stratum 1 is by and large less productive than affixation at stratum 2. This also correlates with the fact that there are fewer lexical exceptions, and fewer cases of semantic opacity in words derived at stratum 2. Thus, *dis-* and *-ment* are affixed at stratum 2 in a productive fashion, creating semantically transparent results, while the same affixes attach unproductively at stratum 1, creating semantically opaque forms. ... My guess is that if a language has two strata of affixation or two strata of compounding, the earlier stratum would be the one that yields more opaque forms. If this is a correct observation, it merits further study. (Mohanan 1986: 57)

The model described here proposes that Mohanan's observation is correct and that it should be formally incorporated into theories of morphophonological structures. Two major kinds of 'productivity' have been described above. One type of productivity is semantic: it encodes the observation that complex words may be interpreted compositionally. The other type of productivity is morphological; formally, it distinguishes affixes and stems which have subcategorisation frames referring only to categories, from those mentioning specific morphemes or sets of morphemes.

Allowing for these two subtypes of 'productivity', (Baker and Harvey 2003) propose the following kinds of conjunctions between productivity and phonological patterns.

Root-level and unproductive
Word-level and unproductive
Word-level and productive
*Root-level and productive

In other words, all complex words involving ROOT-level relations are characterised by non-compositionality and/or arbitrary morphological restrictions on the range of roots and/or affixes. The model specifically excludes the possibility that productive morphology could display ROOT-level phonology.

3.8.1 The two-level theory applied to OT

The model proposed here has clear implications for phonological theory. One of the major concerns of phonological analyses couched in Lexical Phonology was to discover the 'level' or stratum to which morphophonological processes of affixation, reduplication, compounding and stress should be assigned, and the characteristics which unified processes at each level.

To some extent, this concern with the differences between morphological relations has disappeared from current phonology, couched in Optimality Theory analyses. The reason for this, as explained in the Introduction, is that OT (for the most part) is a single level theory: there is no passing of representations from one level to another to undergo further phonological operations. Furthermore, all phonological operations are evaluated in parallel: there is no serial derivation within the single level of the phonological component.

Some of the data which preoccupied Lexical Phonologists was reanalysed in an OT framework, by such authors as Kenstowicz (1995), Benua (1997), and Cohn and McCarthy (1998), using additional machinery such as 'Paradigm Uniformity', 'Output-Output Correspondence', and 'Local Constraint Conjunction', respectively. Chapter 4 examines Local Constraint Conjunction critically, while Output-Output Correspondence is discussed in Baker (2005).

Evidently there is a relationship between productivity and lexical strata, as implied by the comments of Borowsky, Kiparsky and Mohanan quoted above. I have proposed that there is direct relationship between productivity and lexical listing. Taken together, these proposals suggest that only the Level 2/3 morphological relations in English, i.e. those which are productive, are visible to phonological constraints in an OT grammar, if OT grammars have any psycholinguistic reality. While this is not the place to pursue such an analysis, it clearly deserves further attention. See Chapter 7 for further discussion.

To conclude, the distinction between WORD-level and ROOT-level morphological relations accounts for the phonological and morphological patterns found in complex words in Ngalakgan and, I predict, other languages, in a straightforward and elegant fashion. Models which treat all internal morphological relations as being of the same type cannot account for the same range of patterns without stipulation.

In the next chapter, I consider the prosodic characteristics of WORD-level affixes and bound stems. These provide evidence that a relationship between all WORD-level morphemes and prosodic structure is general to the language.

4

Affixation and prosodic domains

In the preceding chapter, I argued that WORD-level stems ('Morphological Words') correspond to a prosodic constituent 'Prosodic Word', which is the domain of pitch accent. I showed that some constituents—ROOT-level stems—which have unpredictable morphological selectional restrictions, do not correspond to Prosodic Words, and therefore do not have a one-to-one association with pitch accents.

Since most WORD-level stems (MWDs) are also free forms, it might be suggested that this accounts for their prosodic characteristics: compounded MWDs simply retain the stress that they have as words. This does not account for the behaviour of WORD-level bound morphemes (affixes and stems) however. These are also distinct prosodic domains: each affix or bound stem potentially takes its own stress (4.2). Since affixes cannot be free forms, it cannot be the case that they are retaining a stress pattern that they have as words. The behaviour of affixes suggests that speakers have access to WORD-level morphological structure, regardless of whether a morpheme is a free or bound form. I encode this pattern in a 'templatic' constraint which parses each WORD-level morpheme to metrical structure individually. This constraint—$\lambda \approx$ PRWD—is presented and discussed in 4.3. The analysis is straightforwardly extended to languages with similar patterns in 4.4.

Such templatic effects have been captured in OT with Alignment constraints: enforcements of the relationship between morphological and prosodic edges. I show in 4.4.2 that Alignment constraints cannot handle the patterns typical of Australian languages. Rather, we require a classic 'templatic' constraint to properly capture these patterns.

The replacement of templatic constraints by Generalised Alignment constraints in McCarthy and Prince (1993a) necessitated a range of 'extra-modular' machinery such as Local Constraint Conjunction (Hewitt and Crowhurst 1996; Moreton and Smolensky 2002), which have been proposed as repairs to the inherent problems of Alignment. I show in 4.4.2 that Alignment by itself cannot accomplish the same job as templatic constraints, and argue further that attempts to constrain Alignment, such as Constraint Conjunction, in fact add an undesirable degree of predictive power to the grammar.

Prefixes, suffixes, and bound stems all have distinct prosodic characteristics; these are summarised in Table (1). While suffixes behave as metrical domains, prefixes are generally stressless, and stems are necessarily associated with pitch accents. I show that these differences follow partly from position in the word, and partly from an association between pitch accents and semantically 'contentful' morphemes (in 4.5).

	Prefixes	Bound stems	Suffixes
Stressed	no	yes	yes
Pitch accented	no	yes	variable

Table 1: Prosodic characteristics of bound morphemes

The prosodic characteristics of prefixes are not the result of special stipulations about prefixes as a class, but follow from general considerations (cf. Selkirk 1995).

I start the chapter with a brief overview of the morphological characteristics of the distinct classes of bound WORD-level morphemes: suffixes, stems and prefixes.

4.1 The morphology of affixes and bound stems

Accounts of Gunwinyguan languages differ in the number and type of morphological classes recognised. Evans (2003) and Merlan (1983) recognise affixes (prefixes, suffixes), bound and free stems, and clitics. The items corresponding to Ngalakgan's Dative pronouns for instance are treated as free forms in BGW which optionally cliticise to nouns and verbs. McKay has a similar analysis for the forms in Rembarrnga, which are even more closely related to those of Ngalakgan. Merlan analyses these same forms in Ngalakgan as affixes. There is very little in the way of justification for these various treatments, or in discussion of morphological classes in general.

On the other hand, Heath (1984: 463), discussing Wubuy, notes that:

> There is no sharp distinction between verbal derivational affixes (especially prefixes like COMIT and MULT) on the one hand, and compound elements on

> the other. For example, the rule ... inserting Epenthetic morpheme /-ŋu-/ at morpheme boundaries (before a stop) treats derivational prefixes and [compound] initials alike (distinguishing them from pronominal prefixes).

I take this Wubuy behaviour to be indicative of a broader pattern. I propose that there are just three classes of morphemes in Gunwinyguan languages: affixes, free stems, and bound stems. The class of 'bound stems' encompasses elements which have been classified elsewhere as 'prefixes', 'clitics' and 'bound stems'. If we distinguish those bound elements which realise obligatory grammatical categories such as tense, agreement/argument indexing, case, and number, then the class of affixes is relatively small and coherent. The class of 'bound stems' is both larger and more diverse. We can also find criteria from prosodic behaviour, phonology, and morphological selectional properties which distinguish affixes on the one hand, from bound stems on the other; these are discussed in 4.1.1. Some bound stems behave as 'true' (phrasal) clitics (Zwicky 1985), in that they attach to words outside the last affix. Such forms are not distinguishable from bound stems except in this characteristic.

Examples of the WORD-level affix and bound stem inventory are provided below. Affixes are presented in (1)-(2), and some examples from the inventory of bound stems in (3)-(9).

WORD-level prefixes

(1) a. Inflectional argument prefixes (c. 70, a few examples given)

/ŋu-/	1st person minimal Subject[1]
/puru-/	3rd person augmented Subject
/ŋun-/	1st person minimal Object
/cun-/	2nd person minimal Subject/1st person minimal Object[2]

b. Noun Class

/ɳu-/	M (masculine/animate)	/ɳu-ku-/	M-TOP
/cu-/	F (feminine)	/cu-ku-/	F-TOP
/mu-/	VEG (vegetable)	/mun-ku-/	VEG-TOP
/ku-/	NEUT (neuter)	/kun-ku-/	NEUT-TOP

[1]The minimal/augmented distinction in all person categories except for the 1st person inclusive corresponds to the usual singular/plural distinction. It is the morphology of the 1st person inclusive category which prompted McKay (1975) to propose the minimal/augmented system for Rembarrnga. 1st person inclusive minimal behaves like a singular number, rather than a plural, e.g. it does not take the morpheme (really a recurrent partial) /-rV/ which is common to other augmented forms in agreement prefixes and other pronominal forms. Instead, the partial /-rV/ appears on the 1st inclusive augmented forms such as /-ŋkore/ (12aDAT), /ŋuru-/ (12aS) which both refer to 'we three or more inclusive'.

[2] Note that the convention '*x*/*y*' in glosses of argument prefixes denotes '*x* (subject) acting on *y* (object)'.

WORD-level suffixes

(2) a. Case

/-kkaʔ/ ~ /-kkakaʔ/	LOC/ALL
/-ʔkVn/	DAT/GEN
/-ʔwala/	ABL
/-jiʔ/	ERG/INST/COMIT
/-kkoʔ/	DYAD
/-wi/	PURP/LAT
/-cciʔ/	PRIV

b. Number

/-ppulu/	PL
/-ppiraʔ/	DUAL

c. Verbal suffixes

/-kVn/	REL/SUB
/-cciʔ/	Future Negative

The following two tables provide the full range of allomorphs found in the inflectional argument prefix paradigm (the full paradigm is presented in Merlan 1983). Just one category, 2nd person singular, has two allomorphs for subject functions, one for transitive subjects, and one for intransitive subjects.

	subject allomorphs	object allomorphs
1min	ŋu-	ŋun-
12min	ji-	jin-
2min	cu- (Erg) ŋiɲ- (Nom)	nun-
1aug	jir-	jiriɳ-
12aug	ŋur-	ŋuruɳ-
2aug	nu-	nuɳ-
3aug	pur-	puruɳ- ~ pun- ~ pu-
3min	ø-	ø-
VEG	ø- ~ mu-	ø- ~ mu-
NEUT	ø- ~ ku-	ø- ~ ku-

Table 2: Argument prefixes: third person paradigm allomorphs (combinations of SAP with 3rd person arguments)

		Object			
		2aug	2min	1aug	1min
Subject	2aug			jini-	jini-
	2min			jini-	cun-
	1aug	jiriị-	jiri-		
	1min	ɳuku-	ŋiɲ-		

Table 3: Person marking prefixes: SAP → SAP

It can be seen that the class of WORD-level affixes is quite well-defined: it consists of a small class of case and number suffixes on the one hand, and noun class and argument-indexing prefixes on the other. The Relative/Subordinating suffix /-kVn/ which occurs on verbs is formally distinct from the DAT/GEN suffix on nouns, but historically related (see Chapter 6), and indeed, other case-marking suffixes are occasionally observed on inflected verbs (see 3.5).

Chapter 3 has already introduced the notion of 'bound stem' as opposed to affix. The class of bound stems is both larger and more diverse than that of affixes, it is also apparently open to some degree, at least historically. I distinguish 'left-binding' stems (3)-(5), which find a host to the left, from 'right-binding' stems (6)-(9), which find one to the right. Right-binding stems are referred to as 'prefixes' in descriptions of other GN languages, e.g. Evans (2003), Merlan (1983), Heath (1978b, 1984), presumably because of the right-binding characteristic. However, as Heath notes above, there are no clear criteria for distinguishing these forms from lexical stems, and indeed, there are phonological processes which class them together. The same is true of Ngalakgan; in particular, both free and bound stems require pitch accents (4.5.4), and both exhibit apical alternation (3.7).

In the examples, WORD-level left-binding stems and clitics are preceded by an '=' boundary, while suffixes, prefixes and right-binding stems are preceded/followed by a '-' boundary.

Left-binding stems

(3) Dative pronouns

/=ŋini/	1st person minimal
/=jikki/	1st person inclusive minimal
/=ŋki/	2nd person minimal
/=ɳowi/	3rd person minimal, nonfeminine
/=ŋoci/	3rd person minimal, feminine
/=jere/	1st person exclusive augmented
/=ŋkore/	1st person inclusive augmented
/=ɳuŋkore/	2nd person augmented
/=pore/	3rd person augmented, human

(4) Other modifying stems (>10)

/=palukkun/	Source
/=pinti/	'real'
/=poŋʔ/	Avoidance (used in referring to avoidance relatives; Merlan 1983: 70)
/=kappul/	Collective
/=pukiʔ/	'only; just'

(5) Bound verb stems

/+me/	'get.PP'
/+po/	'hit.PP'
/+wo/	'give.PP'

Right-binding stems (>20)

(6) Quantifiers

/wac-/	(DU) 'a pair'
/kara- ~ karakkara-/	(COLL-UNIT) 'together; whole lot'
/man-/	(COLL-DIST) 'everybody (separately)'
/mala-/	(COLL) 'together; group'
/weleŋ-/	'together'
/koreʔ-/	'alone'

(7) Syntactic applicatives

/paʈʈa-/	COM/APPL
/ɻej-/	APPL
/pak-/	APPL

(8) Modal/affective

/caʔ-/	'now'
/waɳa-/	'continuously'
/meleʔ-/	'lest'
/piʈic-/	'nearly'
/ɳamulu-/	'really, properly'
/waɲʔ-/	'should not'
/waɳa-/	'wanted to'
/wiɭi- ~ ɭi-/	'poor thing'

Bound nominal stems

(9) /piɲi-/, /mili-/	'water; liquid' (suppletive for /weʔ/)[3]
/pala-/	'side'
/kuʔ-/	'raw; dead'
/kerɲe-/	'body; alive'

4.1.1 Distinguishing bound stems and affixes

Ngalakgan possesses a large number of bound or semi-bound morphemes. Many of these are derived ultimately from independent stems, and are in

[3] Interestingly, in BGW, 'water' is likewise the only word to have a suppletive incorporating stem, though neither form is related to Ngalakgan—BGW has free /kukku/ vs bound /po/. The latter is presumably related to Ngalakgan /po/ 'river', Rembarrnga /puwa/. In Wubuy, the class of suppletive bound nominal stems is rather bigger (see Heath 1984: 465), but it also includes 'water'—the bound form is /aɻ/, the free form /kuuku/.

various stages of losing their ability to appear independently. Left- and right-binding stems are synchronically at the border between stem and affix-like behaviour. In the vast majority of cases, what I class as 'bound stems' are realised as bound elements to some other stem. In just a few examples they occur independently as words themselves, revealing that this process of grammaticalisation is not entirely complete. True affixes, by contrast, never occur independently. There are certain other differences between bound stems on the one hand, and inflectional affixes on the other. On the whole, where the characteristics of inflectional affixes and bound stems differ, bound stems approach more closely the characteristics of words. These differences are set out in Table (4):

Bound stems	Affixes
Optional modifiers	Obligatory grammatical categories
Prosodically freer	Prosodically bound
Not subject to allomorphy	Subject to allomorphy
Unrestricted phonotactics	Restricted phonotactics
Necessarily pitch accented	Not necessarily pitch accented

Table 4: Bound stems vs affixes

The prosodic differences between bound stems and affixes are discussed in 4.2. I will briefly discuss the other differences here.

Grammatical functions

Most bound stems, such as /pit̪ic-/ 'nearly', /mala-/ 'group', can be characterised as optional modifiers with adverbial or modal meanings. With a few exceptions, they do not in general realise obligatory grammatical categories in the clause: agreement, case, and tense. The main exception is the class of Dative pronouns, such as /=ŋkore/ 'ours', which are the most commonly occurring left-bound stems. These perform functions similar to those of inflectional person prefixes. Compare (10)a-b. The Dative pronoun /=ŋkore/ in (a) realises three morphosyntactic categories: person (1st inclusive; contrast /=ɳuŋkore/ 2nd person augmented), number (augmented; contrast /=jikki/ 1st inclusive minimal), and case (Dative). The pronominal prefix /ŋuruɳ-/ in (b) realises the same three morphosyntactic categories: (1st inclusive; contrast /ɳuɳ-/ 2nd person augmented object), number (minimal; contrast /jin-/: 1st inclusive minimal object), and case (Object; contrast /ŋuru-/: 12aug. Subject). The selection of the prefix over the Dative pronoun is a matter of syntactic subcategorisation: prefixes saturate (or agree with) argument positions, Dative pronouns project nonsubcategorised adjuncts.[4]

(10) a. /ɳu-ɳe=**ŋkore**/
2aS-cook.PR-12aDAT
'You mob cook **for us**!'

b. /**ŋuruɳ**-pu-woʔ+wo/
12aO-3a-RED+give.PP
'They gave [it] **to us**.'

There are some right-binding stems which function as part of the tense/aspect/modality system in complex verbs, these stems are listed here:

(11) /caʔ-/ 'now, just, IMMED'
/meleʔ-/ 'lest, EVIT'
/waɲʔ-/ 'should not, NEG.OBL'
/waɳa-/ 'wanted to, should, POT'

Notably, none of these stems is obligatory in signalling these functions however, with the possible exception of /meleʔ-/. All of them exist as optional, additional markers of the mood or aspect concerned, which otherwise is marked overtly or as an implicature in the verb suffixing system (see Merlan 1983: 108 for details).

Also, three bound stems have applicative functions:

(12) /paʈʈa-/ COM/APPL
/ɻej-/ APPL[5]
/pak-/ APPL

The functions and realisations of these stems are discussed more fully in 4.5.4.

Prosodic freedom

Many bound stems can occur independently as words, or have historically related independent forms. The extent to which an otherwise bound stem

---

[4] Hence, /pur-woʔwo=ŋkore/ 3a-give.PP=12ADAT is not a possible realisation of the meaning of (10)b. Extension of dative pronominals from nominal to verbal words seems to be a common development in many languages; e.g. Gooniyandi (McGregor 1990: 224).

[5] Here I differ from Merlan (1983) who represents this morpheme as /ɻe-/. The phonetic realisation of this form is [ɻeɪ], with a long syllable, and it is always pitch-accented. It differs from the otherwise similar bound stem /caʔ/ ~ /ceʔ/ ~ /ce/ 'now; IMMED' which is realised as a short syllable, and is rarely pitch accented. With mid-vowel vocalism, this stem is realised as [ɟɛ], with a lax vowel, unlike /ɻeɪ/, which always has a tense vowel. The latter also sounds distinct from monosyllabic open stems such as /ke/ '(man's) son', /ce/ 'nose' which do not have a perceptible high off-glide, but are rather [gɛː], [ɟɛː], with the vowel varying somewhat in tenseness. /ɻej-/ sounds like /ŋej/ 'name', rather than /ce/ 'nose'. The related stem is /ɻi-/ in Ngandi, where is similarly behaves as a bimoraic foot, also /ɻe-/ in Rembarrnga and /ɻe-/ ~ /je-/ in BGW.

can occur independently varies a great deal in the data, from rare once-off attestations, to common occurrences. Given the difficulty of eliciting these distinctions, and the limitations of the database, this will remain an unexplored area of Ngalakgan morphology. However, closely related languages such as Rembarrnga, BGW, and Wubuy evince similar behaviour, and further investigation may reveal something of the motivations behind this variation.

There is one attestation of a Dative pronominal bound stem occurring independently in my data. In example (6), the Dative pronoun /=ŋkore/ ~ /=kore/ 'for us' is realised as a word under contrastive intonation.

(13) [ŋumiɟa̱kɔ̀rickɔ́re][6] [gɔ́re ŋumugɔ́ric]
/ŋu-mu-caʔ-koric=ŋkore, ***ŋkore*** ŋu-mu-koric/
1mS-VEG-now-grind.PR-12aDAT 12aDAT 1mS-VEG-grind.PR
'I'm grinding it now for us, I'm grinding it *for us*.' [2/7/96: 1B]

Since only words can be associated with contrastive intonation, example (13) indicates that Dative bound stems are regarded as marginal words by speakers. Inflectional prefixes and suffixes are not attested as independent words in my data.[7]

McKay (1975: 110) cites similar examples in Rembarrnga of Dative pronouns used as free forms. He summarises the situation in Rembarrnga thus: 'The status of the DAT PRON as a surface morpheme is somewhat ambiguous in that it appears to be treated as a suffix in some situations and as a free form in others' (1975: 108). The Rembarrnga forms are virtually identical to those of Ngalakgan, allowing for regular vowel and consonant correspondences. One example is reproduced here (in surface phonemic form):

(14) /poṯi miccintaʔ **kə-ni**/
spear long.ago 2mDAT-STAT.PP
'That spear was yours before.'

In this example, the Dative pronoun is inflected with the stative auxiliary (derived from /na+/ 'to sit'). The stative auxiliary derives stative predicates

[6] The realisation of class VEG prefix, underlying /mu-/, as [mi] here is due to the following laminal. Fronting of the high back vowel before laminals is regular, particularly in prefixes, but only in unmonitored speech.

[7] Merlan (1983: 26) cites a counterexample: /cu-ku-piraʔ-jiʔ/ 'they two (FEM, ERG)', where the dual suffix /-piraʔ/ acts as nominal head to the prefix /cu-ku-/ (F-TOP) and case suffix /-jiʔ/ (ERG). Merlan does not cite the full sentence in which this form appeared, so it is difficult to draw any conclusions from it.

from nominal stems. Therefore, the Dative pronoun is behaving like a stem in this example.

While Ngalakgan and Rembarrnga are similar in many respects, including the respective order of bound elements in nominal forms (15), they differ in the extent to which Dative pronouns can be stems (McKay n.d.). In Rembarrnga, Dative pronouns can be inflected as predicates, as in (14) above. This is impossible in Ngalakgan. Rather, predication of possession is realised through the cardinal pronouns (Merlan 1983: 62), as in (16).

(15) /takku-ŋənə-ppara?-ji?-ma/
nephew-1mDAT-DU-ERG-*ma*
'my two nephews' [Rembarrnga: McKay, ex. 7-13]

(16) /ɳu-kun?piri puluki jirkkaɳi?-kin/
M-that cow 1aDAT-GEN
'That cow is ours.' [Ngalakgan: M: 3-150]

This indicates that Dative pronouns in Rembarrnga are more independent than they are in Ngalakgan.

In both Ngalakgan and Rembarrnga I regard the underlying form of the 2nd minimal (and in Ngalakgan, also the 1st inclusive augmented) Dative pronoun as beginning in a nasal+stop cluster /ŋk/. The alternative (e.g. McKay 1975: 108) is to regard the initial nasal as an epenthetic segment. The reasons for including the nasal in underlying representation are twofold. Firstly, the 1st inclusive augmented form /=ŋkore/ in Ngalakgan also begins with a nasal+stop cluster. This is cognate with the Rembarrnga form /=ŋakorə/ (same meaning) and Dalabon /=ŋokorŋ/ (where the final /ŋ/ is an extrinsic element appearing on several Dative pronouns in Dalabon). In both cases, the initial nasal reflects the corresponding verb agreement prefix (Ngkn /ŋur(u)-/, Rmba /ŋar(a)-/), and independent emphatic pronoun forms (Ngkn /ŋurkkaɳi?/, Rmba /ŋakurkaɳə?/, where the element /+kaɳi?/, /+kaɳə?/ is common to emphatic pronouns in both languages).[8] Hence, the nasal has a historical basis, at least in the 1st inclusive augmented forms. The same is probably true of the 2nd minimal Dative pronoun, since the intransitive prefix in both languages is /ŋiɲ-/, and the emphatic pronouns are /ŋiɲcaɳi?/ (Ngkn) and /ŋiɲkaɳə?/ (Rmba). Secondly, it is not the case that every stop-initial Dative pronoun has an allomorph with initial homorganic

[8] It appears the Ngalakgan independent form is (re-)modelled on the basis of the argument prefix, while the Rembarrnga form is more similar to the Dative pronoun (see Harvey 2003 for discussion). Other independent pronouns in both languages in general retain the characteristics of the older, pan-Australian set (for instance the first person pronoun /ŋajkka?/ appears to be a relic of the proto-Australian first person pronoun form */ŋaj/ reconstructed by Dixon (2002: 284).

nasal. The 3rd augmented Dative pronoun is /=pore/ in Ngalakgan and /=parə/ in Rembarrnga. In neither language do we find an allomorph /=mpore/, /=mparə/. Hence, the epenthesis rule would still need to be specified to apply only to the 2mDAT pronoun in Rembarrnga, and the 2mDAT and 12aDAT in Ngalakgan. In Ngalakgan, it would be the only such epenthesis rule in the language. Such a stipulatory rule seems unwarranted. By contrast, the deletion of the nasal following [–continuant] segments follows from the general phonotactic patterns of the language, discussed in 2.3.2.

Several other right-binding stems are attested as independent words (17), (18). As independent words, they have their own primary stress. These examples show that, like left-bound stems, right-bound stems have word-like properties.[9]

Prefix

(17) /ku-caʔ-**ɳamulu**-ɻu+ŋa/
NP-now-really-burn+FUT
'[It] will really get cooking now.' [27/6/96: 1B]

Independent word

(18) /macci Ø-poʈewk-me+n **ɳamulu** ku-Ø-ɻapon-ci/
indeed 3m-bad-be+PR really NP-3m-go+PR-NEG
'Because he's sick and he really can't get around.' [31/5/96: 1B]

Prefix

(19) /puru-**mala**-maŋi+cci+niɲ/[10]
3aS-COLL-get+RR+PC
'They gathered, collected themselves.' [M: 3-106]

Independent word

(20) /**mala** jiri-ɳaŋa+n/
group 1aS-sit+PR
'We sit *as a group*.' [3/9/97: 1A]

Some right-bound stems can be realised as constituents of compound words (21), cf. (19), or reduplicated words (23). In (21), the right-binding stem /mala-/ 'group' is attached to a left-binding stem /-poɳo/ 'another', which is itself obligatorily bound. In (22), a right-binding stem /koreʔ-/ 'alone' modifies a predicate word-internally, while in (23) it is reduplicated

[9]One prefix has a historically-related independent form: /waɲʔ-/ 'should not, ought not' (bound stem) cf. /waɲba/ 'id.' (word).

[10]This PC form of the Reflexive-Reciprocal is anomalous. The usual form is /+ccini/.

to modify a predicate as an external adverb. This stem has also been attested itself as a predicate, in (24).

Compound

(21) /kuɳmaɳʔ **mala-poɳo** puru-koɻ-miɲ, puru-joŋon+iɲ/
maybe group-another 3aS-sick-AUX.PP 3aS-lie+PC
'Maybe some people were lying there sick.' [5/9/97: 1B]

Prefix

(22) /macci ɲiɲ-**koreʔ**-ɳaŋa-ɳaŋa+n/
indeed 2mS-alone-ITER-sit+PR
'Really you're too much alone/by yourself.' [M: 3-285]

Reduplicated word

(23) /**koreʔ-koreʔ** puru-man-ɳaŋa+n/
INTENS-alone 3aS-group-sit+PR
mijelb-mijelb[11]
'Every group sits by itself.' [3/9/97: 1A]

Predicate

(24) /mokkol-koʔ **koreʔ**=pore-ppiraʔ/
father-DYAD alone-3aDAT-DU
dubela mijelb [3/7/96]
'Father and son are alone, the two of them.' [Lit.: 'Aloneness is to the pair of them.'][12]

There are several instances of right-binding stems taking an unreduplicated stem form of a finite verb (25); the examples in (26) are from Merlan (1983).

(25) /mako! ŋiɲ-***caʔ*-wo** cacapaɻɲʔ!/
no![13] 1mS/2mO-IMMED-give.PP yesterday
No, ai bin ***gibit*** *yu yesdi*
'No! I just *gave* it to you yesterday!' [2/9/97: 1B]

(26) a. /ŋun-**paʈʈa-me** mu-wappawappaʔ ŋonto-jiʔ/
1mO-APPL-get.PP VEG-clothing wind-ERG
'The wind took the dress from me.' [M: 3-65]

[11] Kriol *mijelb* is a general reflexive or contrastive pronoun, unspecified as to person.

[12] The predicate /koreʔ/ 'alone' takes an existential argument here.

[13] The interjection /mako/ negates a preceding assertion, hence the gloss.

b. /jiriɳ-**caʔ-wo** ɳu-ku-poloʔ-jiʔ/
1aO-now-give.PP M-TOP-boss-ERG
'Now the boss gave it to us.' [M: 3-291]

These examples are significant because the unreduplicated PP form of these verbs can only otherwise occur in a compound as noted in 3.3.4; see further 4.5.4. Therefore, bound stems can occur in the kinds of morphological structures that are otherwise restricted to free stems—compound and reduplicated words—indicating that they have relatively greater prosodic freedom than affixes, which are never attested in such structures.

Affix allomorphy
The majority of affixes have two allomorphs. Allomorphy is not observed consistently in bound stems, and in this respect bound stems are again similar to free stems, which likewise do not exhibit allomorphic variation.

All stop-initial WORD-level suffixes alternate between geminate and singleton realisations of the initial consonant, but no bound stems do so. The geminate/singleton alternation is predictable. Chapter 6 argues that the stop is underlyingly geminate in these suffixes; it is realised as a singleton in satisfaction of constraints on the form of words. In this respect, bound stems are more like free stems than affixes. WORD-level stems are not realised with initial geminates (see 6.3.4).

Two related WORD-level suffixes exhibit vowel harmony with the preceding stem. The Dative/Genitive suffix /-ʔkVn/ (27)a-b and the Relativising suffix on verbs /-kVn/ (27)c, are both realised with a copy of the vowel of the preceding syllable.

(27) a. /caŋku-ʔkVn/ [ɟaŋgu̯kʊn]
meat-DAT 'for meat'
b. /mu-maj-ʔkVn/ [mumaɪ̯kan]
VEG-food-DAT 'for vegetable food'[14]
c. /ŋun-pu-mecce ʈaɭwaɳi-kkaʔ ŋu-**ɳaŋan-kan**/,
1mO-3a-nurse.PR ceremony.ground-LOC 1m-sit.PR-REL
/macci ŋajkkaʔ ŋu-miŋiriŋki/
because 1min 1m-[ceremonial.role]
'They 'nurse' me when I'm at the *Darlwarni* place, because it's me who's the *Mingirringgi* ...'

[14] Examples such as this one constitute evidence that sequences of vowel+glide in Ngalakgan are treated as nucleus+coda sequences, rather than as complex nuclei. If the nucleus was treated as a diphthong, we might expect a surface form *[mumai̯kin] from underlying form */mu-mai-ʔkVn/.

/pur-mu-**ne?ne-ken** mun-ku-maj/
3a-VEG-cook-PR-REL VEG-TOP-food
/pur-mu-**ler?ler?-ken** kun-ku-ŋoj/
3a-VEG-DIST-set.alight-PR-REL NEUT-TOP-fire
'when they cook the food and light the fires ...'
/jir-ma?ma nu-ku-raj jiri-**ɹapun-kun**/[15]
1aS-get.PR M-TOP-meat 1a-go.PR-REL
'we get meat when we go [there] ...'
/ɳu-ku-wur?wuruɳu puru-ɹapo-**ɹaponiɲ-kin**/
M-TOP-old.people 3a-DIST-go.PC-REL
'when the old people go.' [9/9/97: 1A]

Inflectional prefixes with underlying high back vowel /u/, e.g. /pu-/ '3rd person augmented', have two allomorphs. In one allomorph underlying /u/ corresponds to surface [u], in the other allomorph underlying /u/ corresponds to surface [i]. For example the 3rd person augmented, 2nd position prefix has allomorphs /-pu-/ and /-pi-/. Following prefixes with /i/, the prefix is realised as /pi-/ (Merlan 1983: 85), as shown in (28)b. The elsewhere form is /-pu-/, shown in (28)a; I assume this is the underlying form also.[16]

(28) a. /ŋun-**pu**-wo?wo/
1mO-3a-RED+give.PP
'They gave [it] to me'

b. /jin-**pi**-wo?wo/
12mO-3a-RED+give.PP
'They gave [it] to us'

No bound stems are attested with either of these vowel harmony patterns, nor are any WORD-level free stems. If allomorphy is a characteristic of affixes, bound stems are not affixes.

Distribution of mid-vowels
Mid-vowels have a restricted distribution in the lexicon of Ngalakgan. While high and low vowels are relatively unrestricted, mid-vowels in roots are almost without exception restricted to peripheral syllables, or, if medial, must be distributed in every syllable from an edge. For example, mid-vowels, if occurring in just one syllable, must occur in an edgemost syllable ((29); these are the only examples):

---

[15] The standard realisation of the Present form of the 'go' verb is [ɹabɔn], but a raised realisation [ɹabʊn], as here, was very common among all my informants.
[16] It is not possible to show this definitively since all inflectional prefixes in Ngalakgan have high vowels /i/ or /u/. Comparison with Rembarrnga and other NPN languages suggests that /pu/ is the historically original form (Harvey 2003).

(29) a. /cera**ʈ**a/ 'women's ceremony'
b. /wiriј**e**l/ 'aquatic weed sp.'
c. /w**o**lawaj/ 'cool off'
d. /curuw**e**+/ 'rush'

If occurring in more than one syllable, mid-vowels must occur in contiguous syllables, and in every syllable from a medial position to at least one edgemost syllable (30). If occurring in both edgemost syllables, then every syllable in the root must be a mid-vowel (31):

(30) a. /caw**oro**/ 'patrilineal clan'
b. /malaʈ**o**ʈ**o**/ 'baby bush turkey'

(31) a. /c**ɛ̀**nt**ɛ**w**ɛ́**r**ɛ**c/[17] 'Willywagtail [bird sp.]'
b. /k**o**w**e**l**e**ŋʔ/ 'beckon to'

Therefore, mid-vowels in roots must be 'edge-linked'.[18] Many bound stems have mid-vowels. Six of the nine Dative pronouns have at least one mid-vowel. Other bound stems also have mid-vowels: /=poŋʔ/ AVOID, /caʔ-/ ~ /ce-/ 'now', /meleʔ-/ 'lest', /koreʔ-/ 'alone', /weleŋ-/ 'together', /ɻej-/ 'APPL'. Most WORD-level affixes contrast just the three vowels /a, i, u/. Only one suffix has a mid-vowel: the Dyadic suffix /-kkoʔ/.[19] Therefore, in affixed words, mid-vowels occur on the whole just in roots and bound stems.

Apical distinctions

Chapter 2 discussed the distribution of apical distinctions in words (2.4), and 3.7 shows that the distribution is sensitive to WORD and ROOT level constituency. Apical distinctions are neutralised in ROOTs and WORDs in initial position, with the elsewhere realisation being postalveolar. Bound stems behave like free stems with respect to apical distinctions: they too show neutralisation of apicals to postalveolar in initial position. By contrast, initial apicals in ROOT-suffixes are all apico-alveolar: there are no postalveolar apicals in this position. As for WORD-suffixes, there are no apical-initial forms at all in this class, making WORD-suffixes quite distinct from free and bound stems.

---

17 This word has several variants. Others I have heard are [cɛ̀ntɛwíric] and [cɪ̀ntiwíric]. All variants conform to the distributional restriction on mid-vowels.

18 There is one apparent exception: an onomatopoeic term for 'curlew' /kuweɭuʔ/. I discount this as a counterexample on the grounds that onomatopoeic terms frequently violate surface-true lexical patterns.

19 It is not entirely clear what the morphological status of /-kkoʔ/ is, since it is not attested in combination with any other affixes. However, it does exhibit geminate alternation, suggesting that it is a WORD-level suffix; see Chapter 6.

Summary

To summarise then, bound stems on the whole are more 'word-like' than inflectional affixes. One further difference between bound stems and affixes is in terms of their respective relationships to pitch accents. This difference is described in the section which follows.

4.2 Prosodic characteristics of affixes and bound stems

This section exemplifies and discusses the prosodic characteristics of suffixes and bound stems. In 4.3, I claim that, like MWDs, WORD-level suffixes and bound stems also constitute morphoprosodic domains, and that this is a characteristic of Ngalakgan generally, accounting for a range of patterns in the language. A similar generalisation can be made for other Australian languages such as Warlpiri (Nash 1986) and Diyari (Austin 1981). The stress patterns of these languages can be accounted for in the same way that I account for Ngalakgan.

4.2.1 General patterns: disyllabic suffixes and bound stems

Every disyllabic suffix and bound stem in Ngalakgan is an independent foot. I propose therefore that every suffix and bound stem constitutes a separate domain for metrical structure. The examples in (32) exemplify the pattern.[20]

(32)	a.	/(jappanʔ)(**-ppiraʔ**)/	[jàppan̰ʔbíɾa̰]
		two-DU	'two (people/animates)'
	b.	/puru-(wulup)+pa(**-ppiraʔ**)/	[bʊɾuwʊ̀lʊppabíɾa̰]
		3aS-swim+FUT-DU	'those two will go swimming'
	c.	/jiri-(ɻapo)+na(**-ppiraʔ**)/	[jiɾiɻábonappìɾa̰]
		1aS-go+FUT-DU	'we'll go, the two of us'
	d.	/puru-(ɳaŋa-)(ɳaŋa)+na(**-ppiraʔ**)/	[bʊɾuɳàŋaɳáŋanappìɾa̰]
		3aS-ITER-sit+FUT-DU	'those two want to sit around'
	e.	/ɳu-(mokkol)(=**ŋini**)(**-ppiraʔ**)/	[numɔ̀kkɔlŋ̀ɪnɪppíɾa̰]
		M-father-1mDAT-DU	'my two fathers'
	f.	/ɳu-(mokkol)(=**jere**)-kkaʔ/	[numɔ̀kkɔljɛ́ɾɛkka̰]
		M-father-1aDAT-DU	'to our father'

[20]The underlying forms in slashes include material which is not present in the surface form in some cases. Suffix-initial geminates are realised as singletons because of constraints on geminates in tonal domains, discussed in Chapter 6. Other differences are due to cluster simplification (2.3.2) and vowel assimilation.

g. /(cu-ja)(ppa=ŋki)(-**ppulu**)/ [ɟìjappàŋgɪppʊ́lu][21]
F-sister-2mDAT-PL 'your sisters'

h. /(ce)(=**ŋkore**)-kkaʔ/ [ɟèːŋgɔ́rɛkka̰]
nose=12aDAT-LOC 'in our noses'

i. /(ce)(=**ɳowi**)/ [ɟèːɳówi]
nose=3nfemDAT 'his nose'

j. /(ke)(=**ŋini**)/ [gèːŋíni]
child=1mDAT 'my child'

While suffixes and bound stems behave alike in terms of foot structure, they differ in terms of association with pitch accent. Words containing stressed bound stems behave like compounds: stressed bound stems are always associated with a pitch accent. In a form such as (33)a, only the realisation in (a)—with penultimate primary stress—is possible. Words containing stressed suffixes behave like quadrisyllabic roots: there is variation between primary stress on the stem and primary stress on the suffix. In a suffixed form like (33)c either of the prosodic realisations in (33)c-d is possible (pitch accents indicated with 'T').

(33) a. T T
[ɟijàppaŋíni]
/cu-(jappa)(=**ŋini**)/
F-sister-1mDAT

c. T T
[ɟijàppabʊ́lu]
/cu-(jappa)(-**ppulu**)/
F-sister-PL

b. T
*[ɟijáppaŋìni]

d. T
[ɟijáppabʊ̀lu]

Suffixed forms, then, can be parsed either as a single PRWD, or two PRWDs—a prosodic compound.

(34) a. cu-[(jàppa)]$_{PRWD}$[(-púlu)]$_{PRWD}$ '(my) sisters'
F-sister-PL

b. cu-[(jáppa-)(pùlu)]$_{PRWD}$ '(my) sisters'
F-sister-PL

---

21 The [u] ~ [i] alternation in the phonetic form here is due to assimilation to the laminal root-initial segment. Forms like these show stress shift onto every alternate syllable preceding the primary as a variant of the usual, morpheme-determined stress pattern. Note that such variants violate MWD ≈ PRWD. In this case, stress shift is encouraged by the form of the stem /jappa/, with initial glide and following geminate. Trisyllabic roots with this form tend to have penultimate stress: /wukkáɻa/ 'frog sp.'; /jippúɲca/ 'a long time ago'; /jukkáciʔ/ 'for a long time'; /akkáʈaʔ/ 'late (tardy)'. See 5.6.

A form containing a bound stem, if the latter is stressed, can only be parsed as a prosodic compound:

(35) a. cu-[(jàppa)]$_{\text{PRWD}}$[(=ɲíni)]$_{\text{PRWD}}$ 'my sister'
F-sister-1mDAT

Other bound stems, such as the Collective /=kappul/, behave in the same way as the Dative bound stems. The behaviour of bound stems with respect to pitch accent is analysed formally in 4.3.

4.2.2 Monosyllabic suffixes and bound stems

Monosyllabic suffixes and bound stems are ignored for footing (36) unless they can be footed with an adjacent morpheme (which will not be a disyllabic suffix) (37).

(36) a. /(ʈotojʔ)=**ŋki**/ [dɔ́dɔɪ̰gi]
uncle-2mDAT 'your "uncle"'
b. /(jappa)-**kkoʔ**/ [jáppago̰]
sister-DYAD 'two sisters; sister and brother'
c. /(ʈotojʔ)=**ŋki**(-ppulu)/ [dɔ̀dɔɪ̰gɪppʊ́lu]
uncle-2mDAT-COLL 'all your "uncle"-mob'
d. /(ʈotojʔ)=**ŋki**(-ppulu)(-**kkaʔ**/ [dɔ̀dɔɪ̰gɪppʊ́lʊkka̰]
uncle-2mDAT-COLL-LOC 'at/to all your "uncle"-mob'
e. /(mokkol)(=ŋini)-**kkaʔ**/ [mɔ̀kkɔlŋínɪkka̰]
father-1mDAT-LOC 'to my father'

(37) a. /(ʈotojʔ)(-**ŋki-kkaʔ**)/ [dɔ̀dɔɪ̰gíkka̰]
uncle-2mDAT-LOC 'at/to your "uncle"'
b. /ɳu-(puj)ppu(=**ŋki-kkaʔ**)/ [nubʊ̀ɪppʊŋgíkka̰]
M-brother-2mDAT-LOC 'to your elder brother'
c. /ɳu-(kakka)(=**ŋki-kkaʔ**)/ [nugàkkaŋgíkka̰]
M-brother-2mDAT-LOC 'to your younger brother'
d. /cu-(jappa)(=**ŋki-kkaʔ**)/ [ɟijàppaŋgíkka̰]
F-sister-2mDAT-LOC 'to your sister'
e. /ku-(puŋ)(=**ŋki-jiʔ**)/ [gubʊ̀ŋgíḭ]
NEUT-knee-2mDAT-ERG 'with your knees'
f. /cu-(jappa)(=**ŋki-ʔkVn**)/ [ɟijàppaŋgḭkɪn]
F-sister-2mDAT-DAT 'for your sister'

Although there are a number of monosyllabic suffixes, there is only one monosyllabic Dative pronoun: /=ŋki/ '2minDAT'. Suffixes include those marking case: /-kkaʔ/ LOC, /-ʔkVn/ DAT, /-jiʔ/ ERG/INST, /-wi/ LAT/PURP; and a derivational suffix /-cci/ PRIV. The only sequence of monosyllabic suffixes or bound stems attested is that where the bound stem /=ŋki/ '1mDAT' is followed by a case suffix. Case suffixes do not co-occur, and there are no attested examples of more than two consecutive monosyllabic suffixes or bound stems; it is doubtful that there are any acceptable combinations.

Monosyllabic suffixes can also be incorporated into a foot with the last syllable of a trisyllabic root (38)a-b below. In this case, however, stress (or pitch accent) assignment is somewhat sporadic, varying with unstressed forms such as (39)a-b:

(38)	a.	[ɟáwaɳɖàŋgi]	'your beard'	
		/(cawa)(**ɳʈa=ŋki**)/	whiskers-2mDAT	[22/5/98]
	b.	[gáppuʄìʄi]	'no old people'	
		/(kappu)(**ci-cci**)/	old.people-PRIV	

(39)	a.	[ɟáwaɳɖaŋgi]	'your beard'	
		/(cawa)ɳʈa=ŋki/	whiskers-2mDAT	[22/5/98]
	b.	[gáppuʄiʄi]	'no old people'	
		/(kappu)ci-cci/	old.people-PRIV	

There is just one left-binding form which is longer than two syllables: /=ɳuŋkore/ '2aDAT'. On the one occasion it was recorded, this form varied between initial and second syllable stress, depending on what followed:

(40)	a.	/ɳu-(ke)=(**ɳuŋko**)**re**/	[nugèːɳʊ́ŋgore]
		M-son-2aDAT	'your son'
	b.	/ɳu-(mokkol)=**ɳu**(**ŋkore**)-kkaʔ/	[numɔ̀kkɔlnʊŋgɔ́rɛkka̰]
		M-father-2aDAT-LOC	'to your father'

It is important to note that the metrical structure of suffixes and bound stems is not dependent on their meaning. Unlike suffixes and bound stems, MWDs are always associated with a pitch accent regardless of their size. For MWDs, we might make a case that this prosodic consistency is due to their inherent semantic *content*: they are associated with major categorial signatures in the lexicon, as proposed in Chapter 3.

But whether or not a suffix or bound stem constitutes a foot is not a function of its meaning. For instance, the Ablative case suffix /-ʔwala/ and the Locative /-kkaʔ/ are both local cases, yet the first is consistently associated with a foot (41)a, while the second only becomes part of a foot contingently (41)b. The same is true of the Dative bound stems /=ŋini/ '1mDAT' and /=ŋki/ '2mDAT'. The first is always a foot (42)a, the second only contingently so (42)b:

(41)	a.	[jɛ̀lɛ̰wála] /(jele-ʔ)(**wala**)/ hole-ABL	b.	[jɛ́lɛkka̰] /(jele)-**kkaʔ**/ hole-LOC
(42)	a.	[numɔ̀kkɔlŋíni] /ɳu-(mokkol)=(**ŋini**)/ M-father-mine	b.	[numɔ́kkɔlŋgi] /ɳu-(mokkol)=**ŋki** M-father-yours

The metrical structure of suffixes *is* dependent on their inherent characteristics, but of *size*, rather than semantics, whereas the reverse is true of MWDs, as I now show.

4.3 Morphemes as prosodic domains

It is possible to sum up the preceding examples with the following generalisation (and cf. Nash 1986: 100):

(43) Polysyllabic WORD-level suffixes and bound stems are *inherently* footable, but the footing of monosyllabic suffixes and bound stems is *contingent* on their surrounding environment.

By 'inherently' here I mean, not 'lexically', but 'consistently'. Polysyllabic suffixes and bound stems are always footed. In essence, it appears that polysyllabic suffixes and bound stems are footed because of their inherent size, regardless of their position in the word.

The stress patterns in (32)-(37) above seem to be widely attested among Australian languages. Similar patterns have been described for Warlpiri (Nash 1986) and Diyari (Austin 1981: 30-31) among others. The essential generalisation—that each WORD-level suffix and bound stem forms its own domain for metrical structure—is, I believe, the right one. Nevertheless, the simple generalisation has been problematic to implement theoretically. In the analysis to follow I take an approach which encodes the generalisation in (43) in a constraint applicable to all WORD-level morphemes, not just suffixes and bound stems.

The second part of this generalisation—that monosyllabic suffixes are footed 'contingently'—can be attributed to the constraint PARSE(σ) (Prince and Smolensky 1993: 58). I define this constraint in (44).

(44) PARSE(σ): 'Every syllable must be parsed'[22]

PARSE(σ) demands that as many syllables as possible be included in feet. It has the effect of 'cleaning up' stray syllables which are not subject to some other constraint demanding they be part of feet. In (45) for instance, MWD ≈ PRWD makes sure that the stem is associated with at least one foot; and PARSE(σ) prefers the form where remaining syllables are also parsed into feet:

		MWD ≈ PRWD		PARSE(σ)
(45)	a.	[(**yappa**)=ŋki-kkaʔ] sister-2mDAT-LOC	b.	[(**yappa**)(=ŋki-kkaʔ)]
	c.	*[**yappa**=ŋki-kkaʔ]	d.	*[(yappa)=**ŋki-kkaʔ**]

The (d) form violates PARSE(σ).

Suffixes behave in a similar way to MWDs in one respect. While suffixes do not always surface as Prosodic Words, they *are* required to constitute distinct domains at some level of prosodic structure. Szpyra (1989, 1992) and Rubach and Booij (1990) propose that prefixes in Polish constitute phonological and prosodic domains independent of the following stem.[23] I suggest that something like this is true of *all* WORD-level morphemes in Ngalakgan. Along with MWD ≈ PRWD, then, there is a more general constraint requiring that every WORD-level morpheme—every *lemma*—constitute a PRWD.

(46) λ ≈ PRWD: 'Every WORD-level morpheme (*lemma*) is a Prosodic Word'

The '≈' relation here, which has not been properly defined yet, now needs some formalisation. I assume here that the relation is one of complete identity, as discussed in (McCarthy and Prince 1993a, 2003). Formally, we can express this relation as follows, building on the definition of Alignment in McCarthy and Prince (1993a):

---

22 I follow Prince and Smolensky (1993: 58) in omitting mention of 'foot' in the constraint. It is unclear whether 'PARSE(SYLL)' should be distinct from e.g. 'PARSE(SYLL, FOOT)' or 'PARSE(SYLL, PRWD)'. Perhaps PARSE(SYLL) can be regarded as the underdetermined form of the constraint.

23 Rubach and Booij propose that prefixes in Polish constitute a prosodic constituent they call the 'mot' (i.e. 'word'; the term is used by Liberman and Prince 1977). Szpyra (1992: 209) shows that Polish prefixes are not domains for stress however; prefixed words are stressed as single prosodic domains.

(47) MCat ≈ PCat

Let A be an element of the set MCat {MWD, λ}, and B be an element of the set PCat {σ, Ft, PRWD, PPH}. Let S be any string. Then, for any substring A of S that *is a* MCat, there is a substring B of S that *is a* PCat, such that there is a decomposition D(A) of A and a decomposition D(B) of B, both sub-decompositions of a decomposition D(S) of S, such that D(A)=D(B).

In other words, every segment which is part of a MCat A (MWD or λ, for our purposes) must find a corresponding segment which is part of a PCat B (PRWD, in this case), such that no segment of A is part of a distinct PCat C, and no segment of PCat B is part of a distinct MCat D.

Hence, the parse of MWD /ce/ 'nose' in (48)a satisfies the constraint MWD ≈ PRWD, but those in (b), (c) do not.

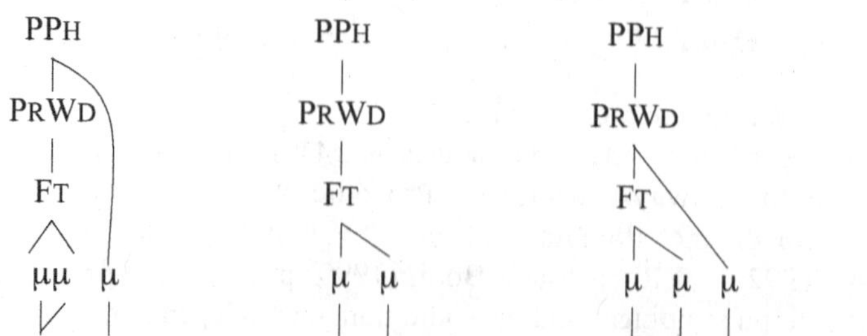

(48) a. ce-ŋki
nose-2mDAT

b. ce-ŋki
nose-2mDAT

c. ku-ce-ŋki
NEUT-nose-2mDAT

In (b), there is a substring B corresponding to PRWD which in this case takes in more than the substring corresponding to the MWD /ce/. Example (c) has the same problem, in this case, three morphemes end up being part of the same PRWD.

The intuition behind λ ≈ PRWD is that speakers use prosodic structure as a way of 'signalling' the morphological structure (Trubetzkoy 1969[1939]: 277). Evidence for this claim is the fact that only WORD-level morphemes, and not ROOT-level ones, are required to be prosodic domains. There is no need to signal the boundaries of ROOT-level morphemes, since ROOT-complex forms are interpreted as units.

In the following section, I set out the analytical mechanisms which can accomplish the patterns we observe in Australian languages. 4.3.1 elaborates on the complexities of the metrical constraints required for Ngalakgan stress in complex words. In 4.4, I discuss some well-known examples of patterns which are similar, in Warlpiri and Diyari, showing that they too can be analysed in the same way. In 4.4.2, I discuss and dismiss some alternative proposals for the Australian stress pattern which have been put forward, including analyses based on Alignment constraints. Templatic constraints such as λ ≈ PRWD can be regarded as constraints which demand simultaneous Alignment at both edges. Indeed, McCarthy and Prince make this comparison explicit in (1993a: 3, 1993b: 145). However, it is not possible to implement templatic constraints of the MCat ≈ PCat variety directly in the formalism of Alignment and derive the right results, as I show in 4.4.2.

4.3.1 Analysis of metrical patterns

In this section I analyse the metrical patterns in suffixes and bound stems using λ ≈ PRWD (prefixes are addressed separately). The constraint hierarchy which derives the pattern we find in Ngalakgan and many other Australian languages is given in (49).

(49) FTBIN, FTFORM (undominated) >> MWD ≈ PRWD >> IDENT[μ] >> λ ≈ PRWD >> ALIGNR(PK, PPH) >> PARSE(σ)

λ ≈ PRWD is distinct from, and must dominate PARSE(σ). This is shown in the tableau in (50). A form (a) which parses suffixes and bound stems isomorphically, but violates PARSE(σ) twice, wins over a competing candidate (c) in which every syllable is parsed, but in flagrant violation of λ ≈ PRWD. This example also demonstrates that, unlike MWD ≈ PRWD, λ ≈ PRWD must in turn be dominated by IDENT[μ], since monosyllabic bound stems do not undergo vowel lengthening except in satisfaction of MWD ≈ PRWD.

(50)

/ʈotojʔ=ŋki-ppulu-kkaʔ/ uncle-yours-PL-LOC	MWD ≈ PRWD	IDENT[μ]	λ ≈ PRWD	PARSE (σ)
☞ a. [(ʈòtojʔ)]=ki[(-ppúlu)]-kkaʔ			**	**
b. [(ʈòtojʔ)][(=kì:)][(-ppùlu)][(-kká:ʔ)]		**!		
c. [(ʈòtojʔ)][(=kì-ppu)][(lú-kkaʔ)			***!	

I return to this example in 4.4.2 to show why ALIGN constraints cannot capture the same facts.

Strings of monosyllabic bound morphemes are parsed together as feet, wherever possible, in order to satisfy ALIGNR(PK, PPH), as shown in (51). However, optimal candidates never violate IDENT[μ] in order to better satisfy ALIGNR (as in candidate c), and hence the latter must be ranked below the former.

(51)

/jappa=ŋki-kkaʔ/ sister-yours-LOC	MWD ≈ PRWD	IDENT[μ]	λ ≈ PRWD	ALIGNR (PK, PPH)
☞ a. [(jàppa)][(=ŋkí-kkaʔ)]			**	σ
b. [(jáppa)]=ŋki-kkaʔ			**	σσσ!
c. [(jàppa)][(=ŋkí:)]-kkaʔ		*!	*	σ
d. [(jáppa)][(=ŋkì-kkaʔ)]			**	σσσ!

However, stress does not shift rightwards from disyllabic affixes in order to better satisfy ALIGNR, suggesting the latter is dominated by λ ≈ PRWD, as shown in (52).

(52)

/jappa-ppulu-kkaʔ/ sister-PL-LOC	MWD ≈ PRWD	IDENT[μ]	λ ≈ PRWD	ALIGNR (PK, PPH)
☞ a. [(jàppa)][(-ppúlu)]-kkaʔ			*	σσ
b. [(jàppa)]-ppu[(lú-kkaʔ)]			**!	σ
c. [(jàppa)][(-ppùlu)][(-kká:ʔ)]		*!		

Suffixes differ from WORD-level major category stems (MWDs) in that the latter *can* force violation of Faithfulness, as we have seen: CV roots show long vowels in surface forms as in (53).

(53) a. /ce/ [ɟé:] 'nose'
b. /ce=ɳowi/ [ɟè:ɳówi] 'his nose'

Long vowels in surface forms in Ngalakgan violate IDENT[μ], since all vowels are underlyingly monomoraic.

In a form which combines a monosyllabic MWD, and a monosyllabic suffix, below in (54), the MWD (a), but not the suffix (b), must be long. The MWD /ce/ 'nose' must constitute a PRWD, and must therefore be bimoraic (by the Prosodic Hierarchy, Strict Layering, and Foot Binarity—Chapter 3). It is more important for MWDs than for other morphemes to constitute a separate metrical domain, and for that domain to be a Prosodic Word. To not lengthen the vowel, as in (c), is to violate this constraint fatally.

(54)

	/ce-kkaʔ/ nose-LOC	MWD ≈ PRWD	IDENT[μ]	λ ≈ PRWD	ALIGNR (PK, PPH)
☞	a. [(cé:)]-kkaʔ		*	*	σ
	b. [(cè:)][(-kká:ʔ)]		**!		
	c. [(cé-kkaʔ)]	*!		**	σ

Note that candidate (54)c, where the MWD is parsed together with the following suffix, violates MWD ≈ PRWD and λ ≈ PRWD, according to the definition given in (47). An MWD which does not constitute its own metrical domain violates both constraints.

To summarise: I have proposed a constraint 'λ ≈ PRWD' which demands isomorphic associations between WORD-level morphemes (lemmas) and PRWDs. The analysis has shown that it can account straightforwardly for the stress patterns of morphologically complex words, with a ranking of MWD ≈ PRWD over IDENT[μ], and IDENT[μ] in turn over λ ≈ PRWD.

This model also successfully accounts for many other Australian languages, such as Warlpiri (Nash 1986), and Diyari (Austin 1981), as I show in the next section.

4.4 Further applications of λ ≈ PRWD

In this section I show how the same constraint λ ≈ PRWD successfully accounts for the stress patterns of other languages. Two are considered here: Warlpiri (Nash 1986) and Diyari (Austin 1981), but many other Australian languages have fundamentally the same kind of metrical system.

Previous analyses of languages like Warlpiri and Diyari, where, as in Ngalakgan, foot structure and morphemes are isomorphic, have concentrated on Alignment approaches (e.g. Kager 1996; Hewitt and Crowhurst 1996; Berry 1999). I argue here that Alignment cannot capture the same facts, and is inherently unsuited to do so.

4.4.1 Warlpiri and Diyari stress

Warlpiri (Nash 1986) and Diyari (Austin 1981) have both been described with stress systems that are like that described for Ngalakgan here. In all three languages, polysyllabic morphemes are footed consistently and independently, while monosyllabic morphemes have inconsistent metrical structure.

For Diyari, Austin (1981: 31) states the following rule:

(55) 'Primary stress falls on the first vowel of a root and secondary stress is assigned to the third vowel of a four syllable root ... and to the first vowel of a disyllabic suffix.'

Some examples are shown in (56) (from Austin 1981: 31):[24]

(56)	a.	káɳa	'man'
	b.	pínatu	'old man'
	c.	wíl̪apìna	'old woman'
	d.	káɳa-wàɻa	'man-PL'
	e.	pínatu-wàɻa	'old man-PL'
	f.	wíl̪apìna-wàɻa	'old woman-PL'
	g.	káɳa-n̪i	'man-LOC'
	h.	káɳa-n̪i-màt̪a	'man-LOC-IDENT'
	i.	káɳa-wàɻa-ŋu	'man-PL-LOC'
	j.	káɳa-wàɻa-ŋùntu	'man-PL-ABL'

It is not clear from Austin's description whether two adjacent monosyllabic suffixes can be footed together. In other respects, foot structure in Diyari and Ngalakgan are the same.

For Warlpiri, Nash (1986: 100) states the following rules (cf. Austin's rule in (55)):

(57) 'Primary stress is uniformly on the initial syllable of a word ... The first syllable of a morpheme of two or more syllables always bears a stress.'

Some examples of Nash's generalisation are given in (58) (from Nash 1986: 102).[25]

		'man'	'tree'	'spinifex plain'	
(58)	a.	wáti	wátija	mánaŋkàra	
	b.	wáti-ŋka	wátijà-ɭa	mánaŋkàra-ɭa	(LOC)
	c.	wáti-ŋkà-ɭu	wátija-ɭà-ɭu	mánaŋkàra-ɭà-ɭu	(LOC-ERG)

As shown by example (58)c Warlpiri behaves like Ngalakgan in allowing foot parsing to 'clean up' stray morphemes where possible: that is,

---

[24] I have supplied morpheme boundaries, based on Austin's glosses, and stress to the phonemic representations, based on Austin's phonetic representations.

[25] (58) replicates Nash's presentation except that I have used a phonemic orthography, rather than the established Warlpiri practical orthography.

where the regular isomorphic relationship λ ≈ PRWD would not be otherwise disturbed.

Both Diyari and Warlpiri are amenable to an analysis using λ ≈ PRWD, as I have done in the previous sections. (59) shows an example tableau for Warlpiri.[26] This example is analogous to the Ngalakgan example (ṭòtojʔ)= ki(-ppúlu)-kkaʔ 'to your "uncles"' analysed previously in (50). As in Ngalakgan, in Warlpiri it is better to parse each morpheme as a separate metrical domain wherever possible, even though to do so leaves more syllables unparsed.

(59) Warlpiri

/wati-ŋka-ɭaŋu-ɭu/ man-LOC-too-ERG	λ ≈ PRWD	ALIGNL (PK, PPH)	PARSE(σ)
☞ a. [(wáti)]-ŋka-[(ɭàŋu)]-ɭu	**		**
b. [(wáti)][(-ŋkà-ɭa)][(ŋù-ɭu)]	***!		

Unlike Ngalakgan, primary stress is always initial in words in Warlpiri, hence, Warlpiri evinces a left edge Peak Alignment constraint.[27]

In the following section, I consider two alternative analyses which have attempted to capture these facts: Kager (1996) and Hewitt and Crowhurst (1996).

4.4.2 Against ALIGN

Kager (1996) and Hewitt and Crowhurst (1996) present analyses of Diyari and Warlpiri using Alignment constraints. In this section I argue that Alignment constraints are inherently unsuited to an analysis of languages like Ngalakgan, Warlpiri and Diyari. This is because Alignment constraints cannot

---

26 David Nash p.c. has confirmed the stress pattern in this form, and it follows his description of stress in Nash (1986: 100). I have made the simplifying assumption here that syllabification in Warlpiri is like that in Ngalakgan, i.e. that homorganic nasal-stop clusters are syllabified as onsets, though this is not crucial to the analysis.

27 I have assumed that stressed polysyllabic morphemes constitute 'Prosodic Words' in Warlpiri (as does Kager 1996), though there may be reasons to think otherwise. For example, the domain of 'word' is the domain of vowel harmony in Nash (1986), and is also the domain within which moraicity is determined for the purposes of prosodically-conditioned case allomorphy. Allowing for word-internal 'PRWD' boundaries may obscure this relationship. On the other hand, if the complex word in Warlpiri constitutes a Phonological Phrase, as in Ngalakgan, then it may be possible to use this as the domain of vowel harmony instead. Determining the domain of moraicity is more complicated, and I will not attempt it here. See Nash (1986) for discussion.

capture the generalisation which applies to these languages: that morphemes are isomorphically associated with metrical structure, as far as possible.

To understand the issue let us return to the definition of 'Generalised Alignment' given in McCarthy and Prince (1993a: 2).

(60) Generalised Alignment
  Align(Cat1, Edge1, Cat2, Edge2) $=_{def}$
  $\forall$ Cat1 $\exists$ Cat2 such that Edge1 of Cat1 and Edge2 of Cat2 coincide

 Where
  Cat1, Cat2 $\in$ PCat $\cup$ GCat
  Edge1, Edge2 $\in$ (Right, Left)

Constraints of this form are designed to enforce association at a designated edge (left or right) between two categories. The categories are drawn from those of prosody and morphology: e.g. PRWD, Foot, Syllable; Root, Stem, Word, Suffix.

However, *contra* (McCarthy and Prince 1993a: 3), these constraints are not equivalent to templatic constraints, such as $\lambda \approx$ PRWD. Alignment constraints do not enforce a one-to-one association between two constituents, say a suffix and foot. Alignment constraints can only refer to the edges of such constituents: every instance of a morpheme boundary '$]_{MWD}$', '$[_{MWD}$' and of a foot boundary '$(_{FT}$', '$)_{FT}$' is evaluated independently for Alignment. This characteristic makes Alignment constraints unsuited to describe isomorphic morpheme-to-prosody associations in languages like Ngalakgan. The qualitative difference between the morpheme boundary of an inherently footable morpheme and that of an inherently unfootable one cannot be captured.

Consider an example of this approach: Kager (1996), who addresses Warlpiri stress. Noting that 'poly-syllabic affixes are stressed on their initial syllable' Kager (1996: 15) proposes the following constraint:

(61) ALIGN-MO-L Align(Morpheme, Left, PRWD, Left)

This constraint demands that every morpheme start a new Prosodic Word. The constraint is reminiscent of something like AlignL(λ, PRWD), but it is not identical, since Kager does not distinguish between types of 'morphemes' for the purposes of prosody. As demonstrated by Baker and Harvey (2003), Warlpiri also evinces a distinction between ROOT-level and WORD-level morphology and, as in Ngalakgan, WORD-level morphology, but not ROOT-level morphology, is relevant to prosody. Hence, Kager's constraint makes the wrong predictions for certain classes of morphological structure, such as complex inflected verb roots.

A further, undominated constraint rules out PRWDs which do not immediately begin in a foot:

(62) ALIGN-WD-L Align (PRWD, Left, Foot, Left)

The analysis works for the Warlpiri examples (58) presented in Nash (1986: 102). I repeat Kager's tableaux (1996: 16) here (square brackets represent PRWD boundaries, parentheses enclose feet):[28]

(63)

/watija-ḷa/ tree-LOC	ALIGN-WD-L	ALIGN-MO-L	PARSE(σ)
☞ a. [(wáti)(jà-ḷa)]		*	
b. [[(wáti)ja]-ḷa]		*	**!
c. [(wáti)ja][-ḷa]	*!		**

(64)

/watija-ḷa-ḷu/ tree-LOC-ERG	ALIGN-WD-L	ALIGN-MO-L	PARSE(σ)
☞ a. [(wáti)ja][(-ḷà-ḷu)]		*	*
b. [(wáti)(jà-ḷa)-ḷu]		**!	*
c. [[[(wáti)ja]-ḷa]-ḷu]		**!	***
d. [(wáti)ja][-ḷa][-ḷu]	**!		*

Kager's analysis works by building PRWD boundaries wherever possible (in accordance with morphological structure). Only those PRWDs which enclose at least one disyllabic foot are licensed. And since only polysyllabic morphemes can satisfy both ALIGN-WD-L and ALIGN-MO-L simultaneously, these morphemes make the best candidates for association to feet. This is how Kager captures the fact that polysyllabic suffixes maintain their metrical integrity.

This aspect of the analysis is shown in (65) (Kager 1996: 16). Both candidates leave one syllable unfooted, violating PARSE(σ). The disyllabic

[28] In his tableaux, Kager includes a further constraint 'All-Feet-Left' which is ranked below Parse(Syll). This constraint does no work in the examples repeated here and I omit it.

suffix /-ŋuɭu/ (ELAT) must be associated with a foot, because to do so better satisfies ALIGN-MO-L.

(65)

/japaɭa-ŋuɭu/ FaMo-ELAT	ALIGN-WD-L	ALIGN-MO-L	PARSE(σ)
☞ a. [(jápa)ɭa][(-ŋùɭu)]			*
b. [(jápa)(ɭà-ŋu)ɭu]		*!	*

Kager's analysis also accommodates Ngalakgan examples like (36)c (ʈòtojʔ)=ŋki(-ppúlu), (37)d cu-(jàppa)(=ŋkí-kkaʔ), and (38)a (cáwaɳ)(ʈà =ŋki) above, which are morphoprosodically analogous to the Warlpiri forms shown here. Notably, his analysis will not work for Warlpiri examples such as (wáti)-ŋka-(ɭàŋu)-ɭu, analysed previously; tableau (66) shows why.

The critical problem is the Alignment constraint 'Align(Morpheme, L, PRWD, L)'. Alignment cannot distinguish between the equal violations of candidates (66)a and (66)b. The unattested candidate (66)b wins because it better satisfies PARSE(σ). This is despite the fact that candidate (66)b runs counter to the general character of the language, which is that morphemes and metrical domains are isomorphic, as far as possible. The analysis therefore also fails for the analogous Ngalakgan example (ʈòtojʔ)=ŋki(-ppúlu)-kkaʔ in (50) (the symbol '💣' indicates a candidate form which is unattested but nevertheless optimal on the given constraint ranking: i.e. a winning candidate we do not want).[29]

(66)

/wati-ŋka-ɭaŋu-ɭu/ man-LOC-too-ERG	ALIGN-WD-L	ALIGN-MO-L	PARSE(σ)
☞ a. [(wáti)-ŋka][(-ɭàŋu)-ɭu]		**	**!
💣 b. [(wáti)][(-ŋkà-ɭa)][(ŋù-ɭu)]		**	
c. [(wáti)][-ŋka][(-ɭàŋu)][-ɭu]	**!		

Hewitt and Crowhurst (1996) is an attempt to 'fix' Alignment with a kind of dependency. They propose to capture the stress patterns of Diyari

[29] To be fair to Kager, examples like that in (66) are not presented in Nash's (1986) discussion of stress. However, the correct candidate, (66)a, is generated by his stress rules (1986: 100), and the unattested, but successful candidate, (66)b violates the rule.

using a 'conjoined' constraint (constraint conjunction was originally proposed in Smolensky 1993). Their constraint is given in (67) (Hewitt and Crowhurst 1996: 109).[30]

(67) AlignL(Morpheme, Foot) $\wedge^{\text{Morph}}$ AlignR(Morpheme, Foot)

The symbol '$\wedge$' is the operator 'and' of Boolean logic. The constraint is satisfied only when both conditions are satisfied, and is violated if either one or both are violated. The superscript 'morph' is designed to relativise both conjuncts to a particular (i.e. existentially-quantified rather than universally quantified) instance of 'morph'. Thus, the constraint is interpreted as 'For any morpheme, it must be true that both the left and right edges are aligned with some foot'.[31]

I take it as an argument in favour of my approach that their constraint does much the same work that $\lambda \approx$ PRWD does. But the two constraints are *not* equivalent. In the first place, the conjoined Alignment constraint predicts that every morpheme should be evenly footable: this is not the case. For instance, Hewitt and Crowhurst note (1996: 113) that their constraint predicts that trisyllabic morphemes will lack stress entirely, since they cannot be footed without violating either of the conjuncts. A typological prediction of the conjoined Alignment approach is that there might be languages where every root is either disyllabic or quadrisyllabic (i.e. evenly footable), but there are no trisyllabic roots. Such languages do not seem to exist.

Secondly, allowing the possibility of conjoined constraints amplifies the power of a constraint-based grammar, by increasing the total number of potential constraints. This makes OT less restrictive as a theory, and less universal. It is not clear whether any two constraints can be conjoined and if there are any principled upper limits on the number of conjoins allowed.[32]

Lastly, we should find evidence in a given language for each of the conjuncts in a conjoined constraint such as (67). It can be argued that there is evidence for AlignL(Morpheme, Foot), since every polysyllabic morpheme begins in a foot. However, there is no such evidence for AlignR(Morpheme, Foot): polysyllabic, odd-numbered morphemes in Ngalakgan, Warlpiri and

30 Hewitt and Crowhurst use the equivalent constraints Align(Morpheme, L, Foot, L) and Align(Morpheme, R, Foot, R). These are notational variants of AlignL(Morpheme, Foot) and AlignR(Morpheme, Foot), respectively.

31 Hewitt and Crowhurst's definition of constraint conjunction therefore differs from the Smolensky conception (1993). In the latter, a conjoined constraint is violated only if both conjuncts are violated.

32 Various restrictions have been proposed on conjunction. Hewitt and Crowhurst (1996) propose that conjoined constraints must share an argument, in this case the 'morph'. Moreton and Smolensky (2002) propose that constraints must share a 'domain' in order to be conjoinable. Regardless of these further stipulations, conjunction exponentially increases the number of total constraints and hence the typological predictions about possible languages.

Diyari do not characteristically end in a foot. Rather, metrical structure is more commonly regularly alternating from the left. Hence, it is unclear how the child learning Warlpiri would ever come to the conclusion that metrical structure was determined by a constraint such as (67), since one of the conjuncts is otherwise unattested in the grammar.

Templatic constraints, such as λ ≈ PRWD, have none of these shortcomings. They can account for morphological prosody regardless of morpheme size. They are also inherently constrained by independently-motivated factors: the morphological analysis of a language, and universal prosodic constituent structure. The first is empirically available to the child learning a language like Ngalakgan, and the second is presumably supplied by Universal Grammar.

In conclusion, I have shown that the templatic approach using λ ≈ PRWD can capture the stress facts in Ngalakgan in a straightforward fashion. The analysis also extends to languages such as Diyari and Warlpiri which have similar systems, as I have shown. In contrast, an Alignment approach requires additional theoretical machinery: either Alignment must be made to behave more like a templatic constraint (Hewitt and Crowhurst 1996), or else it must fail where the inherent differences in bound morphemes become crucial (Kager 1996).

4.5 The pre-head string

The string of elements before the *morphological head* of a word is morphologically and prosodically diverse.[33] It includes compounded major category stems, modifying stems and inflectional prefixes. The fact that needs to be accounted for is that right-binding stems behave like left-binding stems—polysyllabic right-binding stems are associated with pitch accents (4.5.1)—but inflectional prefixes are never associated with pitch accents (4.5.2).

Inflectional prefixes *do* have metrical organisation: the initial syllable of an inflectional prefix string is audibly more prominent than the rest.[34] But

33 The 'morphological head' is the stem morpheme which determines syntactic category and inflectional class. This was defined in Chapter 3 as the rightmost stem immediately dominated by a major category.

34 For instance, like stressed syllables in general, the vowel of the first syllable of an inflectional prefix is normally phonetically 'centralised' (i.e. lower and 'laxer'): [jɪriɳáŋan] 'we (excl.) are sitting', where the 1st augmented intransitive prefix /jiri-/ takes a centralised allophone of the vowel in the first syllable. In phonological terms, the initial syllable of an inflectional prefix may be the head of a metrical foot, but cannot be the head of a PRWD; see 4.5.3.

inflectional prefixes are almost never associated with pitch accents, and the whole prefix string is associated with a steady, low tonal contour.[35] Selkirk (1995) claims that tonal contrasts are optimally associated with lexical, 'content' words, and not with function words. In 4.5.3 I propose that the asymmetry between content and function words extends to the constituents of words in Ngalakgan: only contentful morphemes, not function morphemes, are eligible to be associated with pitch accents. This constraint, interacting with the right edge bias for primary stress in complex words, derives the observed asymmetry between suffixes and prefixes.

4.5.1 Prosody of right-binding stems

Right-binding stems show variable behaviour for stress, depending on their size, frequency, and morphosyntactic function. The most consistent predictor of stress in these stems is size: in this respect right-binding stems behave like left-binding stems. All polysyllabic right-binding stems are (pitch) accented, monosyllabic ones are unaccented.

Examples of accented, polysyllabic bound stems (in bold) are shown in (68).

(68) a. [nunbɨɖ̆icŋariɲbéɲ]
/ɳun-**piʈic**-ŋariɲ-pe+ɲ/[36]
2mO-nearly-hand-bite+PP
'[It: dog] nearly bit your hand.' [31/5/96: 1B]

b. [nuguwàɳabakwakkɛ́na]
/ɳuku-**waɳa**-pak-wakke+na/
1mS/2aO-still-APPL-return+FUT
'I might still come back to you (pl.).' [3/7/96]

c. [guɟa̰ɳàmuluɻʊ́ŋa]
/ku-caʔ-**ɳamulu**-ɻu+ŋa/
NP-now-really-burn+FUT
'[It] will get really cooking now.' [27/6/96: 1B]

I have already noted (4.1.1) that several of the attested right-binding stems can occur as independent adverbial words, or display other 'stem-like' behaviour.[37]

---

[35] Exceptions to this characterisation are noted at the end of 4.5.2.

[36] Pitch accent on the syllable [ʈic] of right-binding stem /piʈic-/ here is due to syllable weight effects on stress examined in Chapter 5. I do not hear a pitch accent on the stem /ŋariɲ/ 'hand', though according to MWD ≈ PRWD it should be there. I speculated in 3.2.3 that this is because of a preference for just two PRWDs (and two pitch accents) per Phonological Phrase. At this point, there are too few words of this kind in the corpus to decide the issue.

[37] Most right-binding stems are rare in naturally-occurring speech. There are a few which are

Some examples of monosyllabic right-binding stems are presented in (69). These stems are not associated with pitch accents, and in this respect are just like inflectional prefixes of any size.

(69) a. [ŋʊnbubakwɔ́cme]
/ŋun-pu-**pak**-woc+me/
1mO-3a-APPL-steal+GET.PP
'They stole [it: glasses] from me.' [2/9/97: 1A]

b. [bʊrʊɳbubakɟʊ̀ɟʊ́ɟja]
/puruɳ-pu-**pak**-cujʔ-cujʔ-ja/
3aO-3a-APPL-ITER-send-FUT
'They'll send [it] back with [?for] them.' [9/9/97: 1A]

c. [ŋʊrʊɳbubakwàkkɻiwʊ́na]
/ŋuruɳ-pu-**pak**-wakkiɻi+wu+na/
12aO-3a-APPL-return.with+GIVE+FUT
'They'll bring [it] back for us.' [31/5/96: 1B]

d. [ŋʊrʊɳbubakbáwʊn̪mɪɲ]
/ŋuruɳ-pu-**pak**-pawunʔ-mi+ɲ/
12aO-3a-APPL-leave+AUX+PP
'They left [it] with us.' [31/5/96: 1B]

e. [ŋumiɟag̱ɔ̀rickɔ́re]
/ŋu-mu-**caʔ**-koric=kore/
1mS-VEG-now-grind-12aDAT
'I'm grinding it (VEG: food) for us now.' [27/6/96: 1B]

The behaviour of right-binding stems can be accounted for with the grammar already proposed, along with a requirement that PRWDs are left-aligned to content morphemes, as I show in 4.5.3. But first let us consider the prosody of inflectional prefixes, which is quite different.

4.5.2 Prosody of inflectional prefixes

The general pattern is for inflectional prefixes to entirely lack pitch accent (70) (the **stems** here are in bold, representing the accented part of the word). Examples (70)a-c show that monosyllabic prefixes lack accent, and (70)d-g show that the same is true of disyllabic prefix strings.

---

quite frequent, such as /meleʔ-/ 'lest', /ca(ʔ)-/ 'now, IMMED', and the productive applicative stem /pak-/. It is notable that these are all quite closely integrated into the aspectual/modal, and agreement marking systems, respectively. The 'lest' stem combined with the Evitative inflection derives the Evitative form of the verb. Since for almost all verbs the Evitative inflection is identical to the Present, the 'lest' stem is indispensible in this function. Similarly, the IMMED stem can distinguish the various interpretations of the Present and Future tense inflections, which can otherwise be ambiguous between Indicative and Potential moods.

(70) a. /pur-**pe+ɲ**/ [bʊrbéɲ]
3aS-bite+PP 'they bit [him]' [30/5/96: 1A]
b. /ku-**je**/ [gujé:]
NP-put.PR '[someone] puts [it]' [27/6/96: 1B]
c. /ɳu-**ma**/ [numá:]
2aS-get.IMPER 'you mob get [it]' [27/6/96]
d. /jir-mi-**je**/ [jɪrmijé:]
1aS-VEG-put.PR 'we put it (VEG)' [DP]
e. /jir-pi-**ʈac**/ [jɪrbiɖác]
1aS-3a-cut 'we cut them' [27/6/96: 1A]
f. /jir-mi-**ma**/ [jɪrmimá:]
1aS-VEG-get.PR 'we get it (VEG)' [DP]
g. /jir-mi-**co**/ [jɪrmiɟó:]
1aS-VEG-chop.PR 'we chop it (VEG)' [DP]

The vowel-lengthening in the stems of the words in (70) shows that the prefix is not part of the Prosodic Word. The reason for their exclusion from PRWD is addressed in 4.5.3 below.

Even when the prefixal string is much longer than the root, as in (71)a-d below, prefixes still lack accent, though the initial syllable of a string of prefixes is audibly more prominent than other syllables in the prefix, as noted. Stressed syllables without pitch, and which are therefore external to a PRWD domain, are not marked with accent diacritics.[38] In example (71)a, two syllables are passed over before accent is assigned to the root, and in (71)b three syllables. Examples (71)c-d both have four syllables worth of prefix before accent.

(71) a. /ŋuruɳ-**ɻu**/ [ŋʊrʊɳɻú:]
12aO-burn.PR 'we're getting burnt'[39]
[13/3/95: 3A]
b. /ŋuruɳ-mu-**ɳe**/ [ŋʊrʊɳmuɳé:]
12aO-VEG-burn.PR 'It [sc. 'sun', VEG] burns us.'
[13/3/95: 3A]
c. /ŋuruɳ-pu-pak-**poɭk+pu+n**/ [ŋʊrʊɳbubakbɔ́ɭkbʊn]
12aO-3a-APPL-noise+HIT+PR 'they are making noise on us'
(i.e. 'talking over the top of us')
d. /jiriɳ-pi-pak-**woc+ma**/ [jɪrɪɳbibakwɔ́cma]
1aO-3a-APPL-steal+GET.PR 'they always steal from us'

---

[38] This only applies to inflectional prefixes, and some bound stems, as discussed in 4.5.3.

[39] This example is interesting from the point of view of agreement, since /ɻu+/ 'burn' is intransitive, but /ŋuruɳ-/ (12aO) is an object prefix.

The effect is not limited to verbs. Nominal prefixes also lack accent, whether monosyllabic (72) or disyllabic (73), and the only productive prefix on adverbs behaves in the same way (74).

(72) a. [muwɔ́m]
/mu-**wom**/
VEG-black.plum (*Vitex glabrata*)

b. [mubák]
/mu-**pak**/
VEG-pond.algae

c. [gubíɳ]
/ku-**piɳ**/
NEUT-rock/money

(73) a. [gʊnguɟɛ́ː]
/kun-ku-**ce**/
NEUT-TOP-nose

b. [gʊngubóː]
/kun-ku-**po**/
NEUT-TOP-river

c. [gʊngubíɳ]
/kun-ku-**piɳ**/
NEUT-TOP-rock/money

d. [nugugóɲ]
/ɳu-ku-**koɲ**/
M-TOP-kangaroo

(74) a. [jibáj]
/ji-**pay**/
ALL-north

b. [jiwálam]
/ji-**walam**/
ALL-south

All inflectional prefixes fail to count for word minimality, and as a result open monosyllabic roots must have long vowels at the surface:

(75) a. [guɟɛ́ː]
/ku-**ce**/
NEUT-nose

b. [gujɛ́ː]
/ku-**je**/
NP-put.PR

The vowel lengthening shows that prefixes, like suffixes, do not contribute to the word minimum. In the following section, I propose an analysis of this pattern.[40]

---

[40] Occasionally I have heard variant pronunciations of some prefixed words, where the prefix is associated with a pitch accent. (a-c) shows some examples of verbs, and (d-f) of nominals.

a. /**ŋuruɳ**-mu-ɳe/ [ŋʊ̀ruɳmuɳéː]
12aO-VEG-burn.PR 'It [sc. 'sun' VEG] burns us.' [13/3/95: 3A]

b. /**mu**-jereʈ-mi+ɲ/ [mɪ̀jɛrɛ́ʈmiɲ] ~ [mijɛ́rɛʈmiɲ]
VEG-grow-AUX+PP 'it [VEG] grew' [3/9/97: 2A]

c. /**ku**-mu-jereʈ/ [gʊ́mujɛ̀rɛʈ] ~ [gumujɛ́rɛʈ]
NP-VEG-grow 'it grows' [3/9/97: 2A]

d. /**ku**-ɽuwur/ [gʊ́ɽuwur] ~ [guɽúwur]
NEUT-ridge [3/9/97: 1B]

e. /**ku**-joccoŋ/ [gɪ́jɔccɔŋ] ~ [gujɔ́ccɔŋ]
NEUT-not.sacred [3/9/97: 2A]

f. /**mu**-wom/ [mʊ́wɔm] ~ [muwɔ́m]
VEG-black.plum (*Vitex glabrata*)

4.5.3 Analysis of prefix prosodic structure

In this section I propose an association between lexemic, content items and pitch accents, governed by a constraint ALIGNL(PRWD, STEM). Given this constraint, the asymmetry between prefixes and suffixes, and the differences between types of right-binding stems in terms of accent, is a straightforward consequence.

The analysis rests on the basis of some assumptions which have already been presented in Chapter 3. The first assumption concerns the nature of pitch accent.

(76) Pitch accent represents a Prosodic Word domain.

I have noted in the preceding section that prefixes have metrical organisation, but cannot be associated with pitch accent. Therefore, if premise (76) is true, they can never constitute PRWDs.

The second assumption concerns the headedness and structural characteristics of the higher prosodic constituents.

(77) Prosodic Words form left-headed, adjacent domains; Phonological Phrases form right-headed, recursive domains.

Importantly, Phonological Phrases cannot form left-branching structures.

So far, there is nothing in the analysis which would prevent prefixes from being PRWDs. $\lambda \approx$ PRWD would in fact *require* prefixes to be PRWDs. In addition, we have seen that there can be more than one PRWD per Phonological Phrase: one for every MWD. So there is no principled upper limit on the number of PRWDs which can be built in a PPH.

It is not uncommon to find that pitch or stress realisation is restricted by what we might term 'semantic weight': 'lexical' or 'content' words are stressed in preference to 'grammatical' or 'function' words (Selkirk 1984, 1995; McCarthy and Prince 1993b: 86).[41] With rare exceptions, it is content elements which may be focused in English and Ngalakgan, that is, associated

---

The exceptions—which are in every case in variation with the unaccented form predicted by the generalisation—fall into two distinct patterns. The pattern in (b-c) and (d-f) is one of stress shift leftwards past the root, where the root-initial consonant is an approximant; I discuss this pattern in 5.4. The pattern in (a) is distinct, and is perhaps due to a constraint against overlong intonational phrase-initial sequences lacking a pitch accent, as discussed for English in Beckman (1996: 31). There might be a contrast in Ngalakgan between prefixes which are phrase-initial (in elicitation for example) as against those which are phrase-medial (e.g. in texts); I have not examined this possibility. These variants do not detract from the basic generalisation applicable to Ngalakgan.

[41] This dichotomy is a traditional one, but in modern form it is explicated notably by Sapir (1921).

with contrastive intonation and (in the case of Ngalakgan) moved to the front of the phrase. McCarthy and Prince (1993b: 86) propose the following constraint:

(78) PRWD ⊃ ROOT 'PRWDs include a Root'

In the current model, 'roots' correspond to 'stems': lexical entries which are immediately dominated by syntactic categories—major or minor—in the morphosyntactic component. This includes both free and bound nouns, verbs, coverbs, adjectives and adverbs, as well as pronouns, but excludes all inflectional affixes.[42] Pitch accents therefore cannot be associated with 'grammatical' or 'function' elements. In what follows, content items are bolded in the examples.

Below, I show that the constraint we require is more specific than (78), in fact, we require that PRWDs are left-aligned at a stem.

(79) ALIGNL(PRWD, STEM): 'Align the left edge of every Prosodic Word with the left edge of some stem'

With this constraint in hand, we can derive the attested pattern whereby prefixes are (variably) footed, but cannot be associated with a pitch accent, as shown in tableau (80). Prefixes are subject to λ ≈ PRWD, the general constraint which derives the patterns we observe in the language: that every WORD-level morpheme should constitute a Prosodic Word. However, prefixes cannot be parsed beyond the level of Foot. They cannot be realised as Prosodic Words because PRWDs cannot be associated with grammatical elements like prefixes. Hence, both candidates (b) and (d) are ruled out.

(80)

/ŋuruɳ-**ɻu**/ 1mO-burn.PR	ALIGNL (PRWD)	λ≈ PRWD	ALIGNR (PK, PPH)	PARSE(σ)
☞ a. (ŋuruɳ-)[(ɻú:)]		*		
b. [(ŋùruɳ-)][(ɻú:)]	*!			
☞ c. ŋuruɳ-[(ɻú:)]		*		*!*
d. [(ŋúruɳ-)][(ɻù:)]	*!		σ!σ	

[42] In English, this constraint serves in part to derive the difference between content and grammatical words discussed in e.g. Selkirk (1984: 343), where content words are always parsed by metrical structure but function words such as 'the', 'a' typically are not, unless under contrastive Focus (McCarthy and Prince 1993b: 84). Selkirk (1995) proposes Alignment constraints to make sure that 'lexical categories' are associated with Prosodic Words and vice versa.

This result indicates that ALIGNL(PRWD, STEM) dominates λ ≈ PRWD. λ ≈ PRWD must in turn dominate ALIGNR(PK, PPH). It is not the case that the peak falls further to the right than the initial syllable of the rightmost footable *lemma*, as shown by (52). Other considerations however—discussed immediately below—motivate a close relationship between ALIGNL(PRWD) and ALIGNR(PK), suggesting that they are ranked adjacently, at least for some level of prosodic phrasing.

The asymmetry between prefixes and suffixes follows from the 'Peak Alignment' and prosodic constituency principles given in Chapter 3; the reasons are detailed here. Suffixes fall to the right of any stem element in the word, and are therefore included in the prosodic domain which begins with the first stem element in the word. Because suffixes, and every other phonological segment, must be parsed to the Phonological Phrase (according to the version of the Strict Layering hypothesis adopted in Chapter 3), the following therefore holds:

(81) Every $\}_{\text{PPH}}$ must be right-aligned with the end of the word.

In words consisting of an inflected root followed by a word-level suffix, two outcomes are attested, represented by (a) and (b) in (82), below. This outcome cannot be derived with the grammar however. While candidate (b) is attested, it should be ruled out by ALIGNL(PRWD, STEM)—suffixes such as /-ppiraʔ/ 'DUAL' are not stems.[43] The fact that this candidate surfaces, at least some of the time, suggests that ALIGNR can outrank this constraint at some level. In the absence of a detailed examination of intonational phrasing in Ngalakgan, I will not examine this possibility here. Candidate (a) satisfies ALIGNL(PRWD, STEM), because the only PRWD is left-aligned with the only stem. It does so at the expense of λ ≈ PRWD, and ALIGNR(PK), however.[44] Candidate (b) satisfies ALIGNR(PK, PPH) (while satisfying undominated FTFORM) because the peak is at the right edge of the word. In this case, it is ALIGNL(PRWD, STEM) which is violated: the suffix is not a stem.

43 McCarthy and Prince (1993b: 86) suggest that PRWD ⊃ ROOT is undominated in word-level phonology, but may be dominated at the phrase level, to allow focussing of and stress shift to grammatical elements in English (Selkirk 1984: 343). An examination of citation forms and forms embedded in intonational phrases may reveal a similar distinction in Ngalakgan.

44 Actually, given the dominance of PEAK-TO-HEAD (Prince's 1983 Continuous Column Constraint) presented in 3.2.3, candidate (a) satisfies ALIGNR as much as is possible within this structure. A pitch accent on the initial syllable of the suffix would violate the Continuous Column Constraint, because this syllable is a head at the Foot level, while the initial syllable of the stem /ɳeŋa/ is a head at the PRWD level. Only the latter is eligible for a pitch accent, under the constraint. Nonetheless, candidate (82)b satisfies ALIGNR better in an absolute sense. The violation marks awarded to each form reflect this intuition.

(82)

/ɳu-**ɳe+ŋa**-ppiraʔ/ 2aS-burn+FUT-DU	ALIGNL (PRWD, STEM)	λ ≈ PRWD	ALIGNR (PK, PPH)
☞ a. ɳu-[(ɳé+ŋa)](-ppìraʔ)		**	σσσ
☞ b. ɳu-[(ɳè+ŋa)][(-ppíraʔ)]	*!	*	σ
c. ɳu-[(ɳé+ŋa)][(-ppìraʔ)]	*!	*	σσσ
d. ɳu-[(ɳé+ŋa)(-ppìraʔ)]		***!	σσσ

Candidate (c) violates both the Alignment constraints needlessly. Candidate (d) presumably violates λ ≈ PRWD more than the other candidates, but the difference between (d) and (a) is purely representational. In neither case will the stress on the suffix /-ppiraʔ/ be realised as a pitch accent, because in neither case is the foot the head of a PRWD.[45]

In contrast to the suffixed form in (82), in forms containing two MWDS there is less reason for variation between primary stress on the first or the second PRWD, since one candidate, (a), satisfies all constraints simultaneously.

(83)

/ŋun-**ŋariɲ-pe+ɲ**/ 1mO-hand-bite+PP	MWD ≈ PRWD	ALIGNL (PRWD, STEM)	ALIGNR (PK, P-WD)
☞ a. ŋun-[(ŋàriɲ-)][(pé+ɲ)]			
b. ŋun-[(ŋáriɲ-)][(pè+ɲ)]			σσ!
c. ŋun-(ŋariɲ-)[(pé+ɲ)]	*!		

Any MWDS included in the PPH must constitute PRWDS, because of high-ranking MWD ≈ PRWD. MWD ≈ PRWD and ALIGNL(PRWD, STEM) do not conflict, and are therefore unranked in (83).

Therefore, ALIGNL(PRWD, STEM) is a constraint which is motivated both by the behaviour of inflectional elements—particularly prefixes—in Ngalakgan, and the similar behaviour of 'function' words in languages such as English.

---

[45] A further consideration might be the effect of Strict Layering (3.1.1). Candidate (82)a violates Selkirk's 'Exhaustivity' constraint (1995: 443), whereby prosodic constituents at level *j* must be exhaustively dominated by constituent *j*+1. In this case, the final Foot is dominated by the Phonological Phrase, bypassing the intervening Prosodic Word constituent. Possibly it is this constraint (rather than ALIGNR) which is in competition with ALIGNL(PRWD, STEM).

4.5.4 Analysis of right-binding stems

As we have seen, right-binding stems behave either like inflectional prefixes, or like major categorial stems, depending on their size: stems larger than a monosyllable project viable PRWDs, but FTBIN rules out most parses of monosyllabic stems.[46]

A three way contrast exists in the prosody of the three Applicative stems, shown in (84).

(84) a. /pak-/ Productive verbal Applicative
b. /paʈʈa-/ Productive nominal Comitative, unproductive verbal Comitative Applicative
c. /ɻej+/ Unproductive verbal Applicative

All three have distinct prosodic characteristics. /pak-/ has the same characteristics as monosyllabic agreement prefixes: it is never pitch accented. /ɻej+/ has the same characteristics as a monosyllabic major category stem. Since the rime is a diphthong, /ɻej+/ constitutes a foot and is always associated to a pitch accent. /paʈʈa-/ also has the characteristics of a stem: it is associated to a pitch accent. Merlan (1983: 48) notes that /pak-/ seems to be taking over the functions of /paʈʈa-/ in verbs, since /pak-/ can appear wherever /paʈʈa-/ can, but not vice versa.[47] /ɻej+/ appears to be entirely lexicalised: it is attested with just two verbs: /ɻej+ɲoʔ-mi+/ 'take away' (cf. /ɲoʔ-mi+/ 'go away') and /ɻej+ccuruwe+/ 'rush away with' (cf. /curuwe+/ 'rush away'). Only the first is attested in my data. The form of the second verb lends support to the proposal that /ɻej+/ is a frozen stem: only in ROOT-compounds are roots attested with geminate-initial forms.

Adverbial stems satisfy ALIGNL(PRWD, STEM) and are expected to be associated with pitch, if polysyllabic. Their behaviour is accounted for by the grammar already proposed, given the following ranking in (85), or more properly the domination diagram in (86), showing the absence of an argument for the domination of ALIGNL(PRWD, STEM) by other constraints:

(85) a. FTFORM, FTBIN , PK-TO-HEAD: undominated
b. MWD ≈ PRWD >> IDENT[μ] >> ALIGNL(PRWD, STEM) >> λ ≈ PRWD >> ALIGNR(PK, PPH) >> PARSE(σ)

[46] We might predict that strings of monosyllabic right-binding stems could be parsed together, as is the case with strings of monosyllabic left-binding stems and suffixes. I examine some instances of this below.

[47] This is only true of verbs. /paʈʈa-/ also appears on nouns, as part of a circumfix marking Proprietive or Instrument, e.g. /paʈʈa-ponʈok-jiʔ/ 'with a woomera [spear-thrower]', /paʈʈa-piɳ-jiʔ/ 'with a rock'. /pak-/ cannot be used in this construction. No doubt the Proprietive construction is related to the use of /paʈʈa-/ as a comitative applicative in verbs.

(86)

MWD ≈ PRWD
↓
IDENT[μ] — ALIGNL(PRWD, STEM)
↓
λ ≈ PRWD
↓
PARSE(σ) — ALIGNR(PK, PPH)

(Arrows: ALIGNL(PRWD, STEM) → λ ≈ PRWD; λ ≈ PRWD → ALIGNR(PK, PPH))

Tableau (87) presents a sample derivation. All three of /caʔ-/, /ɳamulu-/, and /ɻu+ŋa/ are stems. The only MWD is /ɻu+ŋa/, the verb. Since all candidates parse this constituent to PRWD they all satisfy MWD ≈ PRWD (not shown). All candidates similarly fail to parse the inflectional prefix /ku-/ to its own PRWD, and thereby violate λ≈ PRWD. Candidate (b) is ill-formed because /caʔ-/ 'now' is too short to constitute a foot. It is not an MWD, because it is not a major category stem, and hence does not license vowel-lengthening.[48] Attempting to parse this stem with the next right-binding stem, as in candidate (c) does not improve the situation, because by doing so the candidate fails to parse each stem isomorphically, fatally violating λ ≈ PRWD. Finally, attempting to parse /caʔ-/ with the inflectional prefix /ku-/ as a PRWD, as in (d), violates ALIGNL(PRWD, STEM). These two morphemes may be parsed as a metrical foot, but this foot cannot be associated with pitch accent because of this constraint.

(87)

	/ku-caʔ-ɳamulu-ɻu+ŋa/ NP-now-really-burn+FUT	IDENT[μ]	ALIGNL (PRWD)	λ ≈ PRWD	ALIGNR (PK)
☞	a. ku-caʔ-[(ɳàmu)lu-][(ɻú+ŋa)]			**	σ
	b. ku-[(cà:ʔ-)][(ɳàmu)lu-][(ɻú+ŋa)]	*!		*	σ
	c. ku-[(càʔ-ɳa)(mùlu-)][(ɻú+ŋa)]			***!	σ
	d. [(kù-caʔ-)][(ɳàmu)lu-][(ɻú+ŋa)]		*!	**	σ

The analysis predicts that monosyllabic right-binding stems should be able to bear pitch just if there is no other eligible item in the word. We also predict that in such cases, ROOT-level bound verb stems (described in 3.3.4) might be able to compound with right-binding stems, in order to be parsed to PRWD level. This prediction is confirmed by the existence of such forms. Right-binding stems are associated with pitch in examples such as [cáʔ-wo]

48 Glottal stops are weightless everywhere in Ngalakgan; see 5.5.

(now-give.PP) and [páʈʈa-me] (APPL-get.PP). The constituents /+wo/ and /+me/ are ROOT-level bound stems, which are not subject to MWD ≈ PRWD, as shown in 3.3.4, and cannot occur independently nor with inflectional affixes alone. The only way they can surface as WORDs is by reduplicating at the ROOT-level—/woʔwo/, /meʔme/—or as elements of a compound, as in (88). Compounds of ROOT-level verb stems with adverbial stems are somewhat marginal. Such bound verb stems are more typical of ROOT-compounds (with other ROOTs).

(88)

	/ŋiɲ-caʔ-wo/ 1mS/2mO-IMMED-give.PP	IDENT [μ]	ALIGNL (PRWD)	λ ≈ PRWD	ALIGNR (PK, PPH)
☞	a. ŋiɲ-[(cáʔ-wo)]			***	σ
	b. ŋiɲ-caʔ-[(wóː)]	*!	*	**	
	c. [(ŋ̀iɲ-caʔ)]-[(wóː)]	*!	*	**	
	d. [(ŋíɲ-caʔ)-wo]		*!	***	σσ

Since neither /caʔ-/ nor /+wo/ are MWDs, neither can be acceptably lengthened to satisfy PRWD-hood by itself, because of IDENT[μ], hence candidates (b) and (c) violate this constraint fatally. Since there is no way to satisfy λ ≈ PRWD without violating IDENT, the difference between candidates (a) and (d) comes down to ALIGNL(PRWD, STEM): candidate (a) aligns the PRWD with the morpheme /caʔ-/, which is a right-binding categorial stem. To align the PRWD with the a-categorial argument prefix /ŋiɲ-/, as in (d), is to violate this constraint.

There are no constraints compelling prefixes to be pitch accented, comparable to MWD ≈ PRWD. There is only the general isomorphic parsing constraint λ ≈ PRWD. This constraint has little effect on prefixes due to the dominance of ALIGNL(PRWD, STEM). Given the right edge bias of primary stress in complex words, the characteristic lack of accent in prefixes in Ngalakgan falls out.

The analysis predicts that prefixing languages with a strong left-edge bias for primary stress should allow accented prefixes. In this case, the constraint on peaks would be ALIGNLEFT(PK, PPH). Even with a constraint ALIGNL (PRWD, STEM) in these languages, prefixes would be stressed, just as suffixes in Ngalakgan are, so long as ALIGNL(PK, PPH) dominates ALIGNL(PRWD, STEM). This appears to be true of Marra and Alawa, at least from my informal impressions based on working with speakers of these languages. In these languages, which are also prefixing, primary stress is associated with the initial syllable of the prefix. Prefixed words in Marra and Alawa are analogous to unprefixed words, which also have primary stress on the initial.

In another prefixing language, Dalabon, ALIGNL(PRWD, STEM) is crucially dominated by $\lambda \approx$ PRWD, leading to a situation where *every* word-level morpheme is a potential PRWD. Evans, Fletcher, and Ross (In press) describe incipient degrammaticalisation in Dalabon, where inflectional prefixes are word-like in several respects: they may be prosodically independent of a following verb, and they are bounded by glottal stop. The latter, as discussed in Chapter 6, is a typical characteristic of word boundaries in Northern languages.

Therefore, being accentless is not *necessarily* a condition of being a prefix (cf. Selkirk 1995: 445). It falls out of general considerations: the penultimate bias for primary stress, and the preference for accents to be associated with semantic content.

4.6 Conclusion

This chapter has shown that all WORD-level morphemes in Ngalakgan optimally constitute Prosodic Words: parsing which is isomorphic to the morphological constituency is a general characteristic of the language, as in most Australian languages. Within this general tendency, there are biases and other constraints which account for the asymmetric distribution of stress and pitch accents we observe. Morphemes with high semantic salience—stems of the major categories Noun, Verb, Adjective—are always privileged in prosodic structure. The most word-like of the bound morphemes—bound stems—are also privileged, but to a lesser extent.

Both prefixes and suffixes are subject only to $\lambda \approx$ PRWD—the general parsing constraint. The differences between them amount to a special relationship between lexical content and pitch, and to the right edge bias for primary stress. The constraints on this relationship restrict the domain of accent to begin as much as possible with the first stem in a word. There are no such constraints on the right edge. Indeed, the right-headedness of PPH entails that any left-bound stems and suffixes must be included in the domain of stress, although this outcome varies with an outcome wherein suffixes remain unaccented. Inflectional prefixes are stressless, then, because they lack lexical content, and purely because of their position to the left of any other such contentful items in the word. There is no need for a special stipulation to the effect that prefixes may not be accented.

The second part of the book focusses on some phenomena which are more particular to Ngalakgan and its immediate neighbours—the nature of geminates and glottal stops. Their interaction with quantity is examined in Chapter 5, and their functions as boundary symbols in Chapter 6.

5

Weight

In Chapter 3 I discussed the stress patterns of words containing only monomoraic syllables. Ngalakgan is however a quantity-sensitive language. In this chapter I present an analysis of this aspect of Ngalakgan's prosodic system.

The central issue in this discussion is the behaviour of geminates and homorganic nasal+stop clusters for the purposes of syllable quantity. In current linguistic theory (e.g. Hayes 1989), geminates have the representation in (1).

(1)
$$\begin{array}{c}\mu \\ | \\ \text{C}\end{array}$$

This representation implies that a geminate consonant should make the preceding syllable heavy, since prosodic 'weight', like segmental quantity, is determined by the number of moras associated to the syllable, or segment, respectively (e.g. Hyman 1985).

However, geminates in Ngalakgan do not make the preceding syllable heavy, even though other codas may do so. There are several possible explanations for this difference between Ngalakgan and most other languages. It could be the case that moras are not, in fact, the basis of quantity-sensitive stress, since not all moraic consonants make heavy codas. Or it could be the case that geminates are not universally moraic. This was the position I argued for in Baker (1999).

Here, I argue instead that the nature of geminates and other homorganic clusters in Ngalakgan is best understood as a relation between articulatory gestures and prosodic structure. This analysis of the weight system of Ngalakgan therefore adds a further complexity to the picture of geminates and weight, already brought into question by Selkirk's (1988) and Tranel's (1991) observations that even in weight-sensitive languages, geminates do not always contribute to weight. While the weight-sensitivity pattern discussed here is best described for Ngalakgan, other neighbouring languages such as Bininj Gun-wok, Ngandi, Rembarrnga, Alawa, and Marra have stress systems which appear to be of a similar type. This is not a pattern which is restricted to Ngalakgan, in other words. Rather, there is something about the phonological system of Ngalakgan and other languages of Central Arnhem Land which drives this unusual relationship between monogesturality and (lack of) weight.[1] I argue that the difference originates in syllabification: monogestural clusters (including geminates) are syllabified as onsets in these languages, as suggested in Chapter 2.

I will first describe which syllables are and are not heavy in Ngalakgan, in 5.1, and show why the Ngalakgan facts do not follow from the Moraic Theory of weight, in 5.2. I propose an alternative model of syllabification in 5.3, to account for the behaviour of monogestural clusters in Ngalakgan. In 5.4 I analyse the Ngalakgan pattern in terms of well-established constraints on syllabification interacting with quantity-sensitivity. Sections 5.4.1-4 describe and analyse heavy syllables in various positions in the word in terms of well-attested processes such as destressing in 'clash' (Prince 1983). In 5.4.5-6, I discuss some further patterns in Ngalakgan and other languages which point to a similar phonological distinction between monogestural and bigestural clusters for weight. 5.4.7 discusses the implications of the analysis for Moraic Theory. 5.5 describes the interaction of glottal stops with stress and analyses their behaviour in terms of their special articulatory properties. 5.6 briefly discusses the effect of onset prominence on stress in Ngalakgan. 5.7 concludes the chapter, with a summary of the discussion.

5.1 The nature of weight in Ngalakgan

In Chapter 3 I showed that metrical stress in Ngalakgan is trochaic, and aligned to the left edge of words and WORD-level morphemes. So the distinction between regular edge-based stress on the one hand, and quantity-sensitive or prominence-based stress in Ngalakgan is easiest to see in trisyllabic roots, where these systems are in conflict.

In trisyllabic roots, we find a consistent distinction between those with medial stress and those with initial stress. With a handful of exceptions, forms with medial stress have a medial closed syllable (L: light syllable, H: heavy; bolding and preceding apostrophe indicate stress).

[1] It could well be that Australian languages from other parts of the country have similar stress systems. At present, in-depth phonological investigations of the prosodic systems of Australian languages are very scarce.

(2)				
a.	[bʊɖɔ́lgo̰]	/pu**ʈol**koʔ/	L'HL	‘brolga’
b.	[miɻárppṵ]	/mi**ɻar**ppuʔ/	L'HL	‘crab’
c.	[lʊɲʊ́rwa]	/lu**ɲur**wa/	L'HL	‘vine sp.’
d.	[mɔɳɔ́cpɔr]	/mo**ɳoc**pɔr/	L'HL	‘mud cod’
e.	[waɻʊ́rkku]	/wa**ɻur**kku/	L'HL	‘club’
f.	[gaɖáɪkka̰]	/ka**ʈaj**kkaʔ/	L'HL	‘stringybark tree’
g.	[bʊrʊ́ʈci]	/pu**ruʈ**ci/	L'HL	‘water python’
i.	[ɟibáɲma]	/ci**paɲ**ma/	L'HL	[personal name]

The reason for the stress pattern in words of this type will be discussed in the first half of the chapter. 5.6 examines other kinds of anomalous medial stress patterns.

I have represented the medial syllable in such cases as ‘heavy’ (H), in accordance with our current understanding of stress systems where aspects of syllable structure interact with stress (e.g. Hyman 1985; McCarthy and Prince 1986; Prince 1990; Hayes 1995). Roots of this form are rare, (2) contains all the attested trisyllabic examples with an initial open syllable.[2]

Forms with *initial stress* fall into two groups. The first group is represented by roots where all syllables are open (CV):

(3)				
a.	[bíɟuɖu]	/**pi**cuʈu/	'LLL	‘big wind’
b.	[wáɖija]	/**wa**ʈija/	'LLL	‘multiparous woman’
c.	[ɟɛ́ɾaɖa]	/**ce**raʈa/	'LLL	‘women’s ceremony’
d.	[ɟílaɾa]	/**ci**lara/	'LLL	‘unidentified tree sp.’
e.	[gámala]	/**ka**mala/	'LLL	‘sky’
f.	[mʊ́naŋa]	/**mu**naŋa/	'LLL	‘European’
g.	[múwaɖa]	/**mu**waʈa/	'LLL	‘canoe’
h.	[ŋʊ́ɭiɾi]	/**ŋu**ɭiri/	'LLL	‘black duck sp.’
i.	[wálama]	/**wa**lama/	'LLL	‘face’

Roots of this form are relatively common in the lexicon.

The second group of *initially-stressed* roots also have what appears to be a medial closed syllable. But in these cases, the medial cluster is homorganic. The examples in (4)a-f below behave as if they consist of sequences of light syllables, and are stressed on the first syllable. The examples in (4)a-f contrast with those in (4)g-k, which consist of heavy as well as light syllables. These words are stressed on the heavy syllable.

---

[2] Examples in this chapter are taken from an electronic lexical database of Ngalakgan (available from the Australian Institute of Aboriginal and Torres Strait Islander Studies ASEDA archive). There are 1268 monomorphemic roots recorded for Ngalakgan, of which 310 have more than two syllables.

(4) a. [mɔ́ɭɔppɔɭ] 'LLL
/**mo**ɭoppoɭ/ ‘shovelhead catfish’
b. [ɟábatta] 'LLL
/**ca**patta/ ‘freshwater tortoise sp.’
c. [ɟáɾʊʈʈu] 'LLL
/**ca**ruʈʈu/ ‘female agile wallaby’
d. [mánappʊɳ] 'LLL
/**ma**nappuɳ/ ‘echidna’ (spiny anteater)
e. [mɔ́ɾɔʈʈɪŋ̰] 'LLL
/**mo**roʈʈinʔ/ ‘wild cassava’
f. [gámakkʊn] 'LLL
/**ka**makkun/ ‘properly’
g. [mɔɳɔ́cpɔr] L'HL
/mo**ɳoc**por/ ‘mud cod’
h. [bʊɖɔ́lgɔ̰] L'HL
/pu**ʈol**koʔ/ ‘brolga’
i. [gɪbíʈkulʊ^{I}c] L'HLL
/ki**piʈ**kuluc/ ‘tawny frogmouth’
j. [gʊ̀ɾiɟáʈpɔŋgo] 'LL"HLL
/**kurica**ʈpoŋko/ ‘olive python’
k. [ɟæ̀ɾaɖáʈpuwa] 'LL"HLL
/**cara**ʈ**at**puwa/ ‘chestnut rail’

Syllables followed by geminates are not the only apparently closed syllables which do not behave as heavy syllables; the same pattern is found with homorganic nasal-stop (NC) clusters.[3] Examples in (5) show that such syllables are not stressed in the medial position of trisyllabic roots (a-c), nor in weak metrical positions in longer roots (d) (that is, in positions which would not be stressed because of foot structure).[4]

(5) a. [ŋɔ́lɔŋgɔ̰] 'LLL
/ŋoloŋkoʔ/ *Eucalyptus camaldulensis* (‘river redgum’)
b. [ɟáganda] 'LLL
/cakanta/ ‘female plains kangaroo’
c. [ŋʊ́ɾʊɳɖʊ^{I}c] 'LLL
/ŋuruɳʈuc/ ‘emu’
d. [gáɻaŋgàŋaɳ̀ini] "LL'LL'LL
/kaɻaŋkaŋaɳini/ ‘macropod sp.’

---

[3] Hereafter, in the interests of readability, these will simply be referred to as ‘NC clusters’, except where they are contrasted with heterorganic clusters.
[4] Such roots are common in the corpus, example (5) represents a small sample.

In longer roots, we observe the same weightlessness of geminates. There are just two quadrisyllabic roots with a geminate between the second and third syllables, which are otherwise open-syllabled (6)a-b. In these forms, the geminate does not attract stress. A syllable in this environment *does* receive stress if it is independently heavy because of another consonant preceding the geminate (6)c-d:

(6)	a.	[wáɻaccàɾa] /**wa**ɻ**accar**a/ ‘flood water’	"LL'LL	c.	[gaɳɖálppuɾu] L'HLL /ka**ɳʈal**ppuru/ ‘female plains kangaroo’
	b.	[ŋámʊccùlo] /**ŋa**mu**ccu**lo/ [subsection term]	"LL'LL	d.	[gulʊ́ɪkkulʊɹ̰] L'HLL /ku**luj**kkulujʔ/ ‘tawny frogmouth’

The examples presented here show that there is an association between place of articulation, syllable structure, and the placement of stress in roots. But it is not the kind of association that crosslinguistic patterns or Moraic Theory would lead us to expect.

Moreover, this pattern is not restricted to Ngalakgan. It is also found in neighbouring language groups such as Marra, Rembarrnga, and Kuninjku. Here, I further illustrate the pattern with examples from Kuninjku, a dialect of Bininj Gun-wok. In roots, BGW has an identical stress pattern to Ngalakgan in most respects, with stress initial in roots (Evans 2003: 100; Bishop 2002). As in Ngalakgan though, heavy syllables disturb this pattern. In particular, syllables which end in a consonant which is heterorganic to any following consonant attract stress:[5]

(7)	a.	/ka**pir**pa/	[gabírba]	‘scats’
	b.	/ko**corʔ**mi/	[goɟóɹ̰mi]	‘orange footed scrub fowl’
	c.	/ku**luj**pir/	[gʊlʊ́ɪbɪr]	‘saratoga’
	d.	/ku**lujʔ**kuluj/	[gʊlʊ́ɹ̰kʊlʊɪ]	‘tawny frogmouth’
	e.	/na**pur**ma/	[nabʊ́rma]	‘striated heron’
	f.	/na**rul**mi/	[naɾʊ́lmi]	‘mythological kangaroo’
	g.	/na**wor**koɭ/	[nawɔ́rgɔɭ]	‘green ant’

[5] The existing research on BGW does not recognise quantity-sensitive stress as a consistent feature of the language. Bishop (2002) notes that some words in her sample have nonstandard stress patterns, which she attributes to ‘limited’ quantity sensitivity, but carried out no systematic investigation of this phenomenon. The stress patterns presented here have been checked with Murray Garde and Nick Evans independently. Garde is a fluent second language speaker of the language, and author of a PhD study of pragmatics in the language (Garde 2003). Evans, with 20 years experience of Bininj Gun-wok in the field, is the author of a comprehensive grammar of the language. I leave it to future research to check these patterns with native speakers. The phonetic representations here are extrapolated from the descriptions of Evans (2003) and Bishop (2002).

h.	/ŋa**laj**ŋu/	[ŋaláɪŋu]	[kun-rdebi kin term]
i.	/ŋa**ɻel**ji/	[ŋaɻɛ́lji]	'long-necked tortoise'
j.	/wa**lirŋ**no/	[walírŋno]	'placenta'[6]
k.	/wa**ʈur**kku/	[waɖʊ́rkku]	'silver barramundi'
l.	/ja**kir**cca/	[jagírcca]	'milkwood'

Just as in Ngalakgan, trisyllabic roots wherein the second vowel is followed by a monogestural cluster—a homorganic nasal-stop cluster or a geminate—do not take penultimate stress.[7] They take the usual initial stress pattern. Example (8) gives forms with homorganic nasal-stop clusters.

(8)	a.	/cawuntu/	[ɟáwundu]	'sea eagle'
	b.	/paɳampi/	[báɳambi]	'fishing net'
	c.	/cinempu/	[ɟínembu]	'fish sp.'
	d.	/capaɳʈa/	[ɟábaɳɖa]	'python'
	e.	/maʅiɲci/	[máʅiɲɟi]	'preying mantis'
	f.	/karampun/	[gáɾambʊn]	'hold hand over eyes'
	g.	/cakaɳʈiɲ/	[ɟágaɳɖiɲ]	'catfish sp.'
	h.	/camaɳʈar/	[ɟámaɳɖar]	'Colocasia sp.'
	i.	/pulaɲcan/	[bʊ́laˈɲɟan]	[subsection term]

As in Ngalakgan, geminates fail to attract stress to the preceding syllable, as shown in (9):

(9)	a.	/palacci/	[bálaˈcci]	'bag' (< Makassarese *balase*)
	b.	/peracca/	[bɛ́ɾaˈcca]	'rice' (< Makassarese *berasaʔ*)
	c.	/poloppi/	[bɔ́lɔppi]	'unidentified tuber sp.'
	d.	/poʅokko/	[bɔ́ʅɔkko]	'water python' (*Bothrochilus fuscus*)
	e.	/cilippa/	[ɟílɪppa]	'light footwear' (< English 'slippers')
	f.	/toloppo/	[dɔ́lɔppo]	'bark of *Eucalyptus tetradonta*'
	g.	/kalukku/	[gálʊkku]	'coconut'
	h.	/manekke/	[mánɛkke]	'that one (VEG class)'
	i.	/maʅakka/	[máʅakka]	'sacred dillybag'
	j.	/marappi/	[máɾappi]	'sand palm' (*Livistonia humilis*)
	k.	/muɳuppar/	[mʊ́ɳʊppar]	'magpie goose' (*Anseranus semipalmata*)
	l.	/ŋalekke/	[ŋálɛkke]	'that one (FEM class)'
	m.	/ŋaʈukki/	[ŋáɖʊkki]	'mine'

[6] The element *-no* is an optional suffix in some BGW dialects, though in Kuninjku it is becoming obligatory for reference to body parts with (overt or implicit) 3rd person possessors (Evans 2003: 196).

[7] Geminates are analysed as long stops in (Evans 2003: 81), in onset position. However, they have the same effect on preceding vowel allophony as a coda (Evans 2003: 73).

This pattern appears to be consistent for my informants, with one or two exceptions, discussed immediately below. The list in (7) represents all of the trisyllabic roots of this form in the Kuninjku dictionary (2900 entries).

Besides lexical roots, most of the proper names of this form in Kuninjku also follow the general pattern:

(10)	a.	/ce**ler**kajo/	[ɟɛlέrgaˡjo]
	b.	/ka**caɻ**ŋu/	[gaɟáɻŋu]
	c.	/ku**mor**polk/	[gumɔ́rbɔlk]
	d.	/ku**rar**me/	[guɾárme]
	e.	/ku**ruɭ**ʈuɭ/	[gʊɾʊ́ɭɖul]
	f.	/mi**pal**met/	[mibálmet]
	g.	/na**kulʔ**mu/	[nagʊ́l̰mu]
	h.	/ku**caɳ**ŋal/	[guɟáɳŋal]
	i.	/ku**ntul**ke/	[gʊndʊ́lge]
	j.	/pu**ʈaɲ**pere/	[buɖáˡɲbɛɾe]
	k.	/ci**mpur**kula/	[ɟɪmbʊ́rgula]
	l.	/ji**rar**kija/	[jɪɾárgija]

There are a handful of exceptions to the rule, listed here. Most of the exceptions are proper names (11). Additionally, there are one or two common noun roots which are exceptions to the pattern, given in (12).

(11)	a.	/caŋackal/	[ɟá**ŋac**kal] ~ [ɟa**ŋác**kal]
	b.	/mumenker/	[mʊ́**mɛn**gɛr]
	c.	/mumulŋoʈ/	[mʊ́**mʊl**ŋɔʈ]
	d.	/kamuɭkpaɳ/	[gá**mʊɭk**paɳ]
	e.	/papoɻji/	[bá**bɔɻ**ji]

(12)	a.	/karakpal/	[gáɾakpal]	'moon'
	b.	/ŋulanjak/	[ŋʊ́lanjak]	'tomorrow'[8]

This pattern in Kuninjku is not limited to roots, it also affects the stress pattern of (historically) complex words such as the ROOT-compound verb forms, like those of Ngalakgan discussed in Chapter 3:[9]

---

[8] In the case of the form /ŋulanjak/, we are tempted to think that here the cluster is assimilated (phonologically if not phonetically) to the palatal nasal /ɲ/. I have no examples of this kind of cluster in Ngalakgan affecting stress in the same way.

[9] The verbs here are given in the NonPast form, which requires an overt agreement prefix of some kind. This has been omitted here, because it does not affect the stress of the root when the latter is polysyllabic. There is a large number of verbs with this phonological pattern in the lexicon, the forms in (13) represent a selection picked at random. I leave it to future research to investigate the phonological nature of stress in complex words in Kuninjku.

(13) a. /ka**perk**+ti/ [gabɛ́rkdi] 'be outside'
b. /ka**perk**+ni/ [gabɛ́rkni] 'be outside'
c /ne**ner**+ke/ [nɛnɛ́rge] 'rattle boomerang sticks together'
d. /ŋa**larp**+me/ [ŋalárpme] 'swim'
e. /ɻa**kalk**+ɻe/ [ɻagálkɻe] 'do sorcery'

While Ngalakgan is now an extinct language, Kuninjku still has several hundred speakers, and is being acquired by children (Evans 2003: 18). Moreover, it belongs to a dialect chain of several thousand speakers which in all probability shares the same general stress pattern. Other languages of the Central and Southern Arnhem Land regions appear to have similar quantity-sensitive stress patterns.[10] Therefore, the pattern described here is a significant one in the Australian context.

Note that there are reasons to believe that this stress pattern is also synchronically active, since loanwords with alternate stress patterns have been modified to fit the pattern. I repeat the relevant examples here:

(14) a. /peracca/ [bɛ́raˈcca] 'rice'; Makassarese /bérasaʔ/
b. /palacci/ [bálaˈcci] 'bag'; Makassarese /baláse/
c. /palanta/ [bálanda] 'European'; Makassarese /balánda/[11]
d. /cilippa/ [ɟílɪppa] 'light footwear' (< English 'slippers')

In one case, (a), the BGW form has the same stress as the form in the donor language, Makassarese.[12] In three cases (b, c, d), however, the donor language has a distinct stress pattern, which has been adapted to conform to the regular pattern. This fact indicates that the stress pattern is not a frozen one, tied to particular roots in the lexicon. Rather, it is one which affects the phonology of these languages synchronically.

This pattern has not been recognised before. Besides being significant in terms of its distribution in Australian languages, it is also significant from the standpoint of phonological theory. I will briefly explain why the Ngalakgan facts are significant in this respect, before offering my explanation for the pattern and its relationship to other crosslinguistic phenomena.

---

10 I have tested stress patterns in roots in citation in both Rembarrnga and Marra. I would say the pattern seems consistent in Marra, based on the items I collected, perhaps less so in Rembarrnga. But in neither case did I extract a complete list of roots with the relevant pattern, and so I will not examine them in detail here. What is clear however, is that in all these languages the stress patterns in roots do not always follow the simple 'stress the initial syllable' rule.

11 This is a word with wide currency in Arnhem Land, although not traditionally associated with BGW or Ngalakgan.

12 Thanks to Anthony Jukes for confirming these stress patterns; for further discussion of this language, see Jukes (2006).

5.2 Geminates in Moraic Theory

Geminates are expected to count for weight everywhere in Moraic Theory (e.g. Hyman 1985; Hayes 1989), so the Ngalakgan pattern contradicts general assumptions. As stated in the introduction, in a moraic theory of syllable weight, heavy syllables are bimoraic, and light ones monomoraic:

(15)

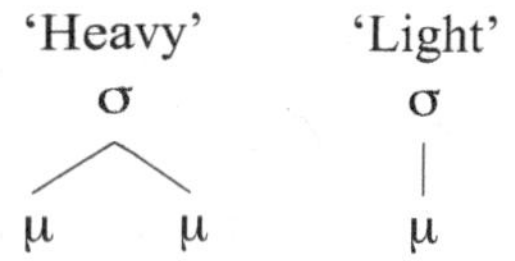

In words with some heavy and some light syllables in a quantity-sensitive language, heavy syllables are stressed in preference to light ones, a condition which is dubbed the 'Weight-to-Stress Principle' in Prince and Smolensky (1993: 53):

(16) Weight-to-Stress Principle (WSP):
'Heavy syllables are prominent in foot structure and on the grid'

Example (2)c above for instance, can be represented as in (17) below:

(17)

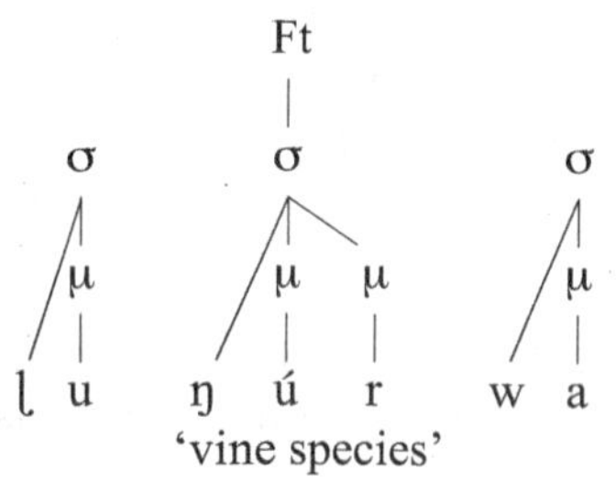

The medial syllable of (17) is associated to two moras, therefore it is a 'heavy' syllable, and the WSP demands that any heavy syllable receive stress.

The WSP principle, and the proposal that heavy syllables are those which are bimoraic, is the standard way of accounting for quantity-sensitive stress systems (e.g. Hyman 1985; Hayes 1989, 1995; Prince 1990; Prince and Smolensky 1993).

The Moraic Theory, as well as being a theory of prosodic *weight*, is also a theory of segmental *length*: long segments are associated to more moras than short segments (Hayes 1989: 256-7), as shown in Figure (1):

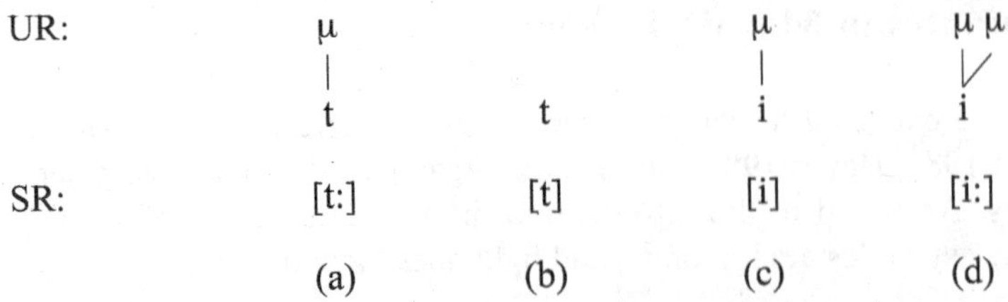

Figure 1: Representation of long segments in Moraic Theory: (a) geminate stop, (b) plain stop, (c) short vowel, (d) long vowel

The geminate stop, in (a) is associated to a moraic position. The geminate is syllabified ambisyllabically, one half (the moraic position) is associated to the preceding syllable node as a coda, and the other half (which is non-moraic) to the following onset:

(18)

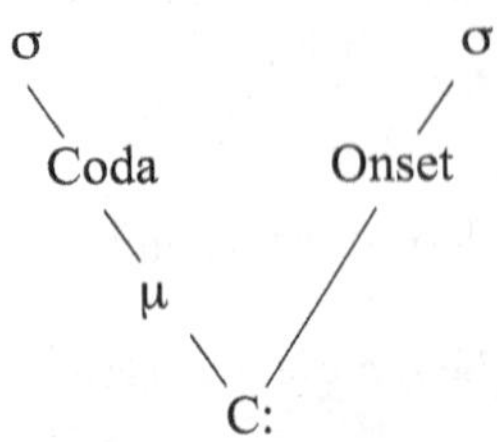

Thus, geminates contribute a moraic coda to the preceding syllable and therefore they are expected to make the preceding syllable bimoraic (since vowels are always moraic). In a quantity-sensitive language then, the following should hold:

(19) Syllables preceding a geminate should be bimoraic, and where stress is associated to heavy syllables, syllables preceding a geminate should be stressed.

So in the word presented in (20), the medial syllable is expected to be heavy, and stressed, based on the prediction in (19).

(20)

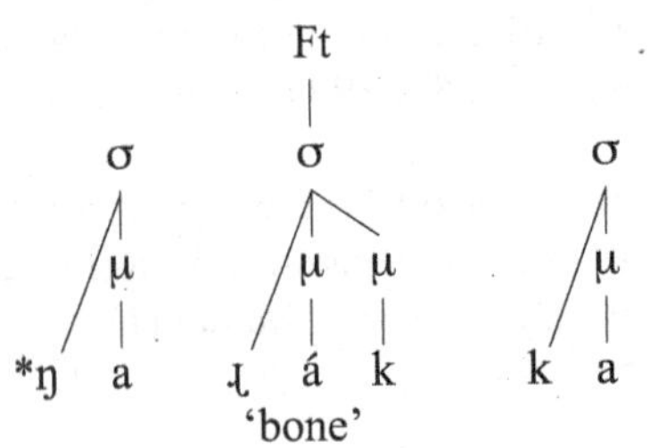

Ngalakgan does not behave in this way, as we have seen.

Tranel (1991) and others (e.g. Lahiri and Kooreman 1988; Selkirk 1988) have observed that the prediction in (19) is empirically false. In Selkup for instance, CVV syllables are heavy, but any syllable closed by a consonant is light, including those closed by a geminate (Tranel 1991: 294, citing Halle and Clements 1983: 189). Stress falls on the rightmost heavy syllable, else the leftmost syllable in Selkup, where heavy syllables are those with long vowels, as shown in (21). Examples (21)a-b show the stress pattern with heavy syllables, c-e with light syllables. Example (21)f shows that a syllable preceding a geminate does not act like a heavy syllable—it is not stressed in preference to the initial syllable.

Heavy CVV syllables
(21) a. qu.mooq.lɨ.**lɨ́ɨ** LHL'H
'your two friends'
b. qu.**móo**.qɨ L'HL
'two human beings'

Light CV, CVC syllables
c. qú.mɨ.nɨk 'LLL
'human being' (DAT)
d. á.mɨr.na 'LLL
'eats'
e. úŋ.ŋɨn.tɨ 'LLL
'wolverine'

Light CVG (G a geminate)
f. **úu**.cɨk.kak 'HLL
'I am working'

Hayes (1995: 302) notes other languages in which geminates do not count for weight (in an otherwise quantity-sensitive system): some dialects of Yupik (Eskimo), Chuvash (Turkic), Ossetic (Iranian), and various Algonquian languages.

Tranel proposed instead a principle of 'equal weight of codas', which states that '*ceteris paribus*, coda portions of geminate consonants behave in the same way as other coda consonants with respect to syllable weight' (1991: 293). The content of Tranel's principle is that in quantity-sensitive languages, if codas are heavy, then the coda portions of geminates are also heavy. But again Ngalakgan does not fulfil this condition: some codas make a syllable heavy, others do not. Note that the weightlessness of geminates must be extended to homorganic NC clusters also. But Tranel's prediction is valid only if these clusters are syllabified in both coda and onset. Chapter 2 has provided reasons for doubting this analysis in the case of Ngalakgan and related languages.

Geminates and homorganic NC clusters have attracted theoretical interest, largely because these articulations often exhibit ambiguous behaviour. They behave like single segments for some phonological processes, and complex segments for others. Hayes (1986, following e.g. Kenstowicz and Pyle 1973; McCarthy 1979; Prince 1984) proposed that geminates are single segments on the melodic tier, but clusters for prosody (including the syllable). Therefore, processes which target melody (such as assimilation) should treat them as single segments, while prosodic processes should treat them as clusters. Stress is a prosodic process, and thus should treat geminates and other homorganic articulations as clusters. However, geminates and NC clusters behave like single segments for prosodic purposes in Ngalakgan: they do not have the same characteristics as other clusters for stress. Chapter 2 has also showed that, in terms of syllable structure, geminates are ambiguous: for many patterns they behave like clusters, but for some phonotactic generalisations they are better analysed as onsets.

Both geminates and homorganic NC clusters are produced with a single articulatory gesture (Hamilton 1996), thus I will refer to both clusters as 'monogestural' in what follows. In a Feature Geometry model (e.g. Sagey 1990), homorganicity (including monogesturality) is represented by association of a single place node to two timing slots on the skeleton:

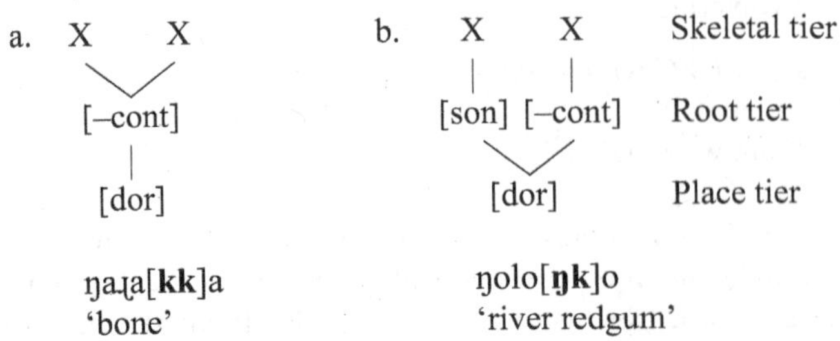

Figure 2 Homorganic consonant sequences in Ngalakgan: (a) geminate, (b) homorganic nasal-stop cluster

Figure (2)a shows a homorganic geminate obstruent, and (2)b a homorganic NC cluster. The two differ in that, while the two timing slots of the geminate have identical melodic features, the NC cluster starts with a lowered velum and ends with a raised velum. Thus, the NC cluster is a sequence of sonorant followed by obstruent.

However, simple homorganicity in the phonological sense is not sufficient to account for the prosodic behaviour of clusters in these languages, as the Kuninjku example in (22) shows.

(22) /kuruɭʈuɭ/ [gʊrʊ́ɭɖʊɭ] [clan name]

In (22), the segment /ɭ/ and the segment /ʈ/ which follows both share the same phonological place: apico-retroflex. But this does not make them monogestural, as pointed out by Hamilton (1996). The segment /ɭ/ is produced with a characteristic lateral gesture, with contact along the middle of the palate but not along the sides, while the stop /ʈ/ is produced with complete closure in the oral cavity. Despite sharing place then, this cluster counts as 'heterorganic'—or more properly, bigestural—for the purposes of quantity-sensitivity in Kuninjku (as noted in Chapter 2, Ngalakgan lacks entirely clusters of liquid+apical).[13]

The fact that geminates and NC clusters are produced with a single oral articulatory gesture distinguishes them from all other supralaryngeal clusters in the language (clusters involving glottal stop are discussed below in 5.5). Therefore, we can observe that syllables which are heavy for stress are those in which a following cluster is bigestural, while syllables which are not heavy for stress, are those in which a following segment, cluster or sequence is monogestural. This kind of quantity-sensitivity has not hitherto been described in the literature.

The Moraic Theory rests on the principle that stress refers only to the characteristics of the syllable node, and in particular, the number of moras each syllable contains. The only thing that stress rules need to know is whether or not the syllable node dominates more than one mora. So the interesting question to be resolved in Ngalakgan is why stress should have anything to do with gesture, while apparently ignoring syllabic properties. In the following sections I argue that the sequence of consonant gestures in Ngalakgan and related languages is crucial for deciding on what counts as a moraic consonant, though indirectly, through syllabification. In section 5.4 I discuss why Australian languages should apparently be different to other, better-known, language groups in this respect, and some related patterns which suggest that the treatment of monogestural clusters as non-moraic segments is correct, at least for these languages. In the section which follows, I expand on the importance of monogesturality for the nature of quantity in Ngalakgan and related languages.

---

[13] We could regard this form as a lexical exception. However, unlike the exceptions listed in (11), there is no apparent reason for this pattern. The exceptions with initial stress can be regarded as the effect of 'majority rule': the fact that the majority of roots in Ngalakgan and Kuninjku are initially-stressed. There can be no such explanation for an exceptional penultimate stress pattern.

5.3 Timing vs gesture in metrical systems

What I will suggest here is that the fundamental difference between languages like Ngalakgan, and other quantity-sensitive languages, is in the relationship between timing, gesture and syllabification. One means of representing timing is through affiliation to moras, making timing equivalent to weight (as shown in Figure 1). However, we have seen that this is an unsupportable assumption on general grounds, given that geminates do not consistently contribute weight in a number of otherwise quantity-sensitive languages. Rather, I will use the 'skeletal slot' theory of timing (Levin 1985), distinguishing this from the moraic theory of weight (cf. Selkirk 1988).

Under the skeletal theory, long segments such as geminates and contrastively long vowels are represented as a single root node associated to two timing slots, represented either as 'X's (Levin 1985) or as 'C's and 'V's (Clements and Keyser 1983), where the root node is the 'core' of a segment's bundle of place and manner features:

(23)	X X	X	X X	X	Timing tier
	\/	|	\/	|	
	/p/	/p/	/a/	/a/	Root tier
	geminate	singleton	long vowel	short vowel	

Rather than the root node, however, in what follows I will refer instead to the 'gesture' in the sense of Browman and Goldstein (1989). Under this model, shown in (24), gestures encode the complex of major articulator together with a three-way distinction in stricture, equivalent to the distinction between total closure (oral or nasal stop), continuant, and glide.

(24) a.	X X	X	X	Timing tier
	\/	|	|	
	/p/	/f/	/w/	Gesture
	|	|	|	
	stop	continuant	glide	Stricture

Hence, homorganic nasal-stop clusters are monogestural because they share both major articulator and constriction type: total closure (25)b, just as geminates do, (25)a. Homorganic clusters of liquid plus stop such as /ɭʈ/, (25)c, are not monogestural because, although they share major articulator (apico-retroflex), they do not share the same constriction features. A liquid does not involve total closure; it does not involve the same kind of constriction as the following stop. Hence, this cluster cannot be produced with a single articulatory gesture.

(25)
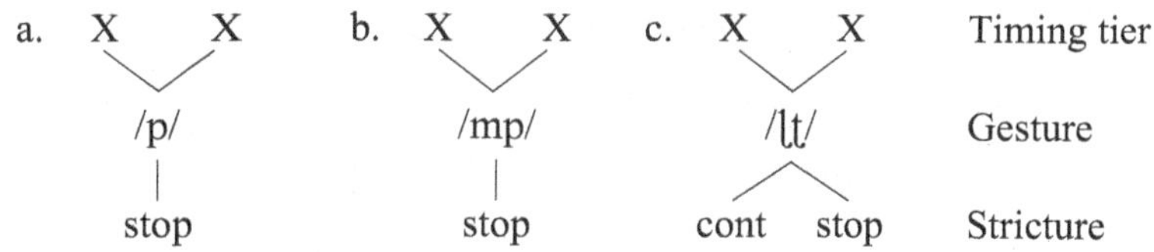

In the majority of languages, it is the timing positions which serve as the input to syllabic structure. In the syllabification algorithm of Itô (1988) for instance, after the universal association of peaks to syllable nodes, onsets are built by associating as many timing slots as are licensed (in a partly language-specific way) to the onset node (the 'Maximal Onset Principle': Kahn 1976). Any remaining material that cannot be syllabified in the onset is syllabified in the coda. If we believe that weight is computed over rimes, then it follows that weight bears a direct relationship to timing slots: the more timing slots within the rime, the heavier the syllable (cf. Blevins 1995).

What makes Ngalakgan, Kuninjku and these other languages different then, is that syllable structure, and hence weight, is computed, not over timing slots, but over gestures. We can represent this difference schematically as in (26) and (27). In (26) we see the typical association between syllable structure and segmental structure: syllables are built on the basis of the timing slots associated to gestures. Hence, geminates, and other monogestural sequences, are syllabified in separate syllables.

(26)
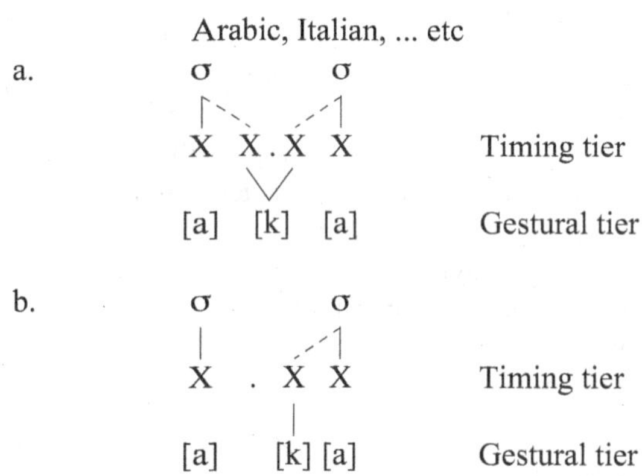

In (27), we see the association that we find in Ngalakgan and other languages of this area, where syllables are built on gestures, not on timing units. Hence, geminates and other monogestural sequences are syllabified in the onset (according to Onset Maximisation) (a), while bigestural sequences are necessarily syllabified in separate syllables (c).

(27) a. b. c.

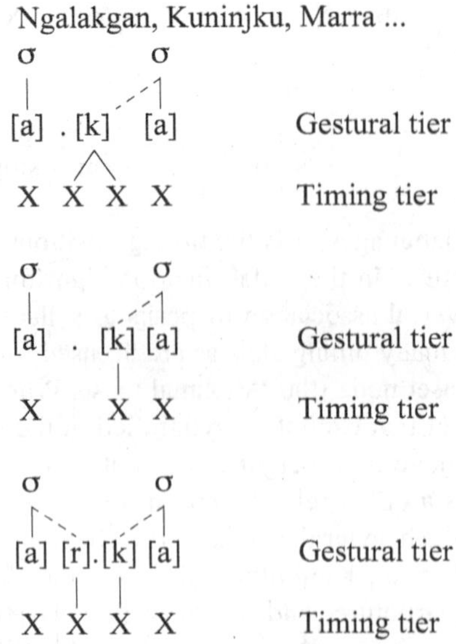

If syllabification is treated as an algorithm which associates margins to syllabic positions, then Ngalakgan and related languages perform this process at a different level to most other languages. Where most languages syllabify on timing positions, Ngalakgan syllabifies at the gestural level.

Note that I am not claiming that geminates or homorganic nasal-stop clusters in Ngalakgan are necessarily segments. In the theory put forward here, they are still clusters, if we define clusters in terms of timing slots (Sagey 1990: 43). This is advantageous, because it allows us to describe their distribution and phonotactic behaviour simply: they behave for the most part like clusters, as shown in Chapter 2. Chapter 2 also showed that, at least in neighbouring languages such as Burarra, these articulations must nevertheless be regarded as occupying an onset position. Similarly, quantity-sensitivity in Ngalakgan and neighbouring languages also suggests that these clusters are onsets. The following section formalises this proposal in an Optimality Theoretic grammar.

5.4 Syllabification in OT

While the intuition about what is happening in Ngalakgan is reasonably clear, it is less clear how to implement this intuition in a formal framework. What follows is a suggestion along these lines, but it will necessarily be subject to further research. There is no escaping the fact that the system found in Ngalakgan and other languages of this area is marked, crosslinguistically.

It has not been described for any other languages of the world. Whatever analysis we can come up with should capture this fact.[14]

In a parallel theory such as OT, we cannot simply stipulate syllable structure and expect to derive the right forms by *fiat*. There must still be a series of constraints which can enforce the distribution that we observe. These constraints should in turn be drawn from the set of constraints made available by Universal Grammar. In particular, since GEN generates a large (or infinite) set of candidate syllabifications, we need constraints which will rule out anything except the syllabification we require for the correct moraic affiliation.

The following constraints are the ones most commonly cited in OT work on syllabification (Prince and Smolensky 1993: 108, 41):

(28) a. ONSET: 'Syllables have onsets'
b. NOCODA: 'Syllables do not have codas'
c. *COMPLEX: 'No more than one C or V may associate to any syllable position node'

The original version of the constraint *COMPLEX refers only to Cs and Vs. Although they do not discuss what they intend here, I assume that Prince and Smolensky meant to refer to segmental timing slots, rather than root nodes. However, if we allow both interpretations of 'C' and 'V' (timing slots or root nodes/gestures), we can capture the Ngalakgan pattern in a simple fashion. I propose therefore that the *COMPLEX constraint be parametrised, as in (29), in a similar way to the parametrisation of the 'FTBIN' constraint, which holds either at the moraic or the syllabic level (Prince and Smolensky 1993). Potentially, this allows for two separate constraints, as shown in (30).

(29) *CXONS (parametrised version): No more than one C or V (at timing or root level) may occupy the onset node.

(30) a. $*\text{CXONS}_T$ (timing): No more than one timing position may occupy the onset node.
b. $*\text{CXONS}_G$ (gesture): No more than one gesture may occupy the onset node.

However, as with the two versions of FTBIN, it is highly unlikely that any languages will make use of both versions of *CXONS, since syllabification never seems to produce contrastive forms in languages (Blevins 1995: 221).

---

[14] I thank Juliette Blevins for reminding me of the importance of this. There are some related patterns found in other languages of the world; these are discussed in 5.4.6.

In the parametrised version of *CXONS, the grammar specifies at which level of the representation the constraint holds: the segmental (timing) tier, or the melodic (gestural) tier. In the majority of languages, it appears, *CXONS holds at the timing tier. Long articulations such as geminates and nasal-stop clusters are syllabified by separate syllables, although it is notoriously difficult to find direct evidence for syllabification (Blevins 1995: 216). In some languages, however, these articulations are possible onsets, leading to analyses of prenasalised stops in the case of nasal-stop clusters (but see Herbert 1975; Downing To appear, for alternative views). Since it is demonstrably the case that languages do allow both geminates and nasal-stop clusters as (word) onsets, then we have to make our model capable of generating this possibility, even in languages with otherwise simple syllable structures. We also need to explain the markedness of word-initial clusters in crosslinguistic terms. I return to this question in 5.4.7.

Consider first the syllabification of medial heavy syllables, shown in (31).

(31)

/ɭuŋurwa/ 'vine sp.'	ONSET	*CXONS$_G$	NOCODA
☞ a. ɭu.ŋur.wa			*
b. ɭu.ŋurw.a	*!		**
c. ɭu.ŋu.rwa		*!	

In this case, syllabification must treat [r] and [w] as belonging to separate syllables. To include them both in the onset, as in (c) is to violate high-ranking *CXONS, in anyone's language. The reason is that there is no way that /rw/ can be articulated with a single gesture. (I must assume in addition here that Faithfulness constraints to the underlying forms of segments outrank these syllabification constraints, in order to prevent parses such as *[ɭu.ŋu.rua]). To include them both in the coda, as in (b), is to violate NOCODA worse than to split them. Moreover, such a parse would violate ONSET, which is demonstrably high-ranking in Ngalakgan as in most Australian languages (Dixon 1980). There is no evidence at this point to enable us to rank ONSET and *CXONS.

I assume that a high-ranking constraint 'Weight-by-Position' (Hayes 1989) forces affiliation of coda consonants to moras exceptionlessly.

(32) Weight-By-Position (WBP): 'Codas are moraic'

With WBP high-ranking, closed syllables are bimoraic. And given the demand that heavy syllables attract stress (the 'Weight-to-Stress Principle' Prince 1990; Prince and Smolensky 1993: 63), then closed syllables will be stressed, all things being equal. The relative ranking of WBP and WSP cannot be determined here.[15]

(33)

/ɭuŋurwa/ 'vine sp.'	WBP	WSP
☞ a. ɭu.ŋúrᵘ.wa		
b. ɭú.ŋurᵘ.wa		*!
c. ɭú.ŋur.wa	*!	

Now consider a trisyllabic word with a geminate, shown in (34).

(34)

/ŋaɻakka/ 'bone'	ONSET	*CXONS$_G$	NOCODA
a. ŋa.ɻakᵘ.ka			*!
b. ŋa.ɻakᵘkᵘ.a	*!		**
☞ c. ŋa.ɻa.kka			

In this case, the fact that geminates are monogestural saves them from violating *CXONS$_G$; crucially, they are simple onsets as far as this constraint is concerned. Because this constraint is high-ranking in Ngalakgan, all monogestural clusters and long monogestural consonantal sequences at the surface will be syllabified by speakers in the following onset, rather than spread across two syllables. Along with WBP (not shown here), this derives the behaviour of weight that we observe in Ngalakgan and neighbouring languages.

In order to capture the behaviour of better-known languages, such as Arabic, with respect to geminate weight, we might propose the same constraint ranking, but with the parameter for *CXONS set to 'timing' rather than 'gesture'. In this case, syllabification of geminates and other long segments in the onset will never be preferred over an ambisyllabic parse, with *CXONS$_T$ high ranking. The following example is of Palestinian Arabic, taken from (Hayes 1995: 126).

15 Codas which are moraic at the surface are shown with superscripted 'μ'. I assume that all vowels are moraic.

(35)

/ʕallamat/ 'she taught'	ONSET	*CXONS$_T$	NOCODA
☞ a. ʕal^μ.la.mat			*
b. ʕal^{μ}l^μ.a.mat	*!		**
c. ʕa.lla.mat		*!	

In both Ngalakgan and Palestinian, the candidate that parses the geminate entirely in the coda (b) violates high-ranking Onset, because it leaves the following syllable without one. Where the two languages differ is in the behaviour of *CXONS: in Palestinian, where this constraint refers to timing slots (as is the unmarked case), a geminate onset violates it. The best solution in Palestinian is to split geminates between neighbouring syllables. And with WBP operating as in Ngalakgan, geminates will always contribute weight to the preceding syllable. Evidently, UG favours syllabification based on timing rather than gesture.

I have made the simple assumption here that GEN generates candidates which freely associate syllabic and moraic structure with input strings (as proposed in Prince and Smolensky 1993 and assumed in much OT work since). These candidates are then weeded by Faithfulness and Markedness constraints. Apart from the constraints on syllabification introduced here, we also require general constraints on the relationship between syllabification, including moraic association, and higher levels of prosodic structure such as feet and PRWDs. The following section provides this analysis.

5.4.1 The organisation of feet in Ngalakgan words

Apart from the evaluation of syllabification and weight in the grammar, there also needs to be a series of constraints referring to the relationship between heavy syllables and the prosodic system in general. This is to account for languages such as Latin and Ngalakgan, where words are parsed into feet, and feet can either consist of one heavy syllable or two light ones. I pursue this question in the remainder of this section.

Prince and Smolensky (1993: 53; cf. Prince 1990) propose that the Weight-to-Stress Principle, already introduced, is a universal constraint on the relationship between syllable weight and the prosodic system.

(36) Weight-to-Stress Principle (WSP):
'Heavy syllables are prominent in foot structure and on the grid'

WSP prefers heavy syllables to be parsed into the strong positions of feet. The existence of WSP in the grammar forces the prosodic system to be uniform: if syllables are stressed because of their inherent characteristics (rather than their position in the word), then they must be considered bimoraic.

The constraints FTBIN and FTFORM(TR) have already been presented in Chapter 3, I repeat them here.

(37) Foot Binarity (FTBIN): 'Feet are binary at some level of analysis (mora μ, syllable σ)'

(38) Foot Form (Trochaic): 'Feet are left headed'

Together, these three constraints in Ngalakgan prefer heavy (bimoraic) syllables to be parsed as bimoraic, stressed feet; as shown in (39).

(39)

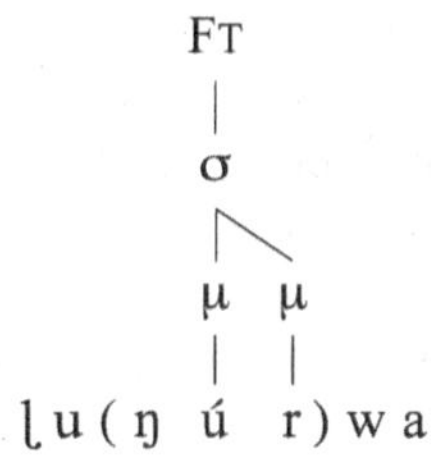

Ngalakgan is a language like those characterised by Prince and Smolensky (1993) as associating stress with the inherent characteristics of syllables, regardless of their position in the word. Therefore, the constraints driving quantity-sensitive stress in Ngalakgan dominate the constraint preferring stress to be edge-based: ALIGNL(PRWD, FT). I repeat its definition here, from Chapter 3.

(40) ALIGNL(PRWD,FT): 'Align the left edge of every Prosodic Word with the left edge of some foot'

ALIGNL is computed gradiently: forms can satisfy this constraint better or worse according to the number of syllables separating the Prosodic Word edge from a foot edge. For every syllable separating a PRWD left edge from a foot left edge the grammar assigns a violation mark. In the tableau, ALIGNL(PRWD, FT) is ranked below the syllabification constraints. FTBIN and FTFORM appear to be undominated in Ngalakgan. WSP must be ranked higher than ALIGNL: it is more important for heavy syllables to be stressed than for stress to be initial in words. The ranking of WSP in relation to the syllabification constraints cannot be determined: these do not conflict with

WSP. In what follows, I simply assume the syllabification and moraic structure argued for in section 5.4 above.

(41)

/ɭuŋurwa/ 'vine sp.'	FTFORM	FTBIN	WSP	ALIGNL (PRWD, FT)
a. [ɭu.(ŋúr$^{\mu}$.wa)]		*!		*
b. [(ɭú.ŋur$^{\mu}$).wa]			*!	
☞ c. [ɭu.(ŋúr$^{\mu}$).wa]				*
d. [(ɭu.ŋúr$^{\mu}$).wa]	*!			
e. [ɭu.(ŋúr$^{\mu}$).(wa)]		*!		*

FTFORM must be ranked above ALIGNL, otherwise we could allow parses of these forms with iambic feet, as in (d), which satisfy the latter but not the former. Since languages do not seem to, on the whole, possess both kinds of foot organisation simultaneously, this should be ruled out on general principles. Given the existence of FTFORM in the grammar, a parse like that in (d) is the most ill-formed candidate, even though phonetically (perhaps) it is indistinguishable from (c).

Chapter 3 suggests that FTBIN is highly-ranked in Ngalakgan, ruling out candidates (a) and (e), though in truth there is no direct evidence that it is active in choosing between (a) and (c) as optimal parses, since the difference is again representational only; both satisfy FTBIN at different prosodic levels. I consider evidence below that in fact (c) is the correct parse, and that feet are maximally, as well as minimally, bimoraic in this language, at least where the difference could lead to a distinct outcome. In this case, there is no better parse which could distinguish them.

(42) displays an evaluation of a geminate-medial form. Again, I assume the syllabification and moraic associations argued for in section 5.4 apply to all candidates shown.

(42)

/ŋaɻakka/ 'bone'	FTFORM	FTBIN	WSP	ALIGNL (PRWD, FT)
☞ a. [(ŋá.ɻa).kka]				
b. [ŋa.(ɻá.kka)]				*!
c. [ŋa.(ɻá).kka]		*!		*

In short, there is nothing to drag stress away from the left edge in the case of words like this, with a geminate or other homorganic cluster between the second and third syllables. High-ranking foot form and binarity constraints prevent alternative parses than the usual one, as in (a).

5.4.2 Heavy syllables elsewhere in the word

We have already seen examples where heavy syllables are medial in trisyllabic roots. This section describes and analyses the distribution of heavy syllables in other positions in words, showing that heavy syllables are stressed regardless of their position in the word, modulo the effects of other constraints.

Heterorganic clusters occur overwhelmingly at the boundary between the first and second syllables of roots. Of 166 occurring roots with a heterorganic cluster, 155 (93%) of them have a cluster in this position. Some examples are presented in (43).

(43) a. /**pal**kkiɲ/ [bálkkiɲ] 'salty; dangerous'
b. /**ŋur**ku/ [ŋúrġu] 'womb, belly'
c. /**par**caɻaj/ [bárɟaɻaɪ] 'large paperbark' (*Melaleuca* sp.)
d. /**ɭar**wa/ [lárwa] 'bush pipe'
e. /**cet**peʈe/ [ɟɛ́tpəɖe] 'archer fish' (*Toxotes* sp.)

A very small proportion of the vocabulary has clusters in a non-initial syllable—we have already encountered all the examples of otherwise open-syllabled trisyllabic roots with a heterorganic cluster following the medial syllable, which provide the strongest evidence of stress effects. In this section I consider the other positions in the word.

5.4.3 Word-final consonants

There is a strong bias against word-final stress in Ngalakgan, which can be formalised in constraint form as 'NONFINALITY' (Prince and Smolensky 1993: 52):

(44) NONFINALITY: 'No final stressed syllables (in Prosodic Word)'

This constraint prevents both primary and secondary stress in PRWD-final syllables.[16]

[16] In Prince and Smolensky (1993:52) NONFINALITY is defined as 'No prosodic head of Prosodic Word is final in Prosodic Word'; where 'prosodic head' is defined as 'strongest foot' in a Prosodic Word, and by transitivity, strongest syllable of the strongest foot: the tonic. The prohibition is stronger than this in Ngalakgan, ruling out *any* prosodic head, including the head of any foot. This interpretation of NONFINALITY is made use of in Prince and Smolensky's (1993: 54) discussion of secondary stress placement in Southern Paiute.

We can see the effects of NONFINALITY in a number of environments. In roots with simple final codas, stress is initial rather than final (45):

(45) a. /ciʈak/ [ɟíɖak] 'coolamon' (a vessel)
b. /cepaŋ/ [ɟɛ́baŋ] 'line, row'
c. /kupuj/ [gʊ́buɪ] 'sweat' (n.)
d. /ŋoʈokoc/ [ŋɔ́ɖɔgoˈc] 'ankle'
e. /kajapam/ [gáɪjabam] 'wild orange' (*Capparis* sp.)
f. /calapir/ [ɟálabɪr] 'red ant sp.'
g. /caʈukal/ [ɟáɖugal] 'male plains kangaroo'
h. /centewerec/ [ɟɛ̀ndɛwɛ́reˈc] 'willy wagtail'

Final coda clusters in disyllables have inconsistent properties. Two examples, shown in (46)a-b, vary between initial and final stress. Four words consistently have initial stress (c-f):

(46) a. /cicciwk/ [ɟíccɪʊk] ~ [ɟɪccíʊk] 'wren sp.'
b. /poʈewk/ [bɔ́ɖɛʊk] ~ [bɔɖɛ́ʊk] 'bad'
c. /waccaɭŋʔ/ [wáccaɭŋ̃] 'mud'
d. /ŋawolŋʔ/ [ŋáwɔlŋ̃] 'navel'
e. /worowk/ [wɔ́ɾoʊk] 'hop' (open class verb stem)
f. /kappuɻk/ [gáppʊɻk] 'dry; not damp'

There are two words which show variation between a final velar and a final glottal stop, both have initial stress:[17]

(47) a. /maʈawk/ ~ /maʈawʔ/ [máɖaʊk] ~ [máɖaʊ̰] 'friarbird'
b. /ʈarawk/ ~ /ʈarawʔ/ [dáɾaʊk] ~ [dáɾaʊ̰] 'tree sp.'

Just three words of this form are stressed finally (48).

(48) a. /kiɳalk/ [gɨɳálk, gɻəɳálk] 'white ibis'
b. /piccurk/ [bɪccʊ́rk] 'edible tuber sp.'
c. /kijark/ [gijǽrk] 'tooth'

I regard the forms in (48) as exceptions to the general rule; their behaviour is discussed in 5.6.

In trisyllables a final syllable ending in a cluster receives what sounds to me like a weak secondary stress (these represent all the examples); primary stress is initial:

[17] There are a few other roots with the same structure whose stress pattern I am unsure of: /camolk/ 'for nothing', /cawelk/ 'grass sp.', /kuɭerŋ/ 'firewood', /kaɭurk/ 'deep'.

(49) a. /peɻemelk/ [bɛ́ɻemɛ̀lk] 'shoulder blade'
b. /cacapaɻɳʔ/ [ɟǽɟæbàɻɳʔ] 'yesterday'
c. /kunuŋuɻk/ [gúnuŋʊ̀ɻk] 'plant sp.'
d. /ciliwurk/ [ɟíliwʊ̀rk] 'guts'
e. /paɻamulk/ [báɻamʊ̀lk] 'wild cucumber'

There is just one disyllabic root with two heavy syllables—stress is initial in this form. I do not hear a secondary stress on the final syllable.

(50) /melwerŋ/ [mɛ́lwɛrŋ] 'insect sp.'

Two trisyllabic roots have adjacent heavy syllables—stress is again on the initial only:

(51) a. /calpurkic/ [ɟǽlbʊrgic] 'jewfish'
b. /ɭaɻkurca/ [láɻgʊrɟa] 'vine sp.'

The dominance of WBP in Ngalakgan would predict final stress in roots like /ciʈak/ and /ŋoʈokoc/. NONFINALITY must therefore be ranked above this constraint. This ranking predicts that closed syllables are heavy and therefore attract stress except where final in the word. This is the generalisation we observe in the forms described in this section.

The result is shown in tableaux (52) and (53) which follow. In (52), we observe that ranking NONFINALITY above the WEIGHT-TO-STRESS-PRINCIPLE and WEIGHT-BY-POSITION derives the result that stress cannot be final despite the presence of a final heavy syllable. The ranking of WBP cannot be determined on this basis, since it does not conflict with either of the other two constraints.[18]

(52)

/ŋoʈokoc/ 'ankle'	NONFINALITY	WSP	WBP
☞ a. (ŋóʈo)koc			*
b. (ŋòʈo)(kóc$^{\mu}$)	*!		
☞ c. (ŋóʈo)koc$^{\mu}$		*	

[18] It could be that WBP is highly ranked, like the syllabification constraints, but NONFINALITY outranks WSP, meaning that final heavy syllables are never stressed. In this case, candidate (c) would be the outcome. Since the difference between candidate (a) and (c) is purely representational, I will not pursue this possibility here.

Whether this word retains a final mora for Ngalakgan speakers is a moot point: there would be no evidence from the grammar that the final syllable was heavy here, and hence both (a) and (c) are shown as optimal candidates in (52).[19]

In the majority of disyllables ending in a cluster, stress is initial. This pattern too falls out from the same constraint ranking. This is again regardless of the fact that the final syllable is heavy.

(53)

	/worowk/ 'jump'	NONFINALITY	WSP	WBP
	a. wo(rów$^{\mu}$k$^{\mu}$)	*!		
☞	b. (wórow$^{\mu}$k$^{\mu}$)		*	
☞	c. (wórowk)			*

Examples such as /páɻamùlk/, with a final 'super-heavy' syllable, are *not* accounted for under this constraint ranking, as shown in (54). In (54), the attested candidate (a) has final secondary stress, violating high-ranking NONFINALITY. The predicted output is (54)c, with no final stress.

(54)

	/paɻamulk/ 'wild cucumber'	NONFINALITY	WSP	WBP
☞	a. (páɻa)(mùl$^{\mu}$k)	*!		
	b. (pàɻa)(múl$^{\mu}$k)	*!		
💣	c. (páɻa)mulk			*

The difference between forms with final cluster and those, as in (52), with a final simple coda, may be due to final consonant extrametricality effects; this was the analysis in Baker (1997). Such effects are common in languages (Hayes 1995 has numerous examples). Due to the limited data, I

19 Where roots take monosyllabic suffixes or other bound forms, however, the final segment of the root would be expected to contribute weight to the preceding syllable. Such effects can be observed in Ngalakgan (and neighbouring languages), but they are somewhat inconsistent, and vary with forms showing the usual initial-stress pattern of the root when independent. For example, /campuɻ-kkaʔ/ 'sand-LOC' varies between [ɟámbuɻkka̰] and [ɟambúɻkka̰], though the latter is more typical. (Further examples are shown in (95).) Such examples bring MWD ≈ PRWD and WBP into conflict. Judging by the attested surface forms, this conflict is unresolved for Ngalakgan speakers.

will not explore this possibility here. Ideally, the difference between (52) and (54) should fall out from the relationship between syllabification and gesture discussed already. The motivation is fairly clear: syllables are heavy where a coda consonant (C_1) is followed by another, heterorganic consonant (C_2). If C_1 is not followed by a consonant (the word-final simple coda case), or if C_2 is not heterorganic (the geminate/NC cluster case), then the preceding syllable is not heavy. It is not clear how to implement this intuition, however, in current models of phonology and prosody. I therefore leave it to future research. Rather, the set of words with final stress will simply have to be entered into the lexicon as exceptions, under the current analysis.

In disyllabic words where a final syllable ending in a cluster is stressed, such as [kiɳálk], the decision between initial and final stress is not due entirely to weight considerations but also to nucleus sonority. The fact that there is a greater degree of variation in disyllabic words ending in a cluster than in others I take to be evidence for this: variation is a characteristic of sonority effects on stress elsewhere in the Ngalakgan lexicon. Prominence-based effects deriving from sonority are examined in 5.6.

5.4.4 NO CLASH

Examples like /mélwerŋ/ and /cálpurkic/ show that adjacent heavy syllables cannot both be stressed. This characteristic, which is common crosslinguistically, is formally stated in terms of a constraint 'NOCLASH' (Liberman and Prince 1977) or '*CLASH', as here.

(55) *CLASH(PRWD): 'Avoid adjacent stressed syllables in a PRWD'

*CLASH encodes the metrical principle that strong beats should alternate regularly with weak beats. *CLASH is ranked above WSP in order to prevent adjacent heavies from receiving stress in (56). WSP is violated where heavy syllables are not stressed. ALIGNL decides the outcome in favour of the leftmost.

(56)

/calpurkic/ 'jewfish'	*CLASH	WSP	WBP	ALIGNL
☞ a. (ɟǽl)(bur)gic		*		
☞ b. (ɟǽl)burgic			*	
c. (ɟǽl)(bùr)gic	*!			
d. (ɟæl)(búr)gic		*		*!

Satisfaction of WBP would entail that both first and second syllable are heavy (and footed) here, as in the (a) candidate. However, to assign weight without stress like this would violate the WEIGHT-TO-STRESS Principle. As with forms affected by NONFINALITY, it is impossible to determine whether candidate (a) or candidate (b) reflects the speakers' grammar.

In this section we have seen that heavy syllables in Ngalakgan behave in ways which have been observed in other languages. Adjacent stresses are avoided (*CLASH), as are final stressed syllables (NONFINALITY). But wherever possible, modulo these conditions, heavy syllables are to be stressed (WSP).

The fact that heavy syllables behave in this way in Ngalakgan is a strong argument that they are part of the general metrical system of the language, not aberrant 'prominence' effects. For instance, Hayes (1995: 272) makes the claim that stress rules which refer to intrinsic prominence, as distinct from (mora-based) syllable weight, should be irrelevant to foot construction. Clearly, this is not true of heavy syllables in Ngalakgan.

The interaction between heavy syllables and the metrical system lends support to the hypothesis that quantity-sensitivity in Ngalakgan is not a drastically different kind of phenomenon from quantity-sensitivity in other languages. What differs in each case is the definition of 'heavy syllable' and the relationship between heavy syllables and the structure of syllables and words generally. In the following sections, I discuss the implications of this approach further.

5.4.5 Other indications of weight

Apart from stress, the other phonological patterns implicated in weight phenomena are word minimality, including reduplication patterns, metrics, and syllable phonotactics in general. There is one context in which we can test the moraicity of monogestural clusters, shown in (57). In these words, monogestural clusters are preceded by phonologically long vowels, because of the requirements of MWD ≈ PRWD, discussed in Chapter 3. In such environments in other languages, it is common for geminates to degeminate or vowels to shorten. This is not what we observe in Ngalakgan, however.

(57)	a.	[ɟéeŋgi]	*[ɟéŋgi]	*[ɟéegi]
		/ce-ŋki/		
		nose-2mDAT	'your nose'	
	b.	[bóokka̰]	*[bókka̰]	*[bóoka̰]
		/po-kkaʔ/		
		river-LOC	'at the river'	
	c.	[numɛlg̰néeppìɾa̰]	'you two better cook it'	
		/ɳu-meleʔ-ɳe-ppiraʔ/	2pl-EVIT-cook.PR-DU	

d. [jinibakjéeppìra̰] 'you two put it down for me'
/jini-pak-je-ppiraʔ/ 2pl/1sg-APPL-put.PR-DU

The fact that vowel length is retained preceding geminates and NC clusters is further evidence that these sequences are not moraic in the phonology of Ngalakgan. If these clusters did contribute a mora to the preceding syllable, we might expect vowels to stay short: there would be no reason to lengthen them. In addition, it has been proposed that syllables are universally restricted to an upper bound of two moras (Prince 1990; Mester 1994). Such syllables would violate this restriction.[20]

The discussion in Chapter 3 makes it clear why the vowel is long in these cases. The CV roots involved here are all 'MWDs' and are thus required to be Prosodic Words. Since they lack codas the only way for them to achieve PRWD size is through vowel lengthening. Chapter 3 has shown that this requirement holds regardless of the size of other morphemes in the word.

5.4.6 Monogestural clusters and weight in other languages

If the analysis of Ngalakgan quantity-sensitivity presented in 5.4 is correct, then we might expect to find other languages in the world which behave similarly. I have already mentioned the other Australian languages of this region which appear to have broadly similar systems of quantity-sensitivity. In order to find a similar system elsewhere, we would be looking for a language which was quantity-sensitive for CVC syllables, and which had 'prenasalised stops' and/or 'fortis stops' which were contrastively long.

Such a combination of characteristics is unfortunately rather rare, and grammars of such languages wherein the stress system is carefully described are even rarer. However, the Chadic language Ngamo appears to satisfy both of these criteria. Ngamo has a reduplication process in which the weight of the stem syllable is reversed in the reduplicant (Schuh 2003: 2).[21] Both CVV and CVC count as heavy syllables. In (58)a, the stem has a short vowel but the reduplicant has a long one. The opposite is true of the (b) example. In (c), the first syllable of the stem is a closed, and hence heavy, syllable. Thus, the reduplicant is short.

(58) a. bìdò bìi-bìdò
'monkey' 'RED-monkey'

[20] We cannot test directly whether heterorganic codas are moraic in the same way, since no morphemes begin in heterorganic clusters.

[21] For clarity, I have used double vowel characters to represent long vowels, rather than the macron. I have also represented homorganic clusters with the appropriate place of articulation of the nasal. Otherwise, I have reproduced these examples as in the source.

b. sàawà — sà-saawà
'large cooking pot' — 'RED-id.'

c. ɲɟàkɗà — ɲɟà-ɲɟakɗà
'stool' — 'RED-stool'

When a prenasalised stop divides the first and second syllables of the stem, the reduplicant affix has a short vowel, as in (59).

(59) a. dìndì — dì-dindì
'toad' — 'RED-toad'

b. gùŋgù — gù-guŋgù
'leopard' — 'RED-leopard'

Homorganic nasal-stop clusters are thus treated as contributing weight to the preceding syllable, and hence they must be syllabified in separate syllables stem-internally. However, when a stem with a light initial syllable begins in a prenasalised stop, the reduplicant affix takes a long vowel, even though, as Schuh notes, we would expect the nasal portion to contribute a coda to the preceding syllable (Schuh 2003: 4), as in the non-occurring (b) forms, based on the behaviour of prenasalised stops (or homorganic NC clusters) stem-internally.

(60) a. ndàkâm — ndàa-ndàkâm
'duck' — 'RED-duck'

b. *ndà-ndàkâm

(61) a. ŋgàdà — ŋgàa-ŋgadà
'gutta percha' — 'RED-gutta percha'

b. *ŋgà-ŋgadà

(62) a. ŋgàrù — ŋgàa-ŋgarù
'servant' — 'RED-servant'

b. *ŋgà-ŋgarù

Ngamo then, appears to treat monogestural clusters in a similar fashion to Ngalakgan for the purposes of weight, at least in stem-initial position. The data here is from the Gudi dialect of Ngamo. In the Yaya dialect, Schuh notes, 'syllabification seems to treat the root-internal nasal+homorganic voiced stop as an onset', because of examples such as (63). In these cases, the vowel of the reduplicant is long, implying that the nasal portion of the NC cluster in the stem does not contribute a mora to the preceding syllable.

(63)	a.	zèŋge	zèe-zeŋge
		'hyena'	'RED-hyena'
	b.	ɟàɲɟa	ɟàa-ɟaɲɟà
		'star'	'RED-star'

He notes further that 'not enough forms were collected to verify this as an across-the-board generalization for Yaya, however' (Schuh 2003: 3). If this pattern is generally true of the Yaya dialect, then the similarity with Ngalakgan is even stronger.

I have already mentioned that other languages of central and southern Arnhem Land appear to have stress systems similar to Ngalakgan's, in their treatment of monogestural clusters for weight. Unfortunately, we still lack detailed phonological and prosodic studies of the vast majority of Australian languages. There are patterns found here and there in the literature which appear to make a similar distinction in other areas of the grammar however.

One such pattern can be found in Yidiny (Dixon 1977). Yidiny has a reduplication process which targets the first two syllables of nominals to form plurals. As Dixon notes (ibid.: 156), homorganic nasal-stop clusters are not treated in the same way as heterorganic clusters for this process.

(64) provides examples of reduplications where syllable two is open. In these cases, the reduplicant is a copy of the first CVCV string of the stem (the copied portion in the stem is in bold).

		Simple stem	*Reduplicated stem*
(64)	a.	buɲa	buɲa-**buɲa**
		'woman'	'women'
	b.	mulari	mula-**mula**ri
		'initiated man'	'initiated men'

When the second syllable is closed by a segment which is word-final, or part of a heteroganic cluster, the reduplicant copies the first CVCVC portion of the stem:

(65)	a.	ŋalal	ŋalal-**ŋalal**
		'big'	'lots of big [ones]'
	b.	gindalba	gindal-**gindal**ba
		'lizard sp.'	'lizards'

In (66), we see an example of a stem containing a homorganic cluster between second and third syllables. In these cases, Dixon states, reduplication treats the cluster in the same way as a simple onset, and the reduplicant is CVCV (Dixon 1977: 156, 233).

(66) a. galambaɽa: gala-**gala**mbaɽa:
'march fly' 'march flies'
b. maɟinda-n maɟi-**maɟ**inda-n
'walk.up-IMPER' 'keep on walking up-IMPER'

The Yidiny reduplication pattern can be described simply if we regard monogestural sequences as onsets. In this case, the reduplicant copies the first two syllables of the word. In cases like /gindalba/, the second syllable is closed by /l/, and hence this segment is included in the reduplicant. In cases like /galambaɽa:/, the second syllable is open (according to this hypothesis), and hence no part of the labial nasal-stop cluster which follows is copied in the reduplicant. Rather, the word reduplicates like other words with a simple segment between second and third syllables, e.g. /mulari/.

On this basis, Nash (1979) argues that Yidiny has a series of prenasalised stops which are treated as simple segments by the phonology. However, there is no suggestion from Dixon (1980) that the homorganic nasal-stop sequences found in Yidiny are any different from the typical clusters we find in other Australian languages, which have two timing slots. The available evidence on Yidiny suggests that it may syllabify monogestural sequences as onsets, as in Ngalakgan, but this does not necessarily mean that such sequences are segments, as I have noted.

A similar distinction between monogestural and bigestural clusters is found in the reduplication pattern of Kugu Nganhcara (Smith and Johnson 2000: 382).[22] In Nganhcara, reduplication copies the first vowel and any following monogestural segment or cluster. In words with a simple segment between first and second syllables of the base, the reduplicant is a V_1C_2 copy of the base, as shown in (67). (The reduplicant is surrounded with brackets here, while the copied portion is in bold.)

(67) a. t̪ena t̪[en]**en**a
'stand'
b. ŋaja ŋ[aj]**aj**a
'I' (1sgNOM)
c. iiru-ma [iir]**iir**u-ma
here-EMPH

When the base contains a monogestural cluster between the first and second syllables, the whole cluster is copied in the reduplicant.

22 Kugu Nganhcara has a voicing distinction. This language is still spoken (Gaby p.c.).

(68) a. muɲɟi m[uɲɟ]**uɲɟ**i
b. yumpi y[ump]**ump**i
c. muŋga m[uŋg]**uŋg**a

Thus, in both cases, reduplication copies C_{inter}, a monogestural segment or cluster, in the terms introduced in Chapter 2.

When what is between first and second syllables is a heterorganic cluster, reduplication copies only the first segment, if this is a stop, as shown in (69).[23]

(69) a. pukpe p[uk]**uk**pe
b. wegbe w[eg]**eg**be

When the first segment of a heterorganic cluster is a nasal, then the nasal is copied as a homorganic cluster, as shown in (70):

(70) a. nunpa n[unt]**un**pa
b. t̪anpa t̪[ant]**an**pa
c. wunpa w[unt]**un**pa
d. uŋpa [uŋk]**uŋ**pa

This last process is optional. Thus /uŋpuŋpa/ is also a possible realisation.

Reduplication patterns similar to the Nganhcara one are found in a restricted number of Australian languages such as Mangarrayi (Merlan 1982; Jones 2000), Alawa (Sharpe 1972), Ngarinyman and Gurindji (Jones 2000), all from the central Top End of the Northern Territory, and, besides Nganhcara, some other languages of Cape York including neighbouring Kuuk Thayorre (Gaby 2006: 22-4). In this pattern, reduplication infixes the first vowel and following consonant or consonant cluster after the first consonant of the stem (McCarthy and Prince 1986, 1993b; Davis 1988; an alternative analysis is proposed by Jones 2000). The examples in (71) are from Mangarrayi (Merlan 1982):

(71) a. maɭuka m[aɭ]**aɭ**uka 'RED-old man'
b. cimkan c[imk]**imk**an 'RED-knowledgeable person'

The Nganhcara pattern is a variant of this. We can analyse it as a pattern that copies the first vowel and the first gesture (rather than the first cluster).

---

23 Ian Smith (p.c.) has provided further information on this process. It appears that the pattern in (69) is restricted just to clusters of this type. Other heterorganic clusters behave like those in (68) or (70).

Monogestural and bigestural clusters are thereby distinguished in this pattern. Monogestural clusters are treated as simple segments, as we have seen, and copied in entirety.

(72) a. muɲɟi m[uɲɟ]**uɲɟ**i
b. ŋaja ŋ[aj]**aj**a

Heterorganic clusters contribute only their first segment to the reduplicant, but the realisation of this segment differs according to the markedness of the cluster. The most marked clusters, with non-coronal non-nasal codas, allow only the first segment in the cluster to be realised between initial consonant and stem:

(73) a. pukpe p[uk]**uk**pe

When the heterorganic cluster has an initial nasal, the reduplicant realises this segment (optionally) as a homorganic cluster between initial consonant and stem:

(74) a. nunpa n[unt]**un**pa

Such patterns are difficult to describe in simple prosodic terms. For one thing, the reduplicant is not a syllable: it consists of a vowel plus following consonantal segments in the string: VC(C). For another, the pattern either copies a whole cluster, or just the first segment in the cluster, depending on whether the cluster is monogestural or not. But such a consideration cannot be described in prosodic terms either: both kinds of cluster consist of a coda plus a following onset, under the usual analysis.

Thus, there is evidence both within Australian languages and in external language families for a similar distinction between bigestural and monogestural clusters for quantity-sensitive phenomena such as reduplication, as well as patterns of syllabification and phonotactics. I have suggested that the simplest way to deal with this pattern is to assume that the phonology of Ngalakgan and similar languages syllabifies monogestural clusters in the onset. By doing so, we enable the quantity-sensitivity of Ngalakgan to be described in the same way as CVC-heavy systems elsewhere. What differs is not the definition of 'heavy syllable' but the class of possible onsets. In the absence of these clusters in word-initial position in Ngalakgan, it is more difficult to sustain an onset analysis. However, the evidence of phonotactics, quantity-sensitive stress patterns and reduplication can provide such evidence from other domains of the phonology. In what follows, I consider the implications for formal models of phonology of the analysis of

Ngalakgan quantity-sensitivity presented in 5.4, as well as the common restriction against word-initial homorganic clusters.

5.4.7 Further implications: the representation of monogestural clusters and weight

In a recent paper, Davis (2003) addresses the issue of whether or not geminates can be universally considered to be underlyingly moraic, as in the representation of (1), repeated here as (75):

(75)
$$\begin{array}{c} \mu \\ | \\ \mathrm{C} \end{array}$$

He considers and rejects alternative analyses based on the representation of contrastive length in terms of root nodes (e.g. Selkirk 1988), as in Baker (1999) or skeletal slots (e.g. Clements and Keyser 1983), as I have proposed above for Ngalakgan and related languages. In this section, I consider Davis' arguments against these alternatives, and I also consider an alternative analysis of Ngalakgan in which geminates and other monogestural clusters are moraic both underlyingly and at the surface. I also discuss the crosslinguistic markedness of word-initial geminates and homorganic NC clusters.

It seems there are three ways in which geminates interact with quantity, crosslinguistically. In many languages which are quantity-sensitive and which have contrastive geminates, these geminates contribute a mora to the preceding syllable; examples are Italian and Arabic (Hayes 1995). I shall refer to these languages as 'Geminate Heavy'. In a smaller group of languages, geminates do not contribute to syllable weight, even though long vowels count as heavy; examples are Selkup, Malayalam, Chuvash, and Ossetic (Selkirk 1988; Tranel 1991; Hayes 1995: 302). These languages I shall refer to as 'Geminate Light'. Thirdly, in a pattern hitherto unknown, geminates and homorganic NC clusters count as light even though consonants in the coda otherwise count as heavy, as in Ngalakgan and BGW. I shall refer to these as 'Onset Geminate' languages.

Despite the existence of Geminate Light languages, it is possible to maintain that geminates are always moraic, given additional provisos in the moraic theory of weight. In order to account for these languages, one proposal is that weight may be computed either at the level of the nucleus, or at the level of the rime as a whole, as in the skeletal theory of Levin (1985), either crosslinguistically, or within the same language for distinct quantity-sensitive phenomena (Steriade 1991). Where weight is restricted to the nucleus, only long vowels will count as heavy. This is the case for Selkup,

Malayalam, and other languages with a similar distinction discussed in Hayes (1995: section 7.3). Where the rime is inspected for weight, then all coda consonants, including geminates syllabifed partly in the coda, will contribute to weight. This accounts for Geminate Heavy languages such as Italian, Arabic and so on. In the case of Onset Geminate languages such as Ngalakgan, we might propose that these languages are just like the Geminate Heavy languages, except that monogestural sequences are never parsed into the coda but only in the onset. Together with the prohibition against onsets contributing to weight (Clements and Keyser 1983; Hyman 1985), this derives the effect that we observe in Ngalakgan and related languages. In this analysis, geminates may still be regarded as moraic, it is simply that their mora cannot contribute to the weight of the syllable, as shown in (76) (where 'O', 'R' and 'N' represent Onset, Rime and Nucleus, respectively):

(76)

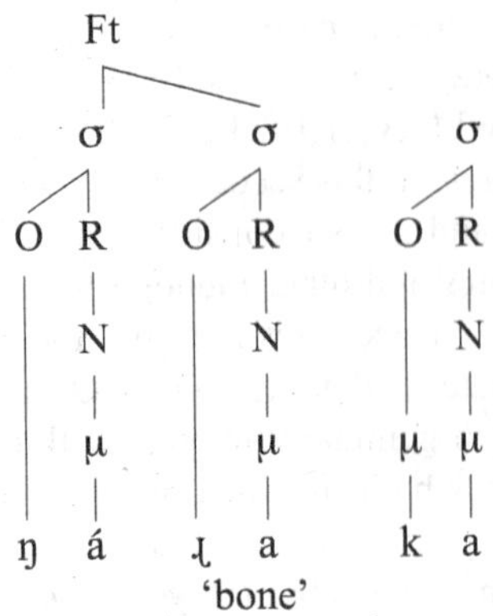

The difference between such a representation and the one I have proposed above, with skeletal slots rather than moras, can only be evaluated with respect to claims about the universality of the moraic affiliation of geminates, as discussed in Davis (2003). There are several arguments against the skeletal theory and in favour of moraic theory (discussed in, for example Hayes 1989, 1995). The first is that moraic theory allows for a unified treatment of the weight of all and only the weight bearing segments of a language, whether consonantal or vocalic (Hayes 1989). While skeletal theories of the 'X' variety can treat vowels and consonants alike, they do not distinguish weight-bearing from non-weight-bearing segments without additional reference to syllable structural elements such as the rime; hence, heavy syllables are those with a branching rime or nucleus in the analyses of e.g. Levin (1985). But while processes which count moras regardless of their affiliation are relatively common, processes which are more discerning about moraic affiliation are also found, as documented in Steriade (1991)

and Gordon (1999). These cases make a moraic analysis more difficult to sustain, since such an analysis requires additional stipulations concerning such elements as nucleus or rime which are already present in skeletal slot theories. That is, the main advantage of the moraic theory—that it makes reference to syllabic constituents unnecessary—is thereby mitigated.

The trade-off is exactly this: whether we allow contrastively moraic consonants in the onset, or whether we allow a distinction between the representation of weight (with moras) and the representation of contrastive length (with timing slots or root nodes). Arguments for the latter position are presented in Blevins (1995). Since the issue is a representational one, and one which is somewhat orthogonal to the description of Ngalakgan that I wish to present here, I will leave it to future research to determine which of these alternatives (or neither) is borne out by the evidence. Studies such as that by Gordon (1999) may make the issue a historical one.

One issue that does deserve further consideration however, is the restriction against word-initial geminates and NC clusters in many (but not all) languages. The proposal that monogestural clusters are onsets in Ngalakgan and related languages raises the question of why they cannot appear in word-initial position. In this case, it is relevant to examine Yidiny again. Besides the pattern of reduplication discussed above in 5.4.6, Nash (1979) adduces other evidence for the status of NC clusters as onsets in Yidiny. In slow speech, speakers syllabify homorganic NC clusters as if they were simple stops, as shown in (77) (Dixon 1977: 100-1, who mentions that 'in a number of other cases' speakers behaved similarly):

(77)	a.	/gilbaj-nda/	'goanna sp.-DAT'	[gílbaj]#[dá]
	b.	/baɻumbar/	'wattle tree grub'	[báɻu]#[bár]

Note that word-level phonotactics cannot entirely explain the differences between these slow speech pronunciations and the usual surface forms; though /jn/ is not a possible word-final cluster, both /m/ and /n/ are possible word-final codas. The question is why speakers would *not* pronounce the second form in particular as in (78).

(78) *[báɻum]#[bár]

The conclusion must be that speakers regard the /m/ as 'belonging' with the following /b/. Our usual understanding of such behaviour is that the /mb/ is syllabified as an onset. In that case, why is the pronunciation not as in (79), with initial NC cluster?

(79) *[báɻu]#[mbár]

A similar effect occurs in Ngalakgan with respect to the NC-initial Dative pronouns /=ŋki/ '2mDAT' and /=ŋkore/ '12aDAT'. As mentioned in Chapter 3, these pronouns when prosodically independent of a preceding stem lose their initial nasal component:

(80) [ŋumijakɔ̀rickɔ́re] [gɔ́re ŋumugɔ́ric]
/ŋu-mu-caʔ-koric=ŋkore, **ŋkore** ŋu-mu-koric/
1mS-VEG-now-grind-12aDAT 12aDAT 1mS-VEG-grind
'I'm grinding it now for us, I'm grinding it *for us*.' [2/7/96: 1B]

Similar effects are found with the related pronominal forms in Rembarrnga and BGW, as well as NC-initial forms in the unrelated Australian language Gaagudju (Harvey 2002: 113-121). What is significant here, as pointed out by Harvey (ibid.: 114-115), is that slow speech normally enhances phonological contrasts. In these cases, however, it reduces them.

Significantly, we also find such effects in other languages with word-initial NC clusters and geminates, such as Leti (Hume, Muller and van Engelhoven 1997), Swiss German (Kraehenmann 2001), and Fijian (Milner 1956). In these languages, according to the descriptions, initial monogestural clusters of geminates or nasal-stop are pronounced when there is a preceding vowel, but not otherwise (depending on language-specific syllabification constraints across morpheme and word boundaries). That is, for both geminates and NC clusters, an immediately preceding vowel (or non-nasal sonorant) is required, presumably within the same intonational phrase, i.e. without intervening pause. This is often interpreted as a requirement that such clusters be partly syllabified into the coda of a preceding syllable (e.g. Hume et al. 1997). However, there are problems with such a proposal (addressed below), and alternative intepretations available.

In order to derive the pattern of Intonation Phrase-initial segment deletion we observe in Ngalakgan and Yidiny, I will again refer to the constraint series proposed by Steriade (1999a), and discussed in Chapter 2 with reference to medial obstruent deletion, repeated here as (81)-(82).

(81) C//V: 'Every C is adjacent to a V'

(82) MAX[–cont]/_K: 'Obstruency must be realised in the output in environment K'

This constraint series can do the job of accounting for initial obstruent deletion in clusters, if we introduce the '#' context as a further elaboration.[24]

[24] Steriade (1999a) similarly introduces '#' as an element of the context that can determine the realisation of segmental contrasts (in place and manner), though not specifically for this

(83) MAX[–cont]/V_C >> MAX[–cont]/#_C >> MAX[–cont]/C_C

The relevant hierarchy in Ngalakgan and BGW is that shown in (84), where the Markedness constraint 'C//V' dominates the Faithfulness constraint to word-initial (or Intonational Phrase-initial) clusters.

(84) MAX[–cont]/V_C >> C//V >> MAX[–cont]/#_C >> MAX[–cont]/C_C

Tableau (85) presents this analysis formally. The input candidate is the NC-initial pronoun, together with the contextual information that it is Intonation Phrase-initial.[25]

(85)

#/=ŋkore/ 12mDAT	*P/N	DEP	MAX[–cont]/ V_C	C//V	MAX[–cont]/ #_C
☞ a. kore					*
b. ŋkore				*!	
c. əŋkore		*!			
d. ŋ̩kore	*!				

The faithful candidate, (b), violates Steriade's (1999) C//V constraint, which bans consonants not adjacent to vowels. The initial nasal, in the absence of an immediately preceding vowel-final word, violates this constraint. Crucially, the Markedness constraint C//V dominates the Faithfulness constraint banning deletion of segments in a word-initial context. The latter constraint is violated by the attested output, (a), which survives because it satisfies higher ranked C//V. A further candidate, (c), attempts to circumvent the problem with initial epenthesis. This is a feature of some languages (such as historical Spanish, and Spanish L2 English), but in Ngalakgan, as in Australian languages generally, constraints banning epenthesis (of the DEP family) outrank the deletion constraints MAX. The final candidate, (d), realises the initial segment as a syllabic nasal. This strategy is found to some extent in Marra (Heath 1981: 12), Leti (Hume et al. 1997), as well as Burarran languages such as Gurr-goni (Green 1995), but again not in Gunwinyguan

constraint series. The constraint ranking here mirrors in important respects that given for the realisation of contrastive aspiration by Steriade (ibid.: 10).

25 I have represented the IP-initial context here simply as '#', abstracting away from the problem of distinguishing phrasal from word-level phonology in OT; see Baker (2005) for one proposal.

languages nor in Gaagudju. While the retroflex glide /ɻ/ is a permitted syllable nucleus in both Ngalakgan and BGW, no other [–syll] segments are. This pattern can be derived with Prince and Smolensky's (1993) 'HNUC' ('Harmonic nucleus') constraint family:

(86) HNUC:
á > *í* > *t́* [generally, λ́ > τ́ if |λ| > |τ|]
'/a/ makes a more harmonic nucleus than /i/, which is more harmonic than.../t/'; or more generally '/λ/ makes a better nucleus than /τ/ if the sonority of /λ/ is greater than that of /τ/'

The ranking of segments by HNUC is universal, according to Prince and Smolensky (2004: 162). Corresponding to the universal harmonic ranking, there is a universally ranked set of markedness constraints of the general form in (87):

(87) *P/τ >> *P/λ (if |λ| > |τ|)

This constraint hierarchy states that the constraint banning association of segment /τ/ to a syllable peak universally outranks the constraint banning association of segment /λ/ to a peak, where the sonority of /λ/ is greater than that of /τ/. The particular constraint in (85), *P/N, bans syllabic nasals. This constraint, like every constraint banning syllabic consonants except /ɻ/ in Ngalakgan, outranks MAX constraints referring to these same classes of segments. Thus, nasals, and all other consonants except /ɻ/, can never be syllabic under this constraint hierarchy.

Ngalakgan's near neighbour Marra (Heath 1981) allows word-initial heteromorphemic heterorganic NC clusters deriving from the NEUT noun class prefix /n-/ as in /n-kumpi/ 'NEUT-meat'. As Heath notes (1981: 12) 'the *n*-prefix is often pronounced as part of a preceding word or is partly syllabic itself, so it is somewhat misleading to speak of these as word-initial clusters'. These heteromorphemic clusters contrast with homorganic, tautomorphemic clusters /mp/, /ŋk/, /nt/ which Heath syllabifies with the following vowel, as in /n-kana n-kumpi/ (NEUT-NEUT.TOP NEUT-meat) 'syllabified as *n-ga-nan-gu-mbi*' (1981: 11). Unfortunately, Heath does not discuss the realisation of word-initial homorganic NC clusters in any detail. My own experience with Marra speakers is that such clusters are subject to a good deal of variation, depending on factors such as speech rate, preceding context, position in the Intonation Phrase and probably others. However, at least some of the time, NC-initial words may be pronounced in isolation with the initial NC cluster intact, e.g. one speaker's pronunciation of /n-ɖawaj/ 'NEUT-language' as #[ndawaɪ]. In this case the NC cluster is necessarily homorganic (monogestural) even though it is tautomorphemic. Initial nasals in NC clusters appear to be necessarily syllabic only when heterorganic and in the absence of a preceding vowel. This is what we would predict given the differences between monogestural and bigestural clusters motivated by the preceding discussion.

In Marra then, MAX[–cont]/#_C outranks C//V, and thus we derive the effect that word-initial NC clusters are realised faithfully. In the case of Marra, *P/N is also outranked by the faithfulness constraint to word-initial clusters, as in (88). The result is shown in (89).

(88) MAX[–cont]/V_C >> MAX[–cont]/#_C >> C//V >> *P/N >> MAX[–cont]/C_C

(89)

#/n-ɖawaj/ NEUT-language	DEP	MAX[–cont]/ V_C	MAX[–cont]/ #_C	C//V	*P/N
a. dawaj			*!		
b. ndawaj				*!	
c. əndawaj	*!				
☞ d. n̩dawaj				*?	*

The winning candidate (d) here is realised with a syllabic nasal. Technically, this candidate violates C//V just as candidate (b) does, but it is relatively clear that making the nasal syllabic should increase the perceptibility of the cluster, compared to candidate (b). If the C//V constraint is interpreted rather as C//[+syll] 'every consonant adjacent to a [+syllabic] segment' then candidate (d) satisfies this constraint while candidate (b) violates it. Following obstruent-final words, the nasal portion of word-initial NC clusters in Marra is deleted, hence C//V must outrank MAX[–cont]/C_C (not shown in (89)), as in Ngalakgan.

Thus, the same constraints that derive the stringwise phonotactics word-medially in Ngalakgan and other Northern languages can also derive the common patterns we observe word-initially, as well as the differences between them in regard to syllabification of initial NC clusters.

As with any alternative proposal, it is incumbent on the proposer to show that the analysis comes with an empirical and explanatory benefit, rather than a cost, compared to the usual analysis. The usual analysis, as noted above, is that initial clusters which require a preceding vowel in order to be realised are syllabified into the preceding syllable projected from the vowel of the preceding word. There are two problems with such an analysis.

One problem is psychological: if initial segments of such words are required to be syllabified into a preceding word, then there is a persistent mismatch between word boundaries and prosodic boundaries in such languages. This means that speech production of any given word *x* at time *n* cannot be faithful to the stored form *x'*, except through a dependency on word *x-1* at time *n-1*. There are in turn two empirical problems with this analysis. One is that allowing for initial extraprosodic segments (however we want to formalise this), predicts the existence of languages with a potentially large set of underlying word-initial clusters which cannot be realised except in a postvocalic context. In fact, with rare exceptions such as Leti, the set of clusters that behave in this fashion is exactly the set of monogestural clusters which I have argued can be syllabified as onsets. This fact would be mysterious under the prosodic theory. The other problem with the prosodic theory is that it predicts we might find languages, the mirror image of Fijian and Leti, in which word-final segments can only be realised by being syllabified with a following (vowel-initial) word. This pattern appears to be unattested as a general strategy for syllabifying words. Even in Oykangand and Arrernte, two Australian languages which have been argued to have canonical VC syllables (by e.g. Sommer 1970; Breen and Pensalfini 1999), there are no word-final clusters which require a phrasal context in order to be realised.

In fact the only case which approaches this kind of situation is again Leti, where, according to (Hume et al. 1997), final consonants are syllabified as onsets to a following vowel-initial word, along with metathesis to avoid phrase-medial vowel-final words, as shown in (90):

(90) /tikil+erun/ [tiklerun]
'to kick+downwards'

Clearly, Leti allows massive violations of word-to-syllable edge isomorphism, on both edges. Other languages are not like this. Tautomorphemically, the only word-initial clusters Marra allows are exactly the homorganic nasal-stop ones, similarly in Fijian. And apart from geminates, Swiss German allows no other 'unsyllabifiable' clusters word-initially.

Some phonological processes are difficult to account for under the prosodic analysis of monogestural clusters. The contrast between monogestural and bigestural clusters for reduplication processes in Australian languages was discussed in the preceding section. As noted there, a prosodic analysis whereby clusters are necessarily divided by a syllable boundary regardless of place-linking cannot derive the difference in behaviour of these two cluster types.

Apart from the synchronic behaviour of monogestural clusters, we observe a similar distinction played out in historical phonology. Here I refer to the well-studied changes in several disjunct groups of Australian languages collectively known as 'initial-dropping' (see Dixon 2002: 589-602 for a survey). Dixon (2002: 653), after noting that word-initial clusters are non-standard in Australian languages, proposes that they can come about in two ways. The first is through loss of both C_1 and V_1 from the initial syllable of a proto-form, exposing the erstwhile medial cluster to the word-initial position. The typical cluster we find here, he notes:

> ... consists of homorganic nasal plus stop, e.g. *djúmbi* > *mbí* 'penis' in Mb̪abaram. If a CC cluster is not of this form then one of two strategies will be employed. In some languages V_1 is retained before other types of cluster [i.e. clusters which are not homorganic nasal plus stop], e.g. *gúrrburu* > *arrbúr* 'full' in Mbabaram. In others the cluster may be simplified e.g. *kálma-* > *má* 'to arrive' and *kúlŋkul* > *ŋkúl* 'heavy' in Ngkoth (Hale 1976: 23).[26] (Dixon 2002: 653-54, see p. 596 for further examples)

This difference in the distribution and behaviour of homorganic (or monogestural) and heterorganic clusters word-initially is not well-captured by a prosodic theory which does not distinguish coda-onset clusters in terms of place. The model proposed here however, where monogestural clusters can exceptionally satisfy *COMPLEXONSET$_G$, predicts that exactly the class of homorganic NC clusters and geminates should be possible onsets in a subset of the world's languages (such as Fijian), and should behave as onsets in other languages where they are nevertheless not permitted in word-initial or IP-initial position (as in Ngalakgan and BGW).

In the following sections, I discuss another problematic feature of weight in Ngalakgan and related languages: the behaviour of glottal stops. I show that their apparently anomalous behaviour follows from their articulatory characteristics.

5.5 The interaction of glottal stop with weight

Glottal stops are weightless in every context in Ngalakgan. In this section I show that the analysis presented for monogestural clusters extends in a straightforward way to the behaviour of glottal stops. Since glottal stops are the only consonantal segments in Ngalakgan which lack a supralaryngeal place feature, this behaviour is expected, if syllabification and weight are dependent on the interaction of root nodes and place gestures. First I discuss the facts of stress in roots and complex words containing glottal stops, and then in 5.5.2, I present an analysis of this behaviour.

---

[26] Dixon (2002) here uses a mixture of standard orthographic representations, e.g. 'rr' for /r/ and 'r' for /ɻ/ as well as phonemic symbols. I have omitted Dixon's non-standard classificatory labels for languages from the quotation.

5.5.1 Glottal stops are weightless

Final clusters of sonorant plus glottal stop consistently fail to act as heavy for stress (91). In polysyllabic words ending in a sonorant+glottal cluster, stress is always initial.

(91)	a.	/canajʔ/	[ɟánaɪ̯]	'goanna sp.'
	b.	/muɳaɲʔ/	[múɳaɲ̃]	[subsection term]
	c.	/jereʔ/	[jɛ́ɾɛ̰]	'downriver'

(92)	a.	/kuttapiɭʔ/	[gúttabɪɭ̰̃]	'bird sp.'
	b.	/kamaciʔ/	[gámaɟḭ]	'swag (bedroll; belongings)'
	c.	/paʈikuluʔ/	[báɖigʊ̀lṵ]	'Eucalyptus sp.'

If glottal stops were treated in the same way as supralaryngeal obstruents, we would expect final secondary stress in forms like (92)a. This is shown in the following examples. Trisyllabic glottal-final forms contrast with trisyllabic roots ending in a cluster; as we have seen, the latter have a final secondary stress; examples are presented in (93).

(93) a. [bɛ́ɻemɛ̀lk]
/peɻemelk/
'shoulder blade'

b. [ɟíliwʊ̀rk]
/ciliwurk/
'guts'

c. [páɻamʊ̀lk]
/paɻamulk/
'wild cucumber'

d. [bɔ́ɻogɔɾ̰]
/poɻokorʔ/
'*Casuarina* sp.'

e. [wʊ́lʊkkʊɾ̰]
/wulukkurʔ/
'sibling-in-law'

f. [bárakkaɭ̰̃]
/parakkaɭʔ/
'plant sp.; spear shaft'

Glottals do not count for weight internally in words either. There is only one trisyllabic root with a medial glottal-final syllable, presented in (94). This form has initial stress.

(94) /ŋaɳaʔpaj/ [ŋáɳ̰apaɪ] 'moreover'

Further evidence comes from complex words. Complex words of a particular structural type display quantity-sensitive stress as one variant. The type in question is a trisyllabic Prosodic Word composed of a disyllabic stem plus monosyllabic suffix, clitic or stem. In one variant, stress is initial, in the other, stress is on the penultimate if it is heavy, as in examples (95)f-j.

If the medial syllable is vowel+glottal stop, it does not count as heavy, and stress is consistently initial in such forms, as in (95)a-e.

(95) a. [jána̰kan]
/janaʔ-ʔkVn/
what-DAT

b. [ɟánda̰ka̰]
/cantaʔ-kkaʔ/
tree-LOC

c. [gáɲa̰ka̰]
/kaɲaʔ-kkaʔ/
little-LOC

d. [jínḭkan]
/jiniʔ-ka+n/
tell-CAUS+PR

e. [gáŋa̰wo]
/kaŋaʔ+wo/
ask+GIVE.PP

f. [ɻagálkkan]
/ɻakalk-ʔkVn/
sorceror-DAT

g. [ɟambʊ́ɻ̰kka̰]
/campuɻ-kkaʔ/
sand-LOC

h. [ŋaccálga̰]
/ŋaccal-kkaʔ/
spring-LOC

i. [mɔkkɔ́lgo̰]
/mokkol-kkoʔ/
father-DYAD

j. [gubʊ́ɪppʊn]
/kupuj+ppu+n/
sweat+HIT+PR

The contrast between forms like those on the left, with vowel+glottal medial syllable, and those on the right, with a closed medial syllable, is consistent. In the next section I offer an explanation for these facts.

5.5.2 Glottal stops as placeless segments

Section 5.4 has argued that syllabification in Ngalakgan and related languages is based on gestures, rather than timing positions. The stress facts presented in 5.5.1 follow if glottal stops are placeless, lacking a position on the gestural tier independent of other gestures in the word.

In autosegmental terms, we can regard the glottal stop as a laryngeal specification [creaky voice], which necessarily associates to the place gesture of a preceding sonorant. Chapter 2 has explained that the only consistent realisation of glottal stops is creaky voice, glottal closure is optional, depending on factors which are yet to be understood but which may well turn out to be a function of phonetic implementation. In autosegmental terms, then, glottal stops lack their own gesture independent of preceding gestures since the one realisation that is never heard is glottal constriction independent of preceding sonorants. Section 2.4.4 suggests they still have a timing slot, however.

Example (96) below represents this proposal, in terms of the association between timing and gesture discussed in 5.3 above.

(96)

The coarticulation of underlying glottal stop with preceding sonorants is enforced by the constraints on perceptibility of glottal constriction in various contexts. A laryngealised vowel is less marked than a phonetic implementation of vowel followed by glottal constriction. We can think of these two implementations as constraints on perceptual difficulty, in the ranking shown:

(97) *CUE[Vʔ] >> *CUE[V̰]

The ranking states that it is easier to perceive cues for glottal stop when it is realised as creaky voice on a preceding sonorant, than when it is separately articulated (cf. Silverman 1997).

A tableau presenting this analysis is shown in (98). The (a) candidate satisfies high-ranking *CUE[Vʔ] by associating the creaky voice specification to the preceding sonorant, a vowel in this case. This violates *CUE[V̰]. By doing so, it can satisfy ALIGNL without violating the Weight-to-Stress principle, because there are no medial closed syllables in this word, in terms of gestural configuration.

(98)

/janaʔ-ʔkVn/ 'what'-DAT	*CUE[Vʔ]	*CUE[V̰]	NOCODA	WSP	ALIGNL (PRWD, FT)
☞ a. já.na̰.kan		*			
b. ja.náʔ.kan	*!		*		*
c. ja.ná̰.kan		*			*!

The output in (a) is thus well-formed for the same reasons that /ŋáɻakka/ 'bone' is: in gestural terms, the stop between syllables 2 and 3 is a simple onset, there is no need to stress the medial syllable. That is, [jana̰kan] has much the same gestural status as [janakan] or [janakkan]. All three involve only simple consonant gestures between syllable peaks, and thus the optimal candidate is one where stress is initial.[28]

27 I have used 'V' and 'C' to represent glide and stop stricture, respectively.

28 In addition we require a constraint banning geminate glottal stop from the output, such a constraint seems crosslinguistically well-founded.

Several other pieces of evidence suggest that glottal stops lack their own gestural node. The pattern of Future and Irrealis inflection in Ngalakgan and Rembarrnga discussed in Chapter 2 is readily explained if stems lack an independent glottal stop gesture: the only input into the Future suffix comes from the place of the final supralaryngeal segment of the stem (vowel or consonant). In (99), the empty C slot contributed by the morphological specification of the FUT suffix is filled by spreading the features of the preceding place gesture. In cases where this place gesture has an additional laryngeal specification, as in (99), only the supralaryngeal place features can be spread, because of the high ranking constraint against syllable initial glottal stop. We can think of this constraint simply in terms of the same ranking presented above in (97), requiring [creaky voice] to be associated to a preceding sonorant.

(99) a.			
	maɳi̤ɲʔ	maɳi̤ɲʔ-CV	Timing tier
		|⁄ |	
	[maɳi̤ɲ̰]	[maɳi̤ɲ̰]-Ca	Gestural tier
	/maɳi̤ɲʔ/	make-FUT	

A further piece of evidence for this claim is that glottal stop is the only (heterorganic) consonant following which apicals can be post-alveolar (also noted by Merlan 1983: 9). Recall from Chapter 2 that the apical contrast is neutralised morpheme-initially, and that following all consonants except apico-postalveolars, apicals can only be alveolar. (100)a, b provide examples of root-medial and root-initial postalveolars preceded by glottal stop. Apicals cannot be postalveolar following other non-postalveolar consonants. Whether root-internally, as in (100)c, or root-initially, as in (100)d, when following non-postalveolar consonants, apicals are neutralised to apico-alveolar.

(100)
a. [wɛ́ɻ**ɖ**ak] ~ [wɛ̰́**ɖ**ak][29]
/weʔʈak/
'dry, waterless'

b. [gɔ́ɻ**ɳ**an] ~ [gɔ̰́**ɳ**an]
/ku-koʔ+ɳa+n/
3NP-have+SEE+PR
'has'

c. [ɟágan**d**a]
/cakanta/
'female plains kangaroo'

d. [bɔ́p**n**an]
/ku-pop+ɳa+n/
3NP-smell+SEE+PR
'smells'

Because of the phonotactic constraints on apicals in second position of a cluster, discussed in Chapter 2, there are no root-internal clusters of non-

[29]This form is recorded as /weɻʔtak/ (in my transcription) in Merlan (1983: 214). The fact that speakers clearly pronounced this word as [wɛ̰́ʔɖak] on more than one occasion indicates that the retroflexion belongs with the following stop, and is not a pre-glottal retroflex glide. The meaning of the word argues in favour of this analysis also: compare /weʔ/ 'water'. There is no apparent etymology for */ʈak/, though Wubuy /ʈaʈark/ 'dried up' may be cognate.

apical+apical. Such clusters are highly restricted in the vast majority of Australian languages. The only clusters where apicals are found in C_2 are those arising from elision of high vowels between peripheral stops and liquids word-initially, discussed in Chapter 2. In this position, apicals are again alveolar, regardless of whether they are retroflex or alveolar underlyingly:

(101)	a.	[blál]	/piɭal/	'waterlily leaf'
	b.	[bláɾak]	/piɭarak/	'for a long time'

The fact that glottals, and glottals alone, allow the postalveolar realisation of a following apical suggests that vowel+glottal stop sequences are treated like vowels by the phonology in this instance.[30] So in the constraint ranking that refers to the neutralisation of apicals, repeated here in (102), forms such as (100), where a laryngealised vowel precedes a retroflex, are subject to the highest ranking Identity constraint, that referring to retroflexes following vowels.

(102) Ident(retro) / V ʈ V >> Ident(retro) / V ʈ # >> Ident(retro) / # ʈ V

The primary cue for glottal stop in Ngalakgan is creaky voice, as I have observed. This is the only primary consonant cue which can be coarticulated with a vowel. While other consonants are cued by transitions into and out of

[30] There are no instances of vowel+glottal stop+alveolar. This follows from two independent factors: the scarcity of morpheme-internal examples of glottal stop, and the neutralisation pattern applying to all stem-initial apicals, as well as those of WORD-level bound elements. The latter pattern means that all post-glottal apicals in the language are invariably postalveolar. The single class of exceptions comes from the inflection of thematic verbs, discussed in Chapter 2, 2.4.2. When the final supralaryngeal consonant of the stem is an alveolar, the Future form ends in glottal+alveolar: /pawunʔ/ 'leave', /pawunʔ-na/ 'leave'-FUT; /ʈulʔ/ 'set alight', /ʈulʔ-la/ 'set alight'-FUT. This pattern can be attributed to the fact that adjacent apicals are never heterorganic in Ngalakgan; the pattern does not alter the generalisation that apico-alveolars are not found after vowel+glottal stop sequences. But it is unclear whether this is an accidental fact. Evans (p.c.) claims that apicals following glottal stop in BGW *must* be postalveolar, even where they are underlyingly alveolar. He provides the following example:

ka-[n]i	'(s)he sits'
ka-ʔ-[ɳ]i	'(s)he sits (with Immediate marker -ʔ-)'

The distribution of apical contrasts in morpheme-initial position is by no means as straightforward in other languages as it appears to be in Ngalakgan. Heath (1978b: 17-18), for example, provides a bewildering array of rules for the realisation of retroflexion in the initial apicals of morphemes in Ngandi, some of them apparently morphophonemic in nature. While noting the existence of such complexities, I maintain that the distribution of postalveolars in Ngalakgan is not affected by preceding glottal stop. The BGW pattern may be related to the fact that prefixes in BGW can take pitch accents, and can therefore form part of the same PRWD as a following root. This makes the boundary between prefixes and roots much less robust in BGW than it is in Ngalakgan, since it is less consistently correlated with a prosodic boundary.

vowels, these transitions are necessarily brief, and cannot affect the vowel so substantially that the vowel quality itself is obscured. But because laryngeal gestures can be made independently of those in the oral cavity, the cue for glottal stop can spread through preceding segments to a much greater extent than is possible for other consonants. Therefore, treating them separately to other consonants for the purposes of constraints on syllabification appears to be justified.

In 6.4.2, we examine the CVʔ reduplication pattern found in Ngalakgan and other Gunwinyguan languages, drawing on the analysis of laryngealisation discussed here.

5.6 Prominence-based stress in Ngalakgan

In this section, I describe medial stress in another group of trisyllabic roots. The words in this group fall into several distinct stress patterns. Each of these patterns finds an explanation in terms of constraints already used elsewhere in the literature. However, there are exceptions to most of these patterns in the lexicon, so they must be regarded as lexicalised to some degree, in the sense that the stress patterns they predict in words are not entirely borne out in the data.

There are strong factors at work in the grammar of Ngalakgan which make trisyllabic roots 'hard to parse'. Ngalakgan belongs to a group of northern Australian languages in which primary stress is found in both word-initial and penultimate positions. That both of these patterns are imposed on roots can be seen by considering the stress patterns in roots with light syllables described in Chapter 3. Disyllabics (with no heavies) are always initially-stressed: these satisfy both initial and penultimate constraints. Quadrisyllabics can be evenly footed bipedally: as noted, most quadrisyllabics vary between initial and penultimate primary.

Trisyllabics represent a special problem: the initial and penultimate motivations are in direct conflict, neither can be satisfied without violating the other. Therefore, it is to be expected that if quantity and sonority effects were to be found anywhere, it would be precisely in trisyllabic roots, where the grammar makes a special effort to regularise stress patterns across the lexicon.

We find a number of reflections of the 'hard to stress' problem. The first is the medial heavy syllables discussed in preceding sections. The second is that a number of trisyllabic roots *do* satisfy both initial and penult stress, by building two feet in the word with the pattern secondary^primary. Examples are shown in (103). The majority of these examples have an initial heavy syllable, followed by two light syllables. Example (103)f is exceptional, in this case a nasal stop cluster apparently makes the initial syllable heavy.

(103) a. [ɟírbili] ~ [ɟìrbíli]
/cirpili/ 'bonefish' (?herring sp.)
b. [gʊ́rmuɭu̻] ~ [gʊ̀rmʊ́ɭu̻]
/kurmuɭuʔ/ 'blue tongue lizard'
c. [màngáɖa̻]
/mankaʈaʔ/ 'woolybutt' (*E. miniata*)
d. [wàrmbája]
/warmpaja/ 'anywhere'
e. [jàrmáɖa]
/jarmaʈa/ 'marsupial sp.'
f. [gàmbʊ́ma][31]
/kampuma/ 'estuarine ray'

Note that the doubly-stressed variants violate *CLASH. Note also that in every case where the initial syllable and the penultimate are stressed, the relationship between them is secondary^primary. This is the stress pattern associated with compounds, as discussed in Chapter 3, such as the examples in (104).

(104) a. [ŋɔ̀o̻mḛ́me] 'got guts'
(ŋoʔ)-(meʔ+me) guts-RED+get.PP
b. [ɻèɪɲóo̻miɲ] 'took away'
(ɻej)-(ɲoʔ)-mi+ɲ) APPL-go.away-AUX+PP

In compounds, violations of *CLASH are also tolerated. In WORD-compounds, each MWD constitutes a PRWD (by MWD ≈ PRWD). I have stipulated previously (in (55)) that *CLASH is relativised to PRWD domains. The words in (103) then are treated by the prosody as compounds: they are 'prosodic compounds' corresponding to a single lexical item. As with the complex words in (95), this pattern violates MWD ≈ PRWD. I noted in 4.5.3 that MWD ≈ PRWD and ALIGNR(PK, PPH) appear to be in an incompletely resolved conflict in the grammar of Ngalakgan. The pattern in (95) and (103) appears to be another example of this phenomenon. Further phonological studies of Northern languages are required to fully account for this pattern.

The same pattern is observed as a variant in the examples in (105) (these are the only monomorphemic examples of such phonotactic structures).

---

31 This form seems odd: the first syllable should not be heavy since what follows is a homorganic cluster. In Wubuy the word is /kaampuma/, so it is possible that the first syllable is lexically heavy. The word is not recorded in Merlan's (1983) dictionary, so it is also possible that it is a recent loan from Wubuy or other languages of the area. Rays are not typical of the environment in which the Ngalakgan traditionally lived (the inland rivers, 80kms or more from the coast), so it would not be surprising for them to have borrowed this word.

(105) a. /miɻppara/ [mìɻppáɾa] ~ [míɻppaɾa] 'child'
b. /palppaɻaʔ/ [bàlppáɻa̰] ~ [bálppaɻa̰] 'friend'
c. /palccuʈaʔ/ [bàlccúɖa̰] ~ [bálccuɖa̰] 'lizard sp.'
d. /purkkaci/ [bùrkkáɟi] ~ [búrkkaɟi] 'real'
e. /waɭkkara/ [wàɭkkáɾa] ~ [wáɭkkaɾa] 'herring spp.'

All these examples have an initial heavy syllable, followed by a geminate.

The examples in (106) below stand out as a different case. In these words, initial stress is *not* a permitted variant:

(106) a. /wukkaɻa/ [wʊkkáɻa] *[wʊ́kkaɻa] 'frog sp.'
b. /jippuɲca/ [jɪppʊ́ɲɟa] *[jíppʊɲɟa] 'a long time ago'
c. /jukkaciʔ/ [jʊkkáɟḭ] *[jʊ́kkaɟḭ] 'for a long time'
d. /akkaʈaʔ/ [akkáɖa̰] *[ákkaɖa̰] 'late (tardy)'

Syllable 1 in these forms has a glide onset, or no onset, and the first vowel is followed by a geminate. Syllable 1 is not heavy, and in all cases the first vowel has sonority of equal or lesser value than the second vowel.

One other root with the same syllable structure has a different stress pattern:

(107) /waccuɳʈu/ [wáccʊɳɖu] 'goanna sp.' (*Varanus gouldii*)

This word never has penultimate stress. It appears that the respective vowel qualities of syllable 1 and syllable 2 may be relevant to the determination of stress in these forms. Similar facts have been reported (often anecdotally) elsewhere in Australia.

The penultimate-stressed forms may be contrasted with the three examples in (108), where stress is always on the initial syllable:

(108) a. /picciri/ [bícciɾi] *[bɪccíɾi] 'file snake'
b. /kappuci/ [gáppuɟi] *[gappʊ́ɟi] 'old person'
c. /kappuɭa/ [gáppuɭa] *[gappʊ́ɭa] 'old, blind person'

These words all have an obstruent as their initial consonant, while those in (106) begin in glides, or are onsetless, as noted.

A similar pattern seems to underlie forms such as those in (109). These are surface variants involving complex onsets. Underlyingly, these forms consist of a sequence of non-coronal stop (/k/ or /p/) followed by /i/ followed by a liquid or the semivowel /ɻ/. In these words, the first vowel is typically elided in casual speech (though it may be present in careful speech, and citation forms).

(109) a. [bɻíŋʊŋ] /piɻiŋuŋ/ [toponym]
b. [blál] /piɭal/ 'waterlily leaf'
c. [bláɾak] /piɭarak/ 'for a long time'
d. [wakkɻíwo] /wakkiɻi+wo/ 'return with+GIVE.PP'[32]

A similar phenomenon is described by (Evans 2003: 90) in BGW. Such clusters are also found, marginally, elsewhere in Australia, the languages around Adelaide in particular (e.g. Yaralde: McDonald 1977).

5.7 Conclusion

In conclusion, Ngalakgan has a weight system for stress of a kind which is hitherto undescribed in the literature. Indeed, in broad respects it is wholly unexpected. For instance, Tranel (1991) makes the claim that, in languages wherein CVC is heavy for stress, then geminates will contribute weight to the preceding syllable. But Ngalakgan and neighbouring languages are not like this. Moreover, there are some languages wherein geminates are the only consonant segments which contribute weight to the preceding syllable. Ngalakgan is a language wherein monogestural sequences (geminates, homorganic nasal-stop clusters) are the only bisegmental consonantal sequences which *do not* contribute weight to the preceding syllable. These characteristics would be otherwise mysterious without an understanding of the phonotactics of Ngalakgan, and related languages, discussed in Chapter 2. Such considerations argue for the proposal that monogestural clusters in Ngalakgan and in other Australian languages are syllabified as onsets by speakers, affecting a range of phenomena, including reduplication, in unexpected ways.

[32] This form typically has the stress pattern given here. I cannot explain it, unless it is another instance of the stress shift pattern attested with other glide-initial roots with geminates in second onset position, as in (106).

6

Geminates and other boundary signals

Chapter 2 briefly described the phonetic and phonological characteristics of the geminate/singleton contrast in Ngalakgan. This chapter reviews this analysis more carefully. I present a range of evidence from phonetics which demonstrates that this analysis is the correct one. The nature of the stop opposition in Ngalakgan is important because, as we shall see in the second half of this chapter, geminates alternate with singletons in suffix-initial position. To understand this process we need to understand the nature of geminates, as well as other obstruent clusters. Understanding the nature of geminates in Ngalakgan is also crucial to understanding their role in quantity-sensitivity, see Chapter 5.

6.1 examines the phonetic correlates of geminates and other obstruent clusters, drawing on both my own acoustic studies and the detailed survey work of Butcher (1993a, and especially 1993b). I argue that all three obstruent cluster types—geminates, heterorganic obstruent+obstruent clusters, and laryngeal+obstruent clusters—are characterised by the feature 'spread glottis'. A proposal for the phonological representation of obstruent clusters in Ngalakgan and related languages is in 6.1.3. In 6.2, I show that geminates and laryngeal segments are associated with morpheme boundaries, and derive from historical fortition and laryngealisation in these positions. In these positions, geminates and laryngeal segments function as 'boundary signals' (Trubetzkoy 1969[1939]: 275): overt phonological signals of morphological structure.

In 6.3, I examine the predictable alternation between geminate and singleton realisations of suffix-initial stops in Ngalakgan and related languages. The realisation is conditioned by the phonological form of the preceding stem, and the location of pitch accent. I analyse these alternations as well-formedness conditions on the location of phonological boundaries in relation to intonation domains, and morphological and prosodic categories. In 6.4, I show that the same grammar also accounts for one of the most common reduplication patterns in Ngalakgan—CVʔ reduplication—and for morpheme structure constraints on geminates in roots (6.6). The same constraints also account for prosodically-conditioned distributions of laryngeal segments and geminate/fortis stops in the neighbouring, unrelated Yolngu and Ndjébbana languages, and in other languages such as Finnish and Yupik (6.5).

6.1 Phonetic correlates of the stop contrast

In this section I show that at the surface, singleton and geminate stops in Ngalakgan contrast in terms of duration. The contrast in Ngalakgan is not a voicing contrast. The discussion closely follows that of Butcher (1993b): a survey of stop contrasts in several languages of the Top End.

6.1.1 Duration

In roots, geminates are consistently longer than singletons at the same place of articulation in the same environment. In what follows I present measurements of singleton and geminate stops at all places of articulation which demonstrate this. Measurements of stops were taken from words in citation in most cases, in intervocalic environments following a primary stress.

Table 1 below presents average durations for post-tonic singletons and geminates ordered by place of articulation. The number of tokens is given in parentheses, followed by the average duration in miliseconds (ms). It can be seen that geminate stops at all places are at least twice the length of the corresponding singleton stop, with the exception of apico-alveolar singletons, for which there are no data. In the case of apico-retroflex, the duration difference between geminates and singletons is 4:1. Similar ratios are presented by Butcher (1993b: 11) for six languages of central Arnhem Land.

	Labial	Alveolar	Retroflex	Laminal	Dorsal
Geminate	(9) = 194	(5) = 139	(2) = 226	(2) = 228	(35) = 211
Singleton	(7) = 71		(23) = 48	(4) = 64	(6) = 63

Table 1: Average durations of geminates and singletons

These duration ratios are consistent with those reported by researchers for length distinctions in other languages. For example, Lehiste (1960) reports ratios of between 1:2 and 1:3 for short vs long stops ('Quantity 1' vs 'Quantity 2') in Estonian.

Lehiste (1970: 27) observes that 'the intrinsic duration of consonants is influenced both by their point of articulation and by the manner of articulation', citing evidence from English, Breton, Estonian, Norwegian and Swedish to back up the claim. Even taking into account these inherent durational differences, the values shown here are significant enough to suggest a systematic phonological difference between geminate and singleton stops.

The duration ratios of geminate/singleton in Ngalakgan are greater than those of voiceless and voiced stops in English and German (e.g. Fischer-Jørgensen 1972), which have also been analysed as having a fortis/lenis contrast. In these languages, voiceless stops are around 1.3 times as long as voiced ones. Phonetically, geminates in Ngalakgan are more like the geminates of languages such as Finnish, Italian, and Estonian, than they are like the 'fortis' voiceless stops of English and German.

v́pv	v́tv	v́ţv	v́cv	v́kv
97	no examples	34	76	76
87		50	48	65
93		60	79	68
46		59	54	52
69		63		46
56		52		69
46		57		
		35		
		35		
		50		
		50		
		56		
		48		
		75		
		68		
		55		
		33		
		41		
		56		
		25		
		26		
		43		
		40		
Av. (7) = 71		Av. (23) = 48	Av. (4) = 64	Av.(6) = 63

Table 2: Durations of post-tonic singletons*

*Table 2 shows figures for singleton stops at all POAs except apico-alveolar, of which I have no citation examples in the relevant environment.[1] The average durations range from 48ms for apico-postalveolars to 71ms for labials. The average over all POAs is 62ms.

[1] There are only four roots in the lexicon with the relevant environment: /karatata/ 'chest brace', /kolototok/ 'peaceful dove', /ciriţiti/ 'bird sp.' (possibly a fly-catcher), and /ţotojʔ/ 'uncle'.

v́ppv	v́ttv	v́ʈʈv	v́ccv	v́kkv
135	166	228	190	116
151	122	224	266	190
172	118			166
209	144			166
170	146			218
230				237
205				104
227				218
247				97
				221
				199
				215
				252
				146
				220
				230
				193
				172
				117
				247
				190
				266
				247
				310
				270
				249
				248
				232
				272
				170
				248
				268
				251
				231
				214
Av (9) = 194	Av. (5) = 139	Av. (2) = 226	Av. (2) = 228	Av. (35) = 211

Table 3: Durations of post-tonic geminates*

*Table 3 presents figures for durations of post-tonic geminates at all five places of articulation. The average durations range between 139ms for apico-alveolar geminates, through to 226 and 228ms for the apico-postalveolar and lamino-alveopalatal geminates, respectively.[2] The average of geminates over all POAs is 200ms.

[2] Durations of geminates can be quite massive. One apico-postalveolar token, for the word /paʈʈiʔ/ 'fly' was 392 ms. This token was omitted from the table.

6.1.2 Voicing

In this section I consider whether the geminate/singleton contrast at the surface can be described in terms of voicing, instead of or in addition to duration. I reject this proposal on the grounds that neither the presence during closure, nor the onset time of voicing at release is a consistent cue to the contrast (cf. Butcher 1993b: 20). Firstly, I briefly discuss how voicing contrasts are implemented in languages. I then show that Ngalakgan stops do not implement a surface contrast in any of the ways that have been observed elsewhere.

I follow Lisker and Abramson (1964) in assuming that voicing contrasts are correlated with differences in 'voice onset time' (VOT): the time between the release of stricture in an obstruent and the onset of voicing in a following sonorant and, to a lesser extent, 'voice termination time' (VTT): the time between the onset of closure and the termination of voicing. That is, voicing contrasts in stops are implemented by varying the timing between glottal abduction and adduction, and stricture formation. In *voiceless aspirated* stops, peak glottal opening is timed to co-occur with release of stricture. Voicing in the following vowel cannot begin immediately on release. These stops have a 'long lag' VOT. In *voiceless unaspirated* or *plain voiceless* stops, peak glottal opening occurs during articulatory closure. No voicing occurs during closure, but vocal folds can begin vibrating almost as soon as closure is released. Butcher (1993a: 2) characterises *voiced stops* thus: 'the vocal folds are not actively abducted, and providing air is able to flow through the glottis, voicing can begin before the release of the articulatory closure. In the case of intervocalic stops this may well result in continuous glottal pulsing throughout the closure'.

If Ngalakgan were a language with a voicing contrast, we would expect to find a consistent difference between singletons and geminates in their implementation of VOT. None of the characterisations in the preceding paragraph describes the Ngalakgan facts. The pages following display spectrograms and waveforms taken from recordings of Ngalakgan words in citation.[3] It is not the case that all intervocalic stops are fully voiced in Ngalakgan. Figure (1) shows an intervocalic singleton in the word /mu-wu**c**ur/ VEG-'flat grindstone' realised as a voiceless unaspirated stop. So the opposition is not like that in French: with fully voiced stops, contrasted with voiceless unaspirated ones.

Nor is the opposition like that in English: where voiceless stops have long VOT, and contrast with short VOT voiced stops. It is not the case that every geminate in Ngalakgan has a long lag VOT. Most geminates have a VOT of around 20 ms. But Figure (2) shows two intervocalic geminates in the same word /jir-puj**pp**uj+ɳe-**pp**iraʔ/; neither are aspirated. The intervocalic singleton in Figure (1) and the intervocalic geminates in Figure (2) both have zero VOT. VOT therefore does not consistently distinguish singletons and geminates in Ngalakgan.

[3] Recordings were digitised on a Macintosh PowerPC and analysed using the Signalyze program.

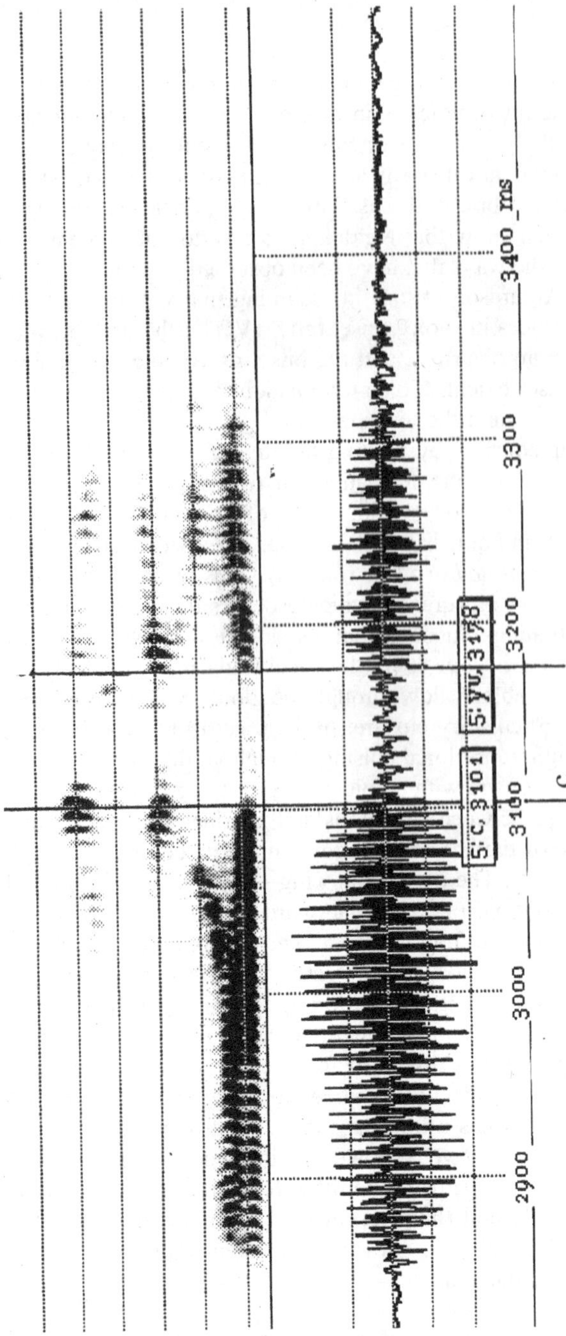

Figure 1: [muwúcur] /mu-wucur/ 'VEG-grindstone'

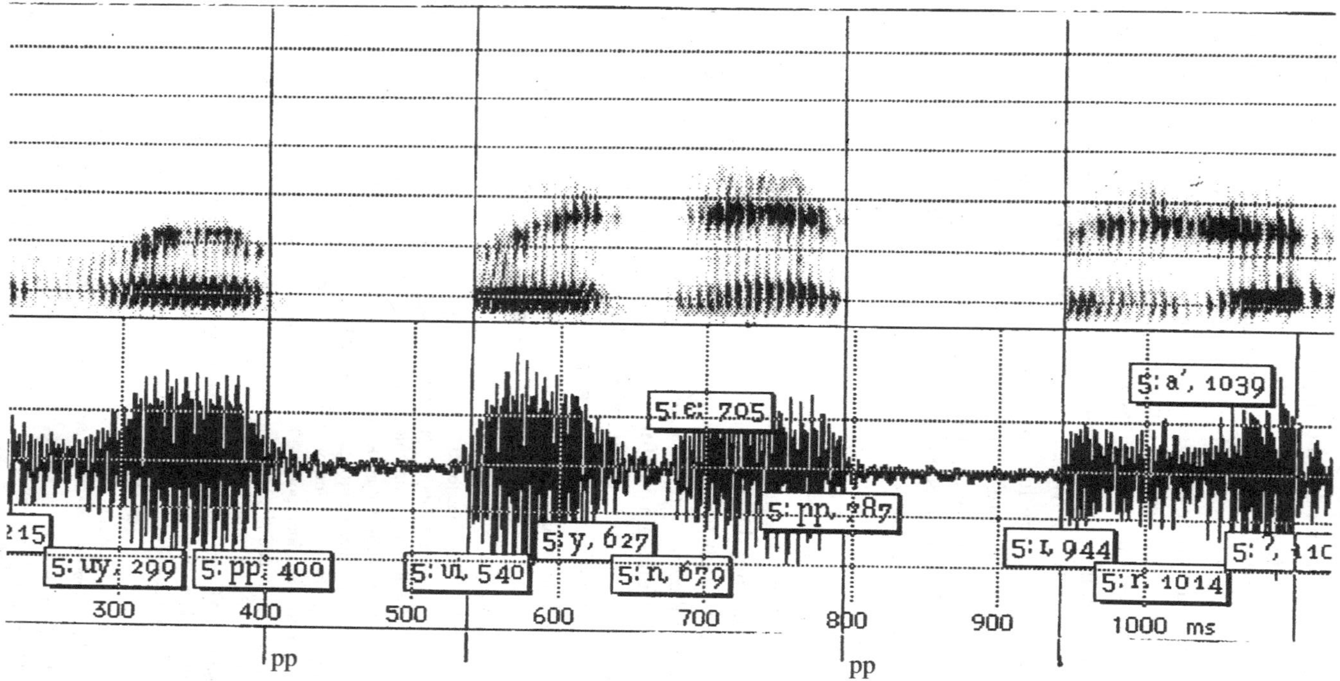

Figure 2: [jɪrbʊɪppʊmeːppɪrɐ̰] /jir-pujppuj-ɳe-ppiraʔ/ 1aS-singe-BURN.PR-DU

Butcher (1993b: 14, 19) found two consistent correlates of stop contrasts in languages of the area (Central Arnhem Land), which he labels as 'fortis' vs 'lenis'. The first of these was duration, as in Ngalakgan. The second consistent correlate of fortis stops was a higher degree, and a higher rate of rise in, intraoral pressure—the air pressure behind the oral stricture—in fortis stops as opposed to lenis stops.[4] Discussing Gunwinyguan and Burarran languages, Butcher (1993b: 20) observes that 'all speakers appear actively to abduct the vocal folds to avoid prolonging voicing into FORTIS stop closures'.[5]

Butcher proposes (2004: 556) that 'speakers consistently aim to achieve a different target peak pressure for each stop category [i.e. fortis vs. lenis], rather than maintaining a more or less constant subglottal pressure and leaving the peak intraoral pressure to be determined by the duration of the articulatory closure'. He bases this conclusion on the fact that, if the pressure differences were the automatic consequence of constriction duration differences, we would expect that duration and pressure should show a regular mathematical relationship, and that the rate of rise should remain constant. But this is not the case, pressure in geminates rises at more than twice the rate in singletons, and in the case of the Daly languages (which have a stop contrast based on voicing), the duration differences between fortis and lenis stops are not great enough to explain the pressure differences, which are *greater* than those of the GN and Burarran languages. Therefore, the intraoral pressure which is correlated with fortis stops is not an automatic consequence of their duration, since the maximum reached and the rate of rise observed are both greater than that of lenis stops.

We have seen that stops contrast consistently in terms of duration: plain stops are at least half, and may be as little as a quarter of the duration of

[4] These claims were based on volume velocity data recorded on a pneumotachograph.

[5] Recent unpublished work by Stoakes (in preparation) suggests that in BGW, it is glottal constriction, rather than glottal abduction, which is a consistent correlate of fortis stops in that language. His results further suggest that heteromorphemic geminates have variable glottal constriction. It is not clear whether heterorganic obstruent clusters have the same characteristics. Since the results are preliminary, and only came to light in the final stages of the writing of this book, they have not been incorporated here. However, if Stoakes is correct (and if this characteristic is true of Ngalakgan also) there are several implications. The first is that such a laryngeal specification makes geminates look more like single, fortis segments, rather than clusters. The second is that it unifies the laryngeal characteristics of the two segments found as boundary signals in Northern languages: fortis stops and glottal stops. It therefore suggests a closer relationship between the articulation of fortis stops and glottal stops than would be otherwise apparent. Wood (1978) suggested that fortis stops were simply ordinary stops occurring in a syllable autosegmentally specified as 'fortis', and that such syllables were otherwise characterised by laryngealised sonorant codas. He ultimately rejected this analysis because of the contrast found in Yolngu (which is also found in Ngalakgan and many Northern languages) between /ʔ/ + C sequences and geminates/fortis stops. The full implications of this intriguing finding must await further research.

geminate stops. These ratios are consistent with duration differences between long/geminate and short/singleton stops in languages such as Estonian, Finnish and Italian (Lehiste 1960).

We have also seen that the contrast cannot be described as a voicing contrast. VOTs are not consistently long enough for the contrast to be characterised as one of voiceless aspirated vs plain voiceless or unaspirated stop. On the other hand, singleton stops are not consistently voiced throughout closure. So neither can the contrast be described as one of plain voiceless vs fully voiced stops. Butcher (1993b) has suggested that intraoral pressure differences between the two categories are also a consistent correlate. However, it is not clear whether and how such differences are perceived by speakers, or whether there is some other acoustic correlate at work.

6.1.3 The phonological representation of geminates

In order to make concrete the phonetic description, I assume a representation of geminates and singletons as presented in Figure (3). Underlying stops are symbolised with capitals here to indicate their status as stops unspecified for laryngeal features.

	Geminate /PP/	Singleton /P/
Timing	[C] [C]	[C]
Gesture	[p]	[p]
Laryngeal	[]	[]

a. Underlying Representation

	Geminate [pp]	Singleton [b̥]
Timing	[C] [C]	[C]
Gesture	[p]	[p]
Laryngeal	[spread glottis]	[]

b. Surface Representation

Figure 3: Underlying (a) and surface (b) representations of geminates and singletons

As discussed in Chapter 5, geminates differ from singletons in having two timing nodes, rather than one. The two timing nodes are associated to a single 'gesture' node (cf. Selkirk 1988).

There are laryngeal differences between the two. Underlyingly, neither geminates nor singletons have laryngeal specifications. At the surface, geminates are specified as 'spread glottis', while intervocalic singletons surface with no laryngeal specification. These phonological specifications adapt Butcher's phonetic characterisation of stop contrasts in Gunwinyguan and Burarran languages (Butcher 1993b: 24) as 'presence vs absence of vocal fold abduction reinforced by different articulatory constriction durations'.[6] The use of [spread glottis] as the surface specification of geminates is designed to encode the fact that geminates in the languages discussed by Butcher all had high intraoral pressure as a primary correlate, along with stricture duration. Spreading the glottis allows the maximum degree of pressure to be attained in the quickest time, as observed by Butcher (1993b: 23-24).

The surface singleton stops are not phonologically specified for laryngeal features. This also accords with the phonetic facts. Butcher (1993b: 20) notes that 'the inconsistent presence of glottal pulsing through lenis [singleton] stop constrictions provides a strong indication that active adduction of the vocal folds is not a prerequisite for these sounds'. Singleton stops require neither an abduction nor an adduction movement of the vocal cords.

Singleton stops in Ngalakgan therefore do not have the same 'markedness value' as voiced stops in languages with a voicing contrast. Speakers do not actively seek to attain voicing throughout closure, or shorter VOT times, as we have seen in 6.1.2. Singleton stops are therefore not specified as [voice]. In Ngalakgan then, it is not the case that the surface 'voiced' stops are the marked members of the stop opposition, and the surface 'voiceless' stops are the unmarked members. If anything the opposite is true; the 'voiceless' (geminate) stops require speakers to make an articulatory effort: to spread the glottis and maintain closure, while the 'voiced' (singleton) stops require less articulatory effort. The effortful nature of geminates, and relative effortlessness of singletons, is reflected in the fact

---

[6] The feature label [spread glottis] was proposed in Halle and Stevens (1971), but I do not assume their classification for stop contrasts, and I am using 'spread glottis' to encode a different contrast to theirs. In Halle and Stevens (1971), 'spread glottis' entails aspiration, that is, maximal glottal abduction timed to co-occur with release of closure. Here, I mean that glottal abduction is part of the articulation of geminates, but is not *necessarily* timed so as to occur with release of closure. Butcher suggests the glottal spreading gesture in the Maningrida group is timed to co-occur *during* the closure, so as to maximise intraoral pressure. In fact, the timing of glottal abduction in Ngalakgan geminates seems to vary, assuming that the duration of post-release VOT is an indication of this timing.

that singletons are commonly approximated in Ngalakgan and the languages studied by Butcher (1993b). Geminates are never approximated in these languages.

The term 'lenis' is therefore appropriate as a characterisation of the phonetic and phonological characteristics of singletons, since they are articulatorily less effortful than geminates, and are unspecified for positive laryngeal features. I represent them phonetically here with the IPA diacritic for voicelessness, but with a voiced symbol, to encode their lenis quality (Pullum and Ladusaw 1986). Elsewhere I simply represent them with the voiced symbol in phonetic representations, though it should be kept in mind that singleton stops have a distinct place in the phonological system from voiced stops in systems of voicing contrasts, as I have observed.

Stops in Ngalakgan consistently contrast in duration; I have characterised the contrast as 'geminate' vs. 'singleton', but one might characterise it as 'long fortis stop' vs. 'short lenis stop' (e.g. Evans 2003 for Bininj Gun-wok dialects; or Green 1995 for Gurr-goni). This seems to be Merlan's (1983) proposal for Ngalakgan. Even though Merlan recognises that duration is the main phonetic correlate of fortis consonants, this does not alter the fact that she is setting up a phonological opposition of *segments*. In her analysis, a lenis syllable *onset* contrasts with a fortis syllable *onset*, not a fortis geminate, as she makes clear (1983: 2): 'If ... the stops represented by voiceless symbols are not taken to be geminate [but rather fortis], then (given restrictions on their distribution ...) a single stop of this kind would always be the onset of a syllable frequently preceded by an open syllable, or sometimes by one with a non-nasal sonorant as the final segment.'

Characterising the contrast as fortis vs lenis implies that the surface contrast corresponds to an underlying segmental contrast between two series of stops. Chapter 2 has shown that the behaviour of geminates in syllable structure is ambiguous. One the one hand, most of their distributional characteristics in Ngalakgan can be easily captured by treating them as clusters. On the other hand, in closely related language groups with geminates, such as the Burarran languages, geminates can occur in positions that are otherwise restricted to simple obstruents. In the following sections, I provide additional phonetic evidence relevant to this question, showing that geminates have similar acoustic characteristics to other obstruent clusters.

6.1.4 Assignment of [spread glottis]

It might be thought that the fact that geminates and singletons contrast in terms of the [spread glottis] feature is grounds for treating geminates as a distinct series of fortis stops. In fact, as I show in this section, [spread glottis] is a characteristic of all obstruent clusters in the language, including geminates.[7]

The accompanying spectrograms (following this section) show that geminates (Figure 5), as well as two types of obstruent clusters—glottal+obstruent (Figure 6), and obstruent+obstruent (Figure 7)—are characterised by a long period in which full voicing ceases. (Henceforth, I use the term 'devoiced', rather than voiceless, to cover situations where modal voicing is lacking, whether this is because of glottal abduction or glottal constriction.) In the geminate in Figure (5) /kama**kk**un/ 'properly', voicing ceases for 200 ms. In the glottal+obstruent cluster of Figure (6) /ɻaj-**ʔk**an/ 'meat-DAT', the devoiced period (creaky voice followed by voicelessness) lasts for 134 ms. In the obstruent+obstruent cluster of Figure (7) /ce**tp**eʈe/ 'archer fish', voicelessness is maintained for 197 ms. The /ʈk/ cluster of Figure (8), /ŋu**ʈ-k**a+na-ppiraʔ/ 'stop-CAUS+FUT-DU' has a duration of 245 ms. Note that in each of these clusters, C_2 /p/ of the cluster /tp/, and /k/ of /ʈk/ is aspirated at release, just like the geminate of Figure (5), possibly indicating glottal spreading in heterorganic obstruent clusters. Figure (8) shows that the suffix-initial geminate /pp/ of /-**pp**iraʔ/ has the same characteristics as stem-internal geminates, with a duration of 225 ms and aspirated release.

A similar relationship between underlying and surface forms therefore holds of obstruent+obstruent, and glottal+obstruent clusters, as for geminates. These representations are given in Figure (4). Again, the underlying supralaryngeal stops are unspecified for laryngeal features, but are filled in with [spread glottis] at the surface. The laryngeal segment is underlyingly specified as [constricted glottis] ([cg]), as discussed in Chapter 2.

Geminates and obstruent clusters—obstruent+obstruent and glottal stop +obstruent—are characterised by a long devoiced period based on deliberate glottal abduction, or constriction and abduction gestures in the last case.

Since all obstruent clusters are [spread glottis] at the surface, the fact that geminates are also [spread glottis] is not necessarily a reason for them to be considered a contrastive series of fortis stops.[8]

---

[7] McKay (1980) to my knowledge was the first to show that heterorganic and homorganic clusters of stops (in Rembarrnga) had similar acoustic characteristics. McKay originally proposed the analysis in (1975). The similarity was also noted informally by Wood (1978), in the Yolngu language Gälpu.

[8] The fact that geminates are [sg] cannot be considered to be positive evidence that they *are* clusters however, since obstruent clusters in Lithuanuan and many other languages agree in voicing also (Steriade 1997: 18). This does not mean that the voiceless stops in these languages are clusters.

	CC cluster		ʔC cluster	
Timing	/C/	/C/	/C/	/C/
Gesture	[t]	[p]	[ ]	[k]
Laryngeal	[]	[]	[cg]	[]

a. Underlying representation

	CC cluster		ʔC cluster	
Timing	/C/	/C/	/C/	/C/
Gesture	[t]	[p]	[ ]	[k]
Laryngeal	[sg]	[sg]	[cg]	[sg]

b. Surface representation

Figure 4: Underlying (a) and surface (b) representations of obstruent-obstruent and glottal-obstruent clusters

6.1.5 Summary

To summarise then, the acoustic evidence suggests that the phonological basis of the stop contrast is gemination. The only consistent acoustic parameter is duration, as Butcher (1993b) found in the case of other Top End languages with a stop contrast. There is no consistent voicing distinction between geminates and singletons: while geminates are always voiceless, singletons may also be voiceless.

Geminates commonly occur at stem boundaries in complex words in Ngalakgan and in other Northern languages. Glottal stops appear in all of the same environments, suggesting that the two—glottal stop, and geminate—perform a similar function. In 6.2, I discuss the distribution and behaviour of these segments in these positions, and argue that they are both well-suited to this role given the acoustic characteristics discussed in the preceding section. These characteristics will in turn suggest an analysis of the unusual phenomenon of geminate alternation, discussed in 6.3.

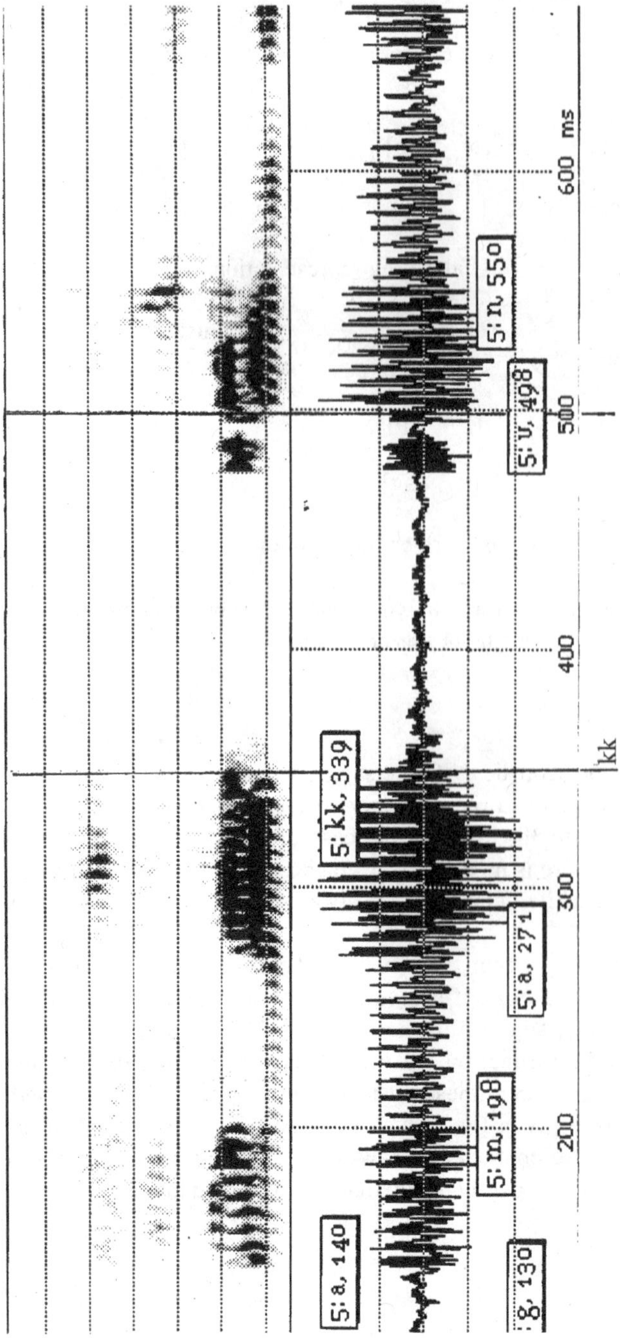

Figure 5: [kɐ́mɐkkʊn] /kamakkun/ 'properly'

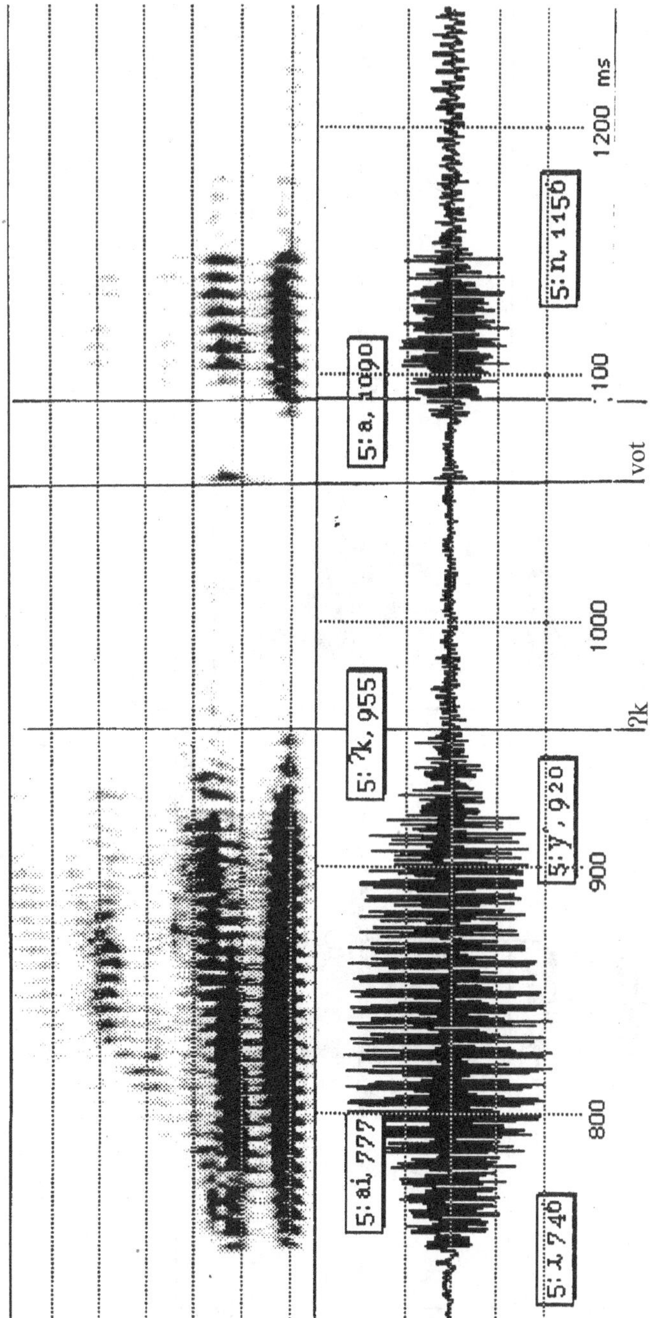

Figure 6: [ɹáḭkan] /ɹajʔ-kan/ 'meat-DAT'

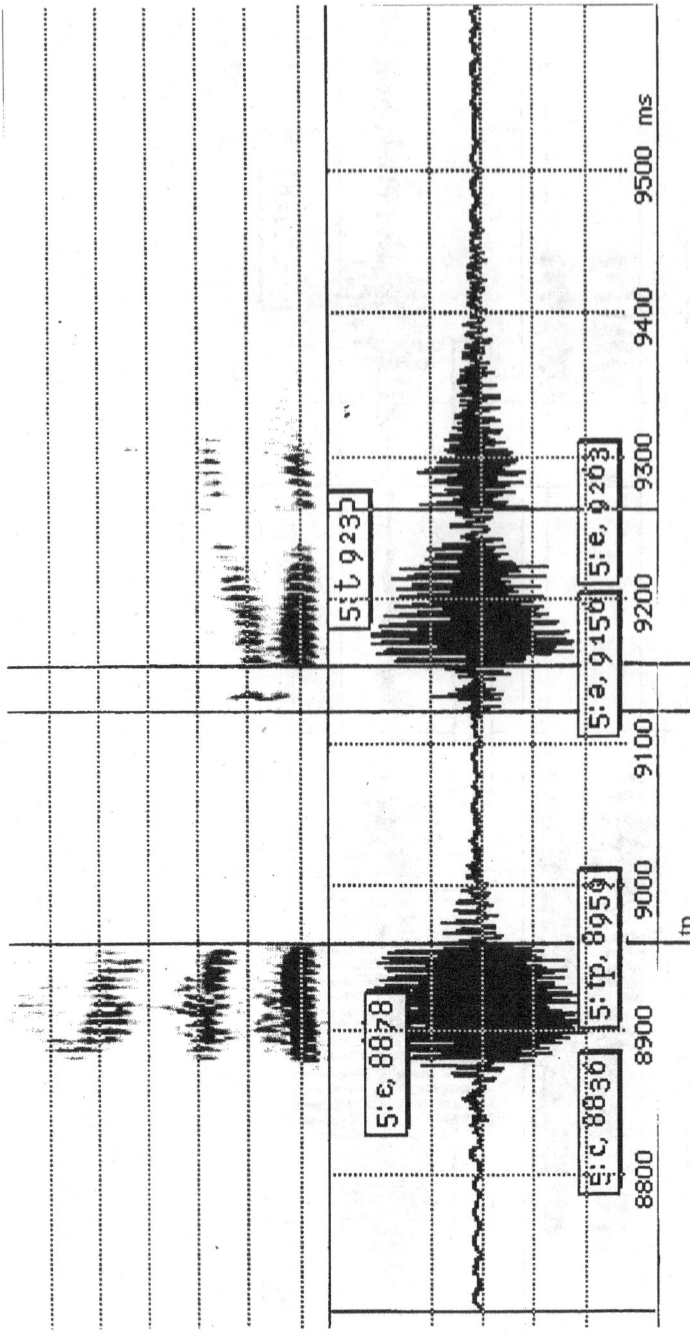

Figure 7: [ɟɛ́tpəɖɛ] /cetpeṭe/ 'archerfish'

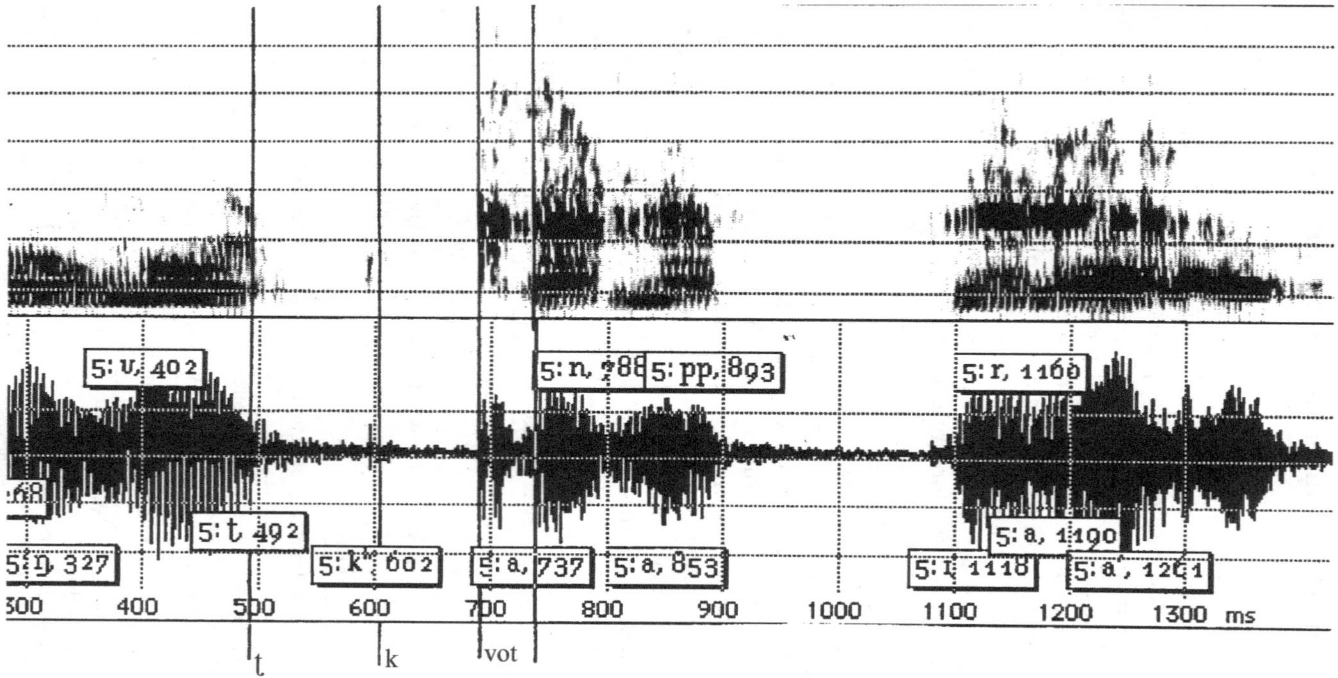

Figure 8: [ŋʊrβuŋʊ̀ʈkɐnɐppíɾɐ̰] ‘we have to stop those two’ /ŋur-pu-ŋuʈ-kana-ppiraʔ/ 12aS-3a-desist-CAUS.FUT-DU

6.2 Gemination and laryngealisation at morpheme boundaries

Geminates appear initially in suffixes, between stems in lexicalised compounds and reduplicated forms, and at the left edges of bound stems. A consideration of the historical evidence suggests that geminates in these positions are derived from an original morpheme-initial simple stop. Glottal stops appear in some cases in the initial position (in suffixes and bound stems), and in others in a morpheme-final position (right-binding stems, reduplicants, verb stems, suffixes). I regard the two phenomena—gemination and laryngealisation—as being two symptoms of the same syndrome.

The reason I regard laryngealisation and gemination as deriving from the same source is because of the form of suffixes. In WORD-level case suffixes, both geminate-initial and glottal-initial forms are found. A comparison of Gunwinyguan (GN) languages suggests that initial geminates in suffixes are innovations in Rembarrnga, Ngalakgan and Ngandi.[9] Suffix-initial glottal stops are found both in these three, and in other languages of the family also (dialects of BGW and Dalabon, to name two). Ngalakgan, Rembarrnga and Ngandi reflexes of the Proto-GN suffix forms in other GN languages do not necessarily show initial glottal stop or geminate, even if glottal stops or geminates are found in other suffixes in the same language. Nor do the geminates and glottal stops appear in the same positions in the cognate suffixes of Ngalakgan, Ngandi and Rembarrnga. This lack of correspondence can be shown by a comparison of two case suffixes in extant GN languages, given in Table (4).

Proto-GN	Ngalakgan	Rembarrnga	Ngandi	BGW[10]
*-kun GEN/DAT	-ʔkVn	-kkan	-kku	-ken(ʔ)
*-kun REL[11]	-kVn		-ʔkuʔ	-ken(ʔ)
Proto-GN	Ngalakgan LOC/ALL	Rembarrnga ALL	Dalabon LOC/ALL	BGW LOC/ALL
*-ka LOC	-kkaʔ	-ʔkaʔ	-ʔkaʔ	-(ʔ)kaʔ

Table 4: Case suffixes in central and eastern Gunwinyguan languages

[9] These are the same three languages in which geminate alternation, described in 6.3, is found. The analysis suggests that this is no coincidence.

[10] This form realises the Genitive meaning in BGW. The form with final glottal stop is from the Kunwinjku dialect (Evans 2003: 142). Glottal-initial forms are also occasionally heard in Mayali, and more regularly in Dalabon. The suffix is also used as a Relative/Subordinator (Evans 2003: 323), though again, with more frequency in Dalabon (Evans p.c.).

[11] I regard the verb Relative/Subordinator suffix as deriving from the nominal Dative suffix. The evidence for this is that in both Ngalakgan and Ngandi, the two suffixes are the same, except for the differences in initial/final laryngealisation, and extend in the case of Ngalakgan to the fact that both suffixes undergo vowel-harmony with the preceding syllable. These are the only two morphemes in Ngalakgan which do so.

For Proto-GN Genitive/Dative */-kun/, which has a glottal-initial reflex in Ngalakgan, both Ngandi and Rembarrnga have geminate-initial reflexes, while most dialects of BGW have a simple stop-initial form. A form of the Dative suffix became specialised as a verb subordinating or relativising suffix in Ngalakgan and Ngandi. Again, the suffixes are different in each language, and moreover, different to the related nominal suffix. The Ngalakgan REL suffix has a singleton-initial form, in Ngandi it is glottal stop-initial and final, where the suffix-initial glottal stop alternates with zero depending on the form of the stem (Heath 1978b: 24). For the Proto-GN Locative */-ka/, Ngalakgan has a geminate-initial form, while Rembarrnga has a glottal stop-initial form.[12] Despite the fact that Ngalakgan, Ngandi and Rembarrnga have both geminate- and glottal stop-initial suffixes, these realisations are distributed among the various suffix forms differently in each language.

The different distribution patterns in each language suggest two things. Firstly, each language applied both initial laryngealisation and gemination to suffixes independently, leading to the various realisations of what was the same suffix originally. Secondly, since both geminate-initial and glottal-initial suffixes are found in the same environment, I suggest that historical laryngealisation and gemination were variant realisations of the same impetus.

Stem-demarcation with gemination, laryngealisation and fortition/lenition alternations appears to be an areal feature of this region (see Harvey 1991 for a discussion and survey of glottal stop distribution in Northern languages).[13] Languages elsewhere show similar patterns. In Finnish for example, glottal stop and geminates both occur as word-boundary markers (Sulkala and Karjalainen 1992: 369):

---

12 The Proto-GN Dative/Genitive */-kun/ is ultimately from Proto-Australian */-ku/ which signalled Purposive as well as Genitive, Dative, and Allative functions (Dixon 1980: 311). The reflex of Proto-GN */-ka/ realises both Locative and Allative cases in Ngalakgan, Dalabon and most dialects of BGW. Rembarrnga and the Gundjeihmi dialect of BGW have a distinct suffix for Locative: /-ca(m)/ ~ /-cca(m)/, and /-cam/, respectively. The Proto-Australian Locative is reconstructed by Dixon as */-ta/ ~ /-la/ ~ /-ŋka/ (1980: 311), with prosodically-determined allomorphy in many Pama-Nyungan languages. The 'Proto-Australian' (really Proto-Pama-Nyungan) form is most probably cognate with the Proto-GN */-ka/. Since the Rembarrnga and Gundjeihmi form has a restricted distribution and function, I regard it as an innovation, and therefore reconstruct both Locative and Allative functions for PGN */-ka/.

13 This group includes GN languages Ngalakgan (Merlan 1983: 6-8), Ngandi (Heath 1978b: 9), Rembarrnga (McKay 1975: 40), Bininj Gun-wok (Evans 2003: 78), Jawoyn (Merlan n.d.), Warray (Harvey 1986); as well as Mangarrayi (Merlan 1982: 182-86), and Wagiman (Cook 1987: 53-62; Wilson 1999: 174); and the Pama-Nyungan Yolngu languages, e.g. Gälpu (Wood 1978), Djinang (Waters 1980), Djapu (Morphy 1983: 20) and Djambarrpuyngu (Wilkinson 1991).

> There is a glottal stop in certain sandhi positions in Finnish, a phonetic marker of the word boundary which has no correspondence in the writing system. When the glottal stop is followed by a word-initial consonant it is realised as gemination of that consonant, e.g. [tulet tællep puolellek kɐtuɐ] 'come to this side of the street' (written: *tule tälle puolelle katua*). When it is followed by a vowel, a true glottal stop may be pronounced [en hɑlua? ?ollɑ? ?ulkonɑ] 'I don't want to be outside' (written: *en halua olla ulkona*).

Synchronically in Ngalakgan, the stem-demarcation impetus derives the following morphological patterns at the WORD-level:

(1) a. Initial geminate alternation (but not glottal stop alternation) in WORD-suffixes
b. Final laryngealisation of thematic coverb stems
c. Final laryngealisation of CV? WORD-reduplicants

Geminate alternation in suffixes is described and analysed in 6.3, and laryngealisation in the CV? reduplication pattern in 6.4.

6.2.1 Reasons for boundary gemination and laryngealisation

Why is there such an association between edges and laryngeal activity? The link, I suggest, is cessation of normal glottal activity. Apart from the obstruent clusters examined here, glottal vibration is more or less continuous within Ngalakgan words. Intercontinuant plain stops do interrupt voicing sporadically, as we have seen; but by far the majority of intercontinuant plain stops are voiced throughout closure, and quite commonly approximated (cf. Butcher 1993b: 11). With respect to voicing, intercontinuant singletons are 'targetless' obstruents in the sense of Browman and Goldstein (1990): speakers make no concerted effort on the laryngeal tier with respect to singletons. They are specified neither for [–voice] nor for [+voice] in Ngalakgan. Speakers do not actively abduct vocal folds in their production, nor do they actively seek to maintain vocal fold vibration (Butcher 1993b: 20).

Therefore, *apart from* word-internal geminates and glottal stops, the kind of targeted cessation of voicing found in these articulations is only otherwise typical of the boundaries of words in isolation. Word boundaries in Ngalakgan correlate, at least some of the time, with pause. Pause is acoustic silence. Therefore, we have the following two equivalences:

(2) a. Voice[On] = Word
b. Voice[Off] = Word edge '#'

I suggest that Voice[Off] with the interpretation of a word boundary, can be signalled either by cessation of phonation (pause), or by cessation of voicing in Ngalakgan, instigated by segments with [spread glottis] and [constricted glottis] specifications. That is, geminates, [sg] clusters, and glottal stop all signal 'word' boundaries, where 'word' corresponds at least to Prosodic Word, and also, as we shall see, to other prominent prosodic positions.

Since both geminates and glottal stops are found at the boundaries of stems in Ngalakgan and other languages, learners might have posited a general association of the following kind:[14]

(3) Voice[Off] = # 'Contrastive cessation of voicing correlates with an MCat/PCat boundary'

I will refer to the constraint which captures this association as 'No spurious devoicing'. The constraint demands that every *deliberate* break in the voicing profile of a word correspond to the boundary of some morphological or prosodic constituent. The constituents I include in this group are PRWD, strongest foot (FT1), and tonic syllable.

If geminates surface with a privative [spread glottis] specification, in opposition to plain stops unspecified for laryngeal features, then the markedness of geminates and other obstruent clusters with respect to plain stops follows. The constraint licenses these clusters just if they occur at the boundary of a morphological or prosodic constituent.

By associating devoiced articulations with constituent boundaries, an acoustically highly-marked phenomenon in the language—acoustic silence—is put to maximum use: signalling morphological boundaries. This has an obvious advantage for acquisition: wherever learners hear significant breaks in voicing they can be safe in assuming a constituent boundary, and conversely they will expect to hear voicelessness, otherwise they will posit no constituent boundary. Properly interpreting morpheme boundaries becomes an important task in languages such as Ngalakgan, since as we have seen, words can be morphologically very complex.

There is a converse well-formedness condition, that every MCat or PCat constituent boundary should optimally correspond to a break in voicing. Consider the following propositions. Many languages mark off the edges of prosodic words in some perceptible way, for example by final obstruent devoicing rules as in German, Russian, Lithuanian and other languages (Steriade 1997). Probably, less languages mark off the edges of feet, and even fewer mark off the tonic syllables. I propose the following constraints to encode these propositions.

---

[14] The statement in (3) is a preliminary one. A more careful definition is provided at (33).

(4) a. #PRWD# 'The boundaries of the Prosodic Word are delimited by a '#' junctural element'

b. #FT1# 'The boundaries of the strongest foot in a PRWD are delimited by a '#' junctural element'

c. #σ́# 'The boundaries of the strongest syllable in a PRWD are delimited by a '#' junctural element'

The three constraints in (4) are interface constraints, determining associations between prosodic structure and morphological strings. The junctural element '#' is defined in Ngalakgan by the constraint in (3) as a devoiced articulation: geminates and [spread glottis] obstruent clusters. Therefore, all three constraints determine that [sg] articulations should be found at the left and right edges of strong prosodic constituents, and are violated if this is not the case.

The general principle seems to be that the most important prosodic constituents should be delimited in this way before less important constituents. These constituents may therefore be ranked as separate constraints, in a 'meta-constraint hierarchy'.

(5) Constituent boundaries must be signalled ('No obscure boundaries')
#PRWD# >> #FT1# >> #σ́#

All of these constituents can be considered prosodic 'heads' of their respective superordinate constituents. The PRWD is the prosodic head of the Phonological Phrase, the strongest foot (FT1) in a PRWD is its head, and the strongest syllable (tonic) is the head of the strongest foot (Prince and Smolensky 1993: 52).[15] The constraints, when satisfied, have the effect that each of these constituents stands out from its environment. Stress is one way of making constituents stand out and, I suggest, the distribution of obstruent clusters and glottal stops performs a similar function.

An example showing how the constraints work is given in (7). In this example, a stem is suffixed with the LOC suffix, which is underlyingly geminate-initial. Because this suffix is geminate-initial, it demarcates the boundary of the PRWD, which corresponds to the Morphological Word. To degeminate the suffix, as in (b) is to leave the PRWD constituent unmarked: a violation of the principle 'No obscure boundaries.' Singletons by themselves do not interrupt voicing to a sufficient degree to constitute salient

[15] It is perhaps for this reason that PPH does not figure in these constraints, since the domain of PPH is the whole word, it is not a head position, it is the domain *within which* heads are defined. Some suffixes and many roots end in glottal stop, suggesting a PPH delimitation constraint. Glottal stops in these positions display no synchronic alternations, unlike the geminate behaviour discussed below, and I therefore omit consideration of #PPH#.

boundaries. Candidate (b), by degeminating the suffix, violates IO-MAX (Affix), preventing deletion of input material from affixes. The definition in (6) follows McCarthy and Prince (1995: 264), relativised to WORD-affixes.

(6) IO-MAX(AFFIX) 'Every segment of the input affix has a correspondent in the output affix' ('No phonological deletion in affixes')

The notation '#' is meant to suggest the voicing break instigated by obstruent clusters and geminates. The braces enclose material within which there are no [sg] or [cg] specifications: voicing is (more or less) continuous.

(7)

/jele-kkaʔ/ 'hole'-LOC	VOICE [OFF]=#	#PRWD#	#FT1#	#σ#	IO-MAX (AFFIX)
☞ a. {jéle}#-kkaʔ				*	
b. {jéle-kaʔ}		*!	*	*	*

Geminate-initial suffixes are 'licensed by' constraints requiring that constituents be delimited. This is a synchronic aspect of Ngalakgan grammar, as demonstrated by the fact that suffixes alternate between geminate and singleton realisations. In the following sections, I describe these alternations, and propose an account using the characterisation suggested here: that geminates are associated with boundaries to prosodic and morphological domains.

6.3 Geminate alternation

All stop-initial WORD-suffixes, such as /-kkaʔ/ LOC, /-kkoʔ/ DYAD, /-ppulu/ PL, have two allomorphs. One allomorph is geminate-initial: /-kkaʔ/, /-kkoʔ/, /-ppulu/. The other allomorph is singleton-initial /-kaʔ/, /-koʔ/, /-pulu/.

Both of these allomorphs are conditioned by the prosodic and phonological structure of the stem to which they attach. In the first place, allomorphs are conditioned by syllable structure, as shown in Chapter 2 and briefly reiterated here. The surface realisations of the Locative suffix /-kkaʔ/ ~ /-kaʔ/ are exemplified in (8) below. The suffix is realised as /-kkaʔ/ with initial geminate following continuant-final stems, as in (a). The geminate is degeminated following non-continuants, as in (b-c).

(8) a. /campuɻ-kkaʔ/ [ɟambʊ́ɻkka̰] 'on sandy ground'
b. /ʈaɻʔ-kkaʔ/ [ɖɻa̰ka̰] 'in a tree'
c. /ŋariɲ-kkaʔ/ [ŋáɾiɲga̰] 'in [my] hand'

The surface phonetic realisation of degeminated /-kaʔ/ depends on the preceding environment: it is a [spread glottis] stop following obstruents including the glottal stop, and a voiced stop following nasals.

Allomorphs are also conditioned by non-local factors. A suffix-initial geminate remains geminate at the surface if there are only voiced and singleton obstruent segments between the suffix and a preceding tonic syllable as in (9)a-e. If there are any obstruent clusters between an underlying suffix-initial geminate and a preceding tonic syllable, as in (9)f-j, the geminate is realised as a singleton at the surface (heterorganic obstruent clusters are exemplified below). I define 'tonic' as a stressed syllable associated with a pitch accent. In the following examples, 'triggers' of the process are indicated with bolding, and 'targets' with italics.

(9) a. [bʊ́lugikka̰]
/puluki-*kk*aʔ/
bullock-LOC (loan)

b. [ɟambʊ́ɻkka̰]
/campuɻ-*kk*aʔ/
sand-LOC

c. [jɛ́lɛkka̰]
/jele-*kk*aʔ/
hole-LOC

d. [láŋgakka̰]
/ɭaŋka-*kk*aʔ/
billabong-LOC

e. [ɟítnɪkka̰]
/citni-*kk*aʔ/
Sydney-LOC (loan)

f. [álakkoga̰]
/ala**kk**o-*kk*aʔ/
later-LOC

g. [wácciga̰]
/wa**cc**i-*kk*aʔ/
sun-LOC

h. [jɛ́rkkega̰]
/jer**kk**e-*kk*aʔ/
bottom-LOC

i. [ŋɔ́lkkoga̰]
/ŋol**kk**o-*kk*aʔ/
big-LOC

j. [bálkkuga̰]
/pal**kk**u-*kk*aʔ/
string-LOC

Of course, stem-internal obstruent clusters do not correspond to a morphological boundary, so in the case of examples (9)f-j, the stem does not constitute a domain in which voicing is uninterrupted. All stem-internal obstruent clusters *do* correspond to a prosodic boundary, either FT1 or tonic syllable, and it is this fact which is sufficient to make them well-formed, as I will show in 6.3.

The conditioning environments for each allomorph are schematically represented in (10) and (11). (10) states that an alternating stop (the 'C' in bold) is realised as a geminate (**C_iC_i**) if the string between the stop and a preceding tonic syllable (σ́) is all [slack vocal cords] ('voiced') at the surface.

(10) [σ́ (CV)*][slk]-**C_iC_i**[V(X)*...]

(11) states that an alternating stop is realised as a singleton (**C_i**) if there is a [sg] cluster in the preceding string, intervening between the alternating stop and a preceding tonic syllable.

(11) [σ́...V$C_iC_{i/j}$[sg]V(CV)*]-**C_i**[V(X)*...]

The process refers to the surface structure of words. Thus, '[sg] clusters' refers to the following kinds of clusters, whether tautomorphemic or heteromorphemic:

(12)
   a. Geminates
   b. Oral obstruent clusters
   c. Glottal stop+obstruent clusters

As we have seen in 6.1.4, all three clusters are [spread glottis] at the surface, in contrast to singleton stops, which are unspecified, and most commonly voiced in both closure and release.

Examples of each of the types of triggers of geminate alternation are presented in (13). In (13)a, a geminate-initial suffix /-cci/ PRIV is singleton-initial when it attaches to a stem which contains a geminate, such as /kappuci/ 'old person'. A geminate-initial suffix is also singleton-initial if the stem contains a glottal+obstruent cluster, as in (13)b, or obstruent +obstruent cluster, as in (13)c. This example, where the stem is a loanword, also illustrates that the phenomenon is fully productive in Ngalakgan.

(13)
a. [gáppuɟìɟi]
   /ka**pp**uci-*cc*i/
   old.person-PRIV
b. [gʊ́n̰piɾiga̰]
   /kun**ʔp**iri-*kk*aʔ/
   that-LOC
c. [wɔ́cpɛlga̰]
   /wo**cp**el-*kk*aʔ/
   hospital-LOC (loan)
d. [mánacci]
   /mana-*cc*i/
   mother-PRIV
e. [ɟáŋgʊkka̰]
   /caŋku-*kk*aʔ/
   meat-LOC
f. [dʊ́ɖʊkka̰]
   /ʈuʈu-*kk*aʔ/
   father's.father-LOC

So glottal+obstruent and obstruent+obstruent clusters behave in the same way as geminates for this process. The stems in (13)d-f do not contain any clusters of this type, so the suffix begins in a geminate. Note that nasal+stop clusters, as in (13)e, do not condition singleton realisations of suffixes.

Singleton realisations triggered by preceding geminates appear to be entirely consistent for all speakers with whom I have worked. At this point, there is not enough information to tell whether types (12)b and (c) are consistent triggers. There are only a few examples of singleton realisation triggered by type (b) and just two of (c). But while there is little positive evidence, there is no negative evidence to prove that they are not triggers.

The contribution of obstruent clusters to geminate alternation is difficult to check because they are rare morpheme-internally. They are reasonably common heteromorphemically at compound boundaries, but in compounds, stress is commonly associated with the second member (14)a, or with a following disyllabic suffix, as in (b-c), as described in Chapters 3 and 4.

(14) a. [ŋubuwɛ̀tbéːnappìɾa̰]
/ŋu-pu-we**t**+**p**aja+na-*pp*iraʔ/
1mS-3a-sneak.up.on+GO.LOOK+FUT-DU
'I'll sneak up on those two.' [4/7/96]

b. [ŋubuɭàkpunappíɾa̰]
/ŋu-pu-ɭa**k**+**p**u+na-*pp*iraʔ/
1mS-3a-split.shell+HIT+FUT-DU
'I'll split the shells of those two' [4/7/96]

c. [ŋubuŋʊ̀ʈkanappíɾa̰]
/ŋu-pu-ŋu**ʈ**-**k**a+na-*pp*iraʔ/
1mS-3a-desist-CAUS+FUT-DU
'I'll make those two stop' [4/7/96]

These do not constitute counterexamples to a claim that obstruent clusters condition geminate alternation. In (14)a, a pitch accent intervenes between the obstruent cluster /tp/ in the stem and the geminate in the suffix, hence the latter is well-formed. In (14)b-c, the suffix itself is associated with a pitch accent, which also sanctions a geminate-initial realisation (see 6.3 below). I have two examples of suffixed nouns with medial obstruent clusters.

(15) [ŋiɲjábʊn ɟáʈpaga̰]
/ŋiɲ-ɻapo+n ca**ʈp**a-*kk*aʔ/
2mS-go+PR eldest-LOC
'you go to the eldest one'

(16) [ŋuɻábona wɒ́cpɛlga̰]
/ŋu-ɻabon+a wo**cp**el-*kk*aʔ/
1mS-go+FUT hospital-LOC
'I've got to go to hospital.'

As with obstruent clusters, glottal stops are rare morpheme-internally, and hence the number of environments in which they would trigger singleton-realisations of suffixes is limited. I tentatively include both heterorganic obstruent clusters and glottal+obstruent clusters in the class of triggers, subject to further investigation. Comparative evidence from Ngandi (Heath 1978b) and Rembarrnga (McKay 1975) also suggests that all three clusters are triggers of the process.

It can be shown that some other kinds of clusters—such as nasal+stop—do not trigger singleton-initial realisations of suffixes, and NC clusters therefore differ from geminates in this respect. Some further examples of this difference are presented in (17).

(17) a. [ɟáŋgʊkka̰]
/caŋku-*kk*aʔ/
meat-LOC

b. [láŋgakka̰]
/ɭaŋka-*kk*aʔ/
billabong-LOC

c. [ɟámbʊɻkka̰]
/campuɻ-*kk*aʔ/
sand-LOC

d. [ɟɔ́lkkoga̰]
/col**kk**o-*kk*aʔ/
ground-LOC

e. [nɔ́ccoga̰]
/ɳo**cc**o-*kk*aʔ/
grass-LOC

f. [ŋáɪccalga̰]
/ŋa**cc**al-*kk*aʔ/
spring-LOC

(17)a-c show that nasal+stop clusters do not condition singleton-initial realisations. Therefore, these kinds of clusters do not have the same effect that obstruent clusters and geminates do. For reasons discussed previously, it is not possible at this stage to show definitively that other kinds of clusters, e.g. glottal+sonorant, do not condition singleton-initial realisations of suffixes.

Note that the schematic representation of the alternation given in (10) violates the lenition [i.e. geminate alternation] rules provided by Merlan (1983: 27) for Ngalakgan, and Heath (1978b: 22) for Ngandi. Merlan's rule is reproduced here (Heath's rule 1978b: 22 is similar).

(18) Stop → [–fortis] / ... $C_1VC_2V(C)$-___V

(Either C_1 or C_2 is a geminate stop or ʔC; final C may be any consonant; '-' = morpheme boundary).

The rule states that stops must be singleton following a geminate stop or glottal+obstruent cluster in the preceding two syllables.[16] Heath's rule includes 'hard clusters' among the triggers for degemination in Ngandi (though curiously, only as C_2, not C_1 triggers). These are (a) glottal stop+oral obstruent, or (b) oral obstruent cluster, as specifed above in (12) for Ngalakgan.

Merlan's and Heath's rules make no mention of the effect of intervening accent on the realisation of geminates. Merlan (1983: 6) denies any connection between the two: 'the presence of a geminate segment is not directly linked to placement of major word stress'. The following section shows that accent *does* affect the realisation of geminates and singletons in suffixes: following a tonic accent, geminates in suffixes are preferred.

There are therefore two conditioning factors: the presence of a preceding obstruent cluster, and the location of tonic syllables. The alternation process only applies to the initial geminates of WORD-suffixes. Initial *glottal* clusters in WORD-suffixes are not affected consistently, see 6.3.3.[17] Initial obstruents and geminates in ROOT-suffixes and bound stems do not alternate, nor do geminates in other positions: stem-initially or -medially, as shown in 6.3.4.

This section has shown that [sg] clusters trigger the appearance of singletons initially in suffixes, while other kinds of clusters have no effect. In the following section I provide evidence that prosodic structure conditions geminate alternation.

6.3.1 Geminate alternation is prosodically-conditioned

The location of tonic syllables alone can determine the realisation of a suffix, as shown by the contrasting pair in (19). (19)a and (b) both have underlying segmental strings /**ʔp**VLV-*kk*aʔ/, where 'L' is a liquid. Yet (a) is realised with singleton-initial suffix [-ga̰] and (b) is realised with geminate-initial suffix [-kka̰]. The difference between the two conditioning environments is prosodic: in (19)a, the tonic accent is before the trigger /ʔp/, while in (19)b the tonic accent occurs between the trigger /ʔp/ and the following target.

(19)	a. [gʊ́n̰ˀpɪɾɪga̰]	b. [bɔ̀lɔ̰ˀpɔ́lɔkka̰]
	/kun**ʔp**iri-*kk*aʔ/	/polo**ʔp**olo-*kk*aʔ/
	that-LOC	woman-LOC

A tonic syllable 'licenses' geminate-initial realisation of the following suffix.

---

16 I have interpreted the (1983) published version of Merlan's conditioning environment '$C_1CV_2V(C)$' as a typographical error.

17 Glottal stops are sporadically deleted from surface forms under conditions similar to the geminate alternation process. See 6.3.3.

Location of pitch accent can distinguish minimally contrastive strings. Consider (20)a and (b) below. In (20), we observe that the same stem+stem sequence /palak=ŋki/ 'wife's.mother-2mDAT' is followed by a geminate-initial suffix in (20)a but a singleton-initial suffix in (b). The difference between the two lies in the location of pitch accents in each case. In (20)a, a pitch accent must occur between the trigger and the target (because of prosodic constraints: see 4.3.1), and the latter is realised as a geminate. In (20)b, the trigger occurs between preceding tonic and suffix-initial geminate, so the latter is realised as a singleton.

(20) a. [bàlakkíkka̰] /pala**k=ŋk**i-*kk*aʔ/ wife's.mother-2mDAT-LOC
b. [bálakkibìɾa̰] /pala**k=ŋk**i-*pp*iraʔ/ wife's.mother-2mDAT-DU

The observation that a tonic accent occurring between a trigger and target allows the target geminate to surface is one that holds generally within words, not just heteromorphemically. In (21)a, the geminate in the stem is separated from the geminate-initial suffix /-cci/ PRIV by a tonic accent, so the geminate is well-formed in the suffix. If there is no tonic accent separating the target and trigger, as in (21)b, the initial-stop of the suffix must be a singleton.

(21) a. [màrkkarálacci] /mar**kk**arala-*cc*i/ headband-PRIV '(having) no headbands'
b. [jáppaɟi] /ja**pp**a-*cc*i/ sister-PRIV '(having) no sisters'

Whether or not a geminate can be realised initially in suffixes is therefore determined by the location of tonic accents *as well as* the existence of preceding triggers in the stem.

Kinterm morphology provides rich ground for testing geminate alternation, since the Dative pronominal stems are associated with pitch accents if stressed (as shown in Chapter 4). Some examples of intervening accent 'defusing' the alternation are presented in (22).[18]

(22) a. [ɟijàppaŋgíkka̰] /cu-ja**pp**a=ŋki-*kk*aʔ/ F-sister-2mDAT-LOC
[jáppaga̰] /ja**pp**a-*kk*aʔ/ sister-LOC

[18] It is difficult to compare minimally contrastive forms here. The Locative suffix /-kkaʔ/ normally occurs with a preceding Dative pronominal stem, so minimal contrasts such as that in example (a) are rare and difficult to obtain. The Dyadic suffix /-kkoʔ/ cannot co-occur with a preceding pronominal stem, so is used in lieu of /-kkaʔ/ in the other forms.

b. [ɳumɔ̀kkɔlŋgíkka̰]
/ɳu-mo**kk**ol=ŋki-*kk*aʔ/
M-father-2mDAT-LOC

c. [nugàkkaŋgíkka̰]
/ɳu-ka**kk**a=ŋki-*kk*aʔ/
M-brother-2mDAT-LOC

d. [ɟumàrkkɛŋgíkka̰]	[márkkego̰]
/cu-mar**kk**e=ŋki-*kk*aʔ/	/mar**kk**e-*kk*oʔ/
F-father's.sister-2mDAT-LOC	father's.sister-DYAD
e. [nubʊ̀ɪppʊŋgíkka̰]	[bʊ́ɪppugo̰]
/ɳu-puj**pp**u=ŋki-*kk*aʔ/	/puj**pp**u-*kk*oʔ/
M-brother-2mDAT-LOC	brother-DYAD

In (22)a-e, a tonic accent is associated with the stem /=ŋki/ 'yours' when followed by a monosyllabic suffix, as it is here with /-kkaʔ/ Locative. The initial-stop of the suffix is geminate, even though in all cases there is a preceding trigger. The tonic accent intervening between target and trigger allows the geminate in the suffix to be realised. The contrasting forms on the right hand side show that without the intervening tonic accent the following suffix /-kkoʔ/ or /-kkaʔ/ must be singleton-initial.

Further evidence for the proposal that geminate alternation is prosodically-conditioned comes from examples where the location of tonic accents co-varies with the realisation of geminates. In Chapter 4 I observed that affixed words, and roots with two feet or more, showed variation in the location of tonic accents. Where primary stress precedes secondary stress(es), there is just one pitch accent (T*), located on the primary. Where secondary precedes primary, pitch accents are located on both primary and secondary. The two possibilities are represented schematically in (23)-(24).

```
           T*
           |
(23)    [...σ́...σ̀...]

           T*  T*
           |   |
(24)    [...σ̀...σ́...]
```

Where a word allows both possibilities—(23) and (24)—as in (25), the realisation of suffixes differs accordingly. Example (a) with initial primary stress has a single tonic accent and the suffix must be singleton-initial. Example (b) shows the same word but with a variant stress pattern. In this variant, main stress is on the penultimate of the stem, allowing the geminate realisation in the suffix. The examples in (c) and (d) contrast similarly. Example (c) is a fast-speech variant, where an unstressed vowel between peripheral stop and following liquid is elided (as discussed in Chapter 5, section 5.6). Examples such as these indicate that the alternation is a surface phenomenon, not an underlying, lexicalised one.

(25)

a. T* (associated with the first syllable)
[bɔ́lɔ̰pɔ̀lɔbɪ̀ɾa̰]
/polo**ʔp**olo-*pp*iraʔ/
woman-DU

b. T* T*
[bɔ̀lɔ̰pɔ́lɔppɪ̀ɾa̰]
/polo**ʔp**olo-*pp*iraʔ/
woman-DU

c. T*
[náɹakkɻàniga̰]
/ɳaɻa**kk**aɻani-*kk*aʔ/
[place name]-LOC

d. T* T*
[nàɹakkaɻánɪkka̰]
/ɳaɻa**kk**aɻani-*kk*aʔ/
[place name]-LOC

Example (26)b shows a second variant for the word in (26)a, besides that in (25)b above. In (26)b, a tonic accent is associated with the initial syllable of the suffix itself. This also allows a geminate realisation in the suffix (sporadically). Another example is given in (26)d.

(26)

a. T*
[bɔ́lɔ̰pɔ̀lɔbɪ̀ɾa̰]
/polo**ʔp**olo-*pp*iraʔ/
woman-DU

b. T* T* T*
[bɔ̀lɔ̰pɔ̀lɔppíɾa̰]
/polo**ʔp**olo-*pp*iraʔ/
woman-DU

c. T* T*
[gɔ̀ɾɛ̰pɔ́ɾɛppɪ̀ɾa̰]
/kore**ʔ=p**ore-*pp*iraʔ/
alone=3aDAT-DU

d. T* T*
[nugʊ̀n̰pɪɾɪppíɾa̰]
/ɳu-kun**ʔp**iri-*pp*iraʔ/
M-that-DU

Therefore, following a trigger, geminates in suffixes can be licensed in two ways. Either they can be the first [sg] cluster after a tonic, as in (26)c, above. Or they can themselves be associated with tonic accent in the following syllable, as in (26)b, d, in which case the initial geminate can sporadically be realised.[19] If neither of these two conditions holds, as in (26)a, the suffix must be singleton-initial.

[19] The sporadic failure of lenition in disyllabic suffixes was observed also by Merlan (1983: 26) and Heath (1978b: 23), though neither made a connection with stress.

An explanation for these patterns is advanced in the following section.

6.3.2 Analysis

In 6.2.1 I proposed that [spread glottis] clusters constituted boundary signals in the grammar, to a range of prominent prosodic constituents: PRWD, strongest foot, and tonic. In this section, I develop the analysis further, to account for the geminate alternation patterns we observed in the preceding sections.

We have seen that obstruent clusters, which trigger singleton realisations in following suffixes, are characterised by a [spread glottis] gesture. These clusters break the voicing 'profile' of the word. One aspect of surface forms which depends on voicing is tone. Tone requires a minimum degree of voicing (Ohala 1978; Silverman 1997) and cannot be implemented simultaneously with [spread glottis]. These clusters therefore interrupt the *intonation* profile, as well as the voicing profile, of the word.

I have observed above (6.2) that [sg] segments and clusters are associated with morpheme boundaries in Ngalakgan, and other languages in the region. There is therefore a common association between stretches of intonation, broken by [sg] clusters, and constituents of prosody and morphology, such as Morphological Word/Prosodic Word. This association is schematised in (27) below.

The intonation contour (the wavy line) is associated to the word as a whole (the Phonological Phrase). The intonation contour is broken by the [spread glottis] gesture associated with the geminate (indicated by '||' which can be thought of as an iconic equivalent to '#'), which is in turn associated to the morpheme boundary. The salient portion of the intonation contour is associated to the salient portion of the word: the Morphological Word/ Prosodic Word.

(27)

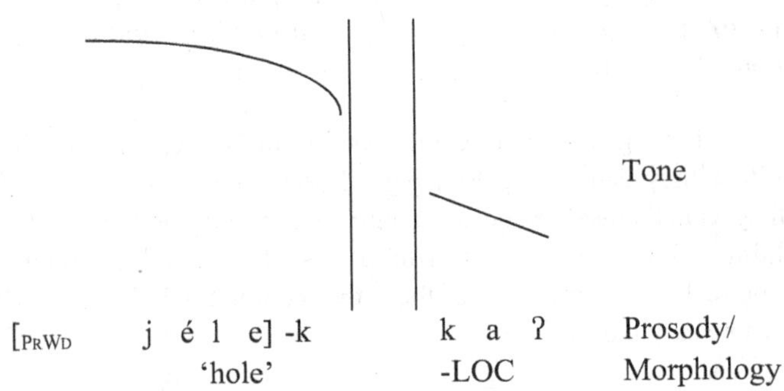

I suggest that it is this bilateral association—between the intonation contour, and prosodic and morphological constituents—which is manipulated by speakers in the process of geminate alternation. Geminates alternate to achieve the best, the optimal match between constituents of morphology, prosody and intonation domains.

The general principles to be expanded on in this section are these:

- Every [spread glottis] gesture is interpreted as a 'domain' boundary.
- Every domain corresponds both to a stretch of intonation, and a constituent: Prosodic Word, strongest foot (of PRWD), or tonic syllable (of PRWD).
- Domains must not be 'broken' by an internal [sg] cluster.

[Sg] and [cg] clusters constitute boundaries to the spread of an intonation contour through the word, and I suggest that this is how they are interpreted by speakers: as boundaries of 'intonation domains'.[20] Every intonation domain extends from a pitch accent as far as it can rightwards through the word. It is blocked by any [spread glottis] clusters.

Optimally, the intonation domains defined by pitch accents on the one hand, and geminates on the other, are isomorphic to MCats and PCats. I translate this as a requirement that domains be properly headed.

(28) DOMAIN(HD) 'Every domain must be headed'

The proper head for an intonation domain is the tonic syllable. The idea is that intonation domains should not be spurious; they should draw attention to the same strong positions in the word that are optimally demarcated with boundaries: PRWD, strongest foot, tonic syllable. The intonational domain headed by the tonic, and the prosodic constituency, together identify the strong morphological positions in the word such as the Morphological Word (≈ Prosodic Word), initial foot or syllable of morpheme (≈ strongest foot and tonic).

I have claimed that clusters which are [spread glottis] interrupt intonation contours in words. The presence of [sg] clusters *within* words leads to an ill-formed domain for the feature [tone]: one which is interrupted in the middle by a [spread glottis] gesture. I follow Kisseberth (1994) in assuming a general constraint that feature domains should not be interrupted by elements which carry an opposite or antagonistic value for that feature.

(29) $*[...[-F]...]_F$ 'Feature domains where [F] elements enclose a [–F] element are ill-formed'

---

[20] These do not necessarily correspond to Prosodic Words.

In this case, the [F] feature is 'tone' and the domain is the intonation contour associated to the word. The [–F] feature is the class of elements which block the spread of intonation in the word: obstruent clusters, which are [spread glottis]. Using '#' as before, to represent [sg] clusters *qua* boundary signals, (30)a is an ill-formed domain configuration, (30)b is an acceptable parse of a string separated by a boundary element #. ('D' represents any domain, '#' represents any domain boundary.)

(30) a. *[...[#]...]$_D$ 'No Broken Domains'
b. ✓[...]$_D$#[...]$_D$

Configurations (30)a-b are well-formedness conditions on surface forms. I will use (30)a as a constraint 'NO BROKEN DOMAINS' (abbreviated as *BRDOM in the tableaux which follow).

I return to the example presented before, to illustrate the constraints. The extent of intonation domains is indicated with underlining in the candidates; PRWD boundaries are indicated with square brackets; # indicates the [sg] domain boundary. In (31)a, the suffix is geminate-initial, and thereby the PRWD and the strongest foot boundaries are demarcated. The Morphological Word, which corresponds to the PRWD, stands out in the word by virtue of being associated to the tonic, and by being demarcated by the geminate in the suffix: the morphological boundary in the form is clear. Were the suffix-initial consonant *not* geminate, as in (31)b, it would leave the PRWD constituent without a phonologically realised boundary, a violation of the 'No obscure boundaries' constraint: #PRWD# (introduced in 6.2.1). Recall that this constraint demands that the edges of PRWDs be associated with [sg] articulations. To parse the intonation domain *beyond* the suffix-initial geminate, as in (31)c, is to create an ill-formed domain structure, which is broken in the middle by an [sg] cluster.

(31)

/jele-*kk*aʔ/ hole-LOC	DOM (HD)	*BRDOM	#PRWD#	#FT1#	#σ́#	IO-MAX (AFX)
☞ a. [jéle]#-kkaʔ					*	
b. [jéle]-kaʔ			*!	*	*	*
c. [jéle]#-kkaʔ		*!			*	

The contrasting examples of suffix 'degemination' violate IO-MAX(AFX); an example is shown in tableau (32) below. The attested output, candidate (32)a, is well-formed despite the fact that it fails to delimit the PRWD or FT1 boundaries. It violates #PRWD# and #FT1# because neither of these positions is associated with a [sg] articulation at the edge. (32)a is nevertheless the most harmonic candidate because it is the only one which parses a single domain, which is properly headed (by the tonic) and unbroken. Every other candidate violates one of the constraints ranked higher than IO-MAX. In the faithful candidates, (32)b and (c), the suffix-initial geminate fails to delimit an intonation domain headed by a tonic. Candidate (32)b parses the domain to the left, and candidate (32)c the domain to the right. Neither of these domains is properly headed by a tonic.[21] Therefore, these candidates both violate DOMAIN(HD): the suffix-initial geminate is unlicensed. Candidate (32)d is an interpretation where the suffix-initial geminate delimits the domain of the PRWD: this creates an ill-formed domain structure, violating NO BROKEN DOMAIN.

(32)

/jappa-*kk*aʔ/ sister-LOC	DOM (HD)	VOICE [OFF]=#	*BR DOM	#PRWD#	#FT1#	#σ#	IO-MAX (AFX)
☞ a. [já#ppa]-kaʔ				*	*		*
b. [já#ppa]#-kkaʔ	*!						
c. [já#ppa]#-kkaʔ	*!						
d. [já#ppa]#-kkaʔ			*!				
e. [já#ppa]#-kkaʔ		*!					

Finally, candidate (e) parses no intonation domains beyond the initial syllable, but realises the suffix-initial geminate faithfully. This is a violation of VOICE[OFF] = # (which was introduced in 6.2.1), I provide a fuller definition here.

(33) VOICE[OFF] = # 'Every [sg] articulation demarcates the boundary of a constituent which is both an intonation domain and a morphological/ prosodic category'[22]

---

[21] If the suffix was disyllabic, and therefore stressed and potentially accented, the suffix *would* constitute an acceptable domain for demarcation at its left boundary. Demarcating the left boundary of prosodic constituents is a possibility examined in (66).

[22] This definition is different from the characterisation given at (3). The former is not meant to be interpreted as a definition.

The geminate here does demarcate the PRWD and FT1 boundaries, but it does so without associating them to a properly-headed intonation domain. The geminate is again unlicensed. Therefore, the constraints regulating the mapping of intonation domains to MCats and PCats dominate the constraints purely demanding [sg] boundaries to these constituents (#PRWD#, #FT1#, #σ́#).

I proposed in Chapter 3 that long roots in Ngalakgan can be parsed into two PRWDS, where the second PRWD domain is associated with primary stress. Since geminates are licensed by a preceding tonic syllable, if a word is parsed as two PRWDS, there are two tonics and hence two geminates may be licensed.

This opens the way for other possible parses of /jappa-kkaʔ/, examined in (35), but these are ill-formed for higher-ranked constraints. Candidate (35)c violates FTBIN (Chapter 3, section 3.1.1), the requirement that feet (and hence PRWDS) be binary at the moraic or syllabic level, since (as Chapter 5 shows) geminates do not contribute a moraic coda in Ngalakgan, and hence the first syllable cannot constitute a foot nor a PRWD. There is no better candidate than (35)c to be found in degeminating the stem-internal geminate, rather than the suffix-initial geminate: candidate (b) violates high-ranking IO-MAX(MWD). Geminate alternation is a property of initial geminates in WORD-suffixes; it is not sanctioned in any other position (see further at 6.3.4).

(34) IO-MAX(MWD) 'Every segment of the input MWD has a correspondent in the output MWD' ('No phonological deletion')

(35)

/ja**pp**a-*kk*aʔ/ sister-LOC	FTBIN	IO-MAX (MWD)	DOM (HD)	#PRWD#	#FT1#	#σ́#	IO-MAX (AFX)
☞ a. [já#ppa]-kaʔ				*	*		*
b. [jápa]#-kkaʔ		*!				*	
c. [jà]#[ppá]#-kkaʔ	*!						

Tonics cannot be adjacent within PRWDS because of the constraint *CLASH, which prevents adjacent stress accents within a PRWD domain.[23] Geminates are thereby banned from adjacent positions in PRWDS. This

[23] *CLASH is defined and exemplified in 5.4.4.

leads to two predictions: if geminates are distant enough to fall in separate PRWD domains, each should be licensed, since each PRWD licenses a tonic. Conversely, if tonics belong to separate PRWDs, regardless of adjacency, then each should license a geminate. Both predictions can be confirmed. Multiple PRWD parses are attested, and indeed preferred, in polypedal roots, as in example (a) below, repeated from (21). In these forms with two pitch peaks, we also find two geminates in the same word.

(36) a. [màrkkarálacci]
/mar**kk**arala-*cci*/
headband-PRIV
'no headbands'

b. [ɟáppaɟi]
/ja**pp**a-*cci*/
sister-PRIV
'no sisters'

Words like (36)a are associated with a secondary^primary (secondary then primary) stress pattern, which I described as having two pitch peaks. Words of this form contrast with those in which primary stress is initial: any following secondary stresses are not associated with a pitch peak. The difference between the two contours is repeated in (37-8).

```
        T*
        |
(37)  [...σ́...σ̀...]

        T*  T*
        |   |
(38)  [...σ̀...σ́...]
```

The general rule is this: a primary stress and any *preceding* secondaries are tonics (pitch accents); any secondaries *following* a primary are not tonics.

Recall from 3.1.4 that each of the pitch accents in a word starts a new Prosodic Word. Each of these PRWDs contains a strongest foot, and a strongest (tonic) syllable. Therefore, each of multiple Prosodic Words in a form should show demarcation effects at the boundaries of these constituents, and each tonic should license a new geminate to perform this function.

(39) shows that the parsing of words into stress and pitch peaks, and the location of geminates in the structure, are two mutually reinforcing aspects of the same grammar. In the attested candidate—(a)—the association of the primary stress with pitch, and the presence of the geminate initially in the suffix, combine to give this stretch of syllables the characteristics of Prosodic Words in Ngalakgan. Prosodic Word boundaries are indicated, as in Chapters

3 and 4, with square brackets.[24] Candidate (c) parses the word with primary stress in initial position. In this parse, the secondary stress cannot be associated with a pitch accent: there is only one tonic in this word, which is the initial syllable. Therefore the intonation domain bounded by the suffix-initial geminate lacks a pitch head.[25]

A foot whose left edge is not aligned with a pitch accent is not an acceptable domain for delimitation; as in (39)c. The intuition is that there is no head strong enough to support the domain delimited by the geminate here: a stressed, but accentless syllable, is not a strong head (Chapter 3).[26] Failing to delimit the second PRWD domain, as in candidate (39)b, again violates #PRWD#: a case of obscure boundaries.

(39)

/mar**kk**arala-*cci*/ 'headdress'-PRIV	DOMAIN (HD)	#PRWD#	#FT1#	#σ́#	IO-MAX (AFFIX)
☞ a. [màr#kka][rála]#-cci		*		*(rá)	
b. [màr#kka][rála]-ci		**!		*(rá)	*
c. [már#kkaràla]#-cci	*!				

A similar analysis obtains for other forms with medial tonics, such as the examples below, repeated from 6.3. The observation was that a tonic syllable licenses a following geminate. This is because each and every PRWD, strongest foot, and tonic syllable should ideally be delimited with a [spread glottis] gesture.

(40) [ɟijàppaŋgíkka̰]
/cu-ja**pp**a=ŋki-*kk*aʔ/
F-sister-2mDAT-LOC

In this case two PRWDs are licensed not just because of the length of the form, but because of constraints demanding isomorphism between morphological and prosodic constituency, as discussed in Chapters 3 and 4.

---

[24] I assume for convenience that every tonic syllable begins a new Prosodic Word domain, which extends as far as the next pre-tonic syllable, or the end of the MWD, whichever is appropriate. The location of PRWD right boundaries internal to MWDs makes no difference to the outcome; because of high-ranking faithfulness to MWDs no segmental changes can be made inside stems.

[25] All candidates shown in (39) happen to satisfy #FT1# in this case, because the initial syllable of the word is a bimoraic foot; see Chapter 5.

[26] Words of this form are never parsed in this stress pattern, perhaps to reinforce the legitimacy of the suffix-initial geminate.

An analysis of (40) is presented in (41). In (41), we see an instance where a bound stem /=ŋki/ licenses a domain delimited by the geminate in the following suffix. Since the bound pronominal stem /=ŋki/ takes primary stress here (as is typical of pronominal stems in this context—Chapter 4), it can and should be delimited by a tonic boundary. The other candidate fails to do this, and is less harmonic for that reason.

(41)

	/cu-ja**pp**a=ŋki-*kk*aʔ/ F-sister-2mDAT-LOC	DOMAIN (HD)	#PRWD#	#FT1#	#σ́#
☞	a. cu-[jà#ppa][=ŋkî#-kkaʔ]		*	*	
	b. cu-[jà#ppa][=ŋkí-kaʔ]		*	*	*!

Finally, the most complex set of examples are those wherein three obstruent clusters are observed. These all have the structure shown in (42).

(42)	[MWD]PRWD	=pro	[-suffix]PRWD	-suffix
	/ʈòʈojʔ	=ŋki	-ppúlu	-kkaʔ/
	uncle	=yours	-DU	-LOC

There are two PRWDs, and two tonics. The second PRWD is bounded on both sides by a geminate, and it is because each geminate bounds a PRWD in this way that it is licensed.

The analysis of this form is presented in (43). In the optimal candidate (a), every internal instance of a PRWD boundary corresponds to a [spread glottis] articulation—a break in the intonation contour. Hence, this form maximally satisfies the top-ranked of the boundary demarcation constraints #PRWD#. The other candidates do not demarcate each PRWD to the same extent as candidate (a), and are less harmonic for that reason. The boundaries which they fail to demarcate in each case are spelled out in the appropriate cell in the tableau.

(43)

	/ʈotoj**ʔ=ŋk**i-***pp***ulu-*kk*aʔ/ uncle-2mDAT-PL-LOC	DOM (HD)	#PRWD#	#FT1#	#σ́#	IO-MAX (AFFIX)
☞	a. [ʈòtojʔ]#=ki[-#ppúlu]#-kkaʔ				**	
	b. [ʈòtojʔ]#=ki[#-ppúlu]-kaʔ		]*!	*)	**	*
	c. [ʈòtojʔ]#=ki-[púlu]#-kkaʔ		[*!	*(	**	*

The analysis predicts that geminates should be licensed at every PRWD boundary, left or right. This is the case; examples such as (26), repeated below, show that a PRWD (the suffix /-ppíraʔ/ in this case) can be geminate-initial instead of or as well as geminate-final. Both constitute boundaries, and a domain which is bounded on both sides is well-formed.

(44) [bɔ̀lɔ̰ˀpɔ̀lɔppíra̰]
/poloʔpolo-*pp*iraʔ/
woman-DU

An analysis is presented in (45). In candidate (45)a, every PRWD is clearly demarcated with a [spread glottis] gesture: each is a salient association of morphology, prosody, and acoustics.[27] The candidate with the singleton-initial suffix, (45)b, is less harmonic than the candidate with the geminate-initial suffix, (45)a.[28]

(45)

/poloʔpolo-*pp*iraʔ/ woman-DU	DOMAIN (HD)	#PRWD#	#FT1#	#σ́#
☞ a. [pòloʔ]#[pòlo]#[-ppíraʔ]				***
b. [pòloʔ]#[pòlo][-píraʔ]		[*!	(*	***

We have seen that the constraints against ill-formed intonation domains dominate one Faithfulness constraint on suffixes—IO-MAX(Affix), ruling out deletion—with the result that suffixes degeminate where they would otherwise demarcate the boundary of a prosodic nonconstituent, as in /jappa-kkaʔ/ (32). In the following section, I show that higher-ranked Faithfulness constraints rule out alternations in glottal stop-initial suffixes, and in bound stems and ROOT-suffixes.

6.3.3 Faithfulness to laryngeal features

Ngalakgan has both geminate-initial and glottal stop-initial suffixes. The geminate-initial suffixes alternate with a singleton-initial realisation, as we have seen. The glottal stop-initial suffixes do not alternate, at least not to the same degree of consistency. Merlan (1983: 8) notes that there is a partial

[27] The stem itself is a relic of the same process. /poloʔpolo/ 'woman' is a frozen reduplicant (since the root /poloʔ/ is a distinct word meaning 'old; old person', /poloʔpolo/ is not a WORD-level reduplication—see 6.4). The internal glottal stop in the stem historically served the same function that the geminate in the suffix does.

[28] Both candidates violate the constraint #σ́# three times, once for each instance of an accented syllable which is not right-aligned with an [sg] articulation.

correlation between stems with internal geminates and ‘delaryngealised’ suffixes. She gives the following example (my transcriptions):

(46)	a.	[wɛ̀rɛkkawála]	b.	[gʊ̀ɳɖuɳɔ̀wi̠wə́la]
		/werekka-ʔwala/		/kuɳʈu=ɳowi-ʔwala/
		where-ABL		country-3NFEMDAT-ABL

Merlan notes however that [werekkḁwala] ‘was found as a less frequent alternative’ to [werekkawala] (1983: 8).[29] Merlan suggests that ‘glottal stop has, over the recent past, been in the process of becoming a fixed initial boundary of the suffix, by being generalised from geminate-free environments to those containing a geminate stop’.

I agree with Merlan in finding that speakers do not synchronically allow alternations in glottal-initial suffixes conditioned by preceding obstruent clusters in the stem. In OT terms, this translates as underlying specification of affixes as [constricted glottis]-initial, together with a high-ranking IO-MAX constraint relativised to segments bearing this feature.

(47) IO-MAX[cg] ‘Every [cg] segment in the input string corresponds to some [cg] segment in the output string’ (‘No [cg] deletion’)

IO-MAX[cg] rules out alternations in the form of glottal clusters. An example of a suffix with initial glottal+obstruent cluster is shown in (48) below. In (48), we see a stem with internal geminate, followed by a suffix with underlying initial glottal stop. On the analogy of [jappa-kaʔ] ‘sister’-LOC, we expect that the glottal should delete at the surface, leaving the intonation contour after the stem-internal geminate unbroken. But the attested candidate leaves the glottal intact, violating the constraint against headless domains: DOMAIN(HD). The IO-MAX constraint demanding no deletion of underlying [cg] material therefore dominates DOMAIN(HD).[30]

---

[29] Heath (1978b: 24) finds that glottal alternation is regular in Ngandi, adducing examples such as the following (phonetic transcriptions are my own). In the (a) examples, the initial glottal stop of the suffix is deleted following a fortis [geminate] in the stem. The (b) examples show the underlying form of the suffix/bound stem in each case.

(1)	a.	[ŋaɖ̤akkugṳ]	b.	[ŋawuɽwuruŋṳkṳ]
		/ŋa-ʈ̤akku-ʔkuʔ/		/ŋa-wurʔwuruŋu-ʔkuʔ/
		1mS-child-REL		1mS-old.person-REL
		‘when I (was) small’		‘when I (become) an old man’
(2)	a.	[awaʈʈuwaɲɟi̠]	b.	[amanbḁwaɲɟi̠]
		/a-waʈʈu-ʔwaɲciʔ/		/a-manpa-ʔwaɲciʔ/
		RESID-dog-LIKE		RESID-armband-LIKE
		‘like a dog’		‘like an armband’

[30] I have ignored the vowel harmony effects which derive [-ʔkan] from /-ʔkVn/ here.

(48)

/jappa-ʔkVn/ sister-DAT	IO-MAX [CG]	DOMAIN (HD)	#PRWD#	#FT1#	#σ#
a. [já#ppa-]kan	*!		*	*	
☞ b. [já#ppa-ʔ]#kan		*			

The dominance of Faithfulness to glottal stops over the constraints deriving geminate alternation must be a fairly recent innovation in the grammar, judging by the sporadic effects observed by Merlan (1983), and the perhaps regular alternations of glottal stops in Ngandi (Heath 1978b). In 6.5.1, I examine an instance of synchronic alternations involving glottal stop in the nearby, genetically distant Yolngu languages.

6.3.4 Faithfulness to Morphological Words

There are both singleton-initial and geminate-initial ROOT-level suffixes; but segments in neither of these positions alternate. Since ROOTs followed by ROOT-level suffixes together constitute a single MWD, ROOT-level suffixes are subject to the same Faithfulness constraint that roots are: IO-MAX(MWD), preventing any deletion of underlying segments (6.3.2); this is shown in (49). Square brackets indicate MWD boundaries (these also correspond to the PRWD boundaries, by MWD ≈ PRWD: Chapter 3). The MWD in this form is the whole inflected and derived ROOT-compound. The attested form, in (a), is ill-formed from the point of view of DOMAIN(HD), since the string [+pu(+c)] is not headed by a tonic. Yet candidate (a) is faithful to the underlying Morphological Word. Being faithful to the MWD is the most important consideration, encoded by the high-ranking of IO-MAX(MWD) here. The other candidates (b) and (c) each violate MWD Faith in one way or another. Candidate (b) degeminates the bound RR root /+cci+/, while candidate (c) deletes the glottal stop from the root /kuḷaʔ/.

(49)

/kuḷaʔ+pu+cci+n/ skin+HIT+RR+PR 'shed one's skin'	IO-MAX (MWD)	DOMAIN (HD)	#PRWD#	#FT1#	#σ#
☞ a. $[\text{kúḷaʔ\#+pu+\#cci+n}]_{\text{MWD}}$		*	*		*
b. $[\text{kúḷaʔ\#+pu+ci+n}]_{\text{MWD}}$	*!		*		*
c. $[\text{kúḷa+pu+\#cci+n}]_{\text{MWD}}$	*!		*	*	*

The fact that geminate alternation is a process restricted to the boundaries of WORD-level constituents should be no surprise. We have seen that it is the WORD-level, and not the ROOT-level which counts for compound stress (Chapter 3) and affixal stress (Chapter 4), as well as apical alternations (3.7). The distribution of geminate alternation in words confirms the primacy of WORD-level constituents as the locus of phonological alternations. ROOT-complex forms are treated as units by the geminate alternation process, just as they are by prosodic structure.

This concludes the formal analysis of geminate alternation in Ngalakgan.[31] I have observed that certain segmental configurations are articulated with a [spread glottis] gesture. These clusters are highly salient, and are perceptually similar to word boundaries. I suggested that speakers have grammaticalised the association between [spread glottis] clusters and boundaries, and that prosodic and morphological constituents prefer to be demarcated, and that these clusters conversely are optimally associated with actual PCat and MCat boundaries, not spurious ones.

I further noted that [spread glottis] is incompatible with implementation of tone. This suggests that [spread glottis] clusters divide a word into stretches of intonation I have referred to as 'intonation domains'. Optimally, these intonation domains are associated with prominent morphological and prosodic constituents: PRWD, strongest foot, and tonic syllable. If an intonation domain is not associated with one of these constituents, it is ill-formed. The 'repair' of this ill-formed structure consists of degemination in suffixes at the surface.

In 6.4 which follows, I show how the analysis of domain demarcation proposed here helps to explain the realisation of one common reduplication pattern in Ngalakgan (also found in other Gunwinyguan languages). In 6.5, I extend the analysis to the distribution of glottal stops and geminates in other Top End languages. In 6.6, I show that the same set of constraints are reflected in the distribution of geminates in roots in Ngalakgan.

6.4 CVʔ WORD-reduplication

In this section I discuss one common WORD-reduplication pattern in Ngalakgan, where the reduplicant is a CVʔ stem. I follow McCarthy and Prince (1993b) and Urbanczyk (1996) in assuming that the shape of reduplicants is not stipulated, but is a consequence of constraint satisfaction. I argue that

[31] The analysis appears to generalise without change to Rembarrnga and Ngandi, however, since stress is not marked in the published accounts I cannot be sure that the relationship between prosody and geminate alternation is the same as in Ngalakgan. A somewhat similar process is also found in Warumungu (Simpson 1998), but the facts are not entirely clear from the available materials, and the basis of the stop contrast in this language is somewhat different to that in the Northern languages.

the reduplicant takes the unmarked shape of MWDs in complex environments, using the boundary signal notion proposed earlier in this chapter.

6.4.1 Morphology of CVʔ-reduplication

CVʔ-reduplication was introduced in 3.3.4, in the context of the differences between WORD and ROOT-level reduplication. In this section, after a brief review of the various forms of reduplication found in Ngalakgan, I propose an analysis of CVʔ-reduplication in particular, drawing on the analysis of glottal stops as boundary signals discussed in preceding sections.

(50) repeats some examples of CVʔ reduplication from 3.3.4. The reduplicant is bolded in the phonemic representations:

(50)	a.	[màa̰máŋiɲ] /**maʔ**-maŋiɲ/ DIST-get+PC 'got here and there'	[máŋiɲ] /ma+ŋiɲ/ get+PC 'got'
	b.	[ɟùʊ̰ɟʊ́ɾuwɛn] /**cuʔ**-curuwen/ DIST-rush+PR 'rushing here and there'	[ɟʊ́ɾuwɛn] /curuwe+n/ rush+PR 'rushes'
	c.	[wàa̰wáŋgiɲ] /**waʔ**-waŋkiɲ/ DIST-one 'one at a time'	[wáŋgiɲ] /waŋkiɲ/ one 'one'
	d.	[jàa̰jappáṉɟa] /**jaʔ**-jappanʔca/ DIST-two 'two at a time'	[jappáṉɟa] /jappanʔca/ two 'two'
	e.	[ĵɪ̰jɪppʊ́ɲɟa] /**jiʔ**-jippuɲca/ INTENS-long.ago 'a very long time ago'	[jɪppʊ́ɲɟa] /jippuɲca/ long.ago 'a long time ago'

As shown in 3.3.4, the reduplicant constitutes a bound WORD-level stem: an MWD. Like other WORD-level operations—compounding and affixation—reduplication is (a) freely available, (b) does not take or select for idiosyncratic forms, and (c) has a regular, compositional interpretation.

There are other reduplication patterns, which are exemplified briefly here. They will not be analysed in what follows. Besides CVʔ, a second major pattern is CVXV: a contiguous string of the Base ending in a vowel, where 'X' is a consonant or cluster. This shape is attested with nouns, verbs, and modifiers. Some examples are given in (51):

(51) a. [bʊrubɔ̀ɖɛbɔ́ɖɛʊk]
/puru-**poʈe**-poʈewk/ /poʈewk/
3aS-INTENS-bad bad
'they are very bad'; or: 'they are habitually bad' [3/7/96]

b. [ŋʊruɖʊ̀muɖʊ́mura̠]
/ŋuru-**ʈumu**-ʈumurʔ-a/ /ʈumurʔ-a/
12aS-DIST-break.up-FUT break.up-FUT
'we will go around breaking up (sticks for the fire)' [2/7/96:1A]

c. [bʊruwɔ̀rowɔ́roʊkmiɲ]
/puru-**woro**-worowk-mi+ɲ/ /worowk-mi+ɲ/
3aS-DIST-jump.along-AUX+PP jump.along-AUX+PP
'they jumped along' [KD: passim]

d. [bʊruwʊ̀luwʊ́luppa]
/puru-**wulu**-wulup-pa/ /wulup-pa/
3aS-DIST-bathe-FUT bathe-FUT
'they are going to splash around'

The other major form of reduplication is total reduplication. For common nouns, this is interpreted as a literal count. This is shown by example (52), where the Kriol translation uses the same mechanism (and the speaker also counted off the tokens of 'catfish' caught on his fingers with each repetition of the word).

(52) [mɒ́ɭɒppɔɭ mɒ́ɭɒppɔɭ mɒ́ɭɒppɔɭ ŋubumɛ̰me]
/moɭoppoɭ moɭoppoɭ moɭoppoɭ ŋu-pu-meʔ+me/
catfish catfish catfish 1mS-3a-RED+get.PP
[ŋubuwàkkɻíwo ɟǽɟæbaɻŋ̰gã]
/ŋu-pu-wakkiɻi+wo cacapaɻŋʔ-kaʔ/
1mS-3a-return.with+GIVE.PP afternoon-LOC
ketfij ketfij ketfij ai bin bringimbek aftanundaim [27/6/96: 1A]
'I caught three catfish and brought them back in the afternoon.'

That this kind of reduplication targets the complete word (rather than the MWD), is suggested by examples like that in (53), where a prefixed noun is reduplicated in entirety (several examples like this are attested in the texts).

(53) [ŋuŋò̰mé::: guɟíwi]
/ŋu-ŋoʔ-me, ku-ciwi/
1mS-guts-get.PP NEUT-liver
[jà̰njána̰ gubáɳɖicgubáɳɖic]
/janʔ-janaʔ ku-paɳʈic ku-paɳʈic/
DIST-whatsit NEUT-kidney NEUT-kidney
gejim gats, liva, kidni kidni
'I got the guts, liver, and whatsit ... two kidneys' [Tx 1/6/96]

Reduplication is not common in nouns, except in the delimited class of kinship terms. Here reduplication has a special function: to derive the plural form of Dyadic kinterms. Since this is a semantically specialised domain, in contrast to the majority of occurring WORD-level reduplications, I will not examine these here; see Merlan (1983: 19).

6.4.2 Prosodic characteristics of CVʔ-reduplication

As stated above, I follow McCarthy and Prince (1986, 1993b, 1995) in assuming that the reduplicant is a morpheme which is not specified for segmental material. Its form is derived from constraint satisfaction. Two principles regulate the form of reduplicants:

(54) a. The reduplicant should be a copy of the base to which it attaches
b. The reduplicant is subject to constraints on the interface between morphology and prosody

Principle (54)a entails that the reduplicant contain some or all of the segmental material of the Base. In McCarthy and Prince (1995), reduplication is subject to a distinct set of Correspondence relations, which are schematically represented below (following McCarthy and Prince 1995: 252):[32]

(55) Input: /Morph$_{RED}$ - **Stem**/
I-R Faithfulness ↑↓ *I-B Faithfulness*
Output: **R**[eduplicant] ←→ **B**[ase]
B-R Faithfulness

Faithfulness between the input *stem* and the *base* of reduplication is regulated by IB-Faith constraints (which are not distinct from IO-Faith in McCarthy and Prince 1995). A distinct set of BR-Faith constraints regulates the copying relation between the *reduplicant* and the *base* at the surface.

A particular instantiation is given for /**maʔ**-maŋiɲ/ 'kept getting' in (56):

(56) Input: /STEM$_{RED}$ - **maŋiɲ**/
I-R Faithfulness ↑↓ *I-B Faithfulness*
Output: **[maʔ]** ←→ **[maŋiɲ]**
B-R Faithfulness

[32] I have represented the reduplicant with a dummy morphological label 'morph' rather than McCarthy and Prince's 'affix' to reflect the Ngalakgan situation argued for here.

The input consists of the word /maŋiɲ/ 'was getting (PC)' with a reduplicative morpheme which is phonologically unspecified for content but has some morphological annotation: its category is the same as the category of the Base, i.e. 'WORD-level stem' of a major morphosyntactic category—an MWD. The output consists of the Base, which is a perfect copy of the input word, plus the Reduplicant, which is required to be a stem which minimally differs from the Base.

Condition (54)b—that reduplicants are subject to constraints on the morphology/phonology interface—leads to the frequently attested pattern that reduplicants are realised as one of the constituents of the Prosodic Hierarchy (McCarthy and Prince 1986, 1993b). In earlier work (e.g. 1986), McCarthy and Prince proposed that reduplicants were specified to correspond to a prosodic constituent. So for example, the reduplicant in /**maʔ**-maŋiɲ/ might be specified as 'bimoraic foot'.

This approach is not taken here. Rather, I follow McCarthy and Prince (1993b), Urbanczyk (1996) who propose that:

(57) a. Reduplicants are specified as to morphological category ('stem', 'root', 'affix', 'word').

b. The shapes taken by reduplicants reflect the unmarked shapes for morphological constituents.

The form of CVʔ reduplicants, for example, can be derived from two conditions. The first takes the form of an entry of the following kind in the lexicon:[33]

(58) a. b.

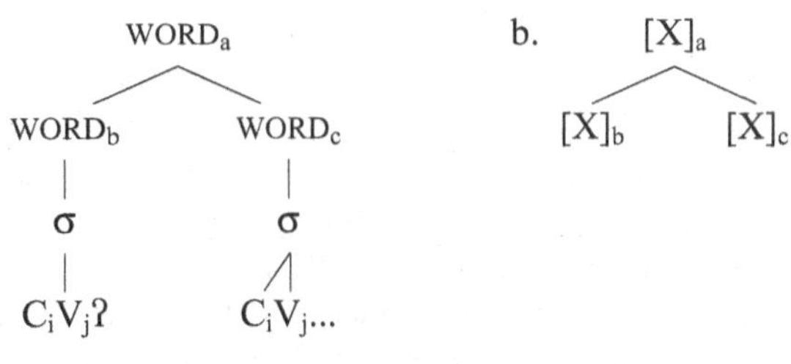

c. If the denotation of 'X' = state, then: [INTENS [$_{State}$]$_c$]$_a$

If the denotation of 'X' = event, then: [DIST [$_{Event}$]$_c$]$_a$

[33] This is a first attempt at a lexical entry for a reduplicant morpheme of the kind that we find in Ngalakgan (and other GN languages). I regard it as a preliminary proposal. One alternative is to leave the phonological form of the reduplicant completely unspecified, and leave its structure to be built by the phonology. At present, I have no evidence to decide this issue either way.

This requirement that Reduplicants be an MWD is thus not a constraint but rather a property of the input. The morphological structure of the input is assigned by the lexicon, and cannot be altered in the phonology.

Being an MWD, reduplicants are subject to whatever constraints other MWDs are subject to. In the first place, reduplicants are subject to the requirement that MWDs constitute PRWDs (Chapter 3), repeated here in (59):

(59) MWD ≈ PRWD

This means that reduplicated forms in Ngalakgan are prosodically identical to compounds. This is a common property of reduplicated forms in Australian languages (cf. Warlpiri—Nash 1986; Baker and Harvey 2003).

Another property of MWDs that concerns us here is that MWDs and other prominent constituents should be demarcated by boundary signals, as proposed in preceding sections; I repeat the constraints here.

(60) Constituent boundaries must be signalled ('No obscure boundaries')
#PRWD# >> #Ft1# >> #σ́#
'Delimit the Prosodic Word' >> 'Delimit the strongest foot' >> 'Delimit the tonic'

By being realised as monosyllabic PRWDs, reduplicants can satisfy all three constraints simultaneously, since the constraints in (60) are relativised to PRWD in Ngalakgan (as I suggested in 6.2.1).

In Ngalakgan, the NO OBSCURE BOUNDARIES constraints are ranked below IO-DEP(MWD). The input form of MWDs cannot be adjusted in order to conform to the ideal shape, as I showed in 6.3.4. But the reduplicant has a segment—glottal stop—which is not found in the base. This glottal stop provides the same function as initial geminates in suffixes—demarcating the stem. Together, these two characteristics argue that the NO OBSCURE BOUNDARIES constraints are ranked above BR-DEP. Just in reduplication, then, MWDs (reduplicants) are universally required to conform to the unmarked shape for MWDs, as shown in tableau (61) below. This characteristic behaviour of reduplicants is dubbed the 'Emergence of the Unmarked' in McCarthy and Prince (1995).

Both the reduplicant and the base are subject to the constraint MWD ≈ PRWD, because they are both WORD-level stems and hence MWDs.[34] Candidates (a), (b), (d) and (f) are ruled out on this basis, because they fail to

[34] We must assume that the reduplicant copies its categorial signature from the base, which means that the reduplicant will always be dominated by a major category, since these are the only stems which reduplicate.

parse one or the other as a well-formed PRWD.[35] (PRWDs are indicated with square brackets.) The only contenders then are (c) and (e). #PRWD# eliminates (e), even though in other respects it is more well-formed. The optimal candidate, (c), satisfies NO OBSCURE BOUNDARIES as much as possible (without violating IO-DEP), by inserting a glottal stop between reduplicant and base, demarcating both domains. The glottal stop is a segment which finds no correspondent in the input, and (c) thereby violates BR-DEP.

(61)

/STEM$_{RED}$-maŋiɲ/	MWD ≈ PRWD	IO-DEP (MWD)	#PRWD#	#FT1#	#σ́#	BR-DEP
a. maʔ#-[(máŋiɲ)]	*!				*	*
b. [(máʔ)]#-maŋiɲ	*!					*
☞ c. [(mà:ʔ)]#-[(máŋiɲ)]						*
d. [(máʔ#-ma)ŋiɲ]	*!			*		*
e. [(mà:)]-[(máŋiɲ)]			*!	*	*	
f. [(mà)]-[(máŋiɲ)]	*!		*	*	*	

Since the CVʔ reduplicant is a PRWD in these forms it must have a long vowel. I assume that vowel lengthening does not violate BR-DEP, but BR-IDENT[μ] (McCarthy and Prince 1995: 265). (This constraint is not shown, but must be ranked below BR-DEP.)

In other respects, reduplicated words behave like compounds in terms of prosody. The reduplicant—the first MWD—takes secondary stress and a pitch accent, and the base—the second MWD—takes primary stress and a pitch accent. These characteristics follow from the same constraints given in Chapter 3 in reference to compounds.

I have shown that a series of constraints referring to the demarcation of domains can derive both geminate alternation and productive reduplication in Ngalakgan. If speakers can recognise, and manipulate, the associations between intonation domains, and prosodic and morphological structure, as I have suggested, then we should find similar associations elsewhere. This is the topic of the following sections.

---

[35] Candidate (f) also violates FTBIN—not shown here. The violation of MWD ≈ PRWD shown here is awarded because a monomoraic form does not constitute a well-formed PRWD.

6.5 Prosodic effects on margins in other languages

Aspects of the phenomena discussed here have been described for a number of other languages both in Australia and elsewhere. They provide further evidence for the constraints proposed here: demanding boundary signals at the edges of prosodic and morphological domains. Named language varieties of the Yolngu dialect chain have a glottal stop alternation process which in many respects is similar to the geminate alternation process found in the three southern Arnhem languages; I discuss the process in the following section.[36] 6.5.2 describes and analyses the alternation of stem-initial segments in Ndjébbana, which McKay (1984, 2000) proposes is prosodically determined by a following tonic. Both processes can be accounted for with the same system of constraints that I have proposed for Ngalakgan.

6.5.1 Glottal stop alternations in Yolngu

Wood (1978: 91) discusses a process of glottal stop alternation in the Yolngu dialect Gälpu. The same process is found in other dialects, such as Djapu (Morphy 1983: 26), and Djambarrpuyngu (Wilkinson 1991).[37] The discussion of Djambarrpuyngu in Wilkinson (1991: 85, 541) is the most extensive, and examples are taken from the latter work except where noted. I will use a phonemic representation, rather than the Yolngu orthography.

Wilkinson describes the distribution of glottal stop as follows (1991: 85).[38]

---

36 The Yolngu /ju:lŋu/ languages form a Pama-Nyungan island surrounded by Non-Pama-Nyungan languages such as Ndjébbana, Burarra, Kune, Rembarrnga, Dalabon, Ngandi, and Nunggubuyu/Wubuy. Yolngu languages are genetically quite distinct from GN languages. There has been extensive diffusion of vocabulary, morphological patterns, and phonological patterns however, including a distinction between two stop series in some Yolngu varieties (e.g. Gupapuyngu), and the occurrence of contrastive glottal stops in many Yolngu varieties (see e.g. Wood 1978; Heath 1978a; Harvey 1991 for discussion). The basis of the stop contrast in Yolngu languages is distinct from that in GN and Burarran languages, as shown by Butcher (1993b). I will represent the distinction phonemically with voiceless vs voiced symbols, though the distinction is based only in part on voicing and in some contexts on duration. I have also represented the glottal stop in the phonetic representations with the usual glottal stop symbol, though only for clarity. The articulation of glottal stop in Yolngu languages so far as I can determine is the same as that in Ngalakgan and other GN languages. That is, it associates a [constricted glottis] feature to a preceding sonorant.

37 Wilkinson (1991) groups Djapu and Djambarrpuyngu dialects under the term 'Southern Yolngu', and I follow her usage here. Gälpu belongs to a different group 'Northern Yolngu'.

38 To the version of Wilkinson's (1991) rule, I have added a second ellipsis before the final word boundary which is in closer accord with Wilkinson's description.

> [W]ith a single class of exceptions one glottal stop is permitted in a word. There is a rule of glottal stop deletion that removes any occurrences of glottal stop after the first in a word. This operates after morphological processes of suffixing and reduplication.
> /ʔ/ → Ø / #.../ʔ/...____...#

The process prevents the realisation of glottal stops which would otherwise be introduced by suffixes and at the reduplicant-base boundary. As in Ngalakgan, reduplication in Djambarrpuyngu, Djapu, and Gälpu is prefixal and regularly introduces a glottal stop between reduplicant and stem, as shown in (62)a-b (the reduplicant is shown in bold, including the glottal stop introduced by reduplication). Some verb stems end in a glottal stop underlyingly, as in (c-d). When these verbs are reduplicated, only the glottal stop at the reduplication boundary is realised, the glottal stop in the base corresponds to surface zero.[39] [40]

(62) a. [n̪ínaʔn̪ìna]
/**n̪ɪnaʔ**-n̪ɪna/
DIST-sit

b. [jú:lŋuʔjùlŋu]
/**ju:lŋuʔ**-ju:lŋu/
DIST-person

c. [ŋálʔŋàljun]
/**ŋalʔ**-ŋalʔ-ju+n/
DIST-climb/rise-AUX+PR

d. [jámanaʔjàmanajun]
/**jamanaʔ**-jamanaʔ-ju+n/
DIST-poke.out.tongue-AUX+PR

Note that stress in reduplicative forms is initial, as in words in general. The change in stress pattern is reflected in the loss of underlying vowel length in the base in (b), and its retention in the surface reduplicant. Long vowels only occur in initial, stressed syllables in Djambarrpuyngu (Wilkinson 1991: 44), where they contrast with short vowels.

Some suffixes introduce glottal stop also; examples in (63) show a similar contrast in realisation of glottal stop, depending on whether there is a stem-internal glottal stop. Of two underlying glottal stops in the words of (c) and (d), only the stem-internal glottal stop is realised at the surface.

(63) a. [jápaʔmìriŋu]
/japa-ʔmiriŋu/
sister-KIN.PROP

c. [má:ɻiʔmumìriŋu]
/ma:ɻiʔmu-ʔmiriŋu/
father's.father-KIN.PROP

[39] The stress in the surface representations is derived from the descriptions and representations in Wilkinson (1991: 62-3) and Wood (1978: 85-87). I have glossed the verb inflection affix /-ju+/ as an 'auxiliary'. This element has a similar function to the auxiliary verb root /-mi+/ in Ngalakgan, or /-t̪u+/ in Ngandi. The tense inflection of /-ju+n/ I have glossed as 'Present', which is one interpretation of the inflection (Wilkinson 1991: 336).

[40] I have glossed the reduplicant in Djambarrpuyngu examples as 'Distributive', like the Ngalakgan reduplicant, since it appears to have a similar interpretation (Wilkinson 1991: 368). Like Ngalakgan, Djambarrpuyngu has both lexicalised and productive reduplication (ibid.: 121).

b. [jápaʔmàɲɟi]
/japa-ʔmaɲɟi/
sister-DYAD

d. [máːɻiʔmumàɲɟi]
/maːɻiʔmu-ʔmaɲɟi/
father's.father-DYAD

In both the reduplication and suffixation cases, the generalisation is that of two underlying glottal stops, only that closest to the primary stress is realised at the surface, whether this glottal stop derives from the reduplication process, as in (62), or is stem-internal, as in (63). Note that it is *not* the case that glottal stops belonging to stems are retained, at the expense of those belonging to affixes, since it is the *reduplicant*-final glottal stop which is retained in (62)c-d, rather than the root-final one.

I regard these patterns as reflecting the interaction of the same set of constraints as were described above for Ngalakgan. In Djambarrpuyngu, Djapu, and Gälpu, the only boundary signal element is glottal stop. These languages all lack a stop contrast morpheme-initially at the surface. Underlying morpheme-initial lenis stops are subject to extensive lenition processes when occurring between continuants, in all three languages.[41] At the surface between morphemes then, there is a single stop series and no contrastive tautomorphemic geminates (in suffixes).

Therefore, the only boundary element to which the NO OBSCURE BOUNDARIES constraints can refer in Djambarrpuyngu is glottal stop. As in Ngalakgan, the boundary closest to the tonic is realised at the surface, and all other boundaries are eliminated from the surface word due to lack of a proper head. It appears that Yolngu has the same Headedness requirement as Ngalakgan, repeated here.

(64) DOMAIN(HD): 'Domains must be headed by a tonic'

Note that primary stress is initial in words in Yolngu, in all but a small class of exceptions. If Yolngu is anything like Ngalakgan, the pitch accent in an intonation contour docks to the first primary stress, and any preceding (but not following) secondary stresses. In both Yolngu and Ngalakgan, the

---

41 There is an underlying distinction between a 'fortis' stop series which does not alternate, and a 'lenis' stop series. Morpheme-initial lenis stops (e.g. in suffixes and verb roots) are realised either as stops or as homorganic continuants, depending on the preceding segment. Underlying lenis stops are realised as obstruents following [–cont] segments (Wood 1978: 71). Gemination of post-tonic consonants is one common implementation of stress in at least some Yolngu languages (Djinang: Waters 1980; Gälpu: Wood 1978). These geminates are non-contrastive, predictable realisations. But since geminates cannot occur elsewhere in the word, I assume they cannot constitute PRWD boundaries effectively. Nor can fortis stops constitute effective boundary signals, since the only position in which they are contrastive is morpheme-internally between continuants. Stops in these positions cannot alternate because of high-ranking Root Faithfulness constraints, as in Ngalakgan.

only tonic syllable in a word with initial primary stress is the primary stressed syllable itself.

The typical domain delimited by glottal stop in Yolngu corresponds to WORD-level stem (MWD) or primary foot.[42] The characteristics of Prosodic Word in Yolngu languages are unclear to me, I will omit consideration of PRWD in what follows. In place of PRWD, I will refer to MWDs as the domain which should be demarcated: #MWD#, and square brackets represent MWD boundaries accordingly.

I will assume the glottal stop is present in the underlying form of suffixes, like the initial geminates in Ngalakgan suffixes, but is introduced by the phonology in reduplicants. I will assume further that reduplicants in Yolngu are MWDs—WORD-level stems—as they are in Ngalakgan (6.4). DOMAIN(HD) conflicts with the same constraint—IO-MAX[cg]—which was introduced in 6.3.3 above, as shown in (67) below. In the case of Yolngu, unlike Ngalakgan, IO-MAX[cg] is ranked below DOMAIN(HD), with the result that glottal stops alternate, according to their location with respect to intonation domains, just as geminates do in Ngalakgan and glottals did historically.

In both Yolngu and Ndjébbana (examined in 6.5.2) it is only segments at the *edges* of morphemes which alternate, rather than those internal to morphemes. Wilkinson (1991: 85) notes explicitly that morpheme-medial glottal stops are never deleted. This is also true of geminate alternation in Ngalakgan, but so far we have not needed to make this distinction between segments at the edge and those which are internal.

McCarthy and Prince (1995: 371) propose two Faithfulness constraints which specifically refer to the internal structure of morphemes. Their definitions are presented in (65)-(66).

(65) I-CONTIG(M) ('No skipping')
The portion of S_1 (a M[orpheme]) standing in correspondence forms a contiguous string.
Domain ($\Re$) is a single contiguous string in S_1.

(66) O-CONTIG(M) ('No intrusion')
The portion of S_2 (a M[orpheme]) standing in correspondence forms a contiguous string.
Range ($\Re$) is a single contiguous string in S_2.

---

[42] I will simply assume that Yolngu has a similar level-ordered morphology to Ngalakgan. Like Ngalakgan, it has a number of irregular verb paradigms (like the finite ROOTs of Ngalakgan), which act as auxiliaries for coverbs, some of which are in an opaque semantic relationship (like ROOT-compounds in Ngalakgan). The reduplicants shown here are all productively derived. As noted above, Djambarrpuyngu also has a number of lexicalised reduplicated forms (Wilkinson 1991: 121).

McCarthy and Prince (1995: 371) characterise the constraints informally as follows:

> The constraint I-CONTIG rules out deletion of elements *internal* to the input string [S_1]. Thus, the map *xyz* → *xz* violates I-CONTIG, because the Range of ℜ is {*x*, *z*}, and *x*, *z*, is not a contiguous string in the input. But the map *xyz* → *xy* does not violate I-CONTIG, because *xy* is a contiguous string in the input. The constraint O-CONTIG rules out internal epenthesis: the map *xz* → *xyz* violates O-CONTIG, but *xy* → *xyz* does not.[43]

An example of glottal alternation is presented in (67). Candidate (67)a has the only allowable association between morphological and prosodic category and the intonation domain which ends at the first glottal stop. This intonation domain is headed by the only tonic—the primary stress. This candidate demarcates *only* the primary foot.[44] Associating a boundary with the suffix, as in (67)b, creates an intonation domain [mu-], which is much worse. This intonation domain is not headed by a tonic, violating DOMAIN (HD), and hence the glottal stop is ill-formed in this position. Candidate (c) deletes the underlying root-internal glottal stop, instead of the glottal stop in the suffix, thereby violating I-CONTIG(MWD) ('NOSKIP'). Candidate (d) adds a glottal stop, following the tonic, which is not present in the underlying form, violating O-CONTIG(MWD) ('NOINTR'): root-internal epenthesis is ruled out in Yolngu.

(67)

/maːɻiʔmu-ʔmiriŋu/ father's.father-KIN.PROP	NO SKIP	NO INTR	DOM (HD)	#MWD#	#FT1#	#σ́#
☞ a. [máːɻiʔ]#mu-mìriŋu				*		*
b. [máːɻiʔ]#[mu-ʔ]#mìriŋu			*!			*
c. [máːɻimu-ʔ]#mìriŋu	*!				*	*
d. [máːʔ]#ɻimu-mìriŋu		*!		*		

At this point, there is no argument for ranking the three constraints shown at the top of the hierarchy in (67): NO SKIPPING, NO INTRUSION, and DOMAIN(HD).

---

43 The symbol 'ℜ' stands for the Correspondence relation between two strings (e.g. input and output, base and reduplicant). The 'Domain' is (the portion of) the string mapped from, the 'Range' (the portion of) the string mapped to.

44 It is worth noting that roots with internal glottal stops are quite rare in Yolngu languages, Wilkinson (1991: 82-3) records twenty such forms.

In the reduplicated examples, such as (62)c shown in (68), the reduplicant makes the best, most minimal domain: it is simultaneously an MWD, primary foot and primary stressed syllable, as with the CVʔ reduplicants in Ngalakgan.[45] Hence, candidate (68)b has a more harmonic association between boundaries and constituents than (68)c. This is the case even though (68)c maintains the underlying glottal stop of the input stem. Since candidate (b), but not (c), violates IO-MAX[cg], we infer that the latter is ranked below the NO OBSCURE BOUNDARIES constraints. The difference between them comes down to how well they demarcate the optimum constituents, and (b) is the winner here.

(68)

STEM-/ŋalʔ-ju+n/ DIST-climb-AUX+PR	NO SKIP	NO INTR	DOM (HD)	#MWD#	#FT1#	#σ#	IO-MAX [CG]
a. [ŋálʔ-]#[ŋàlʔ]#-ju+n			*!				
☞ b. [ŋálʔ-]#[ŋàl]-ju+n				*			*
c. [ŋál-][ŋàlʔ]#-ju+n				*	*!	*	

In the reduplicated examples with longer stems, the effects of O-CONTIG(M) (NO INTRUSION) become more visible. Candidate (69)c has a perfect association between the primary foot and a following boundary signal, but it fatally violates O-CONTIG. The optimal candidate here is (69)b, since it delimits the first boundary (MWD) (assuming reduplicants are WORD-level stems) without violating O-CONTIG. In other respects, the evaluation of (69) proceeds like that of (68).

(69)

STEM-/jamanaʔ-ju+n/ DIST-poke.out.tongue-AUX+PR	NO SKIP	NO INTR	DOM (HD)	#MWD#	#FT1#	#σ#	MAX [CG]
a. [jámanaʔ-]#[jàmanaʔ]#-ju+n			*!		*	*	
☞ b. [jámanaʔ-]#[jàmana]-ju+n				*	*	*	*
c. [jámaʔ#na-][jàmana]-ju+n		*!		*		*	**

45 However, this is not the preferred reduplicant shape in Djambarrpuyngu. Rather, the majority of polysyllabic bases take a reduplicant of the shape CVXVʔ.

The distribution of glottal stop in words in Southern Yolngu languages therefore parallels that of geminates in GN languages of adjacent south-eastern and central Arnhem Land (Ngalakgan, Ngandi, Rembarrnga) in a close way. In both cases, the PRWD, the strongest foot, or the tonic, in that order, are optimally demarcated by a boundary signal. Boundaries in Ngalakgan are signalled with either [spread glottis] or [constricted glottis] gestures, or both, while in Yolngu only [constricted glottis] gestures signal boundaries. The difference in boundary signal realisations appears to be related to the contrasting presence vs absence of contrasting obstruent geminates at morpheme boundaries in each language.

As with Ngalakgan, the boundary of a domain headed by the tonic in Yolngu words need not be immediately adjacent to the tonic, and need not correspond to a morpheme boundary. The fact that the Yolngu pattern can be accounted for with the same constraint hierarchy which derives geminate alternation in Ngalakgan supports the approach taken here.

In the following section, I discuss the case of Ndjébbana, which McKay argues has geminate alternations determined by a *following* tonic. The Ndjébbana pattern can be regarded as another instance of the same series of constraints as proposed for Ngalakgan and Yolngu.

6.5.2 Pre-tonic gemination in Ndjébbana

Ndjébbana is a non-GN, Non-Pama-Nyungan language of the Arnhem Land spoken on the coast to the north of Rembarrnga.[46] Ndjébbana favours geminates in the initial position of stems following prefixes, but just if the initial syllable of the stem is stressed. Contrast examples (70)a and (b) with (c) and (d) (from McKay 2000: 185).[47] Alternating stops in corresponding positions of roots are italicised. In (70)a, the verb /cuwe/ 'be sick, suffer, die' shows a geminate initial form when the initial syllable of the verb stem is stressed, otherwise the initial stop of the root is a singleton (and initial peripheral and laminal singletons of most verbs lenite intervocalically); other verbs behave similarly (70)b, d.

(70)	a.	ka-*cc*úwa	c.	ka-*j*awé+la
		3m-sick.NP		3m-sick+PC

[46] Green (2003) groups it with Burarra, Gurr-goni and Nakkara in the 'Maningrida' family.

[47] I have used phonemic representations, rather than McKay's orthographic ones. Only surface forms are shown. Vowels show prosodically- and morphologically-determined alternations which are not relevant here: McKay (2000: 180) states that 'there is a tendency for all vowels to be reduced to 'a' [this is [ə]: BB] when not bearing the phonemic stress and length'. Morpheme boundary symbols have roughly their meanings in Ngalakgan, e.g. '+' signals a finite verb root+tense suffix boundary.

b. ka-*pp*úceja 3m-shout.NP		d. ka-*p*ací+na 3m-shout+PC

Similar examples are found among nominals. If stress is not root-initial, the root-initial stop is not geminate (McKay 1984: 186); contrast (71)a-b with (71)c-d. In (71)a, stress is associated with the second syllable of the stem /parapara/ 'big'. In (71)b, the Feminine prefix /ɲa-/, rather than the root, is stressed. In both cases, the initial stop of the stem is realised as a singleton stop. Where stress is initial in the stem, the stem-initial stop is geminate, as in (c) and (d).

(71)	a. ɲa-*p*arápara F-big	c. ɲa-*cc*ícappa F-same
	b. ɲá-*k*aɻo F-fat	d. ɲa-*pp*ókka F-bad

Geminates in Ndjébbana are subject to phonotactic constraints, as in Ngalakgan. Contrast (72)a with (c), and (b) with (d) (from McKay 2000: 186). In (72)a, the initial stop of the stem /pokka/ 'bad' is geminate when the following syllable is stressed, and the stop follows a continuant (a vowel, in this case). Following a nasal, as in (72)c, the singleton/geminate contrast is neutralised. The same contrast is found in (72)b and (72)d.

(72)	a. ɲa-*pp*ókka F-bad	c. n-*p*ókka M-bad
	b. ɲa-*cc*ícappa F-same	d. n-*c*ícappa M-same

The same series of constraints that account for Ngalakgan can be used to derive the Ndjébbana pattern. Ndjébbana is analysed by McKay (1984, 2000) with a singleton/geminate opposition. McKay (2000) states that the opposition has the same phonetic basis as Rembarrnga, where geminates and other obstruent clusters are voiceless throughout closure and typically aspirated; I assume that as in Ngalakgan, Ndjébbana geminates are [spread glottis] at the surface.

McKay (2000: 184) assumes that stems are underlyingly singleton-initial. The geminate-initial form is derived by rule. The Ndjébbana alternations fulfill the same criteria as the Ngalakgan and Yolngu alternations: the process triggers [spread glottis] (respectively, [cg]) clusters or segments at morpheme boundaries, and is conditioned by the location of the tonic syllable. In Ndjébbana, the stem-initial consonant geminates if and only if it demarcates the PRWD, the primary foot, and the tonic all at once. If one of the three constraints demanding these associations is not satisfied, stems are not geminate-initial, because they fail the same headedness requirement which was proposed previously—DOMAIN(HD)—as I show below.

It is significant that geminate alternations are only observed at stem-edges in Ndjébbana: the internal structure of stems does not change, as in Ngalakgan and Yolngu. Again I assume that stems in Ndjébbana are subject to Output-Contiguity (NO INTRUSION), following McCarthy and Prince (1995: 371).

I referred above to the fact that stem-initial obstruents lenite to the homorganic glide when the primary stress is not on the first syllable of the stem. I leave aside the question of what kind of condition should account for the lenition pattern, and simply stipulate the requirement in the following constraint.

(73) *VCV 'No intervocalic (plain) obstruents'

Lenition does not apply to geminates, and does not apply exceptionlessly to plain stops in Ndjébbana (McKay 2000: 184).[48]

Tableau (74) presents an analysis of an alternating verb form. In Ndjébbana, I propose, geminates demarcate intonation domains, as in Ngalakgan. I assume that a tonic starts a new PRWD in Ndjébbana as in Ngalakgan. Therefore candidate (74)a is optimal here, the stem-initial geminate simultaneously demarcates the Prosodic Word, the strongest foot, and the tonic.[49] The domain thus formed satisfies the headedness requirement, since it is a PRWD headed by a tonic syllable. These constraints dominate IO-DEP (MWD), since the stem has an extra timing slot in the output. The Faithful candidate (b), fails to demarcate any constituents, violating the principle of NO OBSCURE BOUNDARIES (the #PCat# series). Candidate (c) fatally violates Contiguity: no changes to the internal structure of stems are permitted. I have represented the violations of candidates (b) and (c) to the #PCat# series with an asterisk and a left boundary marker for the appropriate constituent. This is to emphasise the fact that it is only the stem left edge which is significant in Ndjébbana, in contrast to what we have seen in Yolngu, and in contrast to the simple examples in Ngalakgan.

48 McKay (2000: 184) notes that the stem-initial alternations between geminates, singletons, and glides are exceptionless for laminal-initial verbs, but have exceptions among peripheral stop /p, k/-initial verbs. McKay does not mention the status of apical stop-initial verbs; but there are none listed in the wordlist in McKay (2000).

49 I assume that unstressed prefixes in Ndjébbana are not associated with PRWD domains, and are not evaluated for the constraints on tone domains, as in Ngalakgan.

(74)

/ka-cuwa/ 3m-sick.NP	DOM (HD)	NO INTR	#PRWD#	#FT1#	#σ#	*VCV	IO-DEP (MWD)
☞ a. ka-#[ccúwa]							*
b. ka-[cúwa]			*[	*(	*[	*	
c. ka-[cú#ppa]		*!	*[	*(	*[	*	

In (75), I show an analysis for a 'leniting' Ndjébbana verb form. The optimal candidate in this case is one where no intonation domains are demarcated, because the MWD and PRWD constituents do not correspond. This is the problem with candidate (a), where the stem-initial segment is geminated. The following domain does not correspond to a PRWD, and therefore violates #PRWD#. Gemination is unlicensed in this case: the form violates DOMAIN(HD). The fact that this candidate demarcates MWD is unimportant. Candidate (d) does demarcate a PRWD, but the gemination is stem-internal, violating high-ranking Output-Contiguity (NO INTRUSION). The difference between the remaining two candidates (b) and (c) comes down to the lenition constraint *VCV. This constraint must dominate IO-IDENT[–cont](MWD) (not shown)—since the output segment [j] has different root node features to the input [c].[50]

(75)

/ka-cuwela/ 3s-sick+was	DOM (HD)	NO INTR	#PRWD#	#FT1#	#σ#	*VCV	IO-DEP (MWD)
a. ka-#cca[wéla]	*!		*	*	*		*
b. ka-ca[wéla]			*	*	*	*!	
☞ c. ka-ja[wéla]			*	*	*		
d. ka-ja#p[péla]		*!					*

I assume that the set of constraints (or lexical specifications) determining stress in surface forms dominates—that is, takes priority over—the set of constraints determining alternations. The same is true of Ngalakgan and Yolngu: there can be no reorganisation of stress in order to better satisfy the realisation of geminates/glottal stop in a form.

[50]I will not attempt to account for the vowel alternations in this form.

In sum, historically and synchronically, Ngalakgan and neighbouring languages provide evidence for the importance of constituent boundaries in these languages, and for the demarcation of boundaries with salient articulations. In Ndjébbana, geminates are the salient articulations, there is no phonemic glottal stop in the language. In Ngalakgan, Ngandi and Rembarrnga, both geminates and glottal stops are found as boundary-marking signals, with geminates being synchronically manipulated in all three languages to provide the best association between intonation and constituency. In Southern Yolngu, with no contrastive geminates, glottal stop is the boundary marker, and is manipulated in a way reminiscent of Ngalakgan geminate alternations. It is noteworthy that demarcation of both the left and right edges of prominent constituents is found among these languages. This ambivalence about which edge should be demarcated is predicted by the constraints.

I have motivated a series of constraints demanding that constituents of morphology and prosody be demarcated by segments/clusters which have boundary signal interpretations. I justified the interpretations of obstruent clusters and glottal stops as boundary signals with reference to their acoustic characteristics: the fact that both obstruent clusters and glottal stops make a salient interruption to the voicing and hence the intonation contour of words. If the NO OBSCURE BOUNDARIES series are constraints of universal grammar, we expect to find evidence of boundary signal phenomena in other languages. In addition, if geminates and glottal stops are salient in Ngalakgan because they are articulated with marked laryngeal gestures, then we should similarly observe associations between laryngeal markedness and boundary phenomena elsewhere. This is the topic of the next section.

6.5.3 Implications for other languages

The use of segments or allophones as boundary signals is well-known since Trubetzkoy (1969 [1939]: 275ff). I briefly note just a few instances of boundary signalling in other languages, to back up my contention that the alternations found in Ngalakgan, Yolngu and Ndjébbana are boundary signal effects on segments, licensed by prosodic and morphological constituents.

There is evidence that prosodic constituents require salient boundaries. In English, it is well known that obstruents preceding stressed vowels and some other positions are aspirated, but elsewhere are unaspirated (Kahn 1976; Hayes 1995: 12ff). Selkirk (1995: 451, citing Cooper 1991) claims that onsets to PRWD are also aspirated.[51] We can interpret this to mean that

[51] There is disagreement about the distribution of aspiration in English. Nespor and Vogel (1986: 91) claim the correct generalisation is the initial obstruent in a foot. However, some of their proposed feet in English, such as the initial syllable of '[t^h]errain', would not meet with general agreement.

English evinces both constraints #σ́# and #PRWD#, with a left-edge bias, as in Ndjébbana.

The pattern in Finnish was described above in 6.2. In this language, according to (Sulkala and Karjalainen 1992), both gemination and laryngealisation are observed at word boundaries in unmonitored speech. In Finnish, primary stress is consistently associated with the initial syllable of words. Hence, gemination/laryngealisation demarcates all three of PRWD, FT1, and tonic at the left edge, similarly to Ndjébbana.

Pretonic fortition is described for several dialects of the Koniag Alutiiq (Yupik) group (Leer 1985: 84ff). The Yupik facts are interesting, since Leer shows that fortition is conditioned by *foot* boundaries: the fortis consonant need not be in the onset of a stressed syllable. Voicing is noncontrastive in obstruents. Fortition is realised phonetically as voicelessness, 'tenseness' and lengthening in obstruents.[52] Lenis obstruents are short and at least partially voiced (Leer 1985: 84). Environments (a) and (b) in (76) both condition fortition (foot boundaries represented with parentheses; fortis consonants are followed by an asterisk).[53]

(76) a. $(c{*}vx\acute{v}c)_{FT}$
b. $(c{*}\acute{v}{:}c)_{FT}$

Examples (from Leer 1985: 84) are presented in (77).

(77) a. (naá)ma#(c*íq)(quá) 'where is her plate?'
b. (naá)(m*ací)(q*uá) 'I will suffice'
c. (naá)ma#(c*iqúq) 'where is the plate?'
d. (naá)ma(c*iqúq) 'it will suffice'; or: 'it will continue to burn'

Leer observes that 'fortition of foot-initial consonants...set[s] apart the accented foot as a highly marked unit and impart[s] phonetic reality to the underlying prosodic structure of the word' (Leer 1985: 83). Thus the Aluutiq pattern satisfies #FT#.

In Ngalakgan, the realisation of boundary signals to tonics is derived from boundary signals occurring elsewhere in the language. Geminates,

[52] Leer does not describe the phonetic realisation of fortis sonorants. From Leer's description, fortis obstruents appear to be identical to geminates, and he notes that the fortis/lenis distinction is neutralised in geminates. He distinguishes the fortis from geminate obstruents on syllable structure possibilities: in a cluster C_1C_2, C_2 can be distinctively fortis, but not geminate. The phonetic difference between these two articulations remains unclear to me.

[53] The orthography is that of the source, except that I have represented fortis consonants with following asterisk and geminates as CC, with syllable boundary and hence foot boundary separating C from following C. Geminates make the preceding syllable heavy, and hence must presumably be syllabified according to timing positions, as in the majority of languages.

glottal stops and obstruent clusters all signal the boundaries to prosodic and morphological constituents. Likewise in Aluutiq, the fortis consonants which are boundary signals to feet act as general boundary signals also. Leer notes that 'systematically and phonetically, word-initial consonants are fortis', and hence that the effect of fortition is to make the left edge of a foot sound like the left edge of a word (1985: 83-4). I have suggested that the same impetus underlies historical gemination/fortition and laryngealisation in GN languages, in 6.2.

The Aluutiq pattern provides evidence that prosodic heads and prosodic domains, as well as morphological domains, can be associated with boundary signals. This is a pattern I have formalised as a series of constraints NO OBSCURE BOUNDARIES which refer to prosodic and morphological constituents alike.

So far, in all the patterns discussed we find that segmental boundary signals have one or more of the characteristics of word edges. There was the correlation I noted between pause and [spread glottis] or [constricted glottis] gestures in Ngalakgan in 6.2.1. The same is true of Ndjébbana (with geminates) and Yolngu (with glottal stop). The correlation between word and foot-initial segments is specifically observed by Leer, as we have just seen. Aspiration in English is also a feature of both word-initial and tonic syllable-initial stops, according to Selkirk (1995).

Geminates and glottal stops are both common as boundary signals in many other languages (Firth 1949: 178). In German, glottal stop precedes all vowel-initial stems, in both words and compounds (Booij 1995). In various Austronesian languages, for example Sundanese and Indonesian, glottal stop is found as a boundary signal either stem-initial or stem-final before or after vowels, respectively (Robins 1953; Cohn 1989). Geminates are found as boundary signals in Malayalam (Mohanan 1986), at the boundary between two stems in a compound. Dialects of Italian geminate word-initial stops following a stressed open syllable in the phenomenon called *raddoppiamento sintattico* (e.g. Chierchia 1982; Nespor and Vogel 1986). And in Finnish, geminates alternate with glottal stops, in a way reminiscent of Top End languages (Sulkala and Karjalainen 1992: 369, cited previously.) All of these patterns may be regarded as satisfying #MWD# or #PRWD# or both.

Similar correspondences therefore exist in other languages, between geminate or fortis segments, glottal stop, and boundaries of morphological and prosodic constituents. I regard the constraints proposed here as justified, on the basis that their effects are observable in other languages. In the final section, I show that the constraints proposed also account for the asymmetric distribution of geminates in roots.

6.6 Geminates and morpheme structure constraints

The distribution of geminates in roots in Ngalakgan is consistent with the same constraints which drive geminate alternations in complex words. The geminates in roots are lexicalised: they do not alternate with singletons, and the extent to which they obey the synchronic constraints is subject to exceptions. Nevertheless the majority of root-internal geminates do obey the constraints, giving the historical lexicon and the synchronic grammar a high degree of consistency.

Geminates in roots have a restricted distribution. There can be no more than one geminate per root (Merlan 1983: 3). Thus, along with words like (78) below, there are no words like those in (79) in Ngalakgan:[54]

(78)	a. /capatta/	[ɟábatta]	'long necked tortoise'
	b. /kappuci/	[gáppuɟi]	'old person'

(79)	a. */cappatta/	*[ɟappatta]
	b. */kappucci/	*[gappucci]

In addition, the single geminate allowed in a root is not freely distributed. In 88% of these roots, the geminate is immediately posttonic; some examples are presented in (80).

(80)	a. /palkkiɲ/	[bálkkiɲ]	'salty; dangerous'
	b. /kappuci/	[gáppuɟi]	'old person'
	c. /maraŋkaɭppa/	[màraŋgáɭppa]	'green tree snake'

In these cases, then, the geminate satisfies the constraint #σ́# 'tonics must be demarcated'. As we saw in Chapter 5, syllables like the primary stressed syllables of examples (80)a, c are bimoraic, so in these cases, the geminate also satisfies #FT1#.

In the remaining 12% of 190 roots with geminates (i.e. 22 examples), the geminate is the onset to the third syllable. All of these examples are presented in (81).

(81)	a. álakko	'later'
	b. cápatta	'freshwater tortoise sp.' (prob. *Emydura* sp.)
	c. cáruʈʈuʔ	'female agile wallaby'
	d. kámakkun	'properly'

---

[54]Ngandi and Rembarrnga both allow roots with more than one geminate, but only around 5% of roots have such a form. The Ngandi form of (78)a is recorded by Heath as /cappatta/.

e. káracci 'spinifex wax'
f. kúruppiḷ 'freshwater tortoise sp.' (prob. *Elseya dentata*)
g. ḷériccel 'freshwater tortoise sp.' (prob. *Elseya dentata*)
h. màḷamáḷappa 'young girl'
i. mánappuɳ 'echidna'
j. méḷeppeʔ 'shoulder blade'
k. menikkaʔ 'unlike'
l. míricci 'barramundi'
m. mîɳicca 'tree sp.'
n. móḷoppoḷ 'catfish sp.'
o. mórotʈinʔ 'bush banana' (prob. *Marsdenia viridiflora*)
p. ŋámuccùlo [subsection term]
q. ŋáɻakka 'bone'
r. =pálukkun SOURCE, ORIGIN [bound stem]
s. wáɻaccàra 'floodwater'
t. wérekka 'where?'
u. wúlukkurʔ 'sibling-in-law'
v. jánippi 'whatsit?'
w. járakka 'bandicoot sp.'

These examples satisfy #FT1#: 'Demarcate the strongest foot'.

Therefore, the structure of roots in Ngalakgan is compatible with the synchronic constraints on geminates in complex words. Given that the distribution respects the same constraint ranking which accounts for geminate alternation, there is no need for a separate 'morpheme structure constraint'. Only the WORD-level morphology is synchronically susceptible to alternation however, as we would expect given the other characteristics of WORD-level morphology described in preceding chapters.

Morpheme structure constraints in other languages have similar properties. In Copala Trique (an Otomanguean language), Hollenbach (1977: 36) claims that the fortis series of obstruents (stops, affricates, sibilants and, in one dialect, sonorants) and the laryngeals /ʔ, h/ only occur in the final stressed syllables of words. Elsewhere, only lenis consonants, and no laryngeals, occur. The fortis consonants Hollenbach notes are articulatorily tense, voiceless unaspirated if obstruent, and longer than the lenis consonants. Lenis obstruents vary between voiced and voiceless, and are commonly fricated intervocalically. Since syllables can only be open, or 'checked' (closed by a single laryngeal), fortis segments are in every case pretonic segments. The salient properties of fortis segments in Trique serve to clearly demarcate the stressed syllable, in a similar distribution to Ndjébbana.

6.7 Conclusion

In this chapter I have shown that there is a single series of stops in Ngalakgan, which can be either singleton or geminate. Geminate stops have all the characteristics of clusters: they are consistently longer than singletons, they have the [spread glottis] articulation common to all obstruent clusters, and—for the most part—they have the distribution of clusters in syllables (as shown in Chapter 2). Moreover, these characteristics apply both to tautomorphemic and to heteromorphemic geminates equally.

Geminates, and glottal stops, are commonly found at morpheme boundaries in Ngalakgan and neighbouring languages, suggesting historical gemination and laryngealisation rules. I have proposed constraints which demand that prominent constituents of prosody and morphology be associated with the same kind of junctural effect as the end of words, making these constituents highly salient within complex words. I have suggested that this correlation between phonological juncture and morpho-prosodic constituents aids the interpretation of complex words by hearers: an important task in such a morphologically complex language. Synchronic alternations demonstrate that these constraints are still active in the language, and in other languages.

7

Conclusion

In this final chapter, I briefly summarise the main results in the book and discuss their significance more broadly within linguistics. In addition, I look ahead to further work bearing on the deeper questions this examination of Ngalakgan has raised about the nature of the interface between morphology and interpretation.

7.1 Word structure in Ngalakgan

The first half of the book discussed structures which are found widely in Australia: the system of segmental contrasts and phonotactics, the structure of words, and the distinction between what I have called ROOT and WORD-level relations (following Selkirk 1984 and Borowsky 1990). The ROOT-level/WORD-level distinction is relevant to many phonological patterns, as the preceding chapters have demonstrated—word minimality (3.3.3), the distribution of feet and pitch accents in complex words (3.2-3.3), the behaviour of reduplication (3.3.4), the distribution of apical contrasts (3.7), and the domain of the degemination process (6.3.4). The distinction also has clear correlates with morphological productivity, and with compositionality of interpretation. These considerations argued for the analysis of the grammar provided in 3.5 (following proposals by Jackendoff 1997).

The ROOT-level/WORD-level distinction is clearly crucial for understanding the behaviour of many grammatical patterns in Ngalakgan. Baker and Harvey (2003) show that it is also relevant to the behaviour of phonology and morphology in other Australian languages; besides Ngalakgan, the two examined in that paper were Warlpiri and Warray. Warlpiri is not closely related to Ngalakgan, and these two languages were spoken in regions quite distant from each other traditionally. It is unlikely that speakers of Ngalakgan and Warlpiri were ever in contact in pre-colonial times. Nevertheless, Ngalakgan and Warlpiri share many similarities in terms of word structure, and in terms of the effect of word structure on prosody. Many other Australian languages appear to share similar interactions between morphology and prosody, where only a subset of morphological relations are relevant to prosodic behaviour. I expect that, as more extensive descriptions of the phonology of Australian languages become available, we will be in a better position to judge how extensively this kind of pattern is found.

7.2 Syllable structure, onsets and prosody

Chapters 5 and 6 discussed some phonological patterns which are more restricted in their distribution: the behaviour of monogestural clusters for quantity sensitivity (Chapter 5) and the distribution of 'hard clusters' with respect to prosodic and morphological boundaries in words. Section 5.1 showed that in Ngalakgan and neighbouring languages, monogestural clusters—geminates, homorganic nasal-stop clusters, and sequences of glottal stop+consonant—fail to attract stress to the preceding syllable, even though other medial clusters do so. This is a pattern which cannot be explained by current approaches to weight, such as Moraic Theory (e.g. Hayes 1989). Indeed, Moraic Theory would predict the opposite pattern: that the coda portion of geminates might contribute weight to the syllable, even if other codas did not. Building on some of the evidence of phonotactics discussed in 2.3.3, I argue in 5.3-4 that Ngalakgan syllabifies on the gestural level, rather than the timing level as in most languages. Monogestural clusters therefore behave like simple onsets, and do not contribute a moraic coda, unlike heterorganic clusters. In 5.4.6 I extended this result to similar patterns found in other languages both in Australia and elsewhere. In 5.4.7 I discussed the general implications of abandoning the moraic model of geminates, also proposed by e.g. Selkirk (1988) and Tranel (1991). General considerations, such as those discussed by Gordon (1999) suggest that, in fact, a simple moraic theory of weight is inadequate to capture the empirical facts. Rather, the computation of quantity must minimally be able to have access to such information as the sonority characteristics of root nodes, both vowels and consonants. The evidence of Ngalakgan and related languages suggest that syllabification too needs to have access to more than just the timing characteristics of the string. Further detailed studies of the prosodic systems of Australian languages from a phonological point of view will no doubt produce additional relevant evidence for this issue.

Chapter 6 discussed the behaviour of 'hard clusters'—geminates, heterorganic stop clusters, and clusters of glottal stop+stop—for the purposes of what I call 'boundary marking' (following Trubetzkoy 1969[1939]). This set of clusters, together with the location of pitch accents, conditions the distribution of geminates in complex words, in a pattern found in Ngalakgan, Rembarrnga, and Ngandi, but in no other languages to my knowledge (6.3). However, similar effects on the realisation of fortition and laryngealisation according to prosodic and morphological boundaries are found in other Australian languages (such as Yolngu Matha and Ndjébbana) as well as many other languages (Finnish, Yupik, English, Malayalam, to name a few), suggesting that these are variations on a theme (6.5). In 6.2.1 I suggested that such articulations are well-suited to function as 'boundary signals' in Trubetzkoy's sense—overt phonological signals of morphological structure. This is particularly the case in Australian languages, since hard clusters interrupt the largely continuous voicing profile found within words otherwise. Such patterns have not received detailed attention in phonology up until now, and the analysis presented in Chapter 6 is necessarily tentative. However, the wide distribution of such effects in languages demands an explanation.

In the next section, I look ahead to further work at the morphological interface which is relevant to the deeper question touched on in this work: the nature of the difference between words and phrases.

7.3 Further evidence for words as phrases: compound interpretation in Ngalakgan and Wubuy

One of the interesting questions raised by languages such as Ngalakgan and Bininj Gun-wok is to what extent words in such languages are equivalent (in some respects) to phrases in configurational languages such as English. It is not just phonological behaviour that is relevant to this question, of course. One important set of data has barely been addressed with respect to this issue, and that is the behaviour and interpretation of compounds (discussed in passing in Baker In press). I discuss the issue here because I believe it provides further evidence for the proposal, tentatively put forward in Chapters 3 and 4, that complex words in Ngalakgan *are*, in some respects, phrasal.[1]

---

[1]The following discussion is in part based on a talk presented at the annual Blackwood Australianists' Workshop, in Sydney, March 2005. I would like to thank the participants, in particular Nick Evans, Rachel Nordlinger, Jane Simpson, and Lesley Stirling, as well as Cliff Goddard, Mark Harvey, Nick Reid, Andrea Schalley, and Andy Spencer for useful discussion. I would also like to thank an anonymous reviewer for the Australian Journal of Linguistics, for first bringing this issue to my attention.

Productive compounding of nouns and adjectives is found in many Gunwinyguan languages; apart from Ngalakgan, these structures are described extensively for BGW (Evans 2003: section 5.4), and Wubuy (Heath 1984: Ch 14).

Some typical examples of such compounds in Ngalakgan are shown in (1).

(1) a. /koɲ-ŋolkko/ 'a big kangaroo'
macropod-big
b. /kuɳʈu-jocco ɲ/ 'clear (not sacred) country'
country-clear
c. /ɭaŋka-kaɲaʔ/ 'a small billabong'
billabong-small

As indicated by the glosses, these compounds have the interpretations of nouns modified by an adjective in English; in short, they have the interpretations of Noun Phrases. Indeed, in all three languages, compounds like these are the standard way of expressing such phrases. Evans (2003) is explicit on this point:[2]

> In all dialects [of BGW: BB], modifying compounds are the preferred method of applying adjectives to nouns capable of compounding or incorporation, and in some dialects (for example, Kuninjku) this is the only way of modifying such nouns. (Evans 2003: 177)

Compounds thus formed are interpretively transparent in all three languages.[3] They simply have the same interpretation as phrasal collocations of noun and adjective.

However, these kinds of interpretations are not typical of compounds in other languages. In English, compounds may be regarded as devices for increasing the number of named types in the lexicon. Allen (1978) proposes that English compounds are subject to an 'IS A condition': that compounds name hyponyms of the right-hand member. Cruse (1986: Ch 6), after some discussion of the issue, concludes that the most general criterion for taxonomic relations is whether two terms satisfy the relation 'is a *kind/type* of'. Clearly, the English compounds like those in (2) satisfy this criterion, at least in those examples which are transparently endocentric. A 'pen-knife' is a kind of knife, in the same kind of way that a 'cocker spaniel' is a kind of spaniel, which is in turn a kind of dog.

---

2 This is my observation of Ngalakgan, based on many years of direct experience, and my observation of Wubuy, based on rather less experience. I can find no explicit discussion of the issue in Heath (1984). Wubuy examples are from my own fieldnotes, unless otherwise noted.

3 The extant lexicons of BGW and Wubuy both contain a small number of lexicalised, and largely exocentric, compounds. Ngalakgan has no clear examples of this kind.

(2) a. blackboard 'a type of board for presenting pedagogical material'
b. blackbird 'a kind of bird'
c. pen-knife 'a type of knife'

It is not clear that the Ngalakgan compounds in (1) satisfy Cruse's criterion, except in a trivial sense. A big kangaroo is certainly a kangaroo, but it is not a *kind* of kangaroo in the way that a cocker spaniel is a kind of (or variety of) dog. Compounds in GN languages, then, do not name types or kinds, they name individuals (of the class identified by the noun) that happen to have the properties ascribed to them by the adjective. So in (1), /koɲ-ŋolkko/ refers to an individual which is both a kangaroo and a big example thereof. /koɲ-ŋolkko/ does not name a species (a specific kind) of kangaroo. But that is exactly what we would expect of compounds in other languages. In English for instance, 'blackbird' cannot be applied to any bird which happens to be black, but only to a particular species of bird (and indeed regardless, for instance, of whether it happens to be an albino). The opposite applies to Ngalakgan and these other languages.

Morphologically, these constructions are certainly compounds, rather than phrases, according to several tests. I mention two here (see also 3.5). The first piece of evidence against a phrasal analysis is that these constructions take affixation only at each edge, and not internally. This is what we expect of words.

(3) /jini-munku-ɻa, **ku-colkko-maʔ-kaʔ/**
2sg/1pl-follow-FUT NEUT-ground-good-LOC
'You follow us, to the soft [lit. 'good'] ground.' [5/9/97: 1A]

When the compound is used referentially, as it is here, the noun class affixation is appropriate to the referent—here /colkko/ 'ground' (NEUT).

Compounds of this form can therefore be distinguished from phrases, which would never take a single set of affixes on each edge, since Ngalakgan does not allow case-marking on a single constituent of a phrase.[4]

(4) */ku-colkko maʔ-kaʔ jini-munku-ɻa/
NEUT-ground good-LOC 2sg/1pl-follow-FUT

[4] Merlan (1983: 81) makes the contrary claim, that only the head of NP need take overt case marking. In fact, this is only true with respect to demonstratives, which may omit a case suffix if the case-marked noun immediately follows. It is not true of sequences of noun and adjective, in my data.

Since N-ADJ compounds are headed by an adjective (as argued in 3.5), these constructions can be inflected with pronominal argument prefixes and inflected inchoative auxiliary /me+/. These forms provide even stronger evidence against a phrasal analysis, since pronominal prefixes can never be used on ordinary nouns. Here I use a Wubuy example from recorded conversation, where the formal distinction between nouns and verbs is clearer than in Ngalakgan. (5)a is a compound of a generic noun /jaŋ/ 'voice' and an adjective /waʈawaʈaʈ/ 'strong, firm'. Since it was used as a predicate in this example it takes a verbal inflectional prefix /ni-/ '3 masculine singular' agreeing with the referent, a man. This prefix cannot occur on common (non-adjectival) nouns, and hence (5)b is ungrammatical.

(5) a. [nijambaɖawaɖawaɖaɖ]
/ni-jaŋ-waʈa-waʈawaʈaʈ/
3M-voice-INTENS-strong
'his voice is strong, he is strong voice-wise' [9/4/07: tk1]
b. */ni-jaŋ/

Secondly, there is phonological evidence from Wubuy for a compound analysis. In Wubuy, there is a phonological rule which inserts a meaningless epenthetic string /-ŋu-/ before stop-initial stems, following another stem or a consonant-final prefix. N-ADJ compounds are subject to the rule, just like verbs (Heath 1982: 277). The rule only applies within words, hence the forms in (6)c are ungrammatical.

(6) a. /ana-jir-ŋu-ʈiku/ 'green leaves, foliage'
NEUT.TOP-leaves-EPENTH-raw
b. /ana-jir-ŋu-ʈaʈark/ 'dried-up leaves'
NEUT.TOP-leaves-EPENTH-dry
c. */ŋu-ʈiku/, */ŋu-ʈaʈark/ (Heath 1982: 277)

Hence, the constructions found in these languages are clearly constructions at the word level, not the phrasal level. Nevertheless, their interpretation is that of phrases in languages such as English, and is not the kind of interpretation that compounds have in the latter language.[5]

[5] I have been unable to find explicit discussion of this issue. It is not the case that BGW, Wubuy, and Ngalakgan lack lexicalised or exocentric compounds naming types. For instance, BGW has a form /kep-tukkur/ (literally 'nose-short') which is applied to the estuarine crocodile, and the orange horseshoe bat is /molo-poɳʈok/ (literally 'tail-woomera'). Similar examples can be found here and there in Wubuy (though not Ngalakgan, to my knowledge) e.g. /ŋuta-l̪arʈark/ 'kingbrown snake' (lit. 'midriff-rough') (Heath 1984: 472). However, what is lacking in these languages is endocentric constructions of the kind represented by English

Formally, compounds in English are interpreted like simple nouns. So 'blackbird' has something like the interpretation in (7).

(7) blackbird′(x)
'x is a blackbird'

English compounds are expressions of type 'e' like other common nouns.

In Ngalakgan, BGW, and Wubuy, the semantics of compounds is more complicated. For a start, the semantics of adjectives is not well-understood, and depends on the lexical semantics of the adjective involved (in particular, whether it is intersective, subsective or nonpredicative: Chierchia and McConnell-Ginet 2000: 459). A 'big kangaroo' for instance, is necessarily a kangaroo, but is not necessarily 'big' in some absolute sense. To simplify matters, I will only consider intersective adjectives here, in this case, 'sacred'.

(8) /kuɳʈu-cappuru/ 'sacred country'
$\lambda x[\text{country}'(x) \wedge \text{sacred}'(x)]$
'That entity which is both country and is sacred.'

It may be the case that some lexical items in English and other languages have a similar semantics. Chierchia and McConnell-Ginet (2000: 446) suggest the following analysis for 'mother':

(9) $\text{mother}' = \lambda x[\text{parent}'(x) \wedge \text{female}'(x)]$

However, my point here is that, while it may be the case that some lexical items in English have complex semantics, the semantics of compounds in Ngalakgan, Wubuy and BGW is *necessarily* complex, and cannot be described in terms of the simple application of predicate and argument in (7).

This appears to be an area which has not been deeply investigated in the literature on formal semantics. But I think the relevance of the interpretation of compounds to the question we are interested in here—the nature of words in polysynthetic languages such as Ngalakgan—is self-evident. I expect that future research on these languages will uncover more about the semantics of this and other 'word constructions'.

'black bear', 'river wallaby', etc. I have found no Australian language to use constructions of this kind to name species, or any other natural kinds (see Baker In press for further discussion). The one exception I know of is Demiin, the special initiation register formerly spoken by Lardil initiates. This language, with a lexicon of around 200 items, *has* created names for species which are analogous to English binomial species names (see McKnight 1999). Clearly Demiin is a special case, in many respects.

7.4 Morphology in Optimality Theory

In Chapter 3, I characterised the WORD-level/ROOT-level distinction in Ngalakgan as a 'dual-access' model of morphology, following Clahsen (1999). Authors such as Jackendoff (1997, 2002), Clahsen (1999), and Pinker (1999) have suggested that the dual-access model of morphology is more generally applicable to languages, citing evidence from English and German. Apart from the current work, I am aware of no detailed studies of the morphology of a single language which attempt to apply this model. The evidence of Ngalakgan and other Australian languages discussed in this book provides confirmation that the predictions of the dual-access model are broadly valid for this group of languages.[6]

Current approaches in phonology and morphology appear to have largely ignored the results of the dual-access program, for what I would suggest are historical reasons. The most widely adopted model for phonology at present is Optimality Theory. As discussed in Chapter 1, and demonstrated throughout the book, OT is most commonly implemented as a single-level model of grammar. This approach runs into problems when attempting to deal with classic problems of cyclicity, such as the Levantine Arabic stress data discussed by Brame (1974). As Kiparsky puts it (2000: 359) 'at the root of this problem is the fact that parallel OT attempts to deal with the morphology/phonology interface without a theory of morphology'.

While authors such as McCarthy and Prince (1993b), Duanmu (1999), and Kiparsky (2000) have implemented OT in a level-ordered model, such models are open to a number of criticisms. As in previous level-ordered models such as Lexical Phonology and Morphology (e.g. Kiparsky 1982), it is not clear what the cognitive status of 'levels' are. If earlier levels such as Level 1 in English (cf. Mohanan 1986) are in fact unproductive, authors such as Pinker (1999) would propose that morphology at this level is entirely inaccessible to speakers, or in any case, is accessed in quite a different fashion to fully productive morphology.

Morphology itself as a branch of study has gone in almost the opposite direction: denying the reality of the 'morpheme' and thus of word-internal structure relevant to phonology. Proponents of this approach, notably Beard (1995), Stump (2001), and Spencer (e.g. 2003) argue that the morpheme as a classical construct cannot easily account for the full range of cross-linguistically attested morphological phenomena, for example Semitic root-and-pattern morphology, English and German ablaut in verbs, and reduplication. They therefore propose to do away with it as a concept

[6] See Laaha, Ravid, Korecky-Kröll, Laaha and Dressler (2006) for a recent discussion of the controversy over single and dual-access morphological models.

altogether. It is not obvious how such an approach can explain either the regularity of isomorphism between WORD-level constituents and prosodic constituents in Ngalakgan, nor the invisibility of ROOT-level constituents to phonological processes in general. Nor is it clear how such an approach would explain facts such as those presented in example (82) in Chapter 3, where speakers pronounce bound morphemes in isolation. More generally, such approaches to morphology do not articulate well with current assumptions in OT, where the input is standardly conceived of as a string of morphemes of the usual kind familiar since Chomsky and Halle (1968).

What should be clear from the preceding discussion, and the ongoing controversy in OT itself, is that it is time once again for morphology, and in particular morphological relations, to be taken seriously by current phonological theory. The facts which amply attest to two morphological levels in Ngalakgan and other Australian languages cannot easily be explained by any other current approach in phonology or morphology (including Lexical Phonology, and hence Kiparsky's (2000) LPM-OT: see Baker 2005). But since these facts are widely attested in Australian languages, this suggests that current phonological and morphological theories are architecturally inadequate. I have suggested that an application of the 'dual-access' model to OT provides a straightforward, and cognitively satisfying, account of these patterns, without significantly extending the architecture already widely-used in standard models of Optimality Theory.

References

Abaev, Vasili Ivanovich. 1964. *A grammatical sketch of Ossetic*. [*International Journal of American Linguistics*, vol. 30, no. 4, pt. 2.] Bloomington: Indiana University Centre in Anthropology, Folklore and Linguistics.

Ackema, Peter, and Neeleman, Ad. 2004. *Beyond morphology: interface conditions on word formation*. [Oxford Studies in Theoretical Linguistics vol. 6.] Oxford: Oxford University Press.

Allen, Margaret R. 1978. Morphological investigations. University of Connecticut: PhD dissertation.

Alpher, Barry, Evans, Nicholas, and Harvey, Mark. 2003. Proto-Gunwinyguan verbal suffixes. In *The non-Pama-Nyungan languages of northern Australia: comparative studies of the continent's most linguistically complex region*, ed. Nicholas Evans, 305-352. Canberra: Pacific Linguistics.

Amberber, Mengistu. 2002. *Verb classes and transitivity in Amharic*. [Lincom Studies in Afro-Asiatic Linguistics 06.] Munich: Lincom Europa.

Amberber, Mengistu, Baker, Brett, and Harvey, Mark. 2007. Complex predication and the coverb construction. In *Language description, history and development: linguistic indulgence in memory of Terry Crowley*, eds. Jeff Siegel, John Lynch, and Diana Eades, 209-219. Amsterdam/Philadelphia: John Benjamins.

Anderson, Victoria Balboa. 2000. Giving weight to phonetic principles. University of California at Los Angeles: PhD dissertation.

Aronoff, Mark. 1976. *Word formation in generative grammar*. [Linguistic Inquiry Monographs 1.] Cambridge, MA: MIT Press.

Aronoff, Mark. 1994. *Morphology by itself*. [Linguistic Inquiry Monographs 22.] Cambridge, MA: MIT Press.

Aronoff, Mark, and Sridhar, S.N. 1983. Morphológical levels in English and Kannada or Atarizing Reagan. In *Papers from the parasession on the interplay of phonology morphology and syntax*, eds. John F. Richardson, Michell Marks, and Amy Chukerman, 3-16. Chicago: Chicago Linguistics Society.

Austin, Peter. 1981. *A grammar of Diyari, South Australia.* [Cambridge Studies in Linguistics 32.] Cambridge: Cambridge University Press.

Austin, Peter, and Bresnan, Joan. 1996. Non-configurationality in Australian Aboriginal languages. *Natural Language and Linguistic Theory* 14: 215-268.

Baker, Brett J. 1998. Edge-Crispness: segment to mora isomorphism. In *Proceedings of the West Coast Conference on Formal Linguistics XVI, Spring 1997*, eds. Emily Curtis, James Lyle, and Gabriel Webster, 33-47. CSLI: Stanford.

Baker, Brett J. 1999. Word structure in Ngalakgan. University of Sydney: PhD thesis.

Baker, Brett J. 2002. How referential is agreement? The interpretation of polysynthetic dis-agreement morphology in Ngalakgan. In *Problems of polysynthesis*, eds. Nicholas Evans and Hans-Juergen Sasse, 51-86. [Studia Typologica 4.] Berlin: Akademie Verlag.

Baker, Brett J. 2004. Stem forms and paradigm reshaping in Gunwinyguan. In *Australian languages: classification and the comparative method*, eds. Claire Bowern and Harold Koch, 313-340. Amsterdam: John Benjamins.

Baker, Brett J. 2005. The domain of phonological processes. In *Proceedings of the 2004 conference of the Australian Linguistics Society*, ed. Ilana Mushin. http://hdl.handle.net/2123/112.

Baker, Brett J. In press. Ethnoclassification and the environment in Northern Australia. In *Mental states: language and cognitive structure*, eds. Andrea C. Schalley and Drew Khlentzos. Amsterdam/Philadelphia: John Benjamins.

Baker, Brett J. To appear. The interpretation of complex nominal expressions in Southeast Arnhem Land Languages. In *Discourse and grammar in Australian languages*, eds. Ilana Mushin and Brett Baker. Amsterdam/Philadelphia: John Benjamins.

Baker, Brett J., and Harvey, Mark. 2003. Word structure in Australian languages. *Australian Journal of Linguistics* 23: 3-33.

Baker, Mark C. 2003. *Lexical categories*. Cambridge: Cambridge University Press.

Beard, Robert. 1995. *Lexeme morpheme base morphology*. Stony Brook, NY: SUNY Press.

Beckman, Mary E. 1996. The parsing of prosody. *Language and Cognitive Processes* 11: 17-67.

Benua, Laura. 1997. Transderivational identity: phonological relations between words. University of Massachusetts: PhD dissertation.

Berry, Lynn. 1999. Alignment and adjacency in Optimality Theory: evidence from Warlpiri and Arrernte. University of Sydney: PhD Thesis.

Bishop, Judith. 2002. Aspects of intonation and prosody in Bininj Gun-wok: an autosegmental-metrical analysis. University of Melbourne: PhD thesis.

Bittner, Maria, and Hale, Ken. 1995. Remarks on definiteness in Warlpiri. In *Quantification in natural languages*, eds. Emmon Bach, Eloise Jelinek, Angelika Kratzer, and Barbara H. Partee, 81-106. Dordrecht: Kluwer.

Bittner, Maria, and Hale, Ken. 1996. The structural determination of case and agreement. *Linguistic Inquiry* 27: 1-68.

Blake, Barry. 1979. *A Kalkatungu grammar.* [Series B, vol. 57.] Canberra: Pacific Linguistics.

Blevins, Juliette. 1995. The syllable in phonological theory. In *The handbook of phonological theory*, ed. John A. Goldsmith, 206-244. Malden, MA: Blackwell.

Blevins, Juliette. 1997. Rules in Optimality Theory: two case studies. In *Derivations and constraints in phonology*, ed. Iggy Roca, 227-260. Oxford: Oxford University Press.

Blevins, Juliette. 2003. The independent nature of phonotactic constraints: an alternative to syllable-based approaches. In *The syllable in Optimality Theory*, eds. Caroline Féry and Ruben van der Vijver, 375-403. Cambridge: Cambridge University Press.

Blevins, Juliette, and Marmion, Doug. 1994. Nhanta historical phonology. *Australian Journal of Linguistics* 14, 2: 193-216.

Boas, Franz. 1947. Kwakiutl grammar with a glossary of the suffixes, ed. by Helene Boas Yampolsky with the collaboration of Zellig S. Harris. *Transactions of the American Philosophical Society* N.S. 37, Part 3: 201-377.

Booij, Geert. 1995. *The phonology of Dutch.* Oxford: Clarendon Press and New York: Oxford University Press.

Borowsky, Toni. 1990. *Topics in the lexical phonology of English.* New York: Garland. [Revision of author's 1986 University of Massachusetts PhD dissertation.]

Bowern, Claire, and Koch, Harold eds. 2004. *Australian languages: classification and the comparative method.* Amsterdam: John Benjamins.

Brame, Michael. 1974. The cycle in phonology: stress in Palestinian, Maltese and Spanish. *Linguistic Inquiry* 5: 39-60.

Breen, Gavan. 1992. Some problems in Kukatj phonology. *Australian Journal of Linguistics* 12: 1-44.

Breen, Gavan, and Pensalfini, Robert J. 1999. Arrernte: a language with no syllable onsets. *Linguistic Inquiry* 30: 1-25.

Bresnan, Joan. 2001. *Lexical-functional syntax.* [Blackwell Textbooks in Linguistics.] Malden, MA: Blackwell.

Browman, Catherine P., and Goldstein, Louis. 1989. Articulatory gestures as phonological units. *Phonology* 6: 201-251.

Browman, Catherine P., and Goldstein, Louis. 1990. Tiers in articulatory phonology, with some implications for casual speech. In *Papers in laboratory phonology I: between the grammar and physics of speech*, eds. John Kingston and Mary Beckman, 341-376. Cambridge: Cambridge University Press.

Butcher, Andrew. 1993a. The phonetics of Australian languages. Ms. Flinders University, Adelaide SA.

Butcher, Andrew. 1993b. Phonetic correlates of contrasting stop series in Non-Pama-Nyungan languages. Ms. Flinders University, Adelaide SA.

Butcher, Andrew. 1995. The phonetics of neutralisation: the case of Australian coronals. In *Studies in general and English phonetics: essays in honour of J.D. O'Connor*, ed. Jack Windsor Lewis, 10-38. London and New York: Routledge.

Butcher, Andrew. 1999. What speakers of Australian Aboriginal languages do with their velums and why: the phonetics of the nasal/oral contrast. Paper presented at *XIVth International Congress of Phonetic Sciences*, Berkeley CA.

Butcher, Andrew. 2004. 'Fortis/Lenis' revisited one more time: the aerodynamics of some oral stop contrasts in three continents. *Clinical Linguistics and Phonetics* 18: 547-557.

Capell, Arthur. 1942. Languages of Arnhem Land, North Australia. *Oceania* XII, 4: 354-392, XIII, 1: 24-50.

Capell, Arthur. 1962. *Some linguistic types in Australia.* [Oceania Linguistic Monographs 7.] Sydney: Oceania Publications.

Carstairs-McCarthy, Andrew. *Current morphology.* London and New York: Routledge.

Chierchia, Gennaro. 1982. An autosegmental theory of Raddoppiamento. Ms. University of Massachusetts, Amherst.

Chierchia, Gennaro, and McConnell-Ginet, Sally. 2000. *Meaning and grammar: an introduction to semantics*, 2nd edn. Cambridge, MA: MIT Press.

Chomsky, Noam. 1970. Remarks on nominalization. In *Readings in Transformational Grammar*, ed. R. A. Jacobs and P. S. Rosenbaum, 184-221. Waltham, MA: Ginn.

Chomsky, Noam, and Halle, Morris. 1968. *The sound pattern of English.* New York, Evanston, and London: Harper and Row.

Clahsen, Harald. 1999. Lexical entries and rules of language: a multidisciplinary study of German inflection. *Behavioral and Brain Sciences* 22: 991-1060.

Cléirigh, Christopher. 1998. The genesis of phonic texture: systemic phonology and universal Darwinism. University of Sydney: PhD thesis.

Clements, G.N., and Keyser, Samuel Jay. 1983. *CV phonology*. Cambridge, MA: MIT Press.

Cohn, Abigail C. 1989. Stress in Indonesian and bracketing paradoxes. *Natural Language and Linguistic Theory* 7: 167-216.

Cohn, Abigail C., and McCarthy, John J. 1998. Alignment and parallelism in Indonesian phonology. In *Working Papers of the Cornell Phonetics Laboratory* 12: 53-137. Cornell: Cornell University.

Cook, Anthony. 1987. Wagiman Matyin: a description of the Wagiman language of the Northern Territory. La Trobe University, Melbourne: PhD thesis.

Cooper, André. 1991. An articulatory account of aspiration in English. Yale University: PhD dissertation.

Cruse, David. 1986. *Lexical Semantics*. Cambridge: Cambridge University Press.

Dart, Sarah N. 1991. Articulatory and acoustic propoerties of apical and laminal articulations. In *UCLA working papers in phonetics*, 79. Los Angeles: University of California Los Angeles.

Dave, Radhekant. 1977. Retroflex and dental consonants in Gujarati: a palatographic and acoustic study. In *Annual report of the Institute of Phonetics, University of Copenhagen*, 11: 27-156. Copenhagen: University of Copenhagen.

Davis, Stuart. 1988. On the nature of internal reduplication. In *Theoretical morphology: approaches in modern linguistics*, eds. Michael Hammond and Michael Noonan, 305-323. San Diego: Academic Press.

Davis, Stuart. 2003. The controversy over geminates and syllable weight. In *The syllable in Optimality Theory*, eds. Caroline Féry and Ruben van de Vijver, 77-98. Cambridge: Cambridge University Press.

Dixon, R.M.W. 1972. *The Dyirbal language of North Queensland.* Cambridge: Cambridge University Press.

Dixon, R.M.W. 1977. *A grammar of Yidiny*. Cambridge: Cambridge University Press.

Dixon, R.M.W. 1980. *The languages of Australia*. Cambridge: Cambridge University Press.

Dixon, R.M.W. 2002. *Australian languages: their nature and development*. Cambridge: Cambridge University Press.

Dixon, R.M.W. ed. 1976. *Grammatical categories in Australian languages*. [Linguistic Series vol. 22.] Canberra: Australian Institute of Aboriginal Studies.

Downing, Laura J. To appear. On the ambiguous segmental status of nasals in homorganic NC sequences. In *The internal organization of phonological segments*, eds. M. van Oostendorp and J.M. van de Weijer. Berlin: Mouton de Gruyter.

Duanmu, San. 1999. Alignment and the Cycle are different. In *The derivational residue in phonological Optimality Theory*, eds. Ben Hermans and Marc van Oostendorp, 129-152. Amsterdam: John Benjamins.

Evans, Bethwyn, and Merlan, Francesca. 2004. Stop contrasts in languages of Arnhem Land: from the perspective of Jawoyn, Southern Arnhem Land. *Australian Journal of Linguistics* 24: 185-224.

Evans, Nicholas. 1995. Current issues in the phonology of Australian languages. In *The handbook of phonological theory*, ed. John A. Goldsmith, 723-761. Malden, MA: Blackwell.

Evans, Nicholas. 1997. Role or cast? Noun incorporation and complex predicates in Mayali. In *Complex predicates*, eds. Alex Alsina, Joan Bresnan, and Peter Sells, 397-430. [CSLI Lecture Notes, 64.] Stanford, CA: CSLI.

Evans, Nicholas. 1998. Emu divorce. In *Papers from the regional meetings, Chicago Linguistic Society, 1998, 34(1)*, eds. M. Catherine Gruber, Derrick Higgins, Kenneth S. Olson, and Tamra Wysocki, 127-142. Chicago: Chicago Linguistics Society.

Evans, Nicholas. 1999. Why argument affixes in polysynthetic languages are not pronouns: evidence from Bininj Gun-wok. *Sprachtypologie und Universalienforschung* 52: 255-281.

Evans, Nicholas. 2003. *Bininj Gun-wok: A pan-dialectal grammar of Mayali, Kunwinjku and Kune*. Canberra: Pacific Linguistics.

Evans, Nicholas, Fletcher, Janet, and Ross, Belinda. In press. Big words, small phrases: mismatches between pause units and the polysynthetic word in Dalabon. *Linguistics*.

Firth, J.R. 1949. Sounds and prosodies. *Transactions of the Philological Society* (1948): 127-152.

Fischer-Jørgensen, E. 1972. "Ptk" et "bdg" français en position intervocalique accentué. In *Papers in linguistics and phonetics to the memory of Pierre Delattre*, ed. A. Valdman, 143-200. The Hague: Mouton.

Foley, William A. 1991. *The Yimas language of New Guinea*. Stanford, CA: Stanford University Press.

Fujimura, O., Macchi, M.J., and Streeter, L.A. 1978. Perception of stop consonants with conflicting transitional cues: a cross-linguistic study. *Language and Speech* 21: 337-346.

Gaby, Alice. 2006. A grammar of Kuuk Thaayorre. University of Melbourne: PhD thesis.

Garde, Murray. 2003. Social deixis in Bininj Kun-wok conversation. University of Queensland: PhD thesis.

Glasgow, Katherine. 1981. Burarra phonemes. In *Australian phonologies: collected papers*, ed. Bruce Waters, 63-89. [Work Papers of SIL-AAB, Series A, vol. 5.] Darwin: Summer Institute of Linguistics.

Glasgow, Katherine. n.d. Burarra—Gun-nartpa dictionary with English finderlist. Ms. Australian Institute of Aboriginal and Torres Strait Islander Studies, Canberra.

Goddard, Cliff, and Wierzbicka, Anna eds. 2002. *Meaning and universal grammar: theory and empirical findings, Vols I & II*. Amsterdam: John Benjamins.

Goldsmith, John A. 1990. *Autosegmental and metrical phonology*. Oxford: Blackwell.

Gordon, Matthew. 1999. Syllable weight: phonetics, phonology, and typology. University of California, Los Angeles: PhD dissertation.

Gordon, Matthew, and Ladefoged, Peter. 2001. Phonation types: a cross-linguistic overview. *Journal of Phonetics* 29: 383-406.

Green, Rebecca. 1995. A grammar of Gurr-goni: a language of north central Arnhem Land. Australian National University: PhD thesis.

Green, Rebecca. 2003. Proto Maningrida within Proto Arnhem: evidence from verbal inflectional suffixes. In *The non-Pama-Nyungan languages of northern Australia: comparative studies of the continent's most linguistically complex region*, ed. Nicholas Evans, 369-421. Canberra: Pacific Linguistics.

Green, Rebecca. 2005. Gurr-goni dictionary. Ms. Darwin: Department of Education.

Groen, B.M. 1977. *A structural description of the Macedonian dialect of Dihovo: phonology, morphology, texts, lexicon*. Lisse: The Peter de Ridder press.

Haiman, John. 1972. Phonological targets and unmarked structures. *Language* 48: 365-377.

Hale, Kenneth L. 1973. Deep-surface canonical disparities in relation to analysis and change: an Australian example. In *Current trends in linguistics, Vol. 11*, ed. Thomas Sebeok, 401-458. The Hague: Mouton.

Hale, Kenneth L. 1976a. Phonological developments in particular Northern Paman languages. In *Languages of Cape York*, ed. Peter Sutton, 7-40. Canberra: Australian Institute of Aboriginal Studies.

Hale, Kenneth L. 1976b. The adjoined relative clause in Australia. In *Grammatical categories in Australian languages*, ed. R.M.W.Dixon, 78-105. Canberra: Australian Institute of Aboriginal Studies.

Hale, Kenneth L. 1983. Warlpiri and the grammar of non-configurational languages. *Natural Language and Linguistic Theory* 1: 5-47.

Halle, Morris, and Clements, G.N. 1983. *Problem book in phonology*. Cambridge, MA: MIT Press.

Halle, Morris, and Stevens, Kenneth. 1971. A note on laryngeal features. *Quarterly Progress Report, MIT Research Laboratory of Electronics 101*, 198-213. Cambridge, MA: Massachusetts Institute of Technology.

Halle, Morris, and Vergnaud, Jean-Roger. 1987. *An essay on stress*. Cambridge, MA: MIT Press.

Hamilton, Philip. 1996. Phonetic constraints and markedness in the phonotactics of Australian Aboriginal languages. University of Toronto: PhD dissertation.

Hankamer, Jorge. 1989. Morphological parsing and the lexicon. In *Lexical representation and process*, ed. William Marslen-Wilson, 392-408. Cambridge, MA: MIT Press.

Harris, J.W. 1986. *Northern Territory pidgins and the origin of Kriol*. [Series C, vol. 89.] Canberra: Pacific Linguistics.

Harvey, Mark. 1986. Ngoni Waray amungal-yang: the Waray language from Adelaide River. Australian National University: MA thesis.

Harvey, Mark. 1991. Glottal stop, underspecification, and syllable structure among the Top End languages. *Australian Journal of Linguistics* 11: 67-105.

Harvey, Mark. 2002. *A grammar of Gaagudju*. [Mouton Grammar Library, vol. 24.] Berlin: Mouton de Gruyter.

Harvey, Mark. 2003. Reconstruction of pronominals among the non-Pama-Nyungan languages. In *The non-Pama-Nyungan languages of northern Australia:*

comparative studies of the continent's most linguistically complex region, ed. Nicholas Evans, 475-513. Canberra: Pacific Linguistics.

Harvey, Mark, and Baker, Brett J. 2005. Coronal place oppositions. Ms. University of Newcastle, NSW and University of New England, NSW.

Harvey, Mark, and Borowsky, Toni. 1991. The minimum word in Warray. *Australian Journal of Linguistics* 19: 89-99.

Hayes, Bruce. 1986. Inalterability in CV phonology. *Language* 2: 321-351.

Hayes, Bruce. 1989. Compensatory lengthening in moraic phonology. *Linguistic Inquiry* 20: 253-306.

Hayes, Bruce. 1995. *Metrical stress theory: principles and case studies*. Chicago: University of Chicago Press.

Heath, Jeffrey. 1976. Simple and compound verbs: conjugation by auxiliaries in Australian verbal systems. North East Arnhem Land. In *Grammatical categories in Australian languages*, ed. R.M.W. Dixon, 735-740. Canberra: Australian Institute of Aboriginal Studies.

Heath, Jeffrey. 1978a. *Linguistic diffusion in Arnhem Land*. Canberra: Australian Institute of Aboriginal Studies.

Heath, Jeffrey. 1978b. *Ngandi grammar, texts, and dictionary*. Canberra: Australian Institute of Aboriginal Studies.

Heath, Jeffrey. 1981. *Basic materials in Mara: grammar, texts, and dictionary*. [Series C, vol. 60.] Canberra: Pacific Linguistics.

Heath, Jeffrey. 1982. *Nunggubuyu dictionary*. Canberra: Australian Institute of Aboriginal Studies.

Heath, Jeffrey. 1984. *Functional grammar of Nunggubuyu*. Canberra: Australian Institute of Aboriginal Studies.

Heath, Jeffrey. 1986. Syntactic and lexical aspects of nonconfigurationality in Nunggubuyu (Australia). *Natural Language and Linguistic Theory* 4: 375-408.

Henderson, John. 1998. Topics in Eastern and Central Arrernte grammar. University of Western Australia: PhD thesis.

Herbert, Robert K. 1975. Reanalyzing prenasalized consonants. *Studies in African Linguistics* 6: 105-123.

Hewitt, Mark, and Crowhurst, Megan. 1996. Conjunctive constraints and templates in Optimality Theory. In *Proceedings of the North East Linguistics Society 26*, ed. Kiyomi Kusumoto, 101-116. University of Massachusetts, Amherst: Graduate Linguistic Student Association.

Hollenbach, Barbara. 1977. Phonetic vs. phonemic correspondence in two Trique dialects. In *Studies in Otomanguean phonology*, ed. William R. Merrifield, 35-67. [Summer Institute of Linguistics Publications in Linguistics, 54.] Dallas: Summer Institute of Linguistics and the University of Texas at Arlington.

Hualde, Jose Ignacio. 1991. *Basque phonology*. London: Routledge.

Hume, Elizabeth, Muller, Jennifer, and van Engelhoven, Aone. 1997. Non-moraic geminates in Leti. *Phonology* 14: 371-402.

Hyman, Larry M. 1985. *A theory of phonological weight*. Dordrecht: Foris.

Itô, Junko. 1986. Syllable theory in prosodic phonology. University of Massachusetts: PhD dissertation. [Published 1988, New York: Garland.]

Jackendoff, Ray. 1975. Morphological and semantic regularities in the lexicon. *Language* 51: 639-671.

Jackendoff, Ray. 1990. *Semantic structures*. [Current Studies in Linguistics vol. 18.] Cambridge, MA: MIT Press.

Jackendoff, Ray. 1997. *The architecture of the language faculty*. [Linguistic Inquiry Monographs 28.] Cambridge, MA: MIT Press.

Jackendoff, Ray. 2002. *Foundations of language*. Oxford: Oxford University Press.

Jaeger, Jeri J. 1983. The fortis/lenis question: evidence from Zapotec and Jawoñ. *Journal of Phonetics* 11: 177-189.

Jones, Caroline. 2000. Contiguity under infixation: Mangarrayi reduplication. In *Papers on Australian languages*, eds. Robert J. Pensalfini and Norvin Richards, 105-118. Cambridge, MA: MIT Working Papers in Linguistics.

Jukes, Anthony. 2006. Makassarese (basa Mangkasara'): a description of an Austronesian language of South Sulawesi. University of Melbourne: PhD thesis.

Kager, René. 1996. Generalized Alignment and morphological parsing. [OTS Working Papers of Theoretical Linguistics 96-009.] Utrecht: Utrecht Institute of Linguistics. [Published 1997, in *Rivista di Linguistica* 9: 245-282.]

Kager, René. 1999. *Optimality Theory*. [Cambridge Textbooks in Linguistics.] Cambridge: Cambridge University Press.

Kahn, Daniel. 1976. Syllable-based generalizations in English phonology. [Outstanding Dissertations in Linguistics.] New York: Garland.

Kenstowicz, Michael. 1995. Cyclic vs. non-cyclic constraint evaluation. *Phonology* 12: 397-436.

Kenstowicz, Michael, and Pyle, Charles. 1973. On the phonological integrity of geminate clusters. In *Issues in phonological theory*, eds. Michael Kenstowicz and Charles Kisseberth, 27-43. The Hague: Mouton.

King, Heather. 1998. The declarative intonation of Dyirbal: an acoustic analysis. [LINCOM Studies in Australian Languages.] Munich: LINCOM Europa.

Kiparsky, Paul. 1982. Lexical morphology and phonology. In *Linguistics in the morning calm*, ed. Linguistic Society of Korea, 3-91. Seoul: Hanshin.

Kiparsky, Paul. 2000. Opacity and cyclicity. *The Linguistic Review* 17: 351-367.

Kisseberth, Charles. 1970. On the functional unity of phonological rules. *Linguistic Inquiry* 1: 291-306.

Kisseberth, Charles. 1994. On domains. In *Perspectives in phonology*, eds. Jennifer Cole and Charles Kisseberth, 133-166. [CSLI Lecture Notes no. 51.] Stanford: CSLI.

Kraehenmann, Astrid. 2001. Swiss German stops: geminates all over the word. *Phonology* 18: 109-145.

Laaha, Sabine, Ravid, Dorit, Korecky-Kröll, Katharina, Laaha, Gregor, and Dressler, Wolfgang U. 2006. Early noun plurals in German: regularity, productivity or default? *Journal of Child Language* 33: 271-302.

Ladd, D. Robert. 1986. Intonational phrasing: the case for recursive prosodic structure. In *Phonology yearbook 3*, eds. Colin Ewen and John Anderson, 311-340. Cambridge: Cambridge University Press.

Ladd, D. Robert. 1996. *Intonational phonology*. Cambridge: Cambridge University Press.

Ladefoged, Peter, and Maddieson, Ian. 1996. *The sounds of the world's languages*. Oxford: Blackwell.

Lahiri, Aditi, and Koreman, Jacques. 1988. Syllable weight and quantity in Dutch. *Proceedings of the West Coast Conference on Formal Linguistics* 7: 217-228.

Laver, John. 1994. *Principles of phonetics*. [Cambridge Textbooks in Linguistics.] Cambridge: Cambridge University Press.

Leer, Jeff. 1985. Prosody in Alutiiq. In *Yupik Eskimo prosodic systems: descriptive and comparative studies*, ed. Michael Krauss, 77-134. Fairbanks, AL: University of Alaska.

Lehiste, Ilse. 1960. Segmental and syllabic quantity in Estonian. In *American studies in Uralic linguistics*, ed. Thomas Sebeok, 21-83. [Uralic and Altaic Series 1.] Bloomington, IN: Indiana University Publications.

Lehiste, Ilse. 1970. *Suprasegmentals*. Cambridge, MA: MIT Press.

Levin, Juliette. 1985. A metrical theory of syllabicity. Massachusetts Institute of Technology: PhD dissertation.

Liberman, Mark, and Prince, Alan. 1977. On stress and linguistic rhythm. *Linguistic Inquiry* 8: 249-336.

Lieber, Rochelle. 1992. *Deconstructing morphology: word formation in syntactic theory*. Chicago: University of Chicago Press.

Lisker, L., and Abramson, A. S. 1964. A cross-language study of voicing in initial stops: acoustical measurements. *Word* 20: 384-422.

Lombardi, Linda. 1994. *Laryngeal features and laryngeal neutralisation*. Garland: New York. [Revision of author's 1991 University of Massachusetts, Amherst PhD dissertation.]

McCarthy, John J. 1979. Formal problems in Semitic phonology and morphology. Massachusetts Institute of Technology: PhD dissertation.

McCarthy, John J. 1995. Extensions of Faithfulness: Rotuman revisited. Ms. University of Massachusetts: Amherst.

McCarthy, John J. 1999. Review of Iggy Roca (ed.) (1997) *Derivations and constraints in phonology*. *Phonology* 16, 2: 265-271.

McCarthy, John J. 2001. *A thematic guide to Optimality Theory*. [Research Surveys in Linguistics.] Cambridge: Cambridge University Press.

McCarthy, John J., and Prince, Alan. 1986. Prosodic Morphology. Ms. University of Massachusetts and Brandeis University.

McCarthy, John J., and Prince, Alan. 1993a. Generalized alignment. In *Yearbook of morphology 1993*, eds. Geert Booij and Jaap van Marle, 79-153. Dordrecht: Kluwer.

McCarthy, John J., and Prince, Alan. 1993b. Prosodic morphology I. Ms. University of Massachusetts at Amherst and Rutgers University New Brunswick.

McCarthy, John J., and Prince, Alan. 1995. Faithfulness and reduplicative identity. In *Papers in Optimality Theory*, eds. Jill N. Beckman, Laura Walsh Dickey and Suzanne Urbanczyk, 249-384. University of Massachusetts, Amherst: Graduate Linguistic Student Association.

McDonald, M. 1977. A study of the phonetics and phonology of Yaraldi and associated dialects. Australian National University: MA thesis.

McGregor, William. 1990. *A functional grammar of Gooniyandi*. Amsterdam and Philadelphia: John Benjamins.

McKay, Graham. 1975. R̲embarŋa: a language of Central Arnhem Land. Australian National University: PhD thesis.

McKay, Graham. 1980. Medial stop gemination in Rembarrnga: a spectrographic study. *Journal of Phonetics* 8: 343-332.

McKay, Graham. 1984. Stop alternations in Ndjébbana (Kunibidji). In *Papers in Australian Linguistics No. 16*, eds. Kathleen Glasgow, A. Capell, Graham McKay, Rod Kennedy, and D. Trefry, 107-117. [Series A, vol. 68.] Canberra: Pacific Linguistics.

McKay, Graham. 2000. Ndjébbana. In *Handbook of Australian languages vol. 5*, eds. R.M.W. Dixon and Barry Blake, 155-354. Oxford: Oxford University Press.

McKay, Graham. n.d. Rembarrnga grammar. Ms. Edith Cowan University, Perth.

McKnight, David. 1999. *People, countries, and the Rainbow Serpent*. Oxford: Oxford University Press.

Merlan, Francesca. 1982. *Mangarayi*. [Lingua Descriptiva Series 4.] Amsterdam: North Holland.

Merlan, Francesca. 1983. *Ngalakan grammar, texts, and vocabulary*. Canberra: Pacific Linguistics.

Merlan, Francesca. 2003. The genetic position of Mangarrayi: evidence from nominal prefixation. In *The non-Pama-Nyungan languages of Northern Australia: comparative studies of the continent's most linguistically complex region*, ed. Nicholas Evans, 353-367. Canberra: Pacific Linguistics.

Merlan, Francesca. n.d. Jawoyn grammar, texts, and dictionary. Ms. Australian National University, Canberra.

Mester, R. Armin. 1994. The quantitative trochee in Latin. *Natural Language and Linguistic Theory* 12: 1-62.

Milner, George B. 1956. *Fijian grammar*. Suva: Government press.

Mohanan, K.P. 1986. *The theory of Lexical Phonology*. Dordrecht: Reidel.

Moreton, Elliott, and Smolensky, Paul. 2002. Typological consequences of local constraint conjunction. In *Proceedings of the West Coast Conference on Formal Linguistics 21*, eds. L. Mikkelsen and C. Potts, 306-319. Cambridge, MA: Cascadilla Press.

Morphy, Frances. 1983. Djapu, a Yolngu dialect. In *Handbook of Australian languages vol. 3*, eds. R.M.W. Dixon and Barry Blake, 1-188. Canberra: Australian National University Press.

Morphy, Howard, and Morphy, Frances. 1981. Yuṯpundji-Djindiwirritj land claim. Darwin: Northern Land Council.

Munro, Jen. 2005. Substrate language influence in Kriol: The application of transfer constraints to language contact in northern Australia. University of New England, Armidale: PhD thesis.

Murray, Robert, and Vennemann, Theo. 1983. Sound change and syllable structure in Germanic phonology. *Language* 59: 514-528.

Mushin, Ilana, and Baker, Brett (eds.) To appear. *Discourse and grammar in Australian languages*. Amsterdam/Philadelphia: Benjamins.

Nash, David G. 1979. Yidiny stress: a metrical account. *Proceedings of the Ninth Annual Meeting of the North Eastern Linguistics Society/CUNY Forum 7-8*, City University of New York. New York: Routledge.

Nash, David G. 1986. *Topics in Warlpiri grammar*. New York: Garland. [Revision of author's 1980 Massachusetts Institute of Technology PhD dissertation.]

Nespor, Marina, and Vogel, Irene. 1986. *Prosodic phonology*. [Studies in Generative Grammar 28.] Dordrecht: Foris

Nordlinger, Rachel. 1998. *Constructive case: evidence from Australian languages*. Stanford: CSLI.

Nordlinger, Rachel. 2006. Spearing the emu drinking: subordination and the adjoined relative clause in Wambaya. *Australian Journal of Linguistics* 26: 5-29.

Ohala, John. 1978. The production of tone. In *Tone: a linguistic survey*, ed. Victoria Fromkin, 5-39. New York: Academic Press.

Pentland, Christina. 2004. Stress in Warlpiri: stress domains and word-level prosody. University of Queensland: MPhil thesis.

Pierrehumbert, Janet B. 1980. The phonetics and phonology of English intonation. Massachusetts Institute of Technology: PhD dissertation. [Distributed 1988 by Indiana University Linguistics Club.]

Pinker, Steven. 1999. *Words and rules: the ingredients of language*. London: Weidenfeld and Nicolson.

Pinker, Stephen, and Prince, Alan. 1988. On language and connectionism: analysis of a parallel distributed processing model of language acquisition. *Cognition* 26:195-267.

Pinker, Steven, and Prince, Alan. 1991. Regular and irregular morphology and the psychological status of rules of grammar. In *Proceedings of the seventeenth annual meeting of the Berkeley Linguistics Society*, eds. Laurel A. Sutton, Christopher Johnson and Ruth Shields, 230-251. Berkeley CA: Berkeley Linguistics Society.

Prince, Alan. 1980. A metrical stress theory for Estonian quantity. *Linguistic Inquiry* 11: 511-62.

Prince, Alan. 1983. Relating to the grid. *Linguistic Inquiry* 14: 19-100.

Prince, Alan. 1984. Phonology with tiers. In *Language sound structure: studies in phonology presented to Morris Halle by his teacher and students*, eds. Mark Aronoff and Richard Oehrle, 234-244. Cambridge, MA: MIT Press.

Prince, Alan. 1990. Quantitative consequences of rhythmic organisation. In *CLS 26-II: Papers from the parasession on the syllable in phonetics and phonology*, ed. Karen Deaton, Manuela Noske, and Michael Ziolkowski, 355-398. Chicago: Chicago Linguistics Society.

Prince, Alan, and Smolensky, Paul. 1993. Optimality theory: constraint interaction in generative grammar. [Rutgers Center for Cognitive Science Technical Reports.] Ms. Rutgers University, New Brunswick and University of Colorado, Boulder. [Published 2004, Blackwell: Malden, MA.]

Pullum, Geoffrey K., and Ladusaw, William A. 1986. *Phonetic symbol guide*, 2nd edn. Chicago: University of Chicago Press.

Reid, Nicholas. 1990. Ngan'gityemerri: a language of the Daly River region, Northern Territory of Australia. Australian National University: PhD thesis.

Repp, B.H. 1978. Perceptual integration and differentiation of spectral information for intervocalic stop consonants. *Perception & Psychophysics* 24: 471-485.

Rice, Keren. 1989. *A grammar of Slave*. Berlin/New York: Mouton de Gruyter.

Rice, Keren. 2000. *Morpheme order and semantic scope: word formation in the Athapaskan verb*. [Cambridge Studies in Linguistics 90.] Cambridge: Cambridge University Press.

Robins, R.H. 1953. The phonology of nasalized verbal forms in Sundanese. *Bulletin of the School of Oriental and African Studies* 15: 138-145.

Rubach, Jerzy, and Booij, Geert. 1990. Edge of constituent effects in Polish. *Natural Language and Linguistic Theory* 7: 121-159.

Sagey, Elizabeth. 1990. *The representation of features in non-linear phonology: the articulator node hierarchy*. [Outstanding Dissertations in Linguistics.] New York, London: Garland.

Sapir, Edward. 1921. *Language*. New York: Harcourt Brace.

Schuh, Russell G. 2003. "-ish" reduplication in Gudi Ngamo. Ms. University of California, Los Angeles.

Schultze-Berndt, Eva. 2000. *Simple and complex verbs in Jaminjung: a study of event categorisation in an Australian language*. Nijmegen: Max Planck Institute.

Selkirk, Elisabeth O. 1980. The role of prosodic categories in English word stress. *Linguistic Inquiry* 11: 563-605.

Selkirk, Elisabeth O. 1982. *The syntax of words*. [Linguistics Inquiry Monographs 7.] Cambridge, MA: MIT Press.

Selkirk, Elisabeth O. 1984. *Phonology and syntax: the relation between sound and structure*. [Current Studies in Linguistics 10.] Cambridge, MA: MIT Press.

Selkirk, Elisabeth O. 1988. A two root theory of length. Ms. University of Massachusetts, Amherst.

Selkirk, Elisabeth O. 1995. The prosodic structure of function words. In *Papers in Optimality Theory*, eds. Jill N. Beckman, Laura Walsh Dickey, and Suzanne Urbanczyk, 439-469. University of Massachusetts, Amherst: Graduate Linguistic Student Association.

Sharpe, Margaret. 1972. *Alawa phonology and grammar*. Canberra: Australian Institute of Aboriginal Studies.

Silverman, Dan. 1997. Laryngeal complexity in Otomanguean vowels. *Phonology* 14: 235-261.

Silverman, K., Beckman, M., Pitrelli, J., Ostendorf, M., Wightman, C., Price, P., Pierrehumbert, J., and Hirschberg, J. 1992. ToBI: A standard for labeling English Prosody, *Proceedings of the 1992 International Conference on Spoken Language Processing*: 867-870.

Simpson, Jane. 1998. Warumungu. In *The handbook of morphology*, eds. Andrew Spencer and Arnold M. Zwicky, 707-736. Oxford: Blackwell.

Simpson, Jane, and Withgott, Margaret. 1986. Pronominal clitic clusters and templates. In *The syntax of pronominal clitics*, ed. Hagit Borer, 149-174. [Syntax and Semantics 19.] Orlando, FL: Academic Press.

Smith, Ian, and Johnson, Steve. 2000. Kugu Nganhcara. In *A handbook of Australian languages vol. 5*, eds. R.M.W. Dixon and Barry Blake, 355-489. Melbourne: Oxford University Press.

Smolensky, Paul. 1993. Harmony, markedness, and phonological activity. Handout of keynote address, *Rutgers Optimality Workshop 1*, Rutgers University NJ.

Sommer, Bruce. 1970. An Australian language without CV syllables. *International Journal of American Linguistics* 36: 57-58.

Sommerstein, A. H. 1974. On phonotactically motivated rules. *Journal of Linguistics* 10: 71-94.

Spencer, Andrew. 2003. Putting some order into morphology: reflections on Rice (2000) and Stump (2001). *Journal of Linguistics* 39: 1-26.

Stampe, David. 1972. How I spent my summer vacation. University of Chicago: PhD dissertation. [Also referred to as A dissertation on Natural Phonology.]

Steriade, Donca. 1991. Moras and other slots. Paper presented at *Formal linguistics society of Midamerica 1*.

Steriade, Donca. 1997. Phonetics in phonology: the case of laryngeal neutralisation. Ms. University of California at Los Angeles.

Steriade, Donca. 1999a. The phonology of perceptibility effects: the P-map and its consequences for constraint organization. Ms. University of California at Los Angeles.

Steriade, Donca. 1999b. Alternatives to the syllabic interpretation of consonantal phonotactics. In *Proceedings of the 1998 linguistics and phonetics conference*, eds. O. Fujimura, B. Joseph and B. Palek, 205-242. Prague: The Karolinum Press.

Steriade, Donca. 2001. Directional asymmetries in place assimilation: a perceptual account. In *The role of speech perception in phonology*, eds. Elizabeth Hume and Keith Johnson, 219-250. San Diego: Academic Press.

Steriade, Donca. 2002. The phonology of perceptibility effects: the P-map and its consequences for constraint organization. Ms. University of California at Los Angeles.

Stevens, Kenneth N. 1998. *Acoustic phonetics*. [Current Studies in Linguistics vol. 30.] Cambridge, MA: MIT Press.

Stoakes, Hywel. In preparation. Phonetic investigation of consonants in Bininj Gunwok. University of Melbourne: PhD thesis.

Stump, Gregory T. 2001. *Inflectional morphology: a theory of paradigm structure*. [Cambridge Studies in Linguistics 93.] Cambridge: Cambridge University Press,

Sulkala, Helena, and Karjalainen, Merja. 1992. *Finnish*. [Descriptive Grammars Series.] London: Routledge.

Szpyra, Jolanta. 1989. *The phonology-morphology interface: cycles, levels and words*. [Croom Helm Linguistics Series.] London and New York: Routledge.

Szpyra, Jolanta. 1992. The phonology of Polish prefixation. In *Phonological investigations*, eds. Jacek Fisiak and Stanislaw Puppel, 185-218. Amsterdam and Philadelphia: John Benjamins.

Tabain, Marija, Breen, J.G., and Butcher, Andrew R. 2004. VC vs. CV syllables: a comparison of Aboriginal languages with English. *Journal of the International Phonetic Association* 34: 175-200:

Tindale, Norman B. 1928. Natives of Groote Eylandt and the west coast of the Gulf of Carpentaria (Part III-Languages of Eastern Arnhem Land). *Transactions of the Royal Society of South Australia* 52: 5-27.

Tranel, Bernard. 1991. CVC light syllables, geminates, and Moraic Theory. *Phonology* 8: 291-302.

Trubetzkoy, Nikolay S. 1969. *Principles of phonology*. Berkeley and Los Angeles: University of California Press. [Translation by Christiane A. M. Baltaxe of *Grundzüge der Phonologie*, 1939, Prague: Travaux du Cercle linguistique de Prague.]

Truckenbrodt, Hubert. 1999. On the relation between syntactic phrases and phonological phrases. *Linguistic Inquiry* 30, 2: 219-255.

Urbanczyk, Suzanne. 1995. Double reduplications in parallel. In *Papers in Optimality Theory*, eds. Jill N. Beckman, Laura Walsh Dickey, and Suzanne

Urbanczyk, 499-532. University of Massachusetts, Amherst: Graduate Linguistic Student Association.

Urbanczyk, Suzanne. 1996. Patterns of Reduplication in Lushootseed. University of Massachusetts: PhD dissertation.

Walsh, Michael. 1997. Cross cultural communication problems in Aboriginal Australia. Discussion Paper No.7/1997. Darwin: North Australia Research Unit.

Waters, Bruce. 1980. Djinang phonology. In *Papers in Australian Linguistics 14*, ed. B.E. Waters and P.A. Busby, 1-71. [Series A, vol. 60.] Canberra: Pacific Linguistics.

Wilkinson, Melanie. 1991. Djambarrpuyŋu: a Yolŋu variety of northern Australia. University of Sydney: PhD thesis.

Wilson, Colin. 2001. Consonant cluster neutralisation and targeted constraints. *Phonology* 18: 147-197.

Wilson, Stephen. 1999. *Coverbs and complex predicates in Wagiman.* Stanford CA: CSLI.

Wood, Ray K. 1978. Some Yuulngu phonological patterns. In *Papers in Australian Linguistics No. 11*, eds. Jean F. Kirton, Ray K. Wood, Luise Hercus, Chester S. Street, Harry P. Kulampurut, Dianne Buchanan, and Bella Charlie, 53-117. [Series A, vol. 51.] Canberra: Pacific Linguistics.

Zwicky, Arnold M. 1985. Clitics and particles. *Language* 61: 283-305.

Subject index

Language index

Name index